GLOBAL PERSPECTIVES ON COUNTERTERRORISM

ASPEN ELECTIVE SERIES

GLOBAL PERSPECTIVES ON COUNTERTERRORISM

Second Edition

Amos N. Guiora
Professor of Law
S. J. Quinney College of Law,
University of Utah

Wolters Kluwer
Law & Business

AUSTIN   BOSTON   CHICAGO   NEW YORK   THE NETHERLANDS

Aspen Publishers
Attn: Permissions Department
76 Ninth Avenue, 7th Floor
New York, NY 10011-5201

To contact Customer Care, e-mail customer.care@aspenpublishers.com, call 1-800-234-1660, fax 1-800-901-9075, or mail correspondence to:

Aspen Publishers
Attn: Order Department
PO Box 990
Frederick, MD 21705

Printed in the United States of America.

1 2 3 4 5 6 7 8 9 0

ISBN 978-0-7355-0742-5

Library of Congress Cataloging-in-Publication Data

Guiora, Amos N., 1957-
    Global perspectives on counterterrorism / Amos N. Guiora. — 2nd ed.
        p. cm. — (Aspen elective series)
    Includes index.
    ISBN 978-0-7355-0742-5
    1. Terrorism — Prevention.   2. Terrorism.   I. Title.

K5256.G85 2011
363.325'17 — dc22

                                                    2011003255

About Wolters Kluwer Law & Business

Wolters Kluwer Law & Business is a leading provider of research information and workflow solutions in key specialty areas. The strengths of the individual brands of Aspen Publishers, CCH, Kluwer Law International and Loislaw are aligned within Wolters Kluwer Law & Business to provide comprehensive, in-depth solutions and expert-authored content for the legal, professional and education markets.

CCH was founded in 1913 and has served more than four generations of business professionals and their clients. The CCH products in the Wolters Kluwer Law & Business group are highly regarded electronic and print resources for legal, securities, antitrust and trade regulation, government contracting, banking, pension, payroll, employment and labor, and healthcare reimbursement and compliance professionals.

Aspen Publishers is a leading information provider for attorneys, business professionals and law students. Written by preeminent authorities, Aspen products offer analytical and practical information in a range of specialty practice areas from securities law and intellectual property to mergers and acquisitions and pension/benefits. Aspen's trusted legal education resources provide professors and students with high-quality, up-to-date and effective resources for successful instruction and study in all areas of the law.

Kluwer Law International supplies the global business community with comprehensive English-language international legal information. Legal practitioners, corporate counsel and business executives around the world rely on the Kluwer Law International journals, loose-leafs, books and electronic products for authoritative information in many areas of international legal practice.

Loislaw is a premier provider of digitized legal content to small law firm practitioners of various specializations. Loislaw provides attorneys with the ability to quickly and efficiently find the necessary legal information they need, when and where they need it, by facilitating access to primary law as well as state-specific law, records, forms and treatises.

Wolters Kluwer Law & Business, a unit of Wolters Kluwer, is headquartered in New York and Riverwoods, Illinois. Wolters Kluwer is a leading multinational publisher and information services company.

To my wife Hagit, whose unflagging support throughout the years is unparalleled, and to our three extraordinary children, all unique in their own way: Tamar, Amitai, and Yoav

BIOGRAPHY

Amos N. Guiora

Amos Guiora is a Professor of Law at the S.J. Quinney College of Law, the University of Utah.

Guiora, who teaches Criminal Procedure, International Law, Global Perspectives on Counterterrorism, and Religion and Terrorism, incorporates innovative scenario-based instruction to address national and international security issues and dilemmas. He is a Member of the American Bar Association's Law and National Security Advisory Committee; a Research Fellow at the International Institute on Counter-Terrorism, The Interdisciplinary Center, Herzeliya, Israel; a Corresponding Member, The Netherlands School of Human Rights Research, University of Utrecht School of Law; and was awarded a Senior Specialist Fulbright Fellowship for The Netherlands in 2008.

Professor Guiora has published extensively both in the U.S. and Europe on issues related to national security, limits of interrogation, religion and terrorism, the limits of power and multiculturalism, and human rights. In addition to this book, he is the author of Fundamentals of Counterterrorism, Constitutional Limits on Coercive Interrogation, and Freedom from Religion: Rights and National Security.

He served for 19 years in the Israel Defense Forces as Lieutenant Colonel (retired), and held a number of senior command positions, including Commander of the IDF School of Military Law and Legal Advisor to the Gaza Strip.

SUMMARY OF CONTENTS

CONTENTS

PREFACE

In the opening lines the first edition's Preface I wrote: This book was a labor of love. It was born during a short conversation with my colleague and good friend, Professor Craig Nard, who urged me to write a book on terrorism. Urged would be the polite term, "ordered" would be more descriptive of the conversation. For that, I will be forever thankful. As inspiration, I strategically placed Craig's casebook, along with one of the many academic publications written by my father, Professor A.Z. Guiora, on my bookshelf in such a manner that they were the first things I would see every morning. In addition, Dean Gerry Korngold was a constant supporter — providing both words of encouragement and generous summer stipends. For both I am very grateful.

Those words indeed captured the spirit of the first edition. With respect to this second edition, I hope the text does justice to the comments received from a wide range of students, academics, and the general public — in the United States, Europe, and Israel. The feedback emphasized the value and uniqueness of comparatively analyzing counterterrorism in an interdisciplinary manner. A recurring theme was the need to incorporate additional countries. For that reason, this edition remains true to the pedagogical approach of the first edition while adding two countries, China and Colombia.

In retrospect, both were obvious choices: China because of its extraordinary geopolitical power and relevance; Colombia because of the unique combination of threats it faces. With China, I was very fortunate that American and Chinese academics were gracious with their time and cooperation. The new material on Colombia enormously benefited from insight offered by American and Colombian experts who graciously responded to my many questions.

With the five previously surveyed countries — the U.S., Israel, Russia, India, and Spain — significant additions have been made that reflect the developments of the past three years. I have sought to present to the reader a continuum of events between the two editions. Terrorism cannot be viewed in a vacuum; rather, historical appreciation enormously facilitates understanding terrorism. The four-legged approach that drives this book — law, policy, operations, and intelligence — requires both geopolitical and historical sensitivity to events, trends, and responses.

Given the extraordinary fluidity of this field of study, there is an obvious need to develop a mechanism where up-to-date information is available to readers. To that end, Wolters Kluwer Law & Business has created a website (www.aspenlawschool.com/books/guiora_counterterrorism) dedicated to this book that will provide on-going developments relevant to the issues covered in this book.

It was very important for me to approach counterterrorism from an interdisciplinary perspective. This decision reflects my 19-year career in the Israel Defense Forces, where I was exposed to some of the most complicated and complex decision making that commanders could face in the realm of operational counterterrorism.

What struck me throughout my career was that counterterrorism decisions require the incorporation of different disciplines — in particular, law, policy, tactics and operations, and intelligence gathering. As the Judge Advocate to senior commanders, I was expected to provide legal advice in an area of law best described as operational international law. This is not an area of law that was studied when I was in law school in the early mid-1980s, nor were there an enormous amount of "guides" or "checklists." What could be considered benchmarks were the decisions rendered by the Israel Supreme Court sitting as the High Court of Justice — international law and a moral compass combined with instinct.

I soon realized I had to provide advice beyond the realm of law; a Major General asked me to participate in a meeting where legal issues were not to be discussed. When I asked why, his response was succinct: because I expect you to provide *both* legal and policy advice. From that point on, integrating operational considerations with legal and policy matters was a given, as was my increasing understanding that the soul of counterterrorism is intelligence gathering. To that extent, I worked closely — and obviously not always in agreement — with commanders and intelligence officials alike. Recommending operational decisions steeped in the law while being mindful of additional valid considerations is the essence of legal advice for military commanders. That was my role.

That extraordinary professional experience serves as the backdrop for this book. I am convinced that the only manner in which counterterrorism can truly be studied and understood is through an interdisciplinary approach. Otherwise, an extremely complicated subject will be given short shrift.

As to why I initially chose to examine the U.S., Israel, Russia, India, and Spain, the answer is relatively simple. I felt they were interesting unto themselves, and I also recognized that each conducted counterterrorism sufficiently differently from one another to enable effective comparison.

While on some matters the five — now seven — nations have similar approaches, on a significant number of issues their differences facilitate examining and learning from the contrasts. Different regimes have different laws and policies. However, civil democratic societies also have significant similarities. Those similarities and distinctions, in the context of the four subject areas—law, policy, operations, and intelligence—are the essence of this book.

When writing the first edition, I tried out various chapters at both the law school and collegiate levels in an effort to gauge the relevancy and applicability of my four-subject approach with respect to the five nations. My conviction, based on courses I have taught at both levels, is that the approach resonates with students. To all those students who were the initial "adopters": my many thanks for your honest feedback during and after the respective courses. It is my hope that the second draft is an accurate reflection of the continuing feedback of the first edition.

Amos Guiora
February 2011

ACKNOWLEDGEMENTS

Obviously a project of this nature is not a one-man show. Many thanks are due. I have benefited from the endless and tireless support of a number of people, without whom this project would not have reached the end zone. The words below with respect to the first edition were true then and are true now. The vibrancy of the students who worked with me then is relevant and important to the second edition as it was to the first. This second edition, then, is a continuation of the first with the caveat that changes discussed in the preface differentiate the two.

At Case Western Reserve University School of Law, I was extraordinarily fortunate to have a team of remarkable student research assistants: two students—Erin Page and Sam Riotte—truly became collaborators; their endless and tireless determination made the book a reality. I benefited enormously not only from their research and editing, but also from their insistence that the student be the focus of the book and that I keep my "eye on this ball" at all times. Rounding out the remarkable team were Niki Dorsky Schaefer, Matt Ezzo, Brian Field, and Rebecca Slazinski, who all made significant contributions to this book. Anne Hollander and Jeff Lowe provided additional assistance in securing copyright permissions.

That same spirit of extraordinary collaboration is true for the SJ Quinney College of Law, University of Utah law students who worked on the second edition. Katee Tyler took it upon herself to create a timetable predicated on meeting tight deadlines, keeping our collective eye on the ball, and integrating an enormous amount of new research information. Because this book incorporates four additional countries, there was a need to determine what new developments in the five initially surveyed countries should be included and, simultaneously, what previously included information should be deleted. With the four new countries we had to develop a broad research network, account for language issues, and integrate the old with the new. With respect to this complicated effort, I am enormously in debt to Katee, Lena Cetvei, and Amra Ferhatbegovic. Without their individual and collective efforts the finished product would be drastically different than it is. In addition, many thanks to my Dean and good friend, Hiram Chodosh, for creating an environment that enormously benefits scholarship and research; this book reflects the atmosphere he has created at the SJ Quinney College of Law, the University of Utah. That said, all errors are solely mine.

I am truly indebted to Case Western Reserve University School of Law research librarian Andrew Dorchak. His ability to consistently find "needles in haystacks" made much of this book possible. The IT staff at Case was patient to a fault; in particular, Suparerk (Sami) Janjarasjitt was literally there every step of the way.

At Aspen Publishers I found the often discussed rumor of an "Aspen family" to be true. Their reputation precedes them. I benefited enormously from their integrative, all-encompassing approach. In particular, I would like to thank my publisher, Carol McGeehan, and John Devins, the best editor for which a writer could hope.

I gratefully acknowledge the permission granted, by the authors, publishers, and organizations to reprint portions of copyrighted materials.

GLOBAL PERSPECTIVES ON COUNTERTERRORISM

CHAPTER 1

INTRODUCTION TO COUNTERTERRORISM

This second edition analyzes terrorism and counterterrorism in an interdisciplinary and comparative manner by surveying how seven different nations conduct operational counterterrorism. Its aim is to analyze the four pillars of counterterrorism — **law, policy, operations**, and **intelligence** — as implemented by the United States, Israel, Russia, India, Spain, China, and Colombia. China and Colombia are additions; the other five were addressed in the first edition. In choosing China and Colombia, the scope of the book is broadened by incorporating domestic-based terrorism. That said, the book's primary focus remains international. Furthermore, the Madrid train bombing of March 2004 demonstrates that the distinction between domestic and international terrorism is, perhaps, hazy.

Reexamining earlier analysis of terrorism/counterterrorism contributes to better understanding previously addressed issues including operational measures, government policy, and judicial holdings. A spectrum analysis of the five countries included in both editions suggests that the most significant changes have occurred in the United States. While that is perhaps a reflection of changes in administrations, an additional and no less important factor is the increasing, albeit inconsistent, role of the U.S. judiciary. Conversely, the U.S. Congress has largely been relegated to a non-player, both in the immediate aftermath of 9/11 and ten years later. Israeli counterterrorism strategy has largely stayed consistent though Operation Cast Lead reflects an expanded articulation of "legitimate target" and re-assessment of proportionality; similarly, the Israeli Supreme Court (sitting as the High Court of Justice) has continued to engage in active judicial review of operational measures. Though Russia declared victory in Chechnya, at what cost to human and civil rights and what will be the Russian response if terrorism is renewed, particularly if innocent Russian civilians are the victims of Chechen suicide bombings? The complexity of the multiple threats facing India was dramatically reinforced during the five-day terrorist attack in Mumbai, December 2008. Direct Pakistani involvement is the crux of the operational dilemma facing Indian decision makers; how they respond will once again require discussion throughout the book. With respect to Spain, as in the first edition, this book does not address Basque separatism but rather concentrates on internal, Islamic-based terrorism. The fundamental question is whether Spanish acquiescence can be defined as a successful policy or whether it has potentially emboldened terrorists.

Readers and colleagues suggested that addressing China is a must given its size, complexity, and importance. Colombia, while perhaps a less obvious choice, raises critical questions regarding the limits of operational counterterrorism in a purely domestic terrorism paradigm directly influenced by powerful financial interests. In addition, I will briefly address Mexico and Somalia in the closing chapter. While other countries could have been included, the seven surveyed nations and the two tangentially discussed provide the reader with a sufficiently encompassing overview of terrorism/counterterrorism as we enter this century's second decade.

I. INTRODUCTION

Lawyers provide the legal justification for a wide variety of counterterrorism measures; sociologists explain the origins of terrorism in the context of human misery, ethno-nationalism, and religion; political scientists explain trends and developments in the field of government; and philosophers discuss the existential motives for suicide bombers. However, none of these disciplines alone can explain the cause of terrorism or how to combat it effectively. Accordingly, a multitrack approach to the study of terrorism is most effective.

In studying counterterrorism from a comparative and interdisciplinary perspective, it is incumbent upon the student to develop sensitivity to large-scale geopolitical considerations. That requires an appreciation for different, if not competing, definitions of effectiveness; an understanding of the limits of power; recognition of the attraction of religion, hatred, and ideology; respect for the determination and dedication of the individual terrorist; and an appreciation of historical, political, and social forces. Understanding terrorism requires both a reading of history and a sophisticated analysis of current events, particularly when examining differing ideas and motivations that demand stepping beyond the world of accepted norms. Various tools can be used to attempt to understand terrorism, including simulations, role-playing, and war games.

Successful counterterrorism strategy incorporates all four pillars referenced above. While the pillars can be studied separately, decision makers must successfully integrate them. Otherwise, operational decisions will neither be predicated on the rule of law nor be subjected to a rigorous cost-benefit analysis regarding its effectiveness. Similarly, counterterrorism requires intelligence gathering and analysis of information received; together these two are the backbone of operational decisions. Ultimately, operational counterterrorism is dependent on correct analysis of intelligence gathered from single or multiple sources. However, even when operational counterterrorism decisions are based on reliable, corroborated intelligence, success is not guaranteed.

Addressing counterterrorism from a global perspective, this book is comparative both in structure and purpose. A word about "comparative" is in order: successful policy for one nation is not necessarily effective for another; however, by examining how different nations' respond to similar dilemmas, decision makers can adopt particular measures relevant to their paradigm. Comparativism can be applied to all four pillars of counterterrorism; that integrated approach is at this book's core.

No one nation has the answer to counterterrorism because no one nation has been able to "defeat" terrorism. In analyzing different national policies, either in an effort to proactively prevent terrorism or reactively in response to terrorism, the book analyzes decisions from a legal and policy perspective alike. The two are intertwined and cannot be considered separately. Furthermore, counterterrorism must be viewed through the lens of practicality. Unlike other areas of the law predicated on abstract theoretical analysis, counterterrorism does not lend itself to such an approach. Effective counterterrorism strategy requires operationally viable policy and operational considerations rooted in the rule of law.

II. WHAT IS TERRORISM?

One of the greatest hindrances to a cogent discussion of terrorism and counter-terrorism is a lack of clear, concise universal definitions. Even different government agencies within the United States have varying definitions of terrorism. Consider, for example, the definitions used by the State Department, Federal Bureau of Investigation (FBI), and the Defense Department.

The State Department definition is based on 22 U.S.C. §2656f(d), which concludes:

> [t]he term "terrorism" means premeditated, politically motivated violence per-petrated against non-combatant targets by sub-national groups or clandestine agents, usually intended to influence an audience. The term "international terroris'" means terrorism involving citizens or the territory of more than one country. The term "terrorist group" means any group practicing, or that has significant subgroups that practice, international terrorism.

The FBI defines terrorism as "the unlawful use of force or violence against persons or property to intimidate or coerce a government, the civilian popu-lation, or any segment thereof, in furtherance of political or social objectives."[1]

The Department of Defense defines terrorism as "the calculated use, or threatened use, of force or violence against individuals or property to coerce or intimidate governments or societies, often to achieve political, religious, or ideological objectives."[2]

While these definitions have obvious and easily recognizable similarities, the *essence* of each definition is different. As noted by Simonsen and Spindlove, the State Department looks to motives the terrorist employs, the FBI empha-sizes methods, and the Department of Defense focuses on the objectives or

---

1. *What Is Terrorism?*, http://www.terrorism-research.com (last visited July 11, 2010).
2. *Id.*

goals of terrorist behavior.[3] Therefore, from the perspective of the United States, it might be argued that there are three fundamental elements to the definition of terrorism.

Limiting the definition to its necessary elements, however, fails to include the broader elements of terrorism. In their classic book on the subject, *Political Terrorism*, Schmid and Jongman reached out to a number of international scholars asking them to define terrorism. The authors received 109 definitions of terrorism.[4] Similar to Simonsen and Spindlove's analysis, Schmid and Jongman identified 22 elements common to the 109 definitions.[5] These elements included, but were not limited to, violence and force, as well as terrorism's clandestine nature, its arbitrariness, and the terrorist's intent to use civilians as victims.

Ultimately, Schmid and Jongman proposed the following comprehensive definition:

> Terrorism is an anxiety-inspiring method of repeated violent action, employed by (semi-)clandestine individual, group, or state actors, for idiosyncratic, criminal, or political reasons, whereby—in contrast to assassination—the direct targets of violence are not the main targets. The immediate human victims of violence are generally chosen randomly (targets of opportunity) or selectively (representative symbolic targets) from a target population, and serve as message generators. Threat- and violence-based communication processes between terrorist (organization), (imperiled) victims, and main target (audience(s)), turning it into a target of terror, a target of demands, or a target of attention, depending on whether intimidation, coercion, or propaganda is primarily sought.[6]

While the rigor of such a definition is impressive, it remains unwieldy, complex, and potentially unworkable. In an attempt to include as many elements as possible, it may have rendered itself overly inclusive.

But definitions that fail to consider elements such as terrorism's political nature, its intent to target civilians, and the use of threats and intimidation are under-inclusive. For this reason, the most effective definitions of terrorism are often direct and straightforward. In particular, scholars have noted definitions put forth separately by Bruce Hoffman and Walter Laqueur that emphasize using "illegitimate force to achieve political ends by targeting innocent people." Determining what is "illegitimate," what a "political end" might include, and who determines whether someone is "innocent" provide numerous opportunities for academic and popular debate without suggesting resolution of the question. As it is often said, one man's terrorist is another man's freedom fighter.

Indeed, the debate over an appropriate definition of terrorism also requires consideration of another issue: who is doing the talking? As Schmid recognized,

---

3. C.E. Simonsen & J.R. Spindlove, *Terrorism Today: The Past, the Players, the Future* (2000).
4. Alex P. Schmid & Albert J. Jongman, *Political Terrorism: A New Guide to Actors, Authors, Concepts, Data Bases, Theories and Literature*, 5-6 (1988).
5. *Id.*
6. *Id.* at 28.

distinct arenas speak differently about terrorism. That is, the definition of terrorism potentially changes depending upon whether an academic, a government, or the media is leading the discussion.[7] Academics need a definition to support rigorous research and its conclusions, the state employs another definition to serve its goals of promulgating laws and advancing strategy (domestic and foreign), and the media uses another to provide easily digestible information to explain terrorism to the general public.

To avoid these underlying motives, scholars such as Jonathan White forgo creating definitions and instead rely on making distinctions between various conflicts found in society.[8] White attempts to place terrorism in a continuum somewhere between low-level "folkway violations" and the all encompassing "mass destruction." His effort relies on identifying and distinguishing sometimes similar and overlapping concepts, such as "riot," "terrorism," and "guerilla war." While effective, such an analysis still begs the question: what defines each of the concepts that are employed, and what distinguishes them?

Yet another school of thought suggests that any internationally agreed upon definition of terrorism hampers counterterrorism operations and therefore the discussion is superfluous. However, to ensure lawful counterterrorism, terrorism must be defined. For the purposes of this book, "terrorism" shall be defined as:

> Acts of violence intended to advance a cause — political, social, religious, or economic — aimed at innocent civilians defined as legitimate targets with the intent to cause physical harm, including death, and/or conducting psychological warfare against a population aimed at intimidating it from conducting its daily life in a normal fashion.

This definition captures the essence of terrorism without becoming over- or underinclusive. In reviewing both scholarship and terrorists' writings, the overwhelming impression is that causing harm (physical or psychological) to the innocent civilian population is the core characteristic of terrorist action. Harming civilians is the most effective manner for terrorists to achieve their goals. Accordingly, it is the centerpiece of this book's definition.

While causing death or injury to the innocent civilian population is the "means to the end," intimidation of the population is of equal importance from the terrorist's perspective. Whether resulting in death, injury, or property damage — the attack itself is successful if it results in intimidation.

The importance of understanding how terrorism impacts daily life cannot — and should not — be underestimated. Terrorism is a daily grind. It must be understood in the context of daily attacks than one-time, dramatic attacks (e.g., 9/11). Smaller, more frequent attacks have a much greater long-term effect on an innocent civilian population than does a one-time major event whose undeniable short-term effect may not linger. Therefore, the book's proposed definition emphasizes the effect on the *daily life* of an

---

7. Alex Schmid, *The Response Problem as a Definitional Problem*, 4 Terrorism and Political Violence 7-25 (1992).

8. *See* Jonathan White, *Terrorism and Homeland Security* (2006).

innocent civilian population and the commensurate requirement imposed on the state to respond to the continuous, constant threats that are the reality of modern-day terrorism.

The dilemma of how to protect individual rights while simultaneously protecting society, in the context of operational counterterrorism and intelligence gathering, is arguably the most complex issue confronting policy and decision makers. In the chapters that follow, how the seven surveyed nations balance legitimate national security considerations with equally legitimate individual rights will be analyzed and discussed.

This book also examines the role of national legislatures in drafting legislative responses to terrorism. An analysis of judicial review of executive action in times of armed conflict by national courts is critical to understanding the limits of lawful counterterrorism. International law principles — collateral damage, proportionality, military necessity, alternatives, and self-defense — are discussed as they relate to terrorism and counterterrorism.

Furthermore, this book analyzes the question of which judicial regime is appropriate for bringing terrorists to trial. Determining the status and rights of suspected terrorists is a major challenge facing decision makers. Those questions are related to the dilemma of what paradigm is relevant to terrorism: criminal law, international law, or a hybrid of the two. A critical question is whether terrorists should be distinguished from the common criminal and the soldier. In other words, is terrorism a distinct category requiring a special set of rules? In the United States, the Bush administration considered terrorism distinct from the traditional criminal law paradigm; it remains to be seen how the Obama administration will address this issue.

Chapters are divided by subject matter with each of the surveyed nations' approach to that issue presented as a basis for discussion. In addition, "Issues to Consider" are presented throughout the chapters in order to stimulate debate and discussion. Unlike other areas of the law, the legal and policy aspects of counterterrorism are often amorphous. While this book seeks to address complex counterterrorism issues, many of the questions presented do not have easy answers. That is the reality of counterterrorism.

III. THE TERRORIST

In many cases, the terrorist views himself or herself as making a significant contribution to a cause — be it Palestinian nationalism, profound hatred of the West, the desire to create an independent Kashmir, or establishing a free Chechnya. The "cause" is at the heart of the terrorists' actions; the requisite follow-up query is how far the individual terrorist goes in support of this cause. After all, not everyone is willing to be a suicide bomber, take innocent civilians hostage in a Moscow opera house, turn planes into guided missiles, or attack tourists in Mumbai over the course of a number of days. Herein lies the fundamental issue: *is having a cause enough or does another intangible exist that leads terrorists to deliberately and consciously endanger themselves and others?*

1. Who becomes a terrorist?
2. How do terrorists define their aims/goals/mission?
3. How do terrorists define success?
4. In terrorism, what does success mean for the terrorists, the public, legislators, politicians, and the military?
5. Are terrorists calculating or spontaneous?
6. Do terrorists adhere to a code of conduct including self-imposed limits?
7. How is terrorism distinguished from other forms of violence?
8. Do terrorists genuinely believe that nationalism/separatism or any other stated goal is genuinely attainable as a result of their actions?
9. Is terrorism necessarily violent and are terrorists accordingly violent?

IV. TYPES OF TERRORISM

Understanding terrorism requires appreciating distinct categories of terrorism and terrorists. Policy and decision makers make a critical mistake lumping terrorists into one catchall category. It is important to recognize different categories and to develop policies intended to address specific groups rather than rely on a generalized response. While particularized responses do not guarantee success, they represent the most effective approach to lawful, operational counterterrorism.

A. ETHNO-NATIONALIST TERRORISTS

Ethno-nationalist terrorist organizations are dedicated to the establishment of an independent state, based on a specific ethnic, religious, and/or national identity. Ethno-nationalist terrorism is defined as seeking to achieve a limited goal, specific to a particular geographic region. In certain cases, ethno-nationalism is strongly influenced by religion. The decision to restrict the geographical range of terrorist acts is predicated on a number of factors, including limited operational capability, financial constraints, and ideological considerations. In subsequent chapters two ethno-nationalist, religious terrorist organizations, Hamas and the Chechens, are examined. Hamas seeks to establish a Palestinian state in the Gaza Strip, the West Bank, and Israel proper based on Islam and nationalism. Chechens seek to create an independent Chechen state, free of Russian control.

B. GLOBAL TERRORISTS

1. AL QAEDA

Global terrorists are a second category of terrorists. These groups conduct terrorist attacks on an international scale rather than limiting themselves to a specific geographic location. However, similar to ethno-nationalist terrorists whose specific goal is the creation of an independent state, global terrorists unite around specific goals. Al Qaeda, both before 9/11 and afterwards,[9] is clearly relevant to this category as it practices terrorism on a global scale dedicated to driving the West from secular Arab regimes. The organization seeks to ensure destruction of its enemy, defined both as Western society and its Arab secular supporters (primary targets include Egypt, Jordan, and Saudi Arabia) on whom it has openly declared war predicated on religious doctrine.

Osama bin Laden in his fatwa issued to all Muslims wrote:

> The ruling to kill the Americans and their allies — civilians and military — is an individual duty for every Muslim who can do it in any country in which it is possible to do it, in order to liberate the al-Aqsa Mosque and the holy mosque (Mecca) from their grip, and in order for their armies to move out of the lands of Islam, defeated and unable to threaten any Muslims. This is in accordance with the words of Almighty Allah, and "fight the pagans all together as they fight you all together" and "fight them until there is no more tumult or oppression, and there prevail justice and faith in Allah."[10]

Al Qaeda is not a nationalist movement with self-determination aspirations; rather, the organizations stated aspiration is to bring about the destruction of those identified either as the infidel and/or its supporters. According to scholars and observers alike, al Qaeda's ultimate objective is to replace secular Arab regimes with Sharia-based Islamic states.

It is instructive to quote from the "Minimanual" of the Brazilian revolutionary Carlos Marigella because it sheds light on bin Laden's design to create a new social order.

> The urban guerilla is not afraid of dismantling and destroying the present Brazilian economic, political, and social system, for his aim is to help the rural guerilla and to collaborate in the creation of a totally new and revolutionary social and political structure, with the armed people in power.[11]

Bin Laden's declaration of war against all things American ultimately required an attack on the scale of 9/11. Anything less would have been inadequate. The totality of al Qaeda's approach regarding the United States is evident in a missive drafted by Ramzi bin al-Shibh, who participated in planning 9/11:

> Concerning the operations of the blessed Tuesday (9/11) . . . they are legally legitimate, because they are committed against a country at war with us, and the people in that country are combatants. Someone might say that it is the innocent, the elderly, the women, and the children who are victims, so how can these operations be legitimate according to shark'? And we say that the sanctity of women, children, and the elderly is not absolute. There are special

---

9. For a listing of al Qaeda attacks after 9/11, *see* Timeline: al-Qaeda, BBC, Aug. 7, 2008, http://news.bbc.co.uk/2/hi/7546355.stm (last visited July 5, 2009).

10. For a complete transcript of bin Laden's fatwa, *see* International Institute of Conterterrorism, http://www.ict.org.il/articles/fatwah.htm, last visited Nov. 28, 2006; *see generally* Walter Laqueur ed., *Voices of Terror: Manifestos, Writings and Manuals of Al Qaeda, Hamas, and Other Terrorists from Around the World and Throughout the Ages* (2004).

11. *See* Laqueur, *supra* note 10.

cases . . . Muslims may respond in kind if infidels have targeted women and children and elderly Muslims, (or if) they are being invaded, (or if) the non-combatants are helping with the fight, whether in action, word, or any other type of assistance, (or if they) need to attack with heavy weapons, which do not differentiate between combatants and non-combatants . . . In killing Americans who are ordinarily off limits, Muslims should not exceed four million non-combatants, or render more than ten million of them homeless. We should avoid this, to make sure the penalty (that we are inflicting) is no more than reciprocal.[12]

Terrorism may be both discriminate and indiscriminate. In the case of political assassination, it is discriminate; killers of democratically elected leaders have identified person-specific targets. By contrast, bin Laden's global terrorism is indiscriminate; the physical target is the West and secular Arab regimes but the identity and ethnicity of actual victims is irrelevant. According to this worldview, Muslims killed on 9/11 were sympathizers, or even collaborators, with the Great Satan (the United States), and their deaths, therefore, are not regrettable.

2. Regional "Franchises"

The globalization of terrorism requires vast resources and a commitment to conducting the campaign widely. It also requires a unifying factor. For al Qaeda, it is religion. Religious-based terrorism divides the world into easily recognizable factions: believers and non-believers. According to bin Laden:

We—with Allah's help—call on every Muslim who believes in Allah and wishes to be rewarded to comply with Allah's order to kill the Americans and plunder their money wherever and whenever they find it. We also call on Muslim ulema, leaders, youths, and soldiers to launch the raid on Satan's U.S. troops and the devil's supporters allying with them, and to displace those who are behind them so that they may learn a lesson.[13]

Religious-based terrorism espouses limitless, indiscriminate violence based on theological doctrine. By addressing issues such as redemption, martyrdom, and salvation, religious-based terrorism appeals to a wider audience than secular terrorism. Violence stemming from these beliefs is legitimized by reference to religious scripture and approval of religious leaders. The core of religious terrorism is extremist interpretation of religious texts, predicated on religious absolutism.

Appreciating the influence of religious absolutism is essential to understanding the link between global terrorism and "homegrown" terrorist groups influenced by the teachings of al Qaeda, but not operating in concert with the organization. It is important to note that the bombing of the Madrid train station (March 2004) was the handiwork of "homegrown" Islamic terrorism. This stands in contrast to 9/11 and the attempted Christmas Day

---

12. Alan Cullison, *Inside Al Qaeda's Hard Drive,* The Atlantic Monthly, Sept. 2004.
13. *See* Laqueur, *supra* note 10; Al-Qaeda Messaging/Attacks Timeline, Intel Center, (Feb. 24, 2009) *available at* http://www.intelcenter.com/qaeda-timeline-v7-1.pdf.

bombing of Northwest Flight 253 (Detroit), both executed by individuals specifically brought to the United States for their respective missions. The London train bombing (July 2005), the attempted destruction of commercial airlines from the U.K. to the U.S. (August 2006), the Ft. Hood massacre (November 2009), and the attempted Times Square bombing (May 2010) follow the Madrid pattern, rather than 9/11 and Detroit.

These incidents emphasize an important development in terrorism: the rise in what can be most accurately described as "bin Laden and his progeny,"[14] demonstrating the localization of terrorism *predicated* on themes of commonality, in particular religious extremism. From a geopolitical perspective the distinction is enormous; a previously external-only threat has become internal. Though some homegrown actors lack the necessary skills to carry out successful attacks, the intention and planning makes it clear that al Qaeda "franchising" is a reality. Were bin Laden to be killed today, the significance would be minimal.

The list of attacks carried out by al Qaeda and its progeny over the years is proof of a commitment to a sustained ideology: Riyadh, November 1995; Khobhar Towers, June 1996; Tanzanina and Kenya, August 1998; U.S.S. *Cole*, October 2000; 9/11, September 2001; Bali, October 2002;[15] Madrid, March 2004; London, June 2005; Mumbai, November 2008. All of these attacks, regardless of where they occurred, targeted Western society or its supporters. This indicates what Ajami labels a desire to create a "radical order free from foreign entanglements"[16] with the clear aim (in the case of the attacks in Saudi Arabia) of driving the United States from Saudi Arabia; in essence, as Ajami suggests, this is xenophobia of a murderous kind dressed up in religious garb.

V. EFFECTIVENESS OF TERRORISTS

Experts suggest terrorist organizations define effectiveness through the prism of long-term strategic considerations. Israel's disengagement from the Gaza Strip was, according to some analysts, a result—directly or indirectly—of Palestinian terrorism. This theory rests on the assumption that Prime Minister Rabin, initially, and Prime Minister Sharon, subsequently, determined that the Israeli public had wearied of constant attacks by Palestinian terrorists,

---

14. *See al Qaeda*, http://www.start.umd.edu/start/data/tops/terrorist_organization_profile.asp?id=6 (last visited July 5, 2009) (list of affiliated groups around the world, including al Qaeda in the Islamic Maghreb (Algeria), Jemahh Islamiya (Indonesia, Malaysia, Philippines, Singapore), Lashkar-e-Taiba (India, Pakistan)).

15. One of the fundamental differences between al Qaeda and ethno-nationalist terrorism is scale; bin Laden's self-perception is of an international actor, whereas the Hamas or Chechen focus is on local goals. An example of the global scale of al Qaeda's terrorism is the bombing of a Bali disco frequented by Australians. The location itself held no poltical value. Perhaps more than any other terrorist attack, Bali illustrates the internationalization of al Qaeda's modus operandi.

16. Fouad Ajami, *The Sentry's Solitude*, Foreign Affairs, Nov./Dec. 2001.

and postulated that disengagement would contribute to a sharp downturn in terrorism.[17]

Similarly, the bombing of the Madrid train station directly contributed to the newly elected Spanish government's decision to withdraw from Iraq. Much to the surprise of many commentators, the government's decision did not have the expected effect of directly contributing to additional acts of terrorism. Whether or not the government would have withdrawn from Iraq regardless of the attack is a matter of speculation; what is clear is that in the aftermath of the attack, Spain withdrew. Conversely, brutal attacks by Chechen terrorists did not contribute to a change in Russian tactical counterterrorism policy largely marked by significant violations of human rights. However, Russian declaration of victory in Chechnya represents a significant strategic decision extending beyond particular tactical considerations. Does this suggest that the Chechen terrorists are ineffective?

The effectiveness of various attacks in India must be analyzed through multiple prisms reflecting three terrorist threats: (1) internal threats based on historical enmity involving Hindus, Muslims, and Sikhs; (2) external-internal threats resulting from Pakistan's support of Muslims in Kashmir who seek independence; and (3) external threats arising out of Pakistani-Indian relations and the fact that both nations have nuclear capability.

To understand the terrorist mind-set, it is necessary to appreciate terrorist's determination and resilience. Terrorists are willing to engage in a "war of attrition" imposing enormous hardship on the individual and his immediate family in order to achieve goals the family may or may not share; family members may be indirect victims of operational counterterrorism measures. Counterterrorism, both strategically and tactically, must be premised on recognition that self-sacrifice is inherent to terrorist behavior. Engaging in a never-ending cycle of violence is one means by which terrorist organizations signal to distinct audiences (the general public, followers, and relevant government) their commitment to the cause. From the perspective of terrorist organizations, pressures on decision makers exerted by an attacked and scared public justify continued attacks on innocent civilians.

Terrorists play to their public as a means to signal resiliency, progress, and determination. "Blowback" is the term used for terrorists' responses to government action against them. For example, if in response to the killing of a terrorist leader in a targeted killing, terrorists perform a suicide bombing, then the (second) attack is called "blowback." This *modus operandi* demonstrates to audiences that aggressive government action is an ineffective counterterrorism policy and that a political response to terrorist demands (what others might call capitulation) is the preferred course.

How terrorist leaders view the effectiveness of their actions is critical; e-mails from bin Laden suggest how he defines effectiveness and highlights the dilemmas U.S. policy faces.

---

17. PM Sharon's Statement on the Day of the Implementation of the Disengagement Plan, (Aug. 15, 2005), *available at* http://www.pmo.gov.il/PMOEng/Archive/Speeches/2005/08/speech150805.htm.

If it refrains from responding to jihad operations, its prestige will collapse, thus forcing it to withdraw its troops abroad and restrict itself to U.S. internal affairs. This will transform it from a major power to a third-rate power, similar to Russia.[18]

And, this simply means that Obama and his administration have instilled new seeds to increase the hatred and revenge towards America. The number of those seeds is the number of harmed and destitute people from Swat valley and the tribal regions in Northern and Southern Waziristan, and the number of their sympathizers. And, with that Obama has walked like his predecessors in increasing hostility towards Muslims . . . establishing long-term wars, so the American public must get ready to continue harvesting what is instilled by the leaders of the White House during the next years and decades.[19]

O' my Islamic nation, the discussion of the weakness and decline of American hegemony and the collapse of the American economy is not based upon mere hope alone. It has been acknowledged by their senior leaders what they can no longer hide. Incoming [U.S.] Vice President Biden has stated, "The crisis is worse than we expected. The entire American economy is in danger of collapse."[20]

The effectiveness of counterterrorism must be viewed from the perspective of government and terrorist alike. Defining effectiveness is one of the most difficult aspects of counterterrorism because it requires an analysis of strategic and tactical goals, means, capabilities, and realistic expectations. Secretary of Defense Donald Rumsfeld stated in October 2003 that there are "no metrics enabling the government to determine if it is winning or losing the war on terrorism."[21] Perhaps the frustration expressed by then Secretary Rumsfeld best articulates the nebulousness associated with counterterrorism. Terrorists may well share a similar sentiment. Did 9/11 contribute to bin Laden's final endgame? Did killing hundreds of school children in Beslan advance the struggle for Chechen independence? Did killing hundreds of Indian businessmen on a Mumbai train contribute to a particular goal?

Each new threat evokes distinct philosophies. Former Israeli Prime Minister Yitzhak Rabin described a two-track approach: "We will work for peace as if there is no terrorism; and fight terrorism as if there is no peace."[22] President Bush's declaration of "war on terror" reflected a contrasting approach to Rabin's, allowing no room for a middle ground. President Obama has articulated a more nuanced approach: "where terrorists offer only the injustice of

18. *See* Cullison, *supra* note 12.
19. Osama Bin Laden: "Speech to the Pakistani Nation" (June 3, 2009), *available at* http://www.nefafoundation.org/miscellaneous/FeaturedDocs/nefa_binladen0609.pdf (last visited July 5, 2009).
20. Osama Bin Laden: "A Call for Jihad to Stop the Gaza Assault" (June 14, 2009), *available at* http://www.nefafoundation.org/miscellaneous/FeaturedDocs/nefabinladen0109.pdf (last visited July 5, 2009).
21. *See Are We Winning in Iraq: Testimony Before the H. Comm. on Armed Serv.*, 109th Cong. (2005) (testimony of Andrew F. Krepinevich), *available at* http://armedservices.house.gov/comdocs/testimony/109thcongress/Full%2520Committee%25202005/3-17-05IraqOperationsUpdate.pdf.
22. H.E. Per Stig Moler & H.E. Marwan Jamil Muasher, *Middle East Roadmap Must Not Fail*, Middle East Institute, Nov. 16, 2003, at http://www.mei.edu/Publications/WebPublications/Commentaries/CommentariesArchive/tabid/624/ctl/Detail/mid/1531/xmid/86/xmfid/13/Default.aspx (last visited July 5, 2009).

disorder and destruction, America must demonstrate that our values and our institutions are more resilient than a hateful ideology"[23] later noting that "[t]he solution . . . is not just military—it is political and economic."[24]

ISSUES TO CONSIDER

1. How do governments define counterterrorism effectiveness?
2. How do terrorist organizations define effectiveness?
3. What are the costs and benefits of blowback?
4. What would be appropriate guidelines to determine effectiveness of operational counterterrorism?
5. What weight should be given to the rule of law in ascertaining counterterrorism policy effectiveness?
6. What should be the appropriate balance between human rights, operational considerations, and the determination of effectiveness?
7. What are effective means to counter a terrorist's willingness to commit acts in the name of a "cause"?
8. How should governments respond—proactively and reactively—to the absoluteness articulated in bin Laden's fatwa?

---

23. Remarks by the President on National Security (May 21, 2009), *available at* http://www. whitehouse.gov/the_press_office/Remarks-by-the-President-On-National-Security-5-21-09/ (last visited July 5, 2009)

24. *See* Senator Obama Delivers Address on National Security (Aug. 1, 2007) http://my. barackobama.com/page/community/post_group/ObamaHQ/CpHR (last visited July 5, 2009); also see, National Security Strategy, (May 2010), http://www.whitehouse.gov/sites/default/files/ rss_viewer/national_security_strategy.pdf (last visited June 1, 2010).

2

INTERNATIONAL LAW

I. INTRODUCTION

International law is a set of agreements, sometimes called conventions, freely entered into by states to regulate relations between themselves on particular issues including extradition, trade relations, and mutual defense. In addition, international agreements can establish an organization, such as the United Nations, whereby like-minded states seek to resolve issues of mutual concern.

When international law was developed, the world was composed largely of nation-states. Non-state actors, such as al Qaeda, were not a factor in the development of international law. Furthermore, customary international law — universally binding law developed from the general and consistent practice of states and adhered to from a sense of legal obligation — was predicated on nation-states developing and implementing agreed upon rules. Customary international law consists of two elements: an agreed practice of a number of states and practice consistent with prevailing law. Customary international law is included in Article 38 of the statute of the International Court of Justice (ICJ), which defines what law ICJ can apply.

According to the 1868 St. Petersburg Declaration, the only legitimate object states should endeavor to accomplish during war is to weaken the military force of the enemy. The declaration's limitation on the use of exploding projectiles attempted to ensure that weapons used would reduce the number of soldiers fighting the war while preventing unnecessary and prolonged injury, pain, and suffering among the combatants.

The relationship between terrorism and international law is analyzed by examining international agreements and conventions, the conduct of states and non-state actors, and the applicability of international law post-9/11. While a number of conventions and agreements regarding terrorism have been signed over the years,[1] this chapter focuses on how the U.N. Charter and Geneva Convention affect operational counterterrorism. International

---

1. *United Nations Treaty Collection: Conventions on Terrorism, available at* http://untreaty. un.org/English/Terrorism.asp (last visited July 11, 2010).

law directly affects policies developed by decision makers and, most important, actions implemented by commanders.

II. TERRORISM CONVENTIONS

The United Nations has drafted twelve multinational conventions and protocols relevant to terrorism addressing the roles and responsibilities of member nations. However, these conventions are characterized by one glaring fundamental weakness: terrorism is not defined. Given the centrality of terror bombing to contemporary terrorism, the International Convention for the Suppression of Terrorist Bombing (1997) is of particular importance.[2]

Terror bombing, at its broadest conception, is the greatest threat presently posed by terrorists. A comprehensive definition of terror bombing includes the following: dirty bombs, suicide bombings, bombs triggered by remote control from a safe distance, and nuclear weapons. Particular attention must be given to the indiscriminate killing of innocent civilians accomplished by these bombing methods. "[B]y its sheer nature, [terror bombing] depends on such 'isolated' incidents to achieve its goals. The fragmented nature of most terrorist organizations makes it virtually impossible for the organizations to conduct anything other than small-scale acts."[3]

The terror bombing threat clearly differs from other forms of terrorist attack. Because of its indiscriminate nature, its increasingly widespread use, the ease of its success, and the difficulty of identifying the perpetrator and preventing attacks, terror bombing warrants special attention.

The Convention for the Suppression of Terrorist Bombings is a United States initiative in response to the 1996 bombing of American military personnel in Saudi Arabia.[4] The convention has two important provisions: (1) it establishes universal jurisdiction over those using explosives and other devices in public places with the intent to kill, cause serious bodily injury, or cause extensive destruction of a public place; and (2) obliges nations to extradite for prosecution persons accused of committing or aiding such offenses.

The convention became effective on May 23, 2001; today, 58 nations are signatories. Because the drafters wanted a legal framework whereby nations could prosecute those involved in bombings, the convention established universal jurisdiction over terror bombings. The convention further sought to contribute to international cooperation in the effort to combat terror

---

2. *International Convention for the Suppression of Terrorist Bombing* (1997), U.N. Office on Drugs and Crime, *available at* http://www.unodc.org/unodc/en/terrorism_convention_terrorist_bombing. html (last visited July 10, 2010).

3. Frank A. Biggio, *Neutralizing the Threat: Reconsidering Existing Doctrines in the Emerging War on Terrorism*, 34 Case W. Res. J. Int'l L. 1 (2002).

4. H.R. Rep. No. 107-307, at 7 (2001) ("The International Convention for the Suppression of Terrorist Bombings was conceived by the United States in the wake of the bombing attack of the U.S. military personnel in Saudi Arabia in 1996."), *available at* http://thomas.loc.gov/cgi-bin/cpquery/ ?&dbname=cp107&sid=cp107JhViS&refer=&r_n=hr307.107&item=&sel=TOC_23201&.

bombing. According to Professor Whitten, "it is anticipated that these additional offenses [noted in Convention Art. 2] will strengthen the ability of the international community to investigate, prosecute and extradite conspirators or those who otherwise direct or contribute to the commission of offenses defined in the Convention."[5]

ISSUES TO CONSIDER

1. How is the effectiveness of an international convention to be determined?
2. What is the significance of universal jurisdiction in the context of counterterrorism?
3. What is the significance of distinguishing terrorism from criminal activity in prosecuting individuals involved in terror bombings?
4. Do international conventions contribute to counterterrorism?

III. SELF-DEFENSE

A. U.N. CHARTER

According to Article 2(4) of the U.N. Charter, "all Members shall refrain in their international relations from the threat or use of force against the territorial integrity or political independence of any state, or in any other manner inconsistent with the Purposes of the United Nations."[6] This article expresses one of the primary tenets of international law: prevention of war between member states. Nevertheless, Article 51 states that

> [n]othing in the present Charter shall impair the inherent right of individual or collective self-defence if an armed attack occurs against a Member of the United Nations, until the Security Council has taken measures necessary to maintain international peace and security. Measures taken by Members in the exercise of this right of self-defence shall be immediately reported to the Security Council and shall not in any way affect the authority and responsibility of the Security Council under the present Charter to take at any time such action as it deems necessary in order to maintain or restore international peace and security.[7]

Determining the extent of self-defense is critical to a discussion examining the relationship between international law and counterterrorism. Unlike traditional warfare where militaries face off with planes, tanks, and warships, counterterrorism is characterized by an unseen enemy; battles take place in

---

5. Whitten, *The International Convention for the Suppression of Terrorist Bombings*, 92 American Journal of International Law, 774-75 (1998).
6. U.N. Charter art. 2.
7. U.N. Charter art. 51.

"back alleys with dark shadows." Self-defense in this environment is enormously complicated. The decision to preemptively attack a highly elusive target, often times in close proximity to civilians, is based on intelligence information. The veracity of the intelligence information is critical to the success or failure of any counterterrorism initiative. Operational decisions are predicated on intelligence gleaned from sources; that information is the basis for states attacking terrorists and their infrastructure.

B. THE LIMITS OF STATE SOVEREIGNTY IN SELF-DEFENSE

In 1837, U.S. Secretary of State Daniel Webster articulated a definition of self-defense, which evolved into customary international law. Webster's definition followed what has come to be known as the *Caroline* incident. The *Caroline* was a U.S. steamboat attempting to transport supplies to Canadian insurgents. A British force interrupted the *Caroline*'s voyage, shot at it, set it on fire and let it wash over Niagara Falls. Webster said that Britain's act did not qualify as self-defense because self-defense is only justified "if the necessity of that self-defense is instant, overwhelming, and leaving no choice of means, and no moment for deliberation." According to Webster, Britain could have dealt with the *Caroline* in a more diplomatic manner. He limited the right to self-defense to situations where there is a real threat, the response is essential and proportional, and all peaceful means of resolving the dispute have been exhausted. The concept known as the *Caroline* doctrine was considered customary international law until a competing definition of self-defense arose in Article 51 of the U.N. Charter, which authorizes self-defense only if an armed attack "occurs."[8]

When can preemptive actions be undertaken? Preemptive action requires that intelligence information be reliable and corroborated. Furthermore, preemptive action to be legitimate must be proportional in the context of the attack it seeks to prevent. In determining proportionality, decision makers must take into consideration both the immediacy of the threat and its severity.

The intent of Article 51 was to limit the invocation of the right to self-defense. Any limitation, however, required a discussion regarding the right to engage in anticipatory self-defense. "The United Nations, and the international community, are wary of potential abuses of the rights inherent under Article 51 and has established four standards to prevent nations from abusing those rights."[9] States need to not only defend themselves against ongoing attacks, but also to act preemptively to prevent aggressive acts from being carried out. Customary international law permits a state to respond to a threat and infringe on the territorial sovereignty of another nation when four criteria are met: (1) it is acting in self defense; (2) the attack is substantial and military (i.e., not an "isolated armed incident"); (3) the offending nation is

8. *Id.*
9. *See* Biggio, *supra* note 3.

complicit, unwilling, or unable to prevent further attacks; (4) the attack is widespread and imminent.[10]

The development of a new body of international law providing legal justification for such actions (active self-defense against a non-state actor) must be consistent with existing principles and obligations including proportionality, military necessity, collateral damage, and exhaustion or unavailability of peaceful alternative.

ISSUES TO CONSIDER

1. Decision makers often are confronted with intelligence that paints a less than full picture; in determining whether to order a preemptive attack how is "immediate" best defined?
2. How are nation-states to justify preemptive self-defense in the context of Article 51?
3. Why was the *Caroline* doctrine narrowed by the United Nations?
4. Can an isolated terrorist attack be "substantial"?

In undertaking operational counterterrorism, decision makers are increasingly faced with the following dilemma: whether an action — be it preventative or responsive — can be undertaken in the event it involves violating the sovereignty of another nation-state.

In response to a terror attack in Israel, the Israeli Air Force (IAF) attacked terrorist bases in Syria. Though Israel was widely criticized, the government explained that the target was not Syria; rather the IAF was attacking terrorist bases located in Syria with no intent to violate Syrian sovereignty. This argument appears disingenuous as Syrian sovereignty was clearly violated by the penetration of Syrian airspace by the IAF.

Similarly, the United States violated Sudanese and Afghanistan sovereignty when the U.S. military, in response to the successful al Qaeda bombing attacks on the U.S. embassies in Kenya and Tanzania (1998), attacked targets in those two countries. The U.S. fired 79 tomahawk missiles at alleged bin Laden outposts in Sudan and Afghanistan, including a factory believed to produce chemical weapons. While the attack may be considered to be retaliatory rather than self-defense in nature, the question of anticipatory self-defense is relevant to this attack. If, as had been reported, the factory was indeed producing chemical weapons, then an argument could be made that America and its allies would potentially be at danger.

President Clinton relied on traditional Article 51 self-defense in justifying the act, adding the strikes "were a necessary and proportionate response to the imminent threat of further terrorist attacks against U.S. personnel and facilities."[11]

---

10. *Id.*
11. Lucy Martinez, *September 11th, Iraq, and the Doctrine of Anticipatory Self-Defense*, 72 UMKC L. Rev. 123, 143 (2003).

In a similar vein, the American drone policy directed against targets in Afghanistan, Pakistan, and Yemen violates the sovereignty of three nation-states, all U.S. allies. U.S. decision makers are careful to characterize the attacks as exclusively targeted against the Taliban and al-Qaeda and not the nation-states. Nevertheless, the result of the bombings is both a violation of national sovereignty and collateral damage directly resulting in the deaths of innocent civilians, citizens of the attacked countries. While self-defense is the justification for the policy, the violation of national sovereignty raises questions regarding both its legality and effectiveness.

ISSUES TO CONSIDER

1. What is the significance of the phrase "if an armed attack occurs" of Article 51?
2. Does Article 51 impose obligations on states that are irrelevant in the age of terrorism?
3. Should states wait until actually being attacked?
4. Does intelligence information indicating a forthcoming attack justify a preemptive strike?
5. According to international law, how reliable must intelligence be for it to be deemed operational?
6. What is anticipatory self-defense and when is it legitimate?

C. FAILED STATE

In conjunction with self-defense, the question of failed states providing material support to terrorism must be addressed in the context of international law. When the United States attacked al Qaeda and the Taliban in Afghanistan following 9/11, the United States was attacking a sovereign nation. It was argued that Afghanistan was not strong enough to try to control or limit terrorists within their borders; therefore, other nations affected by those terrorists could take action. The United States warned the Taliban regarding the consequences of cooperating with al Qaeda. However, as the Taliban government failed to take steps against al Qaeda, the United States and its coalition partners claimed self-defense in attacking Afghanistan. The same argument—albeit problematic—has been used by U.S. decision makers to justify American attacks in Yemen and Pakistan.

Some have suggested the attacks are occurring with compliance—tacit or direct—of the three nation-states. While this argument addresses the violation of sovereignty, it begs the failed state question. On the premise that bin Laden is presently in Western Pakistan, the failed state argument suggests that the region is a legitimate target because the Pakistani government (or elements within the government) has either proactively facilitated his safety or turned a blind eye. In either case, American articulation of self-defense justifies the attacks at the risk of violating Pakistani sovereignty. In an effort to limit the impact on Pakistani sovereignty, some have espoused the theory of a partial failed state, thereby legitimizing the attacks by minimizing the impact on the nation-state, not defined as the target by the attacking state.

ISSUES TO CONSIDER

1. In attacking a sovereign that, at best, is marginally involved in 9/11 has the U.S. significantly expanded the definition of self-defense?
2. What warning must be given either to terrorists or the state providing material support before undertaking such an attack?
3. How much support must the sovereign provide in order to justify an attack such as that carried out by the U.S. in Afghanistan, Pakistan, and Yemen?
4. When is a state defined as failed and how is that determination to be made and by whom?
5. What are the rights of the failed state?

IV. CIVILIAN COMBATANT

In the aftermath of the horrors of World War II, the Geneva Conventions were drafted. The Conventions directly address the protection of the civilian population by clearly defining the rights and obligations of both combatants and civilians.

According to Article 43 of the First Protocol Additional to the Geneva Conventions, "members of the armed forces of a Party to a conflict are combatants," suggesting, they have the right to participate directly in hostilities.[12] Article 44 stipulates:

> 1. Any combatant, as defined in Article 43, who falls into the power of an adverse Party shall be a prisoner of war.
> 2. While all combatants are obliged to comply with the rules of international law applicable in armed conflict, violations of these rules shall not deprive a combatant of his right to be a combatant or, if he falls into the power of an adverse Party, of his right to be a prisoner of war, except as provided in paragraphs 3 and 4.
> 3. In order to promote the protection of the civilian population from the effects of hostilities, combatants are obliged to distinguish themselves from the civilian population while they are engaged in an attack or in a military operation preparatory to an attack. Recognizing, however, that there are situations in armed conflicts where, owing to the nature of the hostilities an armed combatant cannot so distinguish himself, he shall retain his status as a combatant, provided that, in such situations, he carries his arms openly:
> > (a) During each military engagement, and
> > (b) During such time as he is visible to the adversary while he is engaged in a military deployment preceding the launching of an attack in which he is to participate.

---

12. Protocol Additional to the Geneva Conventions of 12 August 1949, and relating to the Protection of Victims of International Armed Conflicts (Protocol 1), 1125 U.N.T.S 135 [*hereinafter* Protocol 1].

> 4. A combatant who falls into the power of an adverse Party while failing to meet the requirements set forth in the second sentence of paragraph 3 shall forfeit his right to be a prisoner of war, but he shall, nevertheless, be given protections equivalent in all respects to those accorded to prisoners of war by the Third Convention and by this Protocol. This protection includes protections equivalent to those accorded to prisoners of war by the Third Convention in the case where such a person is tried and punished for any offences he has committed.[13]

Counterterrorism conducted by civil democratic society is necessarily predicated on principles outlined in the Geneva Conventions. To that end, one of the most important principles established by the Geneva Conventions is the requirement to distinguish between combatants and non-combatants.[14]

Unlike traditional warfare, which pits army against army, military commanders confront terrorists who dress and look like civilians. The responsibility to distinguish between combatants and non-combatants remains a critical principle of international law that commanders are obligated to honor. These obligations are codified in the Geneva Convention Protocols, sometimes referred to as the "laws of war." The foremost principle is the following: "when in doubt whether person is a civilian, that person shall be considered to be a civilian."[15]

An additional principle commanders are required to honor is protection of the civilian population:

> In order to ensure respect for and protection of the civilian population and civilian objects, the Parties to the conflict shall at all times distinguish between the civilian population and combatants and between civilian objects and military objectives and accordingly shall direct their operations only against military objectives.[16]

The obligation to protect non-combatants consists of the following: (1) the civilian population shall not be the target of attacks; (2) civilians shall enjoy protections unless they take part in attacks; (3) indiscriminate attacks on a civilian population are prohibited; (4) attacks shall be limited to military targets; (5) cultural objects shall be protected; (6) objects indispensable to a population's survival shall be protected; (7) the natural environment shall be protected. According to the 4th Hague Convention, the right to use weapons is not unlimited as weapons that cause unnecessary suffering are prohibited.

Furthermore, the following international law principles must guide commanders in their operational decision making: (1) the requirement to minimize collateral damage; (2) the obligation that the action to be taken meets the test of military necessity; (3) that the damage — whether loss of life or damage to property — is proportional to the threat posed by the individual who the state intends to attack; (4) that, prior to the undertaking of a military operation, all reasonable alternatives must be considered.

---

13. *Id.*
14. *Id.* art. 48.
15. *Id.* art. 50.
16. *Id.* art. 48.

V. OBLIGATIONS OF STATES

According to international law, non-state actors (combatants, not innocent civilians) have neither rights nor obligations. However, states are obligated to act in accordance with international law even if other parties to the conflict do not. Does international law provide a category under which non-state actors may be held accountable for their actions? As discussed earlier, when international law was developed the dominant institution was the nation-state; accordingly, no provisions were made for the non-state actor.

Though the Geneva Convention obligates the state to distinguish between combatants and civilians, the lines are blurred when the combatant is not wearing a uniform, does not carry his weapon openly, and has no identifying insignia. While a chain of command in a terrorist infrastructure arguably exists, that is the sole definition of a lawful combatant that terrorism meets.

According to Article 28 of the Fourth Geneva Convention, human shielding, defined as the deliberate placement of civilians in or around targets to deter an enemy, willful endangerment of an innocent civilian by a combatant by hiding behind them, is unlawful. Nevertheless, terrorist organizations use innocent civilians as human shields for a number of reasons, primarily to protect themselves, with the underlying assumption that states will not attack them if there is a possibility that innocent civilians will be killed as a result. In that vein, the Israeli High Court of Justice ruled in *Adalah — The Legal Center for Arab Minority Rights in Israel v. GOC Central Command, IDF*[17] that commanders may not use Palestinians as human shields. Though there was an attempt by the IDF to wiggle by developing alternatives, the Court was adamant: human shielding is a violation of international law and therefore forbidden.

Nevertheless, terrorist organizations, not beholden to law, act in direct contravention of this article of the Geneva Convention using innocent civilians, particularly children, as human shields.[18] Since terrorist organizations are not subject to international sanction, should nation-states apply similar principles when responding to threatening non-state actors? This question suggests a fundamental weakness in international law as terrorist organizations assume immunity regarding their actions.

Issues to Consider

1. Is the United Nations the appropriate forum for resolving violations by non-state actors?
2. What sanctions can be imposed on terrorists?
3. What is the role of states that either provide haven or support to terrorists?

---

17. HCJ 3799/02, Adalah — The Legal Center for Arab Minority Rights in Israel v. GOC Central Command, IDF [2005] (Isr.).
18. Chris Bury, *Battle of Jenin: The Search for Truth*, ABC News, Apr. 30, 2002.

4. Should international law be adopted to reflect the increasing role of terrorists and their violations of international law?
5. Should the restriction regarding human shielding be waived to enable states to more effectively conduct counterterrorism?

VI. CHANGING TIMES

In the immediate aftermath of 9/11, the United Nations Security Council passed Resolutions 1368 and 1373, intended, in part, to redefine the limits of self-defense.[19] Resolution 1368 specifically recognized the "inherent right of individual or collective self-defence" articulating determination to "combat by all means threats to international peace and security caused by terrorist acts."[20]

> Resolution 1373 requires all states to take steps to combat terrorism; it creates uniform obligations for all 191 member states to the United Nations, thus going beyond the existing international counterterrorism conventions and protocols binding only those that have become parties to them. This is an unprecedented step for the Security Council to take. The Council has taken provisions from a variety of international legal instruments that do not yet have universal support, such as the Terrorism Financing Convention, and incorporated them into a resolution that is binding on all UN member states. Some mistakenly think Resolution 1373 is directed mainly at terrorist financing. It does address this crucial area, but it also requires or urges other steps by states against terrorists, their organizations, and supporters — for example, to update laws and to bring terrorists to justice, improve border security and control traffic in arms, cooperate and exchange information with other states concerning terrorists, and provide judicial assistance to other states in criminal proceedings related to terrorism. More generally, it requires all member states to review their domestic laws and practices to ensure that terrorists cannot finance themselves or find safe havens for their adherents or their operations on these states' territory.[21]

In the post-9/11 world, nations such as the United States have encouraged a broader reading of international law to justify a policy of aggression either following an attack or in attempting to thwart a suspected threat. The broad latitude the United States seeks was used by the Bush administration to justify attacking Iraq and Afghanistan, and used by the Obama administration for aggressive implementation of the drone policy in Afghanistan, Pakistan, and

---

19. S.C. Res. 1368, U.N. SCOR, 56th Sess., 4370th mtg., U.N. Doc. S/RES/1368 (2001); S.C. Res. 1373, U.N. SCOR, 56th Sess., 4385th mtg., U.N. Doc. S/RES/1373 (2001).

20. S.C. Res. 1368, U.N. SCOR, 56th Sess., 4370th mtg., U.N. Doc. S/RES/1368 (2001), *available at* http://daccess-ods.un.org/doc/undoclg_en/n01/533/82/pdf/n0153382.pdf (last visited July 22, 2007).

21. Eric Rosand, *Security Council Resolution 1373, the Counter-Terrorism Committee, and the Fight Against Terrorism*, 97 A.J.I. L. 333, 334 (Apr. 2003).

Yemen. To that end, self-defense as expressed in Article 51 of the UN charter and the inherent limitations placed on states under Article 2(4) have been clearly challenged by U.S. actions of post-9/11.

ISSUES TO CONSIDER

1. Has an expanded interpretation of self-defense served the policy interests of the United States?
2. What have been the legal or policy considerations of nations who have not adopted a similar approach?
3. Does U.S. policy suggest the irrelevance of international law?
4. What flexibility does international law allow for?
5. What safeguards, if any, does international law provide for in the face of such a broad re-interpretation of basic principles?
6. How expansively can self-defense be defined?

VII. CONCLUSION

U.N. resolution 1373 and other terror-related agreements and conventions address a variety of counterterrorism issues. The failure of the international community to develop an agreed upon definition of terrorism is but one symptom of a larger issue that directly affects how the world both prevents and responds to terrorism. For international law to impact how nations conduct counterterrorism efforts while protecting innocent civilians, traditional principles must be modified to reflect the new reality.

Collateral damage is an inevitable byproduct of counterterrorism;[22] the Geneva Convention principle that it be held to a minimum is conceivably an impractical obligation when terrorists surround themselves with innocent civilians. As will be discussed in forthcoming chapters, targeting specific individuals suspected of involvement in acts of terrorism inevitably results in loss of innocent life. By example, the targeted killings of Salah Shehada and Ayman al-Zahawiri resulted in significant loss of innocent civilian life. It is a reasonable assumption that targeting of particular individuals will continue; similarly, one of the predictable results is continued loss of innocent lives.

Distinct from traditional warfare, which implied large armies engaged in mutual attack and counterattack with infantry, planes, and warships, sophisticated counterterrorism is far more target specific and localized. Military commanders and decision makers must determine what risks and costs are acceptable according both to domestic and international law.

---

22. *See* Amos N. Guiora & Martha Minow, *Guess Who's Coming to Dinner?*, Boston Globe, Jan., 21, 2006.

CHAPTER 3

BALANCING NATIONAL SECURITY AND INDIVIDUAL RIGHTS

I. INTRODUCTION

Balancing legitimate national security rights and equally legitimate individual civil and political rights is the most significant issue faced by liberal democratic nations developing a counterterrorism strategy. Without balancing these two tensions, democratic societies lose the very ethos for which they fight. As Benjamin Franklin once said, "those who would give up essential liberty, to purchase a little temporary safety, deserve neither liberty nor safety."[1] While imperative for democracies to avoid infringing on political freedoms and civil liberties government's ultimate responsibility is protecting its citizens.

How—and whether—each of the seven surveyed nations balances these competing interests is the focus of the chapter. To that extent, how—and whether—each struggles with the self-imposed restraints that inherently limit their response to terrorism is examined. Regimes that act with impunity and disregard norms are distinguishable from nations that internalize the reality of limits of state power. In that vein, the discussion that follows considers responses to major terror attacks in each of the reviewed countries illustrating how—and whether—national security and individual rights are balanced.

In the United States, both the Bush and Obama administrations have struggled to play "catch up." The treatment of illegal aliens in the United States demonstrates the tenuous balance between national security and individual rights. Israel's balancing efforts are analyzed by examining implementation of the house demolition policy. Both Russian and China have action oriented policies, responding to attacks with an instantaneous narrowing of individual rights intended to protect national security. India's balancing is analyzed by

---

1. Benjamin Franklin, *Pennsylvania Assembly: Reply to the Governor, Nov. 11, 1755, in* The Papers of Benjamin Franklin 242 (Leonard W. Labaree ed., 1963).

examining legislative responses to terrorist attacks favoring national security over individual civil rights. Spain's balancing efforts are examined by addressing the issue of incommunicado detention, whereby individual rights are minimized, for a limited time, in the interest of national security. Columbia has chosen to favor national security, providing little protection to individual rights focusing almost exclusively on eliminating the terrorist threat.

ISSUES TO CONSIDER

1. How far should democracies go with self-imposed restraints in the context of counterterrorism?
2. What price are democracies willing to pay for freedom? How much should they be willing to pay?
3. Does surrendering liberty guarantee security?
4. Should nations adopt special/emergency legislation in response to terrorism?
5. Should government be able to listen in on conversations of persons in federal incarceration if there is a reasonable suspicion that the communication might further terrorism?
6. Are there other circumstances when the government would want to listen into conversations of those in federal incarceration?
7. How do we distinguish between actions and thoughts and when are nations allowed to impinge upon certain liberties including, for example, the right to contribute to a charity of an individual's choice?

II. UNITED STATES

A. HISTORICAL DISCRIMINATION AND ETHNIC PROFILING

Though the United States is a nation of immigrants, many of whom traveled far and wide to reach America's shores and achieve the American dream, U.S. history is replete with examples of mistreatment of immigrants. Until the mid-1800s, employment ads and help wanted signs in many cities included notations saying "No Irish Need Apply" and several states refused to allow Jewish immigrants to vote. Mistreatment of aliens extended beyond private actions; the U.S. government implemented policies that limited alien rights. In the Palmer Raids following World War I, suspected radicals were rounded up, held without bail and often deported without trial.[2] These "radicals" were often Eastern European Jews; the raids resulted in the deportation of more than 3,000 aliens.[3] During World War I, the government imprisoned dissidents for

---

2. Haynes Johnson, *The Age of Anxiety: McCarthyism to Terrorism* 107-10 (2005).
3. Laura K. Donohue, *Terrorist Speech and the Future of Free Expression*, 27 Cardozo L. Rev. 233, 245 (2005).

"merely speaking out against the war"; most of those imprisoned were immigrants.[4] In the immediate aftermath of Pearl Harbor more that 120,000 Japanese Americans were interned in camps solely because of their ancestry. Individual determinations of national security threats were not made prior to internment.[5]

David Cole has compellingly written:

> This [post-9/11] is not the first time our nation has responded to fear by targeting immigrants and treating them as suspect because of their group identities rather than their individual conduct. In World War I, we imprisoned dissidents for merely speaking out against the war, most of them immigrants. In 1919, the federal government responded to a politically motivated bombing of Attorney General A. Mitchell Palmer's home in Washington, D.C. by rounding up more than 6,000 suspected immigrants in 33 cities across the country — not for their part in the bombings, but for their political affiliations. They were detained in overcrowded "bull pens" and beaten into signing confessions. Many of those arrested turned out to be citizens. In the end, 556 immigrants were deported, but for their political affiliations, not for their part in the bombings.
>
> In World War II, we interned 110,000 persons, over two-thirds of whom were citizens of the United States, not because of individualized determinations that they posed a threat to national security or the war effort, but solely for their Japanese ancestry. And in the fight against Communism, which reached its height in the McCarthy era, we made it a crime even to be a member of the Communist Party, and passed the McCarran-Walter Act, which authorized the government to keep out and expel noncitizens who advocated Communism or other proscribed ideas, or who belonged to the Communist Party or other groups that advocated proscribed ideas.[6]

Over the years, the Supreme Court has ruled on several issues related to aliens. In *Yick Wo v. Hopkins*, the Supreme Court held that discrimination based on race and nationality was illegal and "all persons within the jurisdiction of the United States shall have the same right in every State and Territory . . . to the full and equal benefit of all laws and proceedings for the security of persons and property as is enjoyed by white citizens."[7] However, within 60 years, the Supreme Court allowed these very rights to be taken away. In *Korematsu v. United States*, the Supreme Court upheld President Roosevelt's decision to place innocent American citizens of Japanese ancestry in internment camps following the Japanese attack on Pearl Harbor.[8]

While those responsible for 9/11 were aliens, not all aliens living in the United States were involved in planning and executing the attack.

---

4. David Cole & James X. Dempsey, *Terrorism and the Constitution* 150 (2002).
5. *Id.*
6. *Id.* at 150.
7. Yick Wo v. Hopkins, 118 U.S. 356, 369 (1882).
8. Korematsu v. U.S., 323 U.S. 214, 65 S. Ct. 193 (1944). The number of people interned ranges from 110,000 to 120,000. *See* http://www.sfmuseum.org/war/evactxt.html. Executive Order 9066 requiring the internment of Americans of Japanese heritage was signed on February 19, 1942. The Order was rescinded by President Franklin D. Roosevelt in 1944 and by the end of 1945 the last internment camp was closed. http://www.infoplease.com/spot/internment1.html.

Furthermore, not all aliens supported the attack; immediately after the attacks, many immigrant groups, including the American-Arab Anti-Discrimination Committee, publicly expressed their outrage.[9] Yet, the United States continues to use ethnic profiling to identify national security risks while potentially infringing on the rights of innocent individuals. Recent examples include the Arizona legislation that gives "the police broad power to detain anyone suspected of being in the country illegally"[10] and the controversy surrounding the construction of a Muslim community center in Lower Manhattan, the so-called "Ground Zero Mosque."

B. ETHNIC PROFILING

In the weeks after 9/11, Gallup polls showed almost 60 percent of Americans favored "requiring people of Arab descent to undergo special, more intensive security checks when flying on American planes" and half said that "they should have to carry special identification cards with them at all times."[11]

> Before September 11, about 80 percent of the American public considered racial profiling wrong. State legislatures, local police departments, and the President had all ordered data collection on the racial patterns of stops and searches. The U.S. Customs Service, sued for racial profiling, had instituted measures to counter racial and ethnic profiling at the borders. And a federal law on racial profiling seemed likely.
>
> After September 11, however, polls reported that 60 percent of the American public favored ethnic profiling, at least as long as it was directed at Arabs and Muslims. The fact that the perpetrators of the September 11 attack were all Arab men, and that the attack appears to have been orchestrated by al Qaeda, led many to believe that it is only common sense to pay closer attention to Arab-looking men boarding airplanes and elsewhere. And the high stakes — there is reason to believe that we will be subjected to further terrorist attacks — make the case for engaging in profiling stronger here than in routine drug interdiction stops on highways. . . .
>
> Press accounts made clear that whether as a matter of official policy or not, law enforcement officials were paying closer attention to those who appear to be Arabs and Muslims. And in November, the Justice Department announced its intention to interview 5,000 young immigrant men, based solely on their age, immigrant status, and the country from which they came.[12]

Historically, racial profiling has not worked, regardless whether to fight crime or to counter terrorism. David Harris argues that when race or ethnic appearance is used in law enforcement, the accuracy of catching criminals actually decreases.[13] In the late 1990s, the New York City police department initiated a "stop and frisk" campaign whereby police would regularly stop

---

9. ADC Press Release, *ADC Joins Fellow Americans in Remembering 9/11 Attacks, Mourning Victims*, March 11, 2002, http://www.adc.org/index.php?id=147&no_cache=1&sword_list[]=9%2F11.

10. Randal C. Archibold, *Arizona Enacts Stringent Laws on Immigration*, N.Y. Times, Apr. 23, 2010, at A1, *available at* http://www.nytimes.com/2010/04/24/us/politics/24immig.html.

11. Maia Davis, *A Painful Reminder for Japanese-Americans*, The Record (Bergen County, NJ), Sept. 20, 2001, at A15.

12. *See* Cole & Dempsey, *supra* note 4, at 168.

13. David Harris, *Profiles in Injustice: Why Racial Profiling Cannot Work* (2002).

people on the street in order to confiscate illegal weapons and reduce crime. Minority communities felt they were unfairly targeted, a belief that turned out to be correct.[14] Only after Amadou Diallo, an unarmed West African immigrant, was killed during such a stop was it demonstrated, according to a study ordered by New York Attorney General Eliot Spitzer, that minorities were unfairly targeted.[15]

However, the federal government did not learn from New York City's experience; in November 2001, Attorney General Ashcroft announced that the FBI and other law enforcement agencies would interview more than 5,000 men mostly from the Middle East, all in the United States on temporary visas.[16] Of the 5,000 individuals initially sought for interviews, only about half could be located.[17] Additionally, interviews the FBI were able to conduct revealed very little information.[18] In fact, this tactic has been greatly criticized by former FBI agents, claiming that it is ineffective and "guts the values of our society."[19]

The ultimate question is whether a policy, however negatively it may impact a particular population group, contributes to national security? If the policy lacks a balanced approach then it is, in all probability, ineffective, decidedly problematic, and potentially unconstitutional.

According to Cole:

> The government has detained over 1200 persons in connection with its investigation of the attacks of September 11, yet as of late December only one had been charged with any involvement in the crimes under investigation, and the government claims that only ten or twelve of the detained are members of al Qaeda, the organization said to be responsible for the attacks. The vast majority are being held on routine immigration charges under unprecedented secrecy. The government will not disclose most of their names, their trials are held in secret, and their cases are not listed on any public docket.
>
> At the same time, ethnic profiling is being broadly engaged in, and widely defended as reasonable. Already, we fear, the government has overreacted in a time of fear, assuming powers in the name of fighting terrorism that are in no way limited to counterterrorist investigations. It has not shown that the new powers it has asserted are necessary to fight terrorism. And it has targeted the lion's share of its infringements on liberty at immigrants, and particularly Arab and Muslim immigrants.[20]

Racial profiling implies "guilt by association," a concept abhorrent to American democratic values raising profound constitutional questions, reflecting an imbalance between national security considerations and personal rights. Guilt by association suggests mere membership in a particular religious, ethnic, or social group is sufficient to determine guilt. The Supreme Court on a

---

14. *Id.*

15. *Id.*

16. Jena Heath, *Bush Defends Anti-Terror Fight, Military Courts*, Atlanta J. & Const., Nov. 30, 2001, at A17.

17. Michael Ratner, *Making Us Less Free: War on Terrorism or War on Liberty?, available at* www.fathom.com/feature/190142/3728_ratner_article.pdf.

18. *Id.*

19. Jim McGee, *Ex-FBI Officials Criticize Tactics on Terrorism*, Wash. Post, Nov. 28, 2001, at A1.

20. *See* Cole & Dempsey, *supra* note 4, at 149.

number of occasions expressly stated the unconstitutionality of guilt by association.[21] In *NAACP v. Claiborne Hardware Co.*, the Court held that the First Amendment "restricts the ability of the State to impose liability on an individual solely because of his association with another."[22] The Court wrote that to "punish association with such a group, there must be 'clear proof that a defendant specifically intends to accomplish the aims of the organization by resort to violence.'"[23]

However, the Supreme Court has upheld the convictions of individuals for membership in a group that advocates overthrowing the U.S. government by force or violence.[24] In order for membership to be illegal, the Court held that the membership must be knowing, active, and purposive as to the organization's criminal ends.[25] The Justice Department maintains that "the racial profiling guidance recognizes that race and ethnicity may be used in terrorist identification, but only to the extent permitted by the nation's laws and the Constitution."[26]

Issues to Consider

1. Is racial profiling constitutional?
2. What are the dangers inherent to such a policy?
3. Does this policy reflect a failure to internalize the lessons suggested by *Korematsu*?
4. Does the policy of profiling and detaining suspects, as described by Cole and Dempsey, guarantee American's safety?
5. Has profiling prevented acts of terrorism?
6. Does this policy reflect American values and the democratic ethos?
7. Is this a balanced policy?

C. DETENTION vs. DUE PROCESS

The PATRIOT Act is relevant to this chapter for aliens rights are directly affected by its provisions. Professor Cole argues the following:

> The PATRIOT Act gives the Attorney General unprecedented power to lock up any immigrant that he certifies as a "suspected terrorist." Such persons are subject to potentially indefinite detention. While "suspected terrorists" may sound like a class that should be locked up, there are several problems with this measure. It applies to "suspected" terrorists, not "proved" terrorists. It allows the Attorney General to lock up individuals where he has "reasonable grounds to believe" that they have committed any of a wide range of immigration violations, without a hearing to determine whether they actually pose any

---

21. *See, e.g.*, NAACP v. Claiborne Hardware Co., 458 U.S. 886, 932 (1982); United States v. Robel, 389 U.S. 258, 265 (1967); Keyishaian v. Board of Regents, 385 U.S. 589, 686 (1967).
22. *Claiborne*, at 918-19.
23. *Id.* at 919 (*citing* Scales v. United States, 367 U.S. 203, 229 (1961) and Noto v. United States, 367 U.S. 290, 299 (1961)).
24. Scales v. United States, 367 U.S. 203, 205-06 (1961).
25. *Id.* at 227.
26. Fact Sheet Racial Profiling, Dep't of Justice, June 17, 2003 (on file with author).

real threat. And the legislation defines "terrorist activity" so expansively that it includes virtually every immigrant who is suspected of being involved in a barroom brawl or domestic dispute, as well as aliens who have never committed an act of violence in their lives, and whose only "crime" is to have provided humanitarian aid to an organization disfavored by the government. The law further provides that such persons may be detained indefinitely, even if they are "granted relief from removal," and therefore have a legal right to remain here permanently. . . . [W]hat the new legislation adds is the authority to detain aliens who do not pose a current danger or flight risk, and who are not removable because they are entitled to asylum or some other form of relief. This provision raises several constitutional concerns.[27]

In the days following 9/11, many Muslim men were detained by the Immigration and Naturalization Service (INS) for a number of reasons including possible violation of immigration laws, suggestions of terrorist activity, pre-existing federal criminal charges, and as material witnesses. The D.C. Circuit Court of Appeals held the government had a right to keep information about the detainees' names secret; subsequently, the Supreme Court refused to take the case on appeal.[28] Nevertheless, complaints were lodged that visitors to the United States were locked up for months in cells lit 24 hours a day simply because their visas had expired.

In the aftermath of 9/11, the Bush Administration seemed to implement a policy of "guilt by association." The detention of thousands of immigrants and the decision to interview thousands of others qualifies as a modern-day version of rounding up the usual suspects.

The Obama administration is struggling with the same dilemma. The PATRIOT Act allows the Department of Homeland Security to detain and deport aliens based on an alien's support—including financial, food, transportation, or supplies—of an organization defined by the United States as a terrorist organization. An alien is assumed to be a national security risk even if the support was to a charitable group that the United State classifies as a terrorist organization. This question was argued before the Supreme Court in *Holder v. Humanitarian Law Project.* In its decision, the Supreme Court ruled that the government may block speech and other forms of advocacy that support groups officially labeled as terrorists organizations, even if the support is aimed at the terrorist group's peaceful or humanitarian actions. The support is only banned if it is given to a group that is coordinated with or controlled by an official terrorist group.

An effective counterterrorism strategy must be based on sophisticated risk assessment; an approach that all threats pose an equal risk is both operationally unfeasible and ineffective. Mass detentions predicated on association with a particular group rather than on an individualized basis, does not better protect the public. To that end, the alien policy adopted by the Bush administration in the aftermath of 9/11 reflects an improper balance between national security and individual rights.

---

27. *See* Cole & Dempsey, *supra* note 4, at 156.
28. Center for National Security v. U.S. Dep't. of Justice, 331 F. 3d 918 (D.C. Cir. 2003), *cert. denied*, 124 S. Ct. 1041 (2004).

ISSUES TO CONSIDER

1. Were the Bush administration's actions with respect to aliens a justified response to 9/11?
2. Is guilt by association necessary to protect Americans?
3. Is guilt by association, through material support, creating an effective method of identifying national security risks?

III. ISRAEL

A. INTRODUCTION

The Israeli experience with terrorism has been extensively documented in academic research, media reports, and by international and Israeli human rights organizations. Many of Israel's counterterrorism methods have been criticized for violating the rights of Palestinians living in the West Bank, the Gaza Strip, and East Jerusalem. The question of balancing national security and individual rights has come under judicial review throughout the years by the Israeli Supreme Court sitting as the High Court of Justice.

An assessment of Israeli policy regarding demolition of Palestinian homes and a discussion of the measure's effect on both terrorists and civilians will facilitate understanding how Israel balances national security considerations and the individual rights.

B. POLICY

In an effort to quell the Palestinian Intifada (1987-1993), the Israeli Government instituted a number of counterterrorism measures including a policy of demolishing houses in which suspected terrorists resided, hoping it would deter other Palestinians from committing similar acts of terrorism. Israel viewed the policy as an administrative sanction in addition to the criminal law process, whereby a terrorist is tried in court.

C. THE PROCESS

In response to a terrorist attack, the General Security Services (today Israel Security Agency (ISA)) recommended demolition of the suspected terrorist's home to the Officer's Command (O.C.) of the West Bank or Gaza Strip, depending on where the home was located. In *Association for Civil Rights in Israel and Others v. Central District Commander*, the Israel High Court of Justice ordered the Israel Defense Forces to establish a mechanism whereby written notification would be given to the family of the intent to demolish the home.[29] The

---

29. HCJ 358/88, The Association for Civil Rights in Israel and Others v. The Central District Commander and Another [1989].

right to appeal the decision to the O.C. to reverse his decision was institution-alized; in those cases when the appeal was denied, the family could petition the High Court of Justice.

A number of criteria were established. For example, if the suspected terror-ist committed an act resulting in the death of innocent civilians, the home would be immediately sealed and the family would be simultaneously notified of the O.C.'s intent to demolish the house. The purpose of immediately sealing the house was to deter others in the terrorist's community from committing a similar act of terrorism. Simultaneous to the sealing, the relevant authorities gathered information — classified and unclassified — regarding the following issues: (1) did the terrorist actually live in the house; (2) how many family members resided in the dwelling; (3) who owned the house; (4) did the terrorist receive assistance — active or passive — from family members; (5) would demo-lition of the house cause structural damage to neighboring homes; (6) how severe were the terrorist acts committed. After the decision was made to seal or demolish the house, the authorities would determine the extent of the sanction imposed. Written notice of the Commander's decision would be given to the family by an Arabic-speaking officer serving in the Civil Admin-istration (an IDF unit).

The chart below illustrates what administrative sanctions were implemen-ted in the West Bank and Gaza Strip during the Intifada.

Criteria for Imposing Administrative Sanctions

Result of Terrorist Act: Sanction:	*Injury, Not Death*	*Less than 5 Individuals Killed*	*More than 5 Individuals Killed*
Sealing	Yes, without intent to demolish	Yes, immediately	Yes, immediately — with intent to demolish
House Demolition	No	Yes, in some cases	Yes
Administrative Detention	No	No	No

D. LEGAL REGIME

Section 119 of the Emergency Defense Regulations 1945 authorizes house demolitions:

> (1) A Military Commander may by order direct the forfeiture to the Gov-ernment of Palestine of any house, structure, or land from which he has reason to suspect that any firearm has been illegally discharged, or any bomb, grenade or explosive or incendiary article illegally thrown, or of any house, structure or land situated in any area, town, village, quarter or street the inhabitants or some of the inhabitants of which he is satisfied have committed, or attempted to commit, or abetted the commission of, or been accessories after the fact to the commission of, any offence against these Regulations involving violence or

intimidation or any Military Court offence; and when any house, structure or land is forfeited as aforesaid, the Military Commander may destroy the house or the structure or anything on growing on the land.

(2) Members of His Majesty's forces or of the Police Force, acting under the authority of the Military Commander may seize and occupy, without compensation, any property in any such area, town, village, quarter or street as is referred to in subregulation (1), after eviction without compensation, of the previous occupiers, if any.[30]

When the IDF entered the West Bank and the Gaza Strip in 1967, the British 1945 Defense Emergency Regulations were in effect; accordingly, commanders were authorized, according to section 119, to order the forfeiture, sealing, and demolition of houses.

Issues to Consider

1. What safeguards are required to ensure the judicious implementation of the house demolitions policy?
2. Is the displacement of innocent family members reasonable?
3. Does the inherent and inevitable collective punishment contribute to counterterrorism?
4. Does the policy reflect balance between national security and individual rights?
5. What are the effects on the Palestinian family?
6. Does the policy deter potential terrorists?

From 1967 to 1989, IDF commanders would order the demolition of homes without granting prior notice to the homeowner or tenants. The High Court's ruling ordering due notice fundamentally changed the process both substantively and procedurally.[31] This ensured both a more lawful process and a more balanced approach to the sanction.

The High Court of Justice forced Israeli decision makers to articulate a house demolitions policy; once the policy was in place, the High Court of Justice largely gave the IDF a free hand in implementing the house demolition sanction.[32] Therefore, the issue was not the legality of the policy; the High Court of Justice had decided that. Rather, the relevant concern was the policy's effectiveness.

To that end, a high level IDF commission recommended to the Minister of Defense that the policy be frozen. The commission concluded that house demolitions had not acted as a deterrent and therefore did not meet its stated purpose. Subsequently, Prime Minister Sharon accepted the recommendation, indicating that the policy could be reactivated were there an extreme change in circumstances.

---

30. Yoram Dinstein, *Israel Yearbook of Human Rights* (1996).
31. HCJ 358/88, The Association for Civil Rights in Israel and Others v. The Central District Commander and Another.
32. *Id.*

Issues to Consider

1. What is the significance of the decision to freeze house demolitions?
2. Does Israel owe some form of compensation to Palestinians whose homes had been demolished, in essence, on false premises?
3. Can a state simply say "sorry, we were wrong"?
4. Did the HCJ too hastily accept the deterrence argument without fully understanding Palestinian society?
5. Did the state truly consider the balancing required of liberal democracies?
6. Was the price of collective punishment and the human toll involved an instigator in encouraging Palestinian terrorism?

Many of the questions raised by house demolitions and the subsequent decision to suspend such tactics are open-ended and reflect the enormous uncertainty involved in developing a counterterrorism strategy in the face of terror attacks. The balancing required, while difficult to implement, must reflect both a mature legal analysis and an equally sober, realistic policy analysis. While some would argue "better late than never," the ultimate question regarding the commission's findings is whether this policy, and the legal arguments designed to explain it, failed.

The cost paid by Palestinian families, whose homes were demolished in response to the actions of a family member, is unquestioned. The development of an effective, balanced counterterrorism strategy that does not collectively punish, but deters others while minimizing blowback, is the true test facing policy and decision makers, who must be sensitive to active judicial review during armed conflict.[33]

The house demolition policy was developed and implemented as a deterrent. According to the internal IDF commission, the policy failed in its primary purpose. Over the years, though the High Court upheld commanders' decisions, human rights organizations strenuously argued that the policy reflected collective punishment and, was therefore, imbalanced. It is indisputable that family members "paid a price" for the terrorist activities of a child, sibling, or parent. If, as according to the internal IDF commission, the house demolitions did not deter others then the price paid by family members would ultimately represent imbalance and a failed policy.

IV. RUSSIA

Russia's approach to balancing national security and individual rights appears to be of greater concern to the international community than to Russian policy makers. In developing a strategy designed to respond to Chechen terrorism, the approach is primarily action-oriented, with significant costs to human rights. The issue of Russian counterterrorism cannot be viewed in a vacuum;

---

33. Amos N. Guiora & Erin M. Page, *The Unholy Trinity: Intelligence, Interrogation and Torture*, 37 Case W. Res. J. Int'l L. 2, 3 (2006).

discussion of Russia's counterterrorism strategy must be understood in the context of post-Soviet-era nascent democracy.

A. POST-SOVIET RUSSIA

Post—Soviet Union Russia initially failed to address allocation of power between branches of government including the President and the Parliament. Under the Soviet system, the judiciary furthered party policy and independent judges and lawyers were not well regarded. While the Russian Constitution seeks to separate power between the three branches of government and provides that justice shall be administered only by courts of law, concerns exist regarding the judiciary's ability to adjudicate issues discussed in this chapter.

According to Article 121 of the Constitution, justices cannot be replaced; nevertheless that does not include High Court justices or Constitutional Court justices who are confirmed for a twelve-year period. Therefore, unlike American federal judges who have lifetime appointments, judges' careers in Russia may depend on whether they uphold or reject executive decisions. In analyzing the balancing of rights in Russia, it is important to understand that the executive is clearly the dominant branch. The lack of lifetime appointments for high judges suggests that the judiciary is beholden to the executive. Accordingly, Russian judicial review in armed conflict will be significantly weaker than both the American and Israeli models, with the latter stronger than the former. The significant human rights abuses in Chechnya committed by Russian forces reflect both an imbalance between national security and individual rights and an imbalance between the different branches of government reflecting the "freedom" accorded the Russian executive.

B. CHECHNYA

The violence of the Chechen conflict in both Chechnya and Russia is undeniable. Attacks in Moscow include the bombings of apartment buildings, suicide bombings at public events, takeover of the Moscow opera, and the rigged bombing of the Beslan schoolhouse.

According to Michael A. McFaul:

> Putin's armed forces continue to abuse the human rights innocents on a massive scale in Chechnya. Russia may have had the right to use force to defend its borders. But the means deployed to fight this war—torture, including summary executions, bombings of villages, the rape of Chechen women, and the inhuman treatment of prisoners of war—cannot be defended. [T]he gross violation of international norms by the Russian government in combating the problem has left a devastation that will take years to overcome and has brought Russia no closer to ending this tragic conflict.[34]

---

34. *See Russia's Transition to Democracy and U.S.-Russia Relations: Unfinished Business*; Testimony before U.S. House of Representatives, Committee on International Relations, Subcommittee on Europe, September 30, 2003, *available at* http://www.globalsecurity.org/military/library/congress/2003_hr/mcf093003.htm (last visited July 21, 2007).

McFaul addresses the issue of how this affects Russia's developing democracy as follows:

> The campaign to erect managed democracy (reforms intended to strengthen Putin's political power without undermining formally the democratic rules of the game) has had serious negatives (sic) consequences for the quality of democracy in Russia . . . there is no demand from society for a more liberal, democratic order.[35]

According to the U.S. Department of State's Report on Human Rights (2009), Russia's record in Chechnya was poor:

> The North Caucasus region of Russia remained an area of particular concern. The government's poor human rights record in the North Caucasus worsened, as the government fought insurgents, Islamist militants, and criminal forces. Local government and insurgent forces reportedly engaged in killing, torture, abuse, violence, politically motivated abductions, and other brutal or humiliating treatment, often with impunity. In Chechnya, Ingushetiya, and Dagestan, the number of extrajudicial killings and disappearances increased markedly, as did the number of attacks on law enforcement personnel. Authorities in the North Caucasus appeared to act outside of federal government control. Although the Chechen government announced a formal end to counterterrorist operations, there was an increase in violence during the summer, which continued through the remainder of the year. Federal and local security forces in Chechnya, as well as the private militia of Chechen president Ramzan Kadyrov, allegedly targeted families of suspected insurgents for reprisal and committed other abuses. There were also reports of rebel involvement in bombing civilian targets and politically motivated disappearances in the region. Some rebels were allegedly involved in kidnapping for ransom. According to the Internet-based news agency Caucasian Knot, 342 members of law enforcement agencies lost their lives and 680 were injured during the year in actions involving insurgents. Thousands of internally displaced persons lived in temporary centers in the region that failed to meet international standards.[36]

The U.S. State Department Report and Human Rights Watch both list a litany of serious human rights violations in Chechnya. The two reports document disappearances of individuals while in detention or otherwise in the custody of government officials, widespread killing of innocent civilians, and a "no surrender" policy.[37]

The terrorist attack on the Beslan schoolhouse in 2004 was the worst attack in modern Russian history and led to increasing erosion of fundamental rights.[38] Even as the conflict in Chechnya entered its sixth year, the Russian government insisted that "it was successfully restoring peace in the republic." However, allegations surfaced that Russian troops "committed hundreds of enforced disappearances and extrajudicial executions, and tortured detainees on a large scale." Chechens have attempted to enlist the help of the European

---

35. *Id.* at 5, 6.
36. Bureau of Democracy, Human Rights, and Labor, *2009 Country Reports on Human Rights Practices: Russia*, Dep't of State (Mar. 11, 2010), http://www.state.gov/g/drl/rls/hrrpt/2009/eur/136054.htm (last visited July 11, 2010).
37. *Id.*
38. Human Rights Watch, World Report 2005, at 406.

Court of Human Rights to halt abuse by Russian troops. However, applying to the Court has proved to be difficult because Russian troops harass the Chechen applicants:

> . . . Government forces continued to abuse individuals seeking accountability for earlier mistreatment in Chechnya and to harass persons who had applied to the ECHR for the redress of grievances. Amnesty International and other human rights groups reported that reprisals against applicants to the court, included killings, disappearances, and intimidation. According to press reports and human rights NGOs, as of September at least six applicants to the ECHR had been killed or abducted. In a 2007 ruling the court emphasized that the relatives of disappeared persons and witnesses should be protected from intimidation and revenge. However, this practice continued during the year. . . .
>
> . . . An HRW report released in September concluded that the central government had failed to act on any of the ECHR rulings that called on it to investigate specific human rights violations in Chechnya. According to the report, the court had issued 115 rulings relating to Chechnya, almost all of which found the country responsible for serious human rights violations and for failure to investigate the crimes. HRW researched 33 of the cases and found that the government had not brought a single perpetrator to justice, even in cases where the court named the persons allegedly responsible[39]

In the aftermath of an attack on the Moscow subway (March 2010) by two female Chechen suicide bombers, the concern is of an excessive response by the Russian executive similar to reactions to previous terrorist attacks.

Ellen Barry, Blasts Could Derail Medvedev's Softer Tack in the Caucus

The New York Times (Mar. 30, 2010)

. . . Monday's bombings came at an uncertain moment for Russia's Caucasus policy, which had been wavering between the muscular clampdown championed by Mr. Putin as president and the cautious liberalization introduced after Mr. Medvedev took office.

If attacks become a regular occurrence in Moscow, as they were for most of Mr. Putin's presidency, "it means war, war against terrorism," said Aleksei V. Malashenko, a Caucasus specialist at the Carnegie Moscow Center. If they are not repeated, he said, Mr. Medvedev could continue to steer away from Mr. Putin's approach, which relied almost entirely on force.

Mr. Malashenko pointed especially to a decision Mr. Medvedev made early this year, when he appointed the businessman Aleksandr G. Khloponin — not a general or a veteran of the F.S.B. security service — as his special envoy to the region, giving him the task of creating new jobs.

"It meant they recognized the old approach was failing," he said. "I think this is the last hope. If it fails once again, it is over."

---

39. Bureau of Democracy, Human Rights, and Labor, *2009 Country Reports on Human Rights Practices: Russia*, Dep't of State (Mar. 11, 2010), http://www.state.gov/g/drl/rls/hrrpt/2009/eur/136054.htm (last visited July 11, 2010).

No group has claimed responsibility for the bombings, which killed 39 people, but the authorities have said they believe that the attackers were from the North Caucasus, the restive border region that includes Chechnya, Ingushetia and Dagestan.

A law enforcement official, speaking on condition of anonymity, told the Interfax news agency on Tuesday that two female suicide bombers and their male companion had arrived in Moscow on Monday morning on a bus that carried shuttle traders from the North Caucasus.

The official said the bus driver had identified the women from photos. He said suicide bombers had used the bus system to carry out two subway attacks in 2004, since "the passenger flow on private buses, unlike trains and planes, is virtually impossible to control," according to Interfax.

Russian politicians on Tuesday pressed their leaders to take a tougher line on terrorism. State prosecutors revived a proposal to collect fingerprints and DNA samples from all citizens of the North Caucasus.

Aleksandr Gurov, a deputy in the State Duma, complained that political correctness was tying authorities' hands when dealing with ethnic minorities.

"How much can we play at so-called tolerance?" said Mr. Gurov, who sits on the Duma's security committee, to the Web site GZT.ru. "How many cases have there been when Caucasians beat up policemen and the police could do nothing about it? What is this outrage?"

Magomed Mutsolgov, who heads a nonprofit organization in the republic of Ingushetia that documents abductions and killings during antiterrorist operations, said he worried that policies in the region were bound to swing back to patterns set under Mr. Putin.

One of Mr. Medvedev's first major appointments was Yunus-Bek Yevkurov, who succeeded Ingushetia's hard-line leader. Mr. Yevkurov reached out to the opposition and invited citizens to tell him their grievances. The new leader, Mr. Mutsolgov said, "really does have liberal views, but he is not supported by the law enforcement structures."

Asked if Monday's attacks meant the experiment was coming to an end, Mr. Mutsolgov said, "I don't think so, and I certainly don't want it, but it is absolutely possible."

It is important to note, as the State Department report suggests, that Chechen fighters have similarly committed abuses:

> Chechen fighters planted landmines that killed or injured federal forces and often provoked federal counterattacks on civilian areas. In other incidents, the rebels took up positions in populated areas and fired on federal forces, thereby exposing the civilians to federal counterattack. When villagers protested, they sometimes were beaten or fired upon by the rebels. . . . Chechen fighters also reportedly abused, tortured, and killed captured soldiers from federal forces.[40]

---

40. Bureau of Democracy, Human Rights, and Labor, *2002 Country Reports on Human Rights Practices: Russia*, Dep't of State (Mar. 31, 2003), http://www.state.gov/g/drl/rls/hrrpt/2002/18388.htm.

Additionally, Chechen fighters have not limited their attacks or abuses to the Chechen territory; they have been responsible for numerous attacks on civilians both inside Chechnya and elsewhere in Russia. In additon, Chechen troops also assassinated Akhmad Kadyrov and other local Chechen leaders who worked with the Russian authorities.

ISSUES TO CONSIDER

1. On the assumption that the reports regarding the conduct of Russian troops are largely accurate, how does this benefit the state?
2. What controls have been instituted over the Russian forces?
3. How do these issues affect the general populace?
4. What is the importance and effect of international condemnation?
5. Is the imposition of Western human rights standards justified?
6. Does an attack such as Beslan justify a no-holds-barred response?
7. Does the fact that Russia is a managed democracy suggest that the executive is unchecked?
8. What legal standards are appropriate for such a democracy?
9. What institution will ensure balancing in such a system?

Given the combination of weak institutions and a public apparently indifferent to brutal attacks committed against innocent civilians, the resulting lack of balance is inevitable. Has this clear imbalance has contributed to the Russian counterterrorism effort?

In the managed democracy system where courts and the legislature do not exercise oversight or act as a restraining force, perhaps executive aggression is inevitable. Only a few days after the Beslan massacre, former President Putin announced new political measures designed to "give the president de facto power to appoint governors, even more sway over the parliament, or state Duma, and increase executive's influence over the judiciary."[41] Many Russians disagreed with the new measures, but checks and balances are too weak to prevent implementation of the measures.

When Putin first came to power there was great public debate among political parties regarding policy issues. The media published a wide variety of opinions, regional governors were strong, the courts had achieved a degree of independence from the executive, and involvement by nongovernmental organizations was growing. This is no longer the case.

> Public debate on key policy issues has all but disappeared. The propresidential United Russia party controls more than two-thirds of all seats in the State Duma, enough to adopt any law or even change the constitution. Opposition parties have been either decimated or eliminated altogether, partially a result of the deeply flawed elections of December 2003. During this election campaign and the presidential election that followed, television

---

41. Open Letter to the UN Counter-Terrorism Committee, Human Rights Watch, Jan. 25, 2005, *available at* http://hrw.org/english/docs/2005/01/25/uzbeki10074_txt.htm.

media shamelessly promoted United Russia and a few other Kremlin-favored parties while constantly vilifying the opposition.

After a two-year long assault on the independent electronic media, all television stations are firmly under Kremlin control, as are most radio stations. Television news has become monotone, perpetually portraying the president in a positive light and avoiding criticism of his policies. Most programs featuring live debate on political issues have been cut. Only a small number of newspapers and Internet publications provide some plurality of opinion, but their readership is marginal.

After convincing regional governors to give up their seats in Russia's senate as a concession to Putin early in his presidency, the Kremlin gradually destroyed them as an independent political force. Through intensive meddling in gubernatorial election campaigns, using its sway over television media and its enormous administrative resources, the Kremlin effectively made the gubernatorial candidates dependent on its support. By September 2004, the governors' power had been reduced to such an extent that not one of them dared publicly to criticize Putin's proposal to scrap gubernatorial elections.[42]

ISSUES TO CONSIDER

1. In the context of checks and balances and rule of law, does the apparent disregard to both in Russia contribute to a more effective counterterrorism policy?
2. Would balancing be appropriate when Chechen terrorists commit acts such as the bombing of the Beslan schoolhouse?
3. What are the limits of state power?

In April 2009, President Dmitry Medvedev stated he was decreasing counterterrorist operations in Chechnya. A week after formally ending the counterterrorism military program, Russia reintroduced it because of alleged activity among illegal armed groups. Continued violence in Chechnya directly leads to continued Russian presence in the region.

In the context of balancing national security considerations and the rights of the individual, measuring effectiveness requires sensitivity both to international law and international opinion. An analysis of the Russian government's conduct in Chechnya suggests willful disregard of both.

An objective assessment suggests that the current policy has not contributed to the defeat of Chechen terrorism; blowback is undeniable, Chechnya's desire to continue their struggle is well documented, and further human rights abuses by both parties is all but inevitable. Weak efforts on the part of domestic institutions, in clear contrast to the Israeli model of active judicial review in armed conflict, clearly contribute to the present state of affairs. Even an American model of circumspect judicial review could contribute to a more balanced, and therefore more effective, Russian counterterrorism strategy.

---

42. *Id.*

V. INDIA

A. INTRODUCTION

The dominant reality is that India faces myriad external and domestic terrorist threats. In examining the development of India's counterterrorism strategy, the question is whether a nation as large and diverse as India is truly capable of a consistent and uniform policy, given its objective circumstances.

This is not meant to justify or defend human rights violations either perpetrated by the government or committed with its acquiescence; rather, it is to present a reality not faced by the other surveyed nations. India's history is rife with conflict and ethnic violence. Upon establishment of India's independence in 1947, neighboring Pakistan was created based on Muslim-majority areas in the eastern and western parts of India. Prior to independence, the land that is now India was mostly Hindu, with some Muslim areas. War between India and Pakistan broke out in 1948 over Kashmir — India wanted to maintain the status quo of its control and Pakistan refused to accept jurisdiction and control by India.

The historical tension between Hindus and Muslims has been the focal point of repeated horrific attacks and violence. Contemporary terrorism first occurred in Punjab in 1978 but "communal and ethnic violence has been to India since independence in 1947."[43] However, that tension has been superimposed on the age in which we live; the age of terrorism. No longer can conflict between the two religions of India be considered a local conflict. The reality of the India-Pakistan relationship, and the primacy of Islamic terror in India, are such that interreligious conflict in India has an importance beyond the local arena.

Given these political and historical circumstances unique to India, is legislation balancing national security and individual rights realistic? India's religious tensions and strict policies in the wake of terrorism attacks do not offer much evidence in favor of individual rights. India's record of striking an appropriate balance is best analyzed by examining legislation promulgated in response to terrorism.

B. PREVENTION OF TERRORISM ACT

On March 26, 2002, India enacted the Prevention of Terrorism Act (POTA) as a response to the December 2001 attack on Parliament. The Act was intended to grant the state wide powers in conducting operational counterterrorism. Indian and international human rights groups, journalists, opposition parties, and minority rights groups all condemned POTA; the Act was repealed two years later in response to this pressure.

Counterterrorism efforts in India are complicated because terrorism is both internally and externally driven. The internal threat involving disputes

---

43. Ved Marwah, India, in *Combating Terrorism* 301 (Yonah Alexander ed., 2002).

between Hindus and Muslims is, in large part, externally driven. Troubled relations with neighboring Pakistan exacerbate domestic terror and create circumstances in which internal disputes can lead to non-domestic terror threats. The suspected Pakistani involvement both in the December 2001 attack on the Indian Parliament and the November 2008 attacks in Mumbai are examples of situations where perceived threats to national security could dangerously escalate, a reality compounded by the nuclear capability of both nations.

> . . . India needs to alter other dimensions of its policy [on terrorism]. The first is the approach to Pakistan, which must start with two premises — that there are limits to what the United States can do, and the impossibility of getting Islamabad to negotiate away its leverage on terrorism. That will lead a different set of options to the top of the Indian agenda vis-à-vis Pakistan.
>
> One is to develop an activist engagement with the Pakistani polity and society that aims at containing the negative forces in that nation. India's constant temptation has been to avoid dealing with Pakistan as a way of punishing those responsible for terrorism. That approach has not worked. Instead, India must actively intervene in the political dynamic inside Pakistan. Tied to this bold policy toward Pakistan must be comprehensive security sector reforms at home. Without a root and branch overhaul of the security forces, intelligence agencies, border management and the higher political command of internal security, India's own war on terrorism will not succeed. There has been too much rhetoric on the threat from terrorism and too little thought on recasting India's internal security strategy.[44]

The tension between Pakistan and India over Kashmir adds another factor to the equation confronting India. There have been widespread reports of serious human rights violations committed in Kashmir by India.[45] From the perspective of the Indian government, the conflict in Kashmir represents an additional threat.[46] Whether India has responded to this threat in a balanced manner is open to debate:

> There have been repeated cases of violation of the Geneva Convention in Jammu and Kashmir. Indian security forces have consistently violated humanitarian law, and do not often comply with its provisions regarding treatment of prisoners-of-war. There were more than 200 incidents of rape in Doda in January 1994 alone. Rape continues to be a major instrument of Indian repression against the Kashmiri people while the majority of casualties in Kashmir are civilians. The Indian authorities have also steadfastly refused to allow any independent monitoring of the situation.
>
> Human rights organizations are routinely denied permission to investigate in a free manner. Although India has recently permitted an assessment visit by

---

44. C. Raja Mohan, *India and the War on Terror*, The Hindu, Sept. 12, 2003, http://www.hindu.com/thehindu/2003/09/12/stories/2003091201571000.htm (last visited Mar. 26, 2006).

45. *See, e.g., Behind the Kashmir Conflict Abuses by Indian Security Forces and Militant Groups Continue*, Human Rights Watch Report, July 1999 *available at* http://www.hrw.org/reports/1999/kashmir/; *India's Secret Army in Kashmir New Patters of Abuse Emerge in the Conflict*, Human Rights Watch Report, May 1996, vol. 8, no. 4(c), *available at* http://www.hrw.org/campaigns/kashmir/1996/.

46. Kashmir, GlobalSecurity, *available at* http://www.globalsecurity.org/military/world/war/kashmir.htm (last visited Oct. 3, 2010).

the International Committee of the Red Cross and another by the International Commission of Jurists, other organizations have had difficulties conducting public investigation. The International Federation of Human Rights and the Amnesty International have also been denied permission to visit.

Newspersons have been attacked and arrested. Humanitarian relief is limited as external agencies are not being allowed to provide medical assistance and other relief materials. There are incidents of destruction of revered shrines and cultural places by the Indian forces. Villages have been razed to the ground.

Many cases of human rights violation stem from abuse of power under repressive laws and police/army brutality unleashed against the Kashmiri people. They are taken into custody for acts that are legitimized by international human rights standards of free speech, freedom of association and assembly, and freedom of the press. While many arrests are without any legal justification whatsoever, the Indian forces also depend on several laws to justify their acts of human rights violation.[47]

ISSUES TO CONSIDER

1. What effect do external threats have on a nation's internal balancing?
2. Does the fact that India's internal terror threat is, in part, externally driven suggest balancing is significantly more difficult?
3. Does the internal/external threat India faces suggest different standards can or should be applied?
4. Does the size of India's population significantly complicate balancing?

According to Human Rights Watch, legislation enacted by India was imbalanced.[48] In addition, the government misused POTA, targeting minorities and political opponents in a manner similar to previous legislation, the Terrorist and Disruptive Activities Act (TADA). One of POTA's most problematic aspects was an overly broad definition of terror enabling the government to detain suspects for up to three months without charging them. With the permission of a special judge, the suspect could be detained for an additional three months. The government tried to remedy some of these problems by implementing safeguards intended to protect due process rights. However, critics argued that safeguards in POTA, intended to protect individual rights, were insufficient and that the legislation was superfluous because existing laws were sufficient.

Human rights abuse continues to be reported, largely the result of a free hand granted to the security forces, especially in Kashmir, by an executive branch subject to minimal scrutiny. While Public Interest Litigation increasingly enables a citizen aggrieved by government action to petition the Supreme Court, the Indian judiciary is not fully engaged in active judicial review during armed conflict.

---

47. Peace Magazine, Jan.-Mar. 2002, at 18; Prasenjit Maiti, *Human Rights Violation in Kashmir*, http://www.peacemagazine.org/archive/v18n1p18.html.

48. *Human Rights Watch, In the Name of Counter Terrorism: Human Rights Abuses World Wide* 15, Mar. 25, 2003, *available at* http://iilj.org/courses/documents/HRW10CountrySurveyofConcerns aboutHumanRightsandCTCMeasures.pdf.

The drafting, repealing, subsequent redrafting, and re-repealing of legislation curtailing the rights of the individual reflects legislative and executive uncertainty. India's effort to balance is clearly a work in progress; the Indian executive branch has been greatly affected by the powerful and persistent enmity between Hindus and Muslims. A Hindu-controlled Indian government convinced that Pakistan and its overwhelmingly Muslim population are intent on military victory does not contribute to a balanced counterterrorism policy.

Perhaps the best example of this very complicated and fragile situation is the following account of recurrent tensions:

> On February 19, 2003, the Gujarat government charged 131 Muslims under POTA for allegedly attacking Hindus. A year earlier, a Muslim mob set fire to a train carrying Hindu activists in Godhra in the western state of Gujarat. Fifty-eight people were killed. In the days that followed, Hindu nationalist groups and their supporters killed more than 2,000 Muslims throughout the state. Muslims were branded as terrorists while armed gangs set out to systematically destroy Muslim homes, businesses and places of worship. Scores of Muslim women and girls were gang-raped before being mutilated and burnt to death. Human Rights Watch investigations revealed that attacks against Muslims were carried out with extensive state participation and support and planned months in advance of the Godhra attack. The Hindu nationalist Bharatiya Janata Party that heads the state government has not charged any Hindus under POTA for violence against Muslims.[49]

This horrific act of random ethnically oriented violence and the tepid — at best — response of the Indian government speaks volumes regarding balance. The incident demonstrates the inability (or unwillingness), of the Indian government to provide measures necessary to protect the rights of all of its citizens. The combination of threats, both internal and external in origin, presents a unique challenge; however, balancing requires protecting individuals from government's inherent inclination to engage in excess regarding national security, despite threats faced.

VI. SPAIN

A. INTRODUCTION

Spain has long faced domestic terrorism; the Basques in the northern part of the nation have demanded an independent state for years. As a result, Euskadi Ta Askatasuna (ETA)[50] has presented a major challenge to Spanish governments and has taken a significant toll on Spanish life. But Spanish counterterrorism relating to the Basques is not discussed here; rather, the balanced

---

49. Asian Center for the Progress of Peoples, *available at* http://www.acpp.org/uappeals/cprofile/india.html (last visited June 26, 2005).

50. ETA, which stands for Basque Homeland and Freedom, established in 1959, states its ultimate goal to be complete independence from Spain. Jean R. Tartter, *Spain: A Country Study* 345-53 (Eric Solsten & Sandra W. Meditz ed., 1990).

response to the multiple bombings at the Madrid train station on March 11, 2004 is examined.

Spanish balancing is paradoxical. On the one hand, Spanish laws enable authorities to implement tough measures; on the other hand, the response of the Spanish government to the train bombing was, in large part, a non-response. Unlike the United States which responded to 9/11 by enacting legislation and implementing measures, some perhaps unconstitutional, and in contrast to Russia which clearly responds with force, as do Israel and India, the Spanish reaction was limited to implementing existing laws. Before September 11, 2001, Spain was one of only six European countries with specific counter-terrorism laws distinct from ordinary criminal codes. The tough statutes allow Spanish magistrates to be "among the most dogged pursuers of al Qaeda suspects."[51] It is important to note that the existing laws were in place precisely because Spain has, for years, experienced internal terrorism. Unlike the United States, which had to literally scramble and enact legislation in response to 9/11, Spain had at its disposal a full panoply of relevant laws.

B. INCOMMUNICADO DETENTION

According to Human Rights Watch,[52] current Spanish law enables the authorities to detain an individual incommunicado for up to 13 days. Incommunicado detention deprives individuals of basic rights, including notifying family members of the detainee's whereabouts, the ability to seek legal counsel, and access to a judge for purposes of objective review of the evidence against him. According to Human Rights Watch, "virtually all terrorism suspects are held in incommunicado detention upon arrest. During this period, they do not have the right to hire a lawyer of their own choosing."[53]

Human Rights Watch further suggests that:

> The principle features of Spain's counterterrorism provisions are the extended period of detention in police custody allowed before the prisoner must be brought before a judge, and the use of the incommunicado detention . . . those detained on suspicion of membership or collaboration with an armed group (including terrorist organization) may be held for an additional 48 hours (others must be brought before a magistrate within 72 hours). This means that terrorism suspects may be under police custody for five days before being seen by a judge.[54]

Similar to concern that arose regarding the status of detainees in Guantanamo Bay and Order 1500 in Israel, Spain has been criticized for legislation enabling authorities to hold a detainee incommunicado.

---

51. Jonathan Stevenson, *How Europe and America Defend Themselves*, 82 Foreign Aff. 75, 81 (2003).
52. Human Rights Watch, *Setting an Example?* 27 (2005) (citing L.E. Crim. Art. 509).
53. *Id.* at 17.
54. *Id.* at 18-19.

ISSUES TO CONSIDER

1. What is the benefit to holding a detainee incommunicado?
2. Is there an operational advantage to such a detention?
3. What rights are being violated?
4. How serious is such an infringement?
5. What have the costs and benefits of such a policy been historically?
6. Why do other nations not implement such a policy?
7. Is such a policy suitable for those suspected of terrorism only?
8. How does such a policy reflect on a liberal democracy?

Given that incommunicado detention has been legislatively enacted, there are two issues to consider: its effectiveness and its possible violation of internationally recognized human rights.

The United Nations commented on Spain's practice of incommunicado detention in *Mikel Egibar Mitxelena v. Spain*:

> Incommunicado detention, when justified by insuperable problems in the investigation of the offence concerned, especially when crimes as serious as terrorism are involved, cannot in itself be regarded as contrary to the Covenant. Furthermore, the Body of Principles for the Protection of All Persons Under Any Form of Detention or Imprisonment authorizes incommunicado detention for a few days in exceptional cases (Principles 15, 16 and 18, paragraph 3), such as "exceptional needs of the investigation", or "exceptional circumstances, to be specified by law or lawful regulations, when it is considered indispensable by a judicial or other authority in order to maintain security and good order". The Group considers charges of terrorism and conspiracy to represent an exceptional circumstance which, according to Spanish legislation, authorizes incommunicado detention for a brief period. It should be added that the judge of Examining Court No. 3 of the National High Court took measures for the physical and psychological protection of the person under arrest, to the point where he received a medical examination daily.[55]

Human Rights Watch also expressed concern regarding incommunicado detention in terrorism cases.

> Spain's anti-terror laws permit the use of incommunicado detention, secret legal proceedings, and pre-trial detention for up to four years. The proceedings governing the detentions of suspected al Qaeda operatives apprehended in Spain in November 2001, July 2002, and January 2003, among others, have been declared secret (causa secreta). The investigating magistrate of the Audiencia Nacional, a special court that oversees terrorist cases, can request causa secreta for thirty days, consecutively renewable for the duration of the four-year pre-trial detention period. Secret proceedings bar the defense access to the prosecutor's evidence, except for information contained in the initial

---

55. Adopted Nov. 29, 1999, E/CN.4/2001/14/Add.1, *available at* http://www1.umn.edu/humanrts/wgad/26-1999.html.

detention order. Without access to this evidence, detainees are severely hampered in mounting an adequate defense.[56]

Incommunicado detention reflects a policy of firmness verging on denial of basic human rights. In denying a detainee basic rights, such as informing family members regarding the detention, the Spanish government is taking measures that imply imbalance. When the Israel Defense Forces invaded the West Bank, the relevant military order decreed that detainees must be brought to a judge within eight days of their detention. Though the military commander reached the conclusion that operational circumstances dictated extension to 18 days, the High Court of Justice held that logistical considerations are irrelevant and that basic rights may not be violated, even during conflict.[57] In a similar vein, the Presidential Order creating the military commissions in Guantanamo Bay and the Department of Defense instructions subsequently promulgated were heavily criticized because detainees were denied the right to be brought before an independent judge.

Furthermore, an analysis from an operational perspective suggests that the benefits of incommunicado detention are unclear. While there has not been another major Islamic based terrorist attack on Spanish soil since the Madrid bombing, there is a lack of evidence as to whether this is a direct result of Spanish counterterrorism policies. Since the equation requires that national security not outweigh civil liberties, the holding of a detainee under such conditions seemingly creates an imbalance.

A comparative transnational analysis would suggest that the policy is illegal, though statutorily enacted. If compared to court holdings in response to Order 1500 and Guantanamo Bay, then its illegality is quite evident; however, Spanish courts have not ruled to date that the policy is illegal.

VII. CHINA

China's national security dilemmas have increasingly come into focus in recent years primarily owing to unrest in Xinjiang Province. The unrest stems in part from ethnic tensions; a majority of the population in Xinjiang are Muslim Uyghurs, an ethnic minority elsewhere in China.

A. HISTORY

During the Cultural Revolution, oppressive policies against the religious and cultural practices of ethnic minorities led to dramatic and draconian limits on individual rights, ruthlessly applied. In the 1980s, the practice was relaxed allowing Uyghurs greater autonomy for their religious and cultural practices. However, this relaxation allowed radical Islamic beliefs to spread; the Chinese

---

56. Human Rights Watch, *In the Name of Counter Terrorism: Human Rights Abuses World Wide* 15, Mar. 25, 2003, *available at* http://iilj.org/courses/documents/HRW10CountrySurveyof ConcernsaboutHumanRightsandCTCMeasures.pdf.
57. HCJ 3239/02, Marab v. IDF Commander in the West Bank (2002) (Isr.).

government alleges that radical Islamic separatists are primarily responsible for a majority of the terrorist attacks in Xinjiang province.

The Xinjiang Province is of importance to China due to significant economic, strategic, and military benefits. Xinjiang has vast natural resources, is the base of economic trade with Central Asian states, and has a border with eight countries magnifying its importance for border security purposes. The eight states also share a common threat of domestic terrorism from radical Islamic groups.

The Chinese response to domestic terrorism has included strong law enforcement crackdown, especially in Xinjiang Province. In 1996 the Chinese implemented "Strike Hard, Maximum Pressure" an anti-crime campaign. The "Strike Hard" campaign was initially intended to crack down on corruption, but included severe restrictions on the practice of religion. Amnesty International has reported serious violations of human rights committed against Uyghurs in the name of counterterrorism. These reported violations included imposition of the death penalty against 190 Uyghurs between 1997 and April 1999. "Strike Hard" was re-launched in 2001 resulting in additional executions, arrests, and prison sentences.

Even with these strict policies in place, there have been numerous incidents of domestic terrorism in Xinjiang province. The Chinese allege that the acts are predominantly the responsibility of the East Turkistan Independence Movement (ETIM). In April 1990, an armed rebellion in Baren township resulted in the deaths of more than 100 protestors and police. In addition, there were numerous riots in 1997 and most recently in July 2009; the riots reflect the constant tension and violence between the Uyghurs and the Chinese government. The response to the 2009 riots highlights China's struggle with balancing national security and individual rights.

B. CHINESE RESPONSE

During the unrest in July 2009, approximately 200 people were killed when Uyghurs and Hans clashed in Urumqi, the capital of Xinjiang Province. The violence occurred when protests by Uyghurs resulted in the destruction of shops and vehicles; subsequently, groups of Han in the province retaliated. In October 2009, several Uyghurs were sentenced for crimes committed during the riots including murder, property damage arson, and robbery. In November 2009, nine men were executed for various crimes including murder and arson. According to a Chinese white paper on Xinjiang, Uygur separatists promoting the independence of the region caused the riots.

When the riots began, thousands of security personnel poured into Urumqi in an attempt to end the riots. One correspondent stated that the city was under "martial law."[58] Immediately after the riots began a curfew was imposed on the Urumqi, and mosques were ordered to remain closed. Additionally, the area was flooded with more troops and armed police that

58. *China Riot City Under Control,* BBC News, July 8, 2009, http://news.bbc.co.uk/2/hi/asia-pacific/8140492.stm.

surrounded Uyghur neighborhoods. In the days following, over 1400 individuals were arrested by the government; by the end of August, the police had arrested over 1500 people. In November 2009, Chinese officials articulated an intention to implement another "strike hard" campaign, aimed to maintain stability and eliminate security dangers.

China's response to the riots is in accordance with a well-documented pattern: the government sweeps in to the region, arrests suspects, quickly holds trials, and executes those convicted. Thereafter, government imposes restrictive policies for a few years intended to deter future violent actions. In times of crisis, China responds with an instantaneous reduction in individual rights articulated essential to national security. The Chinese response, in contrast with other countries, is less of a preemptive attempt intended to prevent terrorist attacks, than an *ex post* response. Severe *ex post* restraints on individual rights, including imposition of curfews and closing of mosques, raise important questions regarding both legitimacy and effectiveness. Perhaps short term national security restrictions on individual rights are effective; however, the fact that approximately every five years there is another large riot, retaliation, or attack suggests policy weakness, if not ineffectiveness. The *ex post* limitation on individual rights and the repeated violent responses in the Xinjiang region reflect a policy that neither effectively nor consistently balances national security and individual rights.

ISSUES TO CONSIDER

1. What is the benefit of an *ex post* response? Is there any situation where it could be more beneficial to respond after an attack?
2. Can a preemptive limitation of rights prevent violence?
3. Is there a way to consistently limit some rights and the interest of national security?
4. Do short term limitations on individual rights, such as freedom of movement or religion, impose a cost on society?

VIII. COLOMBIA

While other countries have attempted — with varying degrees of success — to balance national security and individual rights, Colombia's emphasis on national security at the expense of individual rights is palpable and institutionalized. That said, Colombia has been subjected to consistent attacks from violent organizations since the 1940s. Groups including the Revolutionary Armed Forces of Colombia (FARC) and the National Liberation Army (ELN) have been operating in Colombia for over 45 years; this has directly contributed to Colombia's defense and security policies focused almost exclusively on counterterrorism.

Democratic Security and Defense Policy was implemented by President Uribe in 2003; the stated goals of the policy were to "reinstate the rule of law in Colombia and protect the population" through consolidation of state control by denying sanctuary to terrorists, increasing state presence, destroying illegal drugs and, maintaining a deterrence-based military.[59] Uribe's policy included granting the military a broad range of police power. Proponents of the policy point to the decrease in the number of people murdered and kidnapped between 2002 and 2006.[60] However, the numbers have increased between 2008 and 2009.

The success of this policy has been measured both in the decline of crime as well as an increase in the number of terrorist killed or captured. This has lead to "false positives" which directly contribute to violations of individual rights of Colombian citizens. To create incentives for capturing or killing terrorists, various promotions and vacations for military personnel have been developed that depend on quotas of terrorists killed or captured. To maximize the numbers, military personal round up peasants dress them in uniforms from FARC or others groups and shoot them allowing the military to count their deaths as successes.

The focus on national security that contributed to a temporary decrease in the number of murders, kidnappings, and drugs has lead to extreme violations of individual rights. The U.S. State Department Human Rights Report for Colombia stated that the human rights abuses by the government included unlawful and extrajudicial killings, forced disappearances, torture and mistreatment of detainees, arbitrary arrest, and a high number of pretrial detainees.[61]

In the interest of national security, Colombia has consistently held national security to be more important than individual rights. The effectiveness of this approach is questionable. For a period crime declined but recently there has been a resurgence in the violence perpetrated by FARC and ELN. The population is caught between the government, the military, and a terrorist organization with little protection for their rights or lives.

ISSUES TO CONSIDER

1. What is the price society can tolerate in the context of aggressive counterterrorism?
2. How is effectiveness of aggressive counterterrorism defined?
3. What is the benefit of temporary relief from terrorism when accomplished by significant violations of human rights?
4. What is the significance of historical enmity between government and terrorist organizations?
5. Is balancing possible if the danger posed to society is constant and pervasive?
6. When, if at all, is aggressive counterterrorism justified?

---

59. Press Release, Embassy of Colombia, *The Uribe Administration's Democratic Security and Defense Policy*, http://www.presidencia.gov.co/sne/visita_bush/documentos/security.pdf (last visited Nov. 14, 2009).

60. Michael Reid, *Forgotten Continent: the Battle for Latin America's Soul* 262 (2007).

61. Bureau of Democracy, Human Rights, and Labor, *2008 Country Reports on Human Rights Practices: Colombia*, Dep't of State (2009), http://www.state.gov/g/drl/rls/hrrpt/2008/wha/119153.htm.

IX. CONCLUSION

A comparative analysis of how the seven surveyed nations balance legitimate national security interests with equally legitimate individual rights suggests an imbalanced approach in the face of terrorism.

In spite of dissimilar threats, not to mention political, geographic, historical, and social differences, the responses of the seven nations are remarkably similar. The United States detains immigrants based on guilt by association; Israel justified house demolitions (a policy considered collective punishment by the international community) by arguing that the action deters potential terrorists only to conclude that the policy, though upheld by the High Court of Justice, was ineffective; Russia's operational counterterrorism efforts are characterized by widespread human rights abuses; India enacts and repeals legislation severely curtailing individual rights while simultaneously committing military abuses in Kashmir; Spain imposes a incommunicado detention policy; China's counterterrorism strategy suggests an emphasis on short-term restrictions contributing to a temporary reduction in terrorism followed by resurgence; Colombia's policy is reflective of Russia's in that protections of human rights take a back seat to human rights.

The balancing discussion — as especially illustrated by Russia, Colombia, and China — reflects a clear emphasis on national security at the expense of human rights. The United States, Israel, India, and Spain's balancing is more nuanced, though all four impose limits on individual rights in an effort to conduct effective counterterrorism.

What are the legal and policy implications of this analysis and what recommendations can be suggested? Fighting terrorism clearly requires developing policies that enable governments to respond to the threat of terrorism, in whatever form. Yet the approach adopted by democracies must uphold democratic values and principles. The former president of the Israel Supreme Court, Aharon Barak, suggests that democracies adopt "self-imposed restraints." Otherwise, according to Barak, the attacked will become like the attacker and lose moral superiority. In developing counterterrorism strategies, nations must be equally cognizant of operational and balancing requirements.

CHAPTER 4

HISTORICAL PERSPECTIVE AND LEGISLATIVE RESPONSES TO TERRORISM

I. UNITED STATES

While Tuesday morning, September 11, 2001, would strike most Americans as the starting date for terrorism — at least as understood by a just-attacked America — the truth is very different from both the national and international perspective. However, the scope and intensity of the attacks that Tuesday morning dramatically reshaped U.S. understanding of and response to terrorism both in the short- and long-term.

The shift in America's response has deeply impacted the American political debate and way of life. How a nation responds to such a terrorist attack offers insight to its unique worldview. This outlook is shaped by numerous factors including political infrastructure, culture, and history.

A. HISTORICAL SURVEY

1. The Nixon Administration

The Nixon administration was confronted with international terrorism when a a Palestine Liberation Organization (PLO) splinter group ("Black September") killed eleven Israeli athletes in the 1972 Munich Olympics.[1] That day, Americans faced issues that had largely not been a part of the American culture: the Middle East, terrorists, and the PLO. The impact of that day, primarily a direct result of ABC's television coverage, was significant. Consequently a

---

1. *See Munich 1972*, International Olympic Committee, *available at* http://www.olympic.org/munich-1972-summer-olympics (last visited Jan. 7, 2011).

survey of America's experience with terrorist attacks begins with the Nixon administration.

According to documents made public, the Nixon administration established a terrorism taskforce.[2] The documents reflect concern regarding potential biological terrorism; however for various reasons — the Vietnam war, Watergate, and Nixon's resignation from office — the taskforce died a natural death.

2. The Ford Administration

In response to the Church Committee, which investigated alleged Central Intelligence Agency (CIA) abuses, particularly in Latin America, the Ford administration issued Executive Order 12333[3] outlawing the assassination of leaders of a sovereign state: "No person employed by or acting on behalf of the U.S. government shall engage in, or conspire to engage in, assassination. . . . No agency of the intelligence community shall participate in or request any person to undertake activities forbidden by this order."[4]

The order, reissued by subsequent administrations, was the Ford administration's principal contribution to counterterrorism. It significantly curtailed counterterrorism options available to decision makers.

3. The Carter Administration

Jimmy Carter was, in large part, elected as a response to the Nixon legacy, particularly Watergate. The Carter administration's primary foreign policy focus was human rights. While a laudable aim, the question that must be addressed, in the context of our survey, is the policy's impact on America's national security. In November 1979, 51 Americans were taken hostage in Iran. The administration's operational effort ended when a rescue mission was aborted; eight servicemen were killed. From a counterterrorism perspective the failed mission should have sent red lights flashing. An elite special forces unit was unable to move beyond the staging area in the Iranian desert because of a sand storm, poor planning, and incompetent command. Certainly, terrorists took note of America's inability to respond while Americans were held hostage.

4. The Reagan Administration

Ronald Reagan's counterterrorism policy sounded firm and decisive: " 'Let terrorists beware that when the rules of international behavior are violated, our

---

2. *See* Frank Bass & Randy Herschaft, *Nixon-Era Terrorism Task Force Envisioned Today's Threats,* Gaffney Ledger, Jan. 24, 2005, *available at* http://www.gaffneyledger.com/news/2005-01-24/AP_News/040.html (last visited Jan. 7, 2011).

3. *See* Exec. Order No. 12333, 3 C.F.R. 200, 46 Fed. Reg. 59941 (Dec. 4, 1981), *available at* http://www.archives.gov/federal-register/codification/executive-order/12333.html (last visited Jan. 7, 2011).

4. *Id.*

policy will be one of swift and effective retribution.' "[5] However, reality was very different from stated policy. In what are considered initial suicide bombings conducted by terrorists, hundreds of Americans Marines were killed in Beirut in two separate attacks. In response, President Regan ordered the withdrawal of the marines from Beirut. According to terrorists and students of terrorism alike, this decision may be the seminal event in the history of modern terrorism. Terrorist leaders realized, and no doubt internalized, a wide gulf between America's stated policy and reality. The deterrence threat may have died before it was born.

Similarly, following the brutal murder of Navy SEAL Robert Stethem by Hezbollah terrorists in Beirut during a plane hijacking, the Reagan administration's primary efforts were to negotiate an end to the hijacking. Though television showed terrorists throwing Stethem, still barely alive, onto the airport tarmac after shooting him in the head, the American response — bluster aside — was one of weakness.

President Reagan responded forcefully to the killing of American servicemen in a Berlin disco by attacking Libyan targets including a presidential palace, allegedly killing one of Mu'amar Kaddafi's children. However, the attack appears to have been retaliatory in both nature and scope and thus in violation of international law, which does not allow for acts of reprisal.

Furthermore, in a part of the world Americans would become all too acquainted with, the United States was actively encouraging, if not aiding, the Mujadin in Afghanistan. The Mujadin was engaged in pitched battle with the Soviet Union following the Red Army's invasion of Afghanistan thereby facilitating Osama bin Laden's ascendency. America's singular focus on the Soviet Union, in the context of the cold war, prevented the Reagan administration from correctly identifying the next threat to world order and stability — terrorism.

5. The First Bush Administration

The first Bush administration's response to the 1988 Pan Am 103 terrorist attack, which claimed 270 innocent lives (189 Americans), was to apply the criminal law paradigm initiating legal proceedings against Libyan agents responsible for the attack. It could be argued that the administration was hamstrung because the attack occurred over Scottish territory; nevertheless, Americans flying in an American commercial airliner were the intended target. Not only did the administration choose not to respond operationally against Libya, but its policy response was limited to initiating traditional criminal law procedure.

The issue of what paradigm applies to terrorism — criminal law, traditional warfare whereby POW status is granted to enemy combatants, or a new paradigm recognizing that terrorism and counterterrorism are neither criminal acts nor acts of war — is discussed in Chapter 9.

---

5. Laura K. Donohue, *In the Name of National Security: U.S. Counterterrorist Measures, 1960-2000,* 13 Terrorism and Political Violence 15 (Fall 2001).

Issues to Consider

1. Has the lack of a coherent U.S. policy given an unintended green light to terrorists?
2. To what can the lack of congressional involvement in the development of a U.S. counterterrorism policy be attributed?
3. Should American decision makers adopt a "walk softly but carry a big stick" policy rather than bluster?
4. What can be learned from U.S. involvement in Afghanistan? How might this affect legislative responses to the current U.S. involvement in Iraq?

6. The Clinton Administration

The first significant legislation against terrorism was the 1996 Antiterrorism and Effective Death Penalty Act.[6] President Clinton had previously submitted antiterrorism legislation, which bogged down in Congress; however, after the Oklahoma City and World Trade Center bombings Congress and the administration agreed on counterterrorism legislation.

The Act established a list of designated foreign terrorist organizations (FTOs) and made it illegal for a person in the United States, or subject to the jurisdiction of the United States, to provide funds or other material to any group on the list. Representatives and members of a designated FTO, if aliens, can be denied visas or otherwise excluded from the United States. Finally, American financial institutions must block funds of designated FTOs and their agents, and report this action to the Office of Foreign Assets Control in the Department of the Treasury.[7]

Against the backdrop of the first World Trade Center bombing, which killed six people, the Subcommittee on International Operations of the House Foreign Affairs Committee held a hearing on July 13, 1993.[8] One of its primary purposes was for the Clinton administration to articulate its counterterrorism strategy. During the course of the hearings Assistant Secretary of State Timothy Wirth set forth that policy:

> The Clinton administration is committed to exerting strong and steady leadership in a rapidly-changing world. History has taught us the United States and all nations can meet that challenge by maintaining a commitment to democratic institutions and to the rule of law. Promoting democratic governments and institutions are full — that are fully accountable to their citizens is our most basic tool for advancing free markets and our long-term national security, and addressing the great and complex global issues of our time. Democracy does not

---

6. *See* Antiterrorism and Effective Death Penalty Act of 1996, Pub. L. No. 104-132, 110 Stat. 1214 (1996).

7. *Id.* at §219(a)(2)(C).

8. *Hearings and Markup of H. Res. 118, To Condemn the Release by the Government of Malta of Convicted Terrorist Mohammed Ali Rezaq: Before the Subcomm. on International Security, International Organizations and Human Rights of the H. Comm. on Foreign Affairs*, 103rd Cong. (1993).

sponsor terrorism. It is no accident that states that do—Iraq, Iran, Libya, Cuba—are also among the most repressive for their own citizens.

Mr. Chairman, let me assure you the Clinton administration will remain vigilant in countering whatever threats may be posed by international terrorists to United States interests. Working in close consultation with the Congress, successive administrations have developed a set of principles which continue to guide us as we counter the threat posed by terrorists. These include making no concessions to terrorists, continuing to apply increasing pressure to state sponsors of terrorism, forcefully applying the rule of law to international terrorists, and helping other governments improve their capabilities to counter the threats posed by international terrorists.[9]

The policy expounded by Wirth was strong on rhetoric but weak both on concrete operational counterterrorism, and practical legal and policy initiatives that would have taken the fight to the terrorists. A common recurrence—as evidenced in President Reagan's response to the bombing of the Marine barracks—in American counterterrorism strategy is rhetoric not matched by sustained action:

Another major element of our counter-terrorism policy is a firm response. When President Clinton ordered the cruise missile strike against the headquarters of Iraq's intelligence service, he delivered a firm, proportional and necessary response to the continuing threat against the United States posed by Iraq, as shown by the outrageous Iraqi attempt against the life of former President Bush. The strike demonstrates that the Clinton administration will respond vigorously, decisively and effectively to the terrorist threat around the world.[10]

To describe this response as "firm" is inaccurate. The administration ordered the raid to be carried out in the middle of the night in order to minimize collateral damage in accordance with international law principles. Nevertheless, from a policy perspective, a nighttime bombing of a largely empty military building by the world's only superpower in response to an attempted assassination of a former president raises acute questions.

From a policy standpoint, the issue is effectiveness. If indeed Iraqi military intelligence played a significant role in the failed assassination attempt, then decision makers must ask whether an attack on the building at night serves the intended purpose of deterence or even of "message sending." A non-response is arguably more effective because the other side is left guessing when, or if, a response will occur. A weak response—such as the bombing of the building at night—may backfire, Wirth's assessment notwithstanding.

B. POST-9/11

1. Introduction

Since 8:43 A.M. on 9/11, the United States has been playing catch-up, trying to make up for lost time by attempting to level the playing field with terrorists. In American history there is a tendency to go engage in a panic response

---

9. *Id.* at 84.
10. *Id.*

when attacked.[11] For example, in response to the attack on Pearl Harbor, 120,000 Japanese-Americans were interned without due process. The Supreme Court upheld President Roosevelt's decision holding it bore a direct relationship to the prevention of espionage and sabotage and was "in accordance with congressional authority."[12]

In an atmosphere of "bringing terrorists to justice" (Former President George W. Bush's frequent phrase), a skewed moral compass is a real possibility, threatening the foundation of liberal democratic society and placing traditional values in, at least, temporary abeyance.

ISSUES TO CONSIDER

1. What is the short and long term effect of ineffective responses?
2. Does the U.S. leadership sufficiently differentiate between real enemies and perceived enemies?
3. Did U.S. decision makers protect the rights of real enemies and protect perceived enemies from the anger of citizens?
4. Were leaders able to restrain their worst instincts and develop a sound policy based on fundamental principles of the rule of law?
5. What is the impact of playing catch up?

2. The Bush Administration Response — Military Commissions, PATRIOT Act, National Security Strategy Document

President George W. Bush's response can best be understood by examining three documents: the PATRTIOT Act, overwhelmingly ratified by Congress on October 25, 2001;[13] the Presidential Order establishing military commissions (November 2001); and the National Security Strategy document establishing the Bush preemption doctrine (NSSD, October 2002). The timeline is significant: while the first two documents were drafted in the immediate aftermath of the attack, the NSSD was signed by the President a year later.

Post-9/11 American policy must be examined from both a domestic and a foreign perspective. The PATRIOT Act is the legislative response to an attack on American soil articulating tools and measures Congress provided the administration to defend America; the Presidential Order established a quasi-judicial process devoid of independent judicial review for detainees suspected of involvement in terrorism in Iraq, Afghanistan, and elsewhere be they foreigners or aliens living in America, including those living legally in the United States;[14]

---

11. *See, e.g.,* The Prize Cases, 67 U.S. 635 (1862); Korematsu v. United States, 323 U.S. 214 (1944).

12. *Korematsu* at 218.

13. Uniting and Strengthening America by Providing Appropriate Tools Required to Intercept and Obstruct Terrorism (USA PATRIOT Act) Act of 2001, Pub. L. No. 107-56, 115 Stat. 272 (2001) [hereinafter PATRIOT Act].

14. Military Order of November 13, 2001, Detention, Treatment, and Trial of Certain Non-Citizens in the War Against Terrorism, 66 F.R. 57833 (Nov. 13, 2001) [hereinafter Military Order Terrorism].

the NSSD reflects the administration's post-9/11 counterterrorism policy of aggressively taking the fight to the terrorists.

3. The USA PATRIOT Act

The PATRIOT Act has been much discussed, debated, criticized, and misunderstood. Critics of the Bush administration argued it reflected disdain for basic civil liberties. Supporters of the administration upheld it as the appropriate legislative response to an attack on America. Sections 203, 206, 213, 215, 218, and 411 are of particular relevance to this chapter.

To summarize, section 203 allows information from grand juries to be shared with the CIA without prior approval of a judge.[15] Section 206 grants roving surveillance authority after requiring a court order approving an electronic surveillance to direct any person to furnish necessary information, facilities, or technical assistance in circumstances where the court finds that the actions of the surveillance target may have the effect of thwarting the identification of a specified person.[16] Section 213, also known as the "sneak and peek" exception to the "knock and announce" rule states that notification of searches can be delayed if it would seriously jeopardize the investigation. Section 215 authorizes the government to seize any tangible items sought for an investigation to protect against international terrorism or clandestine intelligence activities.[17] This may include records from banks, credit bureaus, telephone companies, hospitals, or libraries. Section 218 amends FISA (Foreign Intelligence Surveillance Act) to require that an application for an electronic surveillance order or search warrant certify that a *significant* purpose (formerly "the sole or main purpose") of the surveillance is to obtain foreign intelligence information.[18]

Section 411 of the Patriot Act addresses the issue of the definition of terrorist activity:

> Includes within the definition of "terrorist activity" the use of any weapon or dangerous device.
> Redefines "engage in terrorist activity" to mean, in an individual capacity or as a member of an organization, to: (1) commit or to incite to commit, under circumstances indicating an intention to cause death or serious bodily injury, a terrorist activity; (2) prepare or plan a terrorist activity; (3) gather information on potential targets for terrorist activity; (4) solicit funds or other things of value for a terrorist activity or a terrorist organization (with an exception for lack of knowledge); (5) solicit any individual to engage in prohibited conduct or for terrorist organization membership (with an exception for lack of knowledge); or (6) commit an act that the actor knows, or reasonably should know, affords material support, including a safe house, transportation, communications, funds, transfer of funds or other material financial benefit, false documentation or identification, weapons (including chemical, biological, or radiological weapons), explosives, or training for the commission of a terrorist

---

15. PATRIOT Act of 2001 §203, Pub. L. No. 107-56, 115 Stat. 272 (2001).
16. *Id.* §206; *see* Foreign Intelligence Surveillance Act of 1978, 50 U.S.C. §1805(c)(2)(B) [hereinafter FISA].
17. PATRIOT Act at §215.
18. PATRIOT Act at §218; FISA §1805(c)(2)(B).

activity; to any individual who the actor knows or reasonably should know has committed or plans to commit a terrorist activity; or to a terrorist organization (with an exception for lack of knowledge).

Defines "terrorist organization" as a group: (1) designated under the immigration and nationality act or by the secretary of state; or (2) a group of two or more individuals, whether related or not, which engages in terrorist-related activities.

Provides for the retroactive application of amendments under this act. Stipulates that an alien shall not be considered inadmissible or deportable because of a relationship to an organization that was not designated as a terrorist organization prior to enactment of this act. States that the amendments under this section shall apply to all aliens in exclusion or deportation proceedings on or after the date of enactment of this act.

Directs the secretary of state to notify specified congressional leaders seven days prior to designating an organization as a terrorist organization.[19]

ISSUES TO CONSIDER

1. Do the provisions of the PATRIOT Act provide the U.S. government with tools previously unavailable?
2. Do the provisions reflect an over-reaching reminiscent of internment of Japanese-Americans in WWII?
3. Does the Act reflect balancing legitimate national security concerns and individual rights?
4. Has the PATRIOT Act substantially contributed to a safer America?
5. Have the rights of aliens been substantially and unconstitutionally restricted?
6. Could the administration have implemented active domestic counterterrorism without the PATRIOT Act?
7. What are the ramifications of sneak and peak?

Steven Schulhofer[20] has written about the necessity of the PATRIOT Act, questioning whether its provisions fundamentally changed the ability of American law enforcement to conduct counterterrorism within the parameters of the Constitution. According to Schulhofer, the pre-September 11 regime of constitutional and statutory limits on surveillance and intelligence gathering was a complex mixture of stringent restraints, permissive powers, and awkward compromises. The PATRIOT Act shifted this balance in the direction of greatly expanded investigative power, especially by increasing opportunities to conduct e-mail and Internet searches, to authorize clandestine physical searches, to benefit from flexible FISA standards, and to apply these new powers to investigate crimes entirely unrelated to terrorism.

An important Fourth Amendment safeguard is the requirement of immediate notification when a search is conducted. Officers executing a warrant must knock and announce their presence before entering, except when

19. PATRIOT Act at §411.
20. Stephen Schulhofer, *The Enemy Within: Intelligence Gathering, Law Enforcement, and Civil Liberties in the Wake of September 11* (2002).

doing so would expose them to danger or risk destruction of the evidence sought. Similarly, the officers must give a copy of the warrant to the occupant or leave it at the premises if she is not present, again subject to a narrow exception for situations where such notice would endanger lives or seriously impede an investigation. These notice provisions serve to ensure that the target of the search will know that it occurred and have an opportunity to ensure that the particularity limitations of the warrant were respected.[21]

Schulhofer argues that until 9/11, exceptions to these notice requirements were governed by judicial decisions that examined, on a case-by-case basis, the need for conducting a clandestine search (a so-called "sneak and peek") without immediate notification. The "Patriot Act adds to federal law a provision that for the first time gives statutory authorization for clandestine intrusions and defines in broad terms the grounds that can justify delay in notifying the target that her home was searched."[22] Schulhofer has further written that:

> [a] reasonable argument can be made that the case law on clandestine searches needed to be clarified by legislation. A reasonable argument can likewise be made that the broad sneak-and-peek authority codified in the Patriot Act is preferable to the more restrictive view endorsed in some of the cases. Arguments can fairly be made in the other direction as well. But however that debate might best be resolved, this problem has nothing to do with the fight against terrorism. For international terrorism cases, authority to conduct clandestine searches already existed—in much broader terms—under FISA. The new authority conferred by the Patriot Act is simply not needed for such cases, nor is it limited to terrorism cases; it is available in *any* criminal investigation. And because the new sneak-and-peek authority is exempted from the Patriot Act's sunset provision, it will remain in effect indefinitely. There was no justification for adding this issue to an already large emergency agenda after September 11 and for using the momentum of that occasion to obtain endorsement for the justice department's preferred approach to an unrelated problem.[23]

ISSUES TO CONSIDER

1. What is the danger to democratic society when the executive is granted broad powers?
2. How should the effectiveness of new policies be measured, and by whom?
3. What should be the role of Congress in the aftermath of an attack?
4. When should the scope of searches be extended?
5. When should clandestine physical searches be allowed?
6. What is the significance of expanding the definition of terrorist activity?
7. Does national security justify expanded intrusions on an individual privacy?

---

21. *Id.* at 43.
22. *Id.*
23. *Id.*

The USA PATRIOT Act was originally scheduled to sunset in 2005. However Congress has consistently reauthorized its provisions, including those that most substantially impose on personal liberty by facilitating invasion of privacy.

CONGRESS REAUTHORIZES OVERBROAD PATRIOT ACT PROVISIONS

ACLU, Feb. 25, 2010[24]

The House today passed a one-year extension of three expiring Patriot Act provisions without making much-needed changes to the overly broad surveillance bill. The provisions of the Patriot Act which were extended—the John Doe roving wiretap provision, Section 215 or the "library records" provision and the never before used "lone wolf" provision—all lack proper privacy safeguards. The Senate passed the extension by voice vote late last night.

"Congress refuses to make reforming the Patriot Act a priority and continues to punt this crucial issue down the road," said Laura W. Murphy, Director of the ACLU Washington Legislative Office. "Once again, we have missed an opportunity to put the proper civil liberties and privacy protections into this bill. Congress should respect the rule of law and should have taken this opportunity to better protect the privacy and freedom of innocent Americans. We shouldn't have to live under these unconstitutional provisions for another year."

Late last year, to avoid expiration on December 31, 2009, Congress extended the provisions through February 28, 2010. Despite bills pending in both the House and the Senate to amend the three expiring provisions and other sections of the Patriot Act, Congress decided instead to move ahead with a straightforward reauthorization.

In addition to reforms needed regarding the three provisions that were just extended, the National Security Letter (NSL) statute, which was broadened with passage of the original Patriot Act, must be narrowed. NSLs allow the FBI to secretly demand personal records about innocent customers from Internet Service Providers (ISPs), communications service providers, financial institutions and credit reporting agencies without suspicion or prior judicial approval. The statute also allows the FBI to bar NSL recipients from disclosing anything about the record demand. Several Patriot Act reauthorization bills introduced last year addressed the need for NSL reform but none of those proposals were acted upon.

Since the Patriot Act's passage in 2001, there have been several consecutive reports (including one released in January) from the Department of Justice Office of the Inspector General that have outlined widespread and blatant abuse of the statute. FBI agents routinely claimed false terrorism emergencies to use "exigent letters," or emergency letters, in order to gain private records for investigations when no emergency existed. The FBI also regularly issued NSLs after the fact in an attempt to legitimize the use of exigent letters. Even

---

24. *Available at* http://www.aclu.org/national-security/congress-reauthorizes-overbroad-patriot-act-provisions/.

after today's vote, there remain bills pending in both the House and Senate that were specifically introduced to narrow the scope of the NSL statute.

"Even with another damning report on the FBI's use of NSLs, Congress couldn't muster the willpower to give Americans the privacy protections they need," said Michelle Richardson, ACLU Legislative Counsel. "Though the debate over reauthorizing the Patriot Act may be over this year, Congress still has the power to narrow the use of NSL powers and help avoid such abuses in the future. It's time to rein in the overbroad power of the NSL and bring the statute back in line with the Constitution."

C. THE PRESIDENTIAL ORDER

The 2001 Presidential Order[25] was based on the presidential order issued by President Roosevelt following the arrest of German saboteurs caught in New Jersey and Florida. In *Ex parte Quirin*,[26] the U.S. Supreme Court upheld presidential authority to establish military tribunals; as a result, the saboteurs, including an American citizen, were executed. President Bush's order, which established military commissions for the purpose of trying non-American citizens alleged to be supporting, aiding, and abetting al Qaeda worldwide, was criticized in the United States and abroad. Critics[27] repeatedly commented on serious violations of due process both in the order and the subsequently issued military instructions.[28]

Initial criticism focused on a number of issues, including:

1. Failure to consult with Congress before issuing the order;
2. The Authorization to Use Military Force ratified by Congress does not provide for the establishment of the Commission;
3. Lack of an independent appeals process;
4. Detainee's inability to challenge the cause for detention;
5. A reduced evidentiary standard allowing the introduction of any evidence found to be of "probative value to a reasonable person."[29]

In retrospect, the decision to hold detainees in Guantanamo Bay seems to have been based on two primary considerations: a desire to detain the individuals geographically distant from the combat zone and not to detain them in the United States where the argument could be made that they must be granted full constitutional rights.

---

25. Military Order Terrorism, *supra* note 14.

26. Ex parte Quirin, 317 U.S. 1, 24 (1942).

27. *See* Ronald Dworkin, *Terror & the Attack on Civil Liberties*, The New York Review of Books, Nov. 6, 2003, at 37-38; *see also* Neal K. Katyal & Laurence H. Tribe, *Waging War, Deciding Guilt: Trying the Military Tribunals*, 111 Yale L.J. 1259, 1277 (2002).

28. Katyal & Tribe, *supra* note 27, at 1277; Department of Defense, Military Commission Order No. 1: Procedures for Trials by Military Commissions of Certain Non-United States Citizens in the War Against Terrorism (Mar. 21, 2002), http://www.dtic.mil/whs/directives/corres/mco/mco1.pdf (on file with author) [hereinafter Military Commission Order, Procedures].

29. *See* Dworkin, *supra* note 27; *see also* Katyal & Tribe, *supra* note 27, at 1266-67, 1277.

1. Congressional Hearings

Hearings held before the Senate Judiciary and Armed Services Committees in December 2001[30] brought to focus many of the criticisms leveled against the Military Commissions. Members of the committees (Senators Leahy, Kennedy, and Levin, among others) and expert witnesses (Professors Tribe, Katyal, and Sunstein) roundly criticized the Bush administration, emphasizing its failure to consult with Congress prior to issuing the order and questioning the order's constitutionality. Administration witnesses — Deputy Secretary of Defense Wolfowitz, Attorney General Ashcroft, and Department of Defense General Counsel Haynes — were adamant that President Bush was constitutionally authorized to issue the order without consulting with Congress based on the "authorization for use of military force."[31] Senators Warner and Sessions argued that the order is an inherent presidential wartime power.

2. Department of Defense Instructions

Notwithstanding the administration's testimony before the Senate, in the months following the Department of Defense issued a series of instructions,[32] intended to serve as rules for the commissions. Unlike the unilateral manner in which the administration issued the Presidential Order, the Department of Defense published the instructions inviting public response prior to their implementation. Many human rights organizations responded, overwhelmingly negatively.

3. Results

Since their establishment, the commissions have tried only three suspected terrorists.[33] The process has been continuously held up both because of intervention by American courts and also because the commissions have been confronted with "avoidable issues." Had the administration consulted with Congress and, no less important, with constitutional and international law experts rather than relying solely on problematic precedent (*Quirin*, whose relevance is doubtful in that WWII was a declared war unlike the present conflict), the Bush administration might have avoided questionable legal advice. Administration advisors (lawyers and non-lawyers alike) whose rush to action was, in the short term, arguably understandable ill-served the President and the nation. The failure to consider that detainees might demand self-representation before an independent judiciary with clear rules of evidence are examples of a rushed internal process.

---

30. *See* Testimony before the Senate Armed Services Committee on Military Commissions (Dec. 13, 2001), *available at* http://www.defenselink.mil/speeches/2001/s20011212-depsecdef1.html.

31. *Id.*

32. Military Commission Order, Procedures, *supra* note 28.

33. Ali H. Soufan, *Tribunal and Error*, N.Y. Times, Feb. 11, 2010.

4. Combatant Status Review Tribunals

As a result of the Supreme Court's holding in *Rasul v. Bush*,[34] the administration was forced to establish "combatant status review tribunals" to determine both the status of the detainees and whether their continued detention was, based on available intelligence information, warranted. According to the Court's decisions in both *Rasul* and *Hamdi*, a detainee must be afforded notice and opportunity to contest the determination that he is an enemy combatant. According to the Department of Defense's combatant status review tribunal summary, between July 30, 2004 and February 10, 2009, in 581 hearings, 539 detainees were deemed enemy combatants and 39 deemed not to be enemy combatants.[35]

D. THE NATIONAL SECURITY STRATEGY DOCUMENT

The following clauses of the NSSD clearly articulate President Bush's proactive operational counterterrorism policy:

1) America will hold to account nations that are compromised by terror, including those who harbor terrorists because the allies of terror are the enemies of civilization . . . must not allow the terrorists to develop new home bases. . . . We will seek to deny them sanctuary at every turn.

2) As a matter of common sense and self-defense, America will act against such emerging threats (we will cooperate with other nations to deny, contain, and curtail our enemies efforts to acquire dangerous technologies) before they are fully formed. . . . In the new world we have entered the only path to peace and security is the path of action.

3) We make no distinction between terrorist and those who knowingly harbor or provide aid to them.

4) We will not hesitate to act alone. . . . To exercise our right to self-defense by acting preemptively against such terrorists to prevent them from doing harm to our people.

5) For centuries, international law recognized that nations need not suffer an attack before they can lawfully take action to defend themselves against forces that present an imminent danger of attack. legal scholars and international jurists conditioned the legitimacy of preemption on the existence of an imminent threat most often a visible mobilization of armies, navies, and air force preparing to attack. We must adapt the concept of imminent threat to the capabilities and objectives of today's adversaries. . . . The US has long maintained the option of preemptive actions to counter a sufficient threat to our national security. . . . To forestall or prevent such hostile acts by our adversaries the us if necessary will act preemptively. . . . The US cannot remain idle while dangers gather.[36]

---

34. Rasul v. Bush, 542 U.S. 466 (2004); Hamdi v. Rumsfeld, 542 U.S. 507 (2004).
35. Combatant Status Review Tribunal Summary, *available at* http://www.defense.gov/news/csrtsummary.pdf.
36. *See generally The National Security Strategy of the United States of America*, The White House, Sept. 23, 2002, *available at* http://www.whitehouse.gov/nsc/nss.html (on file with author) [hereinafter *National Security Strategy*].

ISSUES TO CONSIDER

1. Do the provisions of the NSSD mean that the United States is undertaking a policy of violating another nation's sovereignty? Does this document violate Article 51 of the U.N. Charter?
2. Does this document introduce a new concept of anticipatory self-defense? According to this document, when may the U.S. attack another sovereign state who willingly or potentially unwillingly harbors a terrorist organization or individual terrorist? Has preemption been extended further than internationally envisioned?
3. Do these two documents reflect a balanced and circumspect response to an attack, or does it reflect an approach potentially throwing world order into chaos?
4. Is the language of the 2002 and 2010 documents specific or deliberately vague in order to leave maximum maneuverability and discretion to the executive?
5. How much potential harm must be envisioned before the government decides to act? How much is reasonable?
6. To what extent were the 2002 and 2010 NSSD created to exhibit America's strength? Who pays the price?
7. Are both documents an accurate reflection of the attitudes of the majority of American people at the time of their enactments?
8. Is the 2002 NSSD preemptive or reactive? The 2010 NSSD?
9. Do both documents grant overbroad powers resulting in overbroad responses? Is one of the documents symbolically focused on reigning in overbroad powers from a previously overly reactive response?

E. PRESIDENT OBAMA

During the 2008 Presidential campaign, President Obama (then the Democratic nominee) promised, if elected, counterterrorism policies distinct from President Bush's including closing Guantanamo Bay and not bringing suspected terrorists before Military Commissions. To that end, in January, 2009, President Obama created three White House Task Forces mandated to address the following issues: identify a proper forum for trying suspected terrorists; articulate a lawful interrogation regime; close Guantanamo Bay. The task forces reflected Obama's stated policy of reversing Bush-era counterterrorism measures. In addition, President Obama sought to strike a different tone: more cooperative, less confrontational, more encompassing, and less unilateral than that of his predecessor. President Obama's National Security Strategy (below) sought to articulate that shift in policy — both with respect to perception and application. However, policy implemented by President Obama is not dissimilar from President Bush's; terrorists and terrorist infrastructure in Pakistan, Afghanistan, and Yemen are aggressively attacked by U.S. drones resulting in loss of life among intended targets and innocent civilians alike. In addition, President Obama has identified a number of High-Value Detainees who will be subject to indefinite detention; furthermore, the

Administration has not determined how or where to try suspected terrorists and has indicated that Khalid Sheijk Mohammed — a prime 9/11 architect — may be tried before a Military Commission.

ADVANCING OUR INTERESTS: ACTIONS IN SUPPORT OF THE PRESIDENT'S NATIONAL SECURITY STRATEGY

Office of the Press Secretary, May 27, 2010[37]

. . . Disrupt, Dismantle, and Defeat Al-Qa'ida and its Violent Extremist Affiliates in Afghanistan, Pakistan, and Around the World: Since this Administration took office, it has been working with key partners around the world — including in the Gulf, Africa, Asia, and Europe — against al-Qa'ida and its extremist affiliates who remain intent on conducting further attacks against the Homeland and against U.S. interests around the globe. In part as a result of this global effort, al-Qa'ida and its affiliates have sustained a dozen leadership losses. In addition, cooperation between our intelligence, homeland security and law enforcement professionals continued to be strengthened, allowing us to identify and disrupt plots here at home; as a result, in 2009, more defendants were charged with terrorism violations in federal court than in any year since 9/11. . . .

. . . Commitment to Closing the Guantanamo Bay Naval Facility: Our nation's senior defense officials and military commanders all support the closure of the detention facility at Guantanamo to help advance our security. The Administration has instituted the most comprehensive review process ever applied to detainees at Guantanamo, with significant improvements including halting the "stove-piping" of classified intelligence and for the first time compiling in a single repository the best information available relating to Guantanamo detainees. Every decision to transfer a detainee to a foreign country in 2009 and 2010 has been made unanimously by all agencies involved in the review process after a full assessment of intelligence and threat information. The Administration has made remarkable progress working with our friends and allies to resettle many detainees in third countries. Since 2008, the State Department has successfully resettled 33 detainees to 13 different destinations. . . .

. . . Prohibited Torture Without Exception or Equivocation: Shortly after taking office, the President issued Executive Order 13491, which unequivocally prohibits torture of individuals detained in any armed conflict. The Executive Order requires that all such persons in U.S. custody or control must be treated humanely and may not be subjected to violence to life and person (including murder of all kinds, mutilation, cruel treatment, and torture), nor to outrages upon personal dignity, including humiliating and degrading treatment.

---

37. *Available at* http://www.whitehouse.gov/the-press-office/advancing-our-interests-actions-support-presidents-national-security-strategy/.

Legal Aspects of Countering Terrorism: In some of his first official acts, President Obama took a series of steps to prohibit torture, begin a process to close Guantanamo Bay prison, and enhance oversight of interrogation and transfers of individuals to other nations. We have also incorporated internationally-recognized law of war principles into decisions regarding who may be detained in an armed conflict. . . .

II. ISRAEL

Over the years, Israel has often been criticized for its operational counter-terrorism policies and measures. For those who believe that according to international law occupation of the West Bank and the Gaza Strip is illegal, counterterrorism is inherently illegal. This casebook does not seek to address the political and legal issues related to the occupation, the result of the 1967 Six-Day War. Rather, the focus is solely on legal and policy responses to terrorism.

A. INTRODUCTION

Israel has been under attack literally from the moment of statehood (May 1948). However, since 2000 (as will be discussed below) Israel has faced a new terrorist threat; therefore, addressing how counterterrorism policy adapts to changing terrorist threats is the focus.

ISSUES TO CONSIDER

1. What is the meaning of significant terror attack?
2. Should a state respond to all terror attacks in a similar fashion?
3. In terms of policy effectiveness, what should be the benchmark for deciding when and how a state should respond?
4. How attuned should a state be to the court of international opinion when deciding on a particular course of action?

It has been Israel's policy since 1967 to respond to terrorism with a combination of measures—some intended to punish the individual terrorist, others aimed at deterring those who might be contemplating an act of terrorism. Israeli methods have included demolishing the home of a terrorist; imposing a curfew on neighborhoods and towns, either in response to intelligence information indicating a potential terrorist attack or in response to an actual attack; deportation of terrorists; placing terrorists in administrative detention when criminal evidence was unavailable or concern for sources prevented the information from being presented to a court of law; and trying terrorists in a court of law. These measures have been based on Israeli law, international law, or regulations inherited from the British mandate.

As all actions undertaken by the executive in Israel are reviewable by the judiciary—the Supreme Court sitting as the High Court of Justice—the Israel

Defense Forces (the executive in the occupied territories) must always be conscious of the possibility that the Court will intervene, including ordering the military not to embark on a particular course of action regardless of its operational efficacy.

B. POST-2000 POLICY

Since 2000, Israel has significantly changed operational counterterrorism tactics and strategy in response both to suicide bombings and the firing of thousands of Kassam missiles from Gaza into southern Israel. Rather than relying on measures considered appropriate and effective between 1967 and 2000, the IDF has implemented a far more aggressive policy reflecting a situation defined as "armed conflict short of war." This is in direct contrast to stone throwing, Molotov cocktails, stabbings, and massive demonstrations that — in large part — previously characterized Palestinian terrorism.

C. SUICIDE BOMBERS

The fundamental change in Israeli counterterrorism policy is a response to the suicide bomber threat. A successful suicide bombing is the working of a well-orchestrated, difficult to penetrate, highly disciplined, financially solvent terror organization — not the act of a lone individual. To that end, a successful suicide bombing requires four distinct actors: the bomber, the leader, the logistician, and the financier. A primary question confronting operational counterterrorism decision makers, tasked with preventing suicide bombers, is determining both which of these four distinct categories is a legitimate actor and when is the state justified to engage them. Suicide bombings are a reality faced by numerous countries including the United States, Russia, Israel, Iraq, Afghanistan, Spain, England, Indonesia, and Saudi Arabia. While suicide bombers do not threaten the existence of these nations, they affect the daily lives of millions of innocent civilians.

D. THE SECURITY FENCE

The approximately 385-mile security fence Israel has erected on the Palestinian side of the Green Line has been described by Israel as a self-defense measure responding to Palestinian terrorism.[38] Different chapters of this casebook address various aspects of the fence including international law, operational counterterrorism, and judicial review. Nevertheless, the decision to build the fence is first and foremost a matter of policy; accordingly, it must be addressed in this chapter.

---

38. *See Israel's Security Fence, available at* http://www.jewishvirtuallibrary.org/jsource/Peace/fence.html (last visited Oct. 6, 2010).

According to the Israeli government, the primary impetus for the construction of the fence was to prevent infiltration into Israel by Palestinian terrorists. Though the fence has been heavily criticized domestically and internationally, both legally and politically, Israel has responded to such criticism by pointing to statistics indicating the fence has been most effective in fulfilling its primary purpose as defined by the government — protecting innocent Israeli civilians. According to statistics provided by the Israeli government, in areas where the fence has been constructed there has been a 90 percent reduction in Palestinian terrorism.[39] From the government's perspective, that statistic alone proves the policy's effectiveness.

In deciding to erect the security barrier, the government argued it was balancing legitimate national security concerns with the equally legitimate rights of residents of the Palestinian Authority on whose land the fence would be built. In arguing that the fence was constructed on the Palestinian side of the West Bank soley for strategic and topographic reasons, the state denied the fence was an illegal grab of Palestinian land.[40] While upholding the fence's legality, the Israeli High Court of Justice wrote that it "affects the fabric of Palestinian life" by separating farmers from their land, children from their schools and friends from neighbors, thereby making it very difficult for Palestinians to move freely within the PA's area.[41] Accordingly, the Court ordered the state to re-contour the fence in order to minimize the damage to individual Palestinians.

The fence, then, is a manifestation of active self-defense. Israel decided to construct the fence because of a belief — ultimately shown to have statistical validity — that the measure would prove effective in preventing infiltration of suicide bombers into Israel.

International law requires the nation-state to minimize collateral damage and seek alternatives; conversely, the state's fundamental obligation is to protect its citizens. Israel's operational response to suicide bombing was two-fold: targeted killing (see Chapter 6) and the fence. As demonstrated by the significant reduction in the number of suicide bombings, the twin-edged policy has proven statistically effective. That said, criticism has been consistent and severe; the negative impact on Palestinian landowners whose land was used (though compensation was offered) for the fence has, as the Court stated, negatively impacted the civilian population.

E. OPERATION CAST LEAD

In January 2006 — once Israel disengaged from the Gaza Strip (August 2005) — Hamas assumed administrative control of Gaza after winning Palestinian legislative elections. In response, Israel closed off all access to Gaza; in addition, Egypt closed the Rafah Border Crossing. The blockade allowed Israel to control the flow of goods and services, including power and water, into Gaza.

---

39. *The Anti-Terrorist Fence — An Overview, available at* http://securityfence.mfa.gov.il/mfm/Data/48152.doc (last visited May 30, 2010).
40. HCJ 2056/04, Beit Sourik Village Council v. The Government of Israel & Commander of the IDF Forces in the West Bank [2004]
41. *Id.* at ¶¶82-85.

Palestinian's sought to bypass the blockade by digging tunnels between Gaza and Egypt; the tunnels, in addition to transporting food and supplies, were a primary means for smuggling Kassam missiles into Gaza.

Between disengagement and December, 2008, Hamas fired approximately 10,000 Kassam missiles into southern Israel thereby placing 750,000 Israelis who live in a 45 kilometer radius of the Gaza Strip in daily threat of direct attack. According to the United Nations, these attacks killed four Israeli civilians and injured an additional seventy-five. In June, 2008, Egypt helped broker a six-month cease fire between Israel and Hamas. According to the agreement, Hamas would end its rocket and mortar attacks and Israel would ease restrictions on goods coming into Gaza and halt military raids in Gaza.

However in November 2008, less than four months after the ceasefire began, the IDF entered the Gaza strip killing a number of Hamas terrorists. Hamas responded by firing rockets into southern Israel; Israel claimed the incursion was not a violation of the ceasefire but rather a legitimate act to eliminate an immediate threat. Fawzi Barhoum, a Hamas spokesman stated that "[t]he Israelis began this tension and they must pay an expensive price."[42]

On December 27, 2008, in response to an increase in the number and frequency of rocket attacks into Israel, the IDF launched Operation Cast Lead targeting both Hamas infrastructure and those responsible for firing the Kassam missiles.

Israel defined as legitimate targets four distinct categories:

1. those responsible for smuggling missiles from Egypt through the tunnels between Gaza and Egypt;
2. those responsible for making Kassam missiles in Gaza;
3. those responsible for firing Kassam missiles; and
4. passive supporters who — knowingly and repeatedly — facilitated firing of the Kassam missile.

Unlike the person-specific counterterrorism policy that had been Israel's *modus operandi*, Operation Cast Lead unilaterally expanded the categories of legitimate targets and re-articulated proportionality in the context of operational counterterrorism.

The operation began with a series of airstrikes simultaneously hitting 100 preplanned targets. Over the following weeks Israel continued airstrikes in Gaza, in addition to naval operations and a ground invasion. According to human rights NGOs, between 1300-1400 people were killed during the attacks; reports estimate 330 were Palestinian combatants.[43] The operation continued until January 18, 2009, when both parties declared a cease-fire.

---

42. Rory McCarthy, *Gaza Truce Broken as Israeli Raid Kills Six Hamas Gunmen*, Nov. 5, 2008, Gaurdian, http://www.guardian.co.uk/world/2008/nov/05/israelandthepalestinians (last visited Feb. 21, 2010).

43. B'Tselem, *B'Tselem's Investigation of Fatalities in Operation Cast Lead*, http://www.btselem .org/Download/20090909_Cast_Lead_Fatalities_Eng.pdf; *Rights Group Names 1,417 Gaza War Dead*, Mar. 19, 2009, Wash. Times, http://www.webcitation.org/5niC4Iiub; Palestinian Centre for Human Rights, *The Dead in the Course of the Israeli Recent Military Offensive on the Gaza Strip*, http://www.pchrgaza.org/files/PressR/English/2008/list.pdf; United Nations Offices for the

III. RUSSIA

A. INTRODUCTION

Post-Soviet Union Russia has faced terrorism similar to that faced by Israel. Chechen terrorism — whether carried out by Chechens alone or assisted by international terrorists — has made enormous efforts to disrupt Russian life.

Understanding Russia's response to Chechen-based terrorism requires a historical overview. After the 1917 Russian Revolution, a declaration of independence by the Chechens was met with occupation by the Bolsheviks who later established the Chechen-Ingush Autonomous Region in 1934. Like their Ingush neighbors, Chechens are predominantly Sunni Muslim. During World War II, Chechen and Ingush units collaborated with invading German Nazis; as a result, in 1944, Stalin deported many of them to Central Asia and Siberia. The mass deportation of Chechens is estimated to number 400,000-800,000 with perhaps 100,000 or more dying due to extreme conditions. After Stalin died in 1953, deportees were repatriated and the republic was reestablished in 1957.

Upon the Soviet Union's collapse in 1991, some regions broke away and gained independence. However, Boris Yeltsin, the president of the newly formed Russian Federation, refused Chechnya's declaration of independence and sent troops who withdrew when confronted by armed Chechens. Tensions between the Russian government and Chechen President Dzokhar Dudayev escalated in late 1994, when Russia invaded Chechnya and a bloody war ensued. In 1996 Russia withdrew, defeated, but Chechnya continued to deteriorate. As the Chechen government's control over its militia eroded, local warlords gained strength over Chechnya's armed but unemployed citizens. The Soviet-Afghan war had attracted Islamic militants and resistance fighters to both Chechnya and neighboring Dagestan; Dudayev (killed in a 1995 rocket attack) was replaced by Aslan Maskhadov, who, in 1999, declared Islamic Shari-ah law.

After a Chechen defeat in Dagestan, Moscow and other cities were victims of bombings killing more than 300 people; Chechens were largely blamed for the attacks. Then Russian president, Vladimir Putin, responded forcefully and brutally as did the Chechens with suicide bombings and increased guerilla warfare. To that end, the pattern of terrorist attacks originating in Chechnya followed by brutal Russian responses condemned by the international community continues largely unabated.

On September 1, 2004, Chechen terrorists took hostage more than 1100 people, including approximately 700 children, in Beslan, North Ossetia. On the third day of the standoff, Russian forces stormed the building; a gun battle ensued between Russian forces and Chechen terrorists, killing 334 hostages, of whom 186 were children. After the attack, President Putin toughened

---

Coordination of Humanitarian Affairs, *Field Update on Gaza from the Humanitarian Coordinator*, http://unispal.un.org/unispal.nsf/85255db800470aa485255d8b004e349a/50a7789ce959e0c 285257554006d3e56?OpenDocument.

terrorism-related laws and expanded governmental powers. In addition, the Kremlin consolidated control over the Russian media and attacked NGOs.

While there are those who argue Chechen terrorism is a homegrown nationalist movement seeking establishment of an independent Chechen state, its Islamic nature—in conjunction with operational, financial, and logistical support provided by non-Chechen Islamic terrorist organizations—suggests Russia faces terrorism that is not exclusively domestic. Therefore, Russian responses directed against Chechnya must not be viewed solely in the context of a response to domestic terrorism. Rather, Russia is confronted with international terrorism, domestic in orientation.

Chechen terrorism is distinguishable from 9/11; those responsible for the latter were in the United States solely for the purpose of committing that single act of terrorism whereas those responsible for the former live in Chechnya but commit acts of terrorism in Russia. Similarly, it is distinct from homegrown terrorist threats like the Madrid training bombing—an act of terrorism committed against Spaniards by individuals living in Spain. The threat Russia faces more closely resembles terrorism faced by Israel (local terrorist organizations with international assistance) or India (Kashmiri terrorists supported by Pakistan).

Until recently, both the Soviet Union and post-Soviet Russia saw themselves as immune to terrorism, domestic and international alike. In the context of the Cold War, the Soviet Union was the prime benefactor—covertly and overtly—of international terrorism. Clearly today, the international geopolitical configuration has changed dramatically, for the terrorist threat Russia faces is international and domestic alike.

B. RUSSIAN POLICY—DETERRENCE AND TOUGHNESS

Mariya Y. Omelicheva, Russia's Counterterrorism Policy:
Variations on an Imperial Theme

Perspectives on Terrorism, Vol III, Issue 1, April 2009[44]

For over a decade, Russia has struggled with persistent domestic insurgency and terrorism. The country has experienced a multitude of terrorist and militant attacks, and the turn of the century was marked by a series of high-profile terrorist incidents involving a large number of civilian casualties. In response to this threat, Russian authorities adopted extensive counterterrorism legislation, established and modified institutions responsible for combating terrorism, and streamlined the leadership and conduct of counterterrorist operations. According to recent statements by the present Kremlin administration, the terrorist problem in Russia has finally receded, and the war on separatism had been definitively won. Yet, the daily reports on the shootouts and clashes between insurgents and Russia's security forces cast serious

---

44. *Available at* http://www.terrorismanalysts.com/pt/articles/issues/PTv3i1.pdf/.

doubts on these official claims. Despite the signs of a slow normalization of life in Chechnya, the security situation remains tense there, and terrorist incidents and guerilla attacks have spread into the broader Southern region previously unaffected by terrorism.

Much ink has been spilled criticizing deficiencies of Russia's forceful, excessive, and poorly-coordinated responses. The state has been blamed for the lack of a comprehensive counterterrorism strategy encompassing socio-economic approaches and an effective system of prevention and protection from terrorism. Yet, judging the Russian campaign's excesses and failures does not improve our general understanding of why it has always favored the tactic of force and suppression as the most appropriate methods of fighting terrorism. Stressing the futility of a short-term reactive approach does not explain Russia's choice of the military approach over the long-term socio-economic solutions for resolving complex security concerns. . . .

. . . In the context of Russia, terrorism has been tightly associated with activities of Islamic militants in Chechnya and the broader North Caucasus region. The latter has been an area with the highest concentration of terrorist attacks, and Chechen guerilla fighters have been implicated in the vast majority of hostage-taking incidents and terrorist crimes in Russia. The development of Russia's counterterrorism legislation and institutional framework has trailed the government's experiences with fighting the Chechen resistance and coping with the threat of terrorism in the North Caucasus.

As a result of the developments in Chechnya, the Russian government adopted the Federal Law "On Combating Terrorism" in 1998, which became the main legal pillar of Russian anti-terrorist efforts. The law attempted to define terrorist activity omitting political motivation as one of the defining characteristics of the crime. It also sketched out the legal regime of the counter-terrorist operation, and defined organizational basis of counterterrorism placing Russia's Federal Security Service (FSB), and the Ministry of Interior (MVD) at the top of the list of agencies responsible for combating terrorism.

The troops of the FSB, MVD, and military units from other "power" ministries—the Defense Ministry, the Ministry of Emergency Situations, and the Border Service—were used in counterterrorism and "mop-up" operations in Chechnya as part of the Combined Group of Forces. To assist the military battalions in carrying out counterterrorism tasks, the FSB, the Interior Ministry, and the Main Intelligence Service of Russia created special task teams for the liquidation of terrorists and militants without trial. With a lack of oversight and the virtual impunity of the military and special task forces, the counterterrorism operation in Chechnya has degenerated into the indiscriminate use of overwhelming military force, characterized by deplorable patterns of brutalizing the local population. Frequent abductions, summary executions, and torture have had a radicalizing effect on the population.

In 1999, Russia entered the second Chechen military campaign, and a new wave of terrorist violence and insurgency engulfed the country in the early 2000s. The government's reaction to a new wave of terrorism was similar to earlier policy responses. President Putin pledged to overhaul the system of

Russia's security services and develop procedures for coordinating the activities of counterterrorism agencies. The Russian government vowed to re-assert its influence in the North Caucasus and restore order in the volatile Southern region. The military strategies were expanded outside of the Chechen republic, and the presence of military troops in the rest of the North Caucasus was substantially increased. Under the pretext of combating terrorism, the Kremlin increased the powers of its security services, strengthened the "power vertical," and expanded controls over mass media and political life. To streamline the changes in the leadership and conduct of counterterrorist operations, the Russian government adopted a new Federal Law "On Counteraction to Terrorism," which replaced the earlier version. Entered into force in 2006, the law legalizes the application of armed forces for counterterrorism operations inside and outside of the country, but provides only scant description of prophylactic measures aimed at defending the Russian people and infrastructure against the threat of terrorism. As the 1998 act "On Combating Terrorism," the 2006 counterterrorism law allows for suspension of certain individual liberties and media freedoms in the zone of counterterrorist operations, and authorizes counterterrorism units to carry out searches and demolition of suspicious airplanes and ships. . . .

Toughness is of paramount importance for the Russian authorities; popular opposition to attacks against civilian targets suggests ready support for uncompromising retaliation. In response to the Chechen attack on the Moscow theater, Putin apparently sanctioned use of an unspecified debilitating gas to neutralize explosive-laden terrorists.[45] Russian leadership considered both the potential for negative public reaction to any concession to the terrorists and the possibility that a harsh and swift response might deter similar acts in the future.[46]

Russia's counterterrorism legislation and policy is telling: politicians and leaders unequivocally and candidly define Russia's counterterrorism policy as active and firm. The government has clearly articulated that it intends to pursue an aggressive counterterrorism strategy, combined with maximum implementation of existing legislation granting the executive broad authority.

After the Moscow subway suicide attacks in March 2010, President Medvedev unequivocally articulated an aggressive counterterrorism policy.

---

45. *See* Matt Bivens, *Chechnya War Making Not Breaking Terrorism*, The Moscow Times, Nov. 1, 2002, at 2557.

46. Andrei Shoumikhin, *Deterring Terrorism: Russian Views*, National Institute for Public Policy, Feb. 2004, at 1.

MEDVEDEV'S STATEMENTS ON THE MOSCOW METRO BLASTS

March 29, 2010[47]

"Prevention of such terrorist acts is a complicated thing, just like maintaining security on public transport. That's what the latest experience teaches us. We need to considerably step up all the measures and to reconsider this problem on the scale of the state — not for a particular type of public transport of for a particular town but for the whole country. Obviously, measures that have been practiced up to now have proven to be insufficient.

Now back to the matter. Of course the first thing to do is to help people and provide support to the families of victims, those who died and, naturally, those who are injured and receiving treatment now–we need to provide all the required assistance both on the regional and governmental level.

Today, the government is going to hold a meeting upon my order to discuss this problem in detail. I have issued an order for the government to do this.

Now on the general situation. We need to be on the guard. It is obvious that such acts, regretfully, are always well planned and aim to cause massive casualties and to unsettle the stability in the country and society. Therefore the police and security forces need to run relevant consultations and informative sessions, and to keep the situation under strict control — while certainly observing the citizen's rights and freedoms — to keep the situation under strict control and, in case of need, to intervene and make on-site decisions to ensure the efficiency of control.

This is a well-known practice both in our country and in the world. Sadly, it's far from the first time such a thing happens to us. Therefore, there should be a very precise and detailed approach to dealing with such situations.

The Prosecutor General's Office and the Investigative Committee should continue gathering evidence and carry out thorough investigation, naturally, without disrupting traffic in the metro. Traffic should resume as soon as the investigative procedures are over so that the city is not affected.

Proposed versions should be given most careful consideration. Evidently, this is the continuation of terrorist activities, and I believe this will be the key version of the investigation. I would like you to keep track of it and report to me.

And the last thing I'd like to say: the policy against terror in our country will continue. We will continue operations against terrorists till the end, with no hesitation. I would like all heads of special services and law enforcement agencies present here to follow the same principle — till the end and with no hesitation.

In a while, we will hold a meeting on specific consequences, but now I suggest going to our workplaces and getting down to our everyday work."

---

47. *Available at* http://rt.com/Politics/2010-03-29/medvedev-statement-blasts-metro.html/.

C. RUSSIAN LEGISLATION

Articles 205-208, 277, and 360 of the Russian Federation criminal code address terrorism-related crimes. Other crimes included in the Russian Federation criminal code may be categorized as terrorist crimes if they are committed for terrorist purposes. Penalties for the commission of such crimes are in accordance with the Russian Federation criminal code; a terrorist is a person participating in the implementation of terrorist activity in any form; a terrorist group is a group of persons united with a view to implementing terrorist activity; a terrorist organization is an organization created with a view to implementing terrorist activity or deeming the use of terrorism possible in its activity. An organization is deemed to be a terrorist organization if one of its structural components carries out terrorist activity with the knowledge of even one of the organization's leading organs.[48]

According to this legislation, terrorist activity is broadly defined: it includes the organization, planning, preparation, and implementation of terrorist action.

The significance of such a definition is that any individual involved in any stage — no matter its significance or ultimate contribution — of a particular terrorist action may be convicted of the crime of terrorism. Similar to the material-support clause of the PATRIOT Act,[49] which led to the conviction of former attorney Lynne Stewart for helping pass messages from a terrorist client,[50] this definition is extremely broad.

ISSUES TO CONSIDER

1. Is a broad definition of terrorist activity conducive to fighting terrorism?
2. Is a broad definition conducive to balancing legitimate national security concerns and rights of the individual?
3. Does the fact that Chechen terrorists attack a variety of targets with a wide range of means suggest that the Russian government can be more repressive in its counterterrorism?

The Russian response to Chechen terrorism has been repeatedly articulated and defended by Russian authorities. In the aftermath of an explosion in a Moscow subway a newspaper headline read "Russian State Duma Intends to Toughen All Laws Relating to Fight Against Terrorism":

> Moscow, February 6 (Ria Novosti) — Russian lawmakers will toughen all laws relating to the fight against terrorism, State Duma (parliament's lower house) Chairman Boris Gryzlov said while commenting on the explosion in the

---

48. *See* Russ. Federation Fed. Law No. 130-FZ, Art. 3, July 25, 1998, translation *available at* http://www.fas.org/irp/world/russia/docs/law_980725.htm (last visited Jan. 7, 2011); *see also* Ugolovnyi Kodeks [UK][*Criminal Code*] arts. 205-08, 277, 360 (Russ.) (translated into English by William E. Butler & Maryann E. Gashi-Butler, *Criminal Code of the Russian Federation*, 3rd ed.).

49. *See* PATRIOT Act, *supra* note 13, §805.

50. *See* Associated Press, *Activist Lawyer Vows to Fight Terror Conviction*, MSNBC Feb. 11, 2005, http://www.msnbc.msn.com/id/6948450/ns/us_news-security/ (last visited Jan. 7, 2011).

Moscow subway. In the speaker's words, he already gave such an instruction to specialized committees of the state Duma, and this work will be conducted as soon as possible." Gryzlov called the act of terrorism, which killed 30 or more people, "another crime of international terrorism forces." However, the explosion was not connected with the coming presidential elections in Russia, the speaker believes. In his words, "international terrorists commit their crimes without linking them to any events or dates."[51]

"Medvedev Seeks 'Brutal' Response to Terror Attacks" is another example of a headline following the subway terrorist attack in Moscow:

> April 1 (Bloomberg) — President Dmitry Medvedev called for a "brutal" response to terrorism during a trip to Dagestan in Russia's mostly Muslim North Caucasus region, where 14 people have died in bomb blasts in the last two days.
> "We've twisted off the heads of the most odious thugs, but clearly that's not enough," Medvedev said during a security meeting in the regional capital Makhachkala. "We'll find them all in a timely manner and we'll punish them all," he said in comments broadcast on state television.
> "That's the only way." . . .
> Medvedev said Russia must expand its arsenal of measures for fighting terrorism. "They must be not only more effective, but tougher, more brutal, if you like, with the goal of preventing terrorist attacks," he said. "People must be punished for that."[52]

According to an April 14, 2004, BBC report, the Russian Federation Council, following a vote in the lower house, adopted amendments to the criminal code increasing the "period for bringing charges from 10 to 30 days in the case of an investigation of a terrorist nature."[53] The Council adopted the resolution overwhelmingly (128 senators voting in favor, 3 against, and 3 abstaining).[54]

In 2006, President Putin signed a decree creating the National Counterterrorism Committee (NCC) following the Beslan massacre. By establishing a single chain of command, the decision making process at the national level was centralized. The law expanded the definition of terrorism under Russian law. According to the legislation, terrorism also included promotion of "terrorist ideas" and distributing materials or information to encourage terrorist activity, or inciting individuals to commit a terrorist act.

The government also, for the first time, released a list of 17 organizations defined as terrorist entities. For an organization to be defined a terrorist entity it must meet the following criteria: (1) activities aimed at changing Russia's constitutional system through violence, including terrorism; (2) links to illegal

---

51. *Russian State Duma Intends to Toughen All Laws Relating to Fight Against Terrorism,* Ria Novosti [Russian News and Information Agency] Feb. 6, 2004, *available at* http://en.rian.ru/onlinenews/20040206/39907054.html (on file with author).

52. Lyubov Pronina and Anastasia Ustinova, *Medvedev Seeks "Brutal" Response to Terror Attacks,* Bloomberg Businessweek, Apr. 1, 2010, *available at* http://www.businessweek.com/news/2010-04-01/chechen-rebel-leader-claims-moscow-suicide-bombings-update1-.html.

53. Mark A. Smith, *Russian Domestic Policy: A Chronology July-September 2003,* Defence Academy: Conflict Studies Research Centre, Jan. 14, 2004, at 5, *available at* http://www.da.mod.uk/colleges/arag/document-listings/russian-chronologies/j37/J37.pt1 (last visited Oct. 6, 2010); *see also Russian Upper House Endorses Changes to Law on Handling Suspect "Terrorists,"* BBC Monitoring, Apr. 14, 2004.

54. *Russian Upper House Endorses Changes to Law on Handling Suspect "Terrorists," supra* note 53.

armed groups and other extremist organizations operating in the North Caucasus; and (3) association with, or links to, groups regarded as terrorists by the international community.

IV. INDIA

A. BACKGROUND

India is one of the world's most terrorism afflicted countries. In 2008, in a pivotal moment called "26/11," terrorists struck at a variety of locations in Mumbai, killing at least 183 people, including 22 foreigners, and 14 members of the police and security forces. In addition, over 300 individuals were injured.

Over the years India has faced complicated terrorist threats from multilateral sources.[55] Israel's threat comes from Palestinian terrorism; Russia's from Chechen terrorism; Spain's, until March 2004, was Basque terrorism. But the threats India faces come in many forms — ethnic separatists, nationalists, and the disenfranchised.[56] India's challenge in developing coherent legal and policy responses is to counter one threat without inviting criticism from another group, which may conclude that a particular policy or legislation unfairly impinges on their rights.

ISSUES TO CONSIDER

1. How does a democracy develop responses to myriad threats?
2. Is maintaining a balance between national security and civil rights possible in such circumstances?
3. What lessons learned from the other countries addressed in this survey are applicable to the Indian experience?
4. How is a terror threat (Kashmir) supported by another sovereign (Pakistan) to be localized so that the terrorism does not become truly internationalized?
5. What actions can be taken without violating international law against a state that supports terrorism?
6. How much should a state compromise and avoid creating an international crisis and risking a global response to a larger threat, particularly when both nations (Pakistan and India) are U.S. allies?

---

55. *The Current Crisis in South Asia: Hearing Before the Subcomm. on the Middle East and S. Asia of the H. Comm. on Int'l Relations*, 107th Cong. at 10 (2002) (statement of Michael Krepon, Founding President, The Henry L. Stimson Center).

56. *See* Law Commission of India, 173rd Report on Prevention of Terrorism Bill, 2000 §II 1.5-9 (2000), *reprinted in* L.K. Thakur, *Essentials of Pota and Other Human Rights Laws* 58-60 (2002) (citing over 2000 militant-related deaths in the northeast region of India during the late 1990s); *see also* U.S. Dept. of State, Patterns of Global Terrorism 2001, 10-11 (2002), *available at* http://www.state.gov/documents/organization/10319.pdf (citing various terrorist threats in India) (last visited Oct. 6, 2010).

A. LEGISLATION

1. Terrorism and Disruptive Activities Act

In 1985 the government approved the Terrorism and Disruptive Activities (Prevention) Act (TADA) (amended 1987).[57] TADA came into law partly in response to the 1984 assassination of Prime Minister Indira Gandhi by militant Sikh extremists. Rajiv Gandhi, Indira's son and successor as prime minister, supported the legislation because various militant groups in India's east, north, and south were engaging in ongoing guerrilla attacks against the state. TADA's provisions expanded the central government's powers with respect to individuals the statute classified as terrorists. For example, at a judge's discretion, trials of accused terrorists could be held *in camera*. Moreover, Section 21 of the Act presumed that suspected terrorists were guilty until proven innocent. In addition, the state could arrest anyone upon mere suspicion of terrorist activity and hold him without bail.

While the Act was created to enable the government to counter terrorism, the legislation died a natural death in 1995 when public pressure forced Parliament not to reenact the Act at its two-year renewal date. Consistent internal and international criticism accused the government of using the legislation as a means to target minorities and political opponents. Although TADA died a "legislative death" its shadow continues to loom for two reasons. First, even though TADA is no longer in effect, the state retains the power to charge suspected persons retroactively for crimes committed during the period of its enactment. Second, the Indian Supreme Court, in 1994, legitimized the statute by holding constitutional one of its central provisions, allowing courts to admit into evidence uncorroborated witness statements gathered by the police. Observers wondered whether the executive branch would push for legislation further enhancing the powers of the police; in the years that followed, these concerns were justified.[58]

2. Prevention of Terrorism Act

The December 13, 2001 attack on the Indian parliament carried out by five Muslim terrorists resulted in legislating the Prevention of Terrorism Act (POTA). According to Human Rights Watch, POTA was a source of great concern:

> POTA creates an overly broad definition of terrorism, prevention of terrorism act while expanding the state's investigative and procedural powers. Suspects can be detained for up to three months without charge, and up to three months more with the permission of a special judge. Its close resemblance to TADA foreshadowed a return to widespread and systematic curtailment of civil liberties. Under TADA, tens of thousands of politically motivated detentions, acts of torture, and other human rights violations were committed

---

57. Terrorist and Disruptive Activities Prevention Act, No. 28 of 1987 (India) [hereinafter TADA].

58. Jayanth K. Krishnan, *India's "Patriot Act": POTA and the Impact on Civil Liberties in the World's Largest Democracy*, 22 Law & Ineq. J. 265, 267-69 (2004).

against Muslims, Sikhs, Dalits (so-called untouchables), trade union activists, and political opponents in the late 1980s and early 1990s. In the face of mounting opposition to the act, India's government acknowledged these abuses and consequently let TADA lapse in 1995.

Indian and international human rights groups, journalists, opposition parties, and minority rights groups have unequivocally condemned POTA. Numerous political parties have alleged the misuse of POTA against political opponents in states such as Uttar, Pradesh, and Jammu and Kashmir. Since it was first introduced, the government has added some safeguards to protect due process rights but POTA's critics stress that the safeguards do not go far enough and that existing laws are sufficient with respect to the threat of terrorism. India's national human rights commission has stated that "existing laws are sufficient to deal with any eventuality, including terrorism, and there is no need for a draconian POTA."

Since its passage, POTA has been used against political opponents, religious minorities, Dalits, tribals and even children. In February 2003 alone, over three hundred people were arrested under the act.

On February 19, 2003, the Gujarat government charged 131 Muslims under POTA for allegedly attacking Hindus. Human rights watch investigations revealed that attacks against Muslims were carried out with extensive state participation and support and planned months in advance of the Godhra attack. The Hindu nationalist Bharatiya Janata party that heads the state government has not charged any Hindus under POTA for violence against Muslims.[59]

Section three of the Act defines terrorist acts:

(1) whoever with intent to threaten the unity, integrity, security or sovereignty of India or to strike terror in the people or any section of the people does any act or thing by using bombs, dynamite or other explosive substances or inflammable substances or firearms or other lethal weapons or poisons or noxious gases or other chemicals or by any other substances (whether biological or otherwise) of a hazardous nature or by any other means whatsoever, in such a manner as to cause, or likely to cause, death of, or injuries to any person or persons or loss of, or damage to, or destruction of, property or disruption of any supplies or services essential to the life of the community or causes damage or destruction of any property or equipment used or intended to be used for the defence of India or in connection with any other purposes of the government of India, any state government or any of their agencies, or detains any person and threatens to kill or injure such person in order to compel the government or any o her person to do or abstain from doing any act; is or continues to be a member of an association declared unlawful under the unlawful activities (prevention) act, 1967 (37 of 1967), or voluntarily does an act aiding or promoting in any manner the objects of such association and in either case is in possession of any unlicensed firearms, ammunition, explosive or other instrument or substance capable of causing mass destruction and commits any act resulting in loss of human life or grievous injury to any person or causes significant damage to any property, commits a terrorist act. For the purposes of

---

59. In the Name of Counter-Terrorism: Human Rights Abuses Worldwide: A Human Rights Watch Briefing Paper for the 59th Session of the United Nations Commission on Human Rights, Mar. 25, 2003, *available at* http://www.hrw.org/en/reports/2003/03/25/name-counter-terrorism-human-rights-abuses-worldwide (last visited Oct. 3, 2010).

this sub-section, "a terrorist act" shall include the act of raising funds intended for the purpose of terrorism.[60]

On September 17, 2004, the new Indian government of Prime Minister Manmohan Singh announced that it would honor an election pledge to repeal POTA and amend existing laws targeting terrorist activity. The new government acknowledged that certain provisions of POTA allowed for widespread abuse, such as dispensing with the presumption of innocence, the compulsory denial of bail, and the admissibility of confessions despite the rampant use of torture and coercion by police and security forces.

ISSUES TO CONSIDER

1. How did POTA define terrorism? Is the definition too broad, curtailing civil liberties?
2. Was the bill aimed at one particular ethnic group, or was it all-encompassing, reflecting India's ethnic and religious diversity?
3. Did the legislation enable the Indian government to arrest with minimal standards?
4. Were the rights of detainees adequately protected?
5. Would special POTA courts fully protect the rights of the accused?
6. Would special POTA courts raise concerns similar to those raised with respect to the military commissions and the rights guaranteed to the detainees at Guantanamo?
7. How did the legislation affect civil liberties and civil rights in India?
8. Can terrorism be deterred by a counterterrorism policy that is largely legislation-oriented?

Home Minister Advani pointed out, during the debate on POTA, that the Supreme Court recommended to the police how to conduct investigations. According to Advani, these recommendations were incorporated into the new bill. For example, under POTA defendants could invoke the right to silence while police had to provide warnings that anything defendants said in the course of the interrogation could be used in court against them.[61] Moreover, POTA explicitly barred the police from using coercion in order to obtain a statement from an individual.[62] The state could punish any police official found abusing this authority with a fine and up to two years incarceration. POTA also assured defendants a statutory right to appeal a criminal conviction to a state high court.[63] For these reasons, both Advani and Prime Minister

---

60. The Prevention of Terrorism Act, 2002, Act No. 15 of 2002, *available at* http://www.satp .org/satporgtp/countries/india/document/actandordinances/POTA.htm (last visited Oct. 1, 2010) [hereinafter Prevention of Terrorism Act].

61. *Id.* at art. 32(2).

62. V. Venkatesan, *POTA Prospects*, 19 Frontline, Mar. 30-Apr. 12, 2002, *available at* http:// www.frontlineonnet.com/fl1907/19070220.htm (last visited July 24, 2007).

63. Prevention of Terrorism Act, *supra* note 60, art. 34.

Vajpayee promised POTA could effectively combat terrorism while protecting defendants' rights to due process and a fair trial.

Some parliamentarians (members of the opposition who argued against the bill's passage) charged that the Bhartiya Janta Party (BJP) was using POTA as a means of pandering to its Hindu fundamentalist constituency. Others suggested that POTA was not so much an antiterrorism measure but rather a "terrorist law [that would be] . . . used to terrorise minorities." Still others worried that the BJP would employ POTA as a tool to harass or threaten political enemies who disagreed with government policy. These dissenting voices failed to carry the day,[64] though ultimately—only two years later—the Act was repealed.

3. India's Current Anti-Terrorism Laws (Post-2008)

In response to the November 2008 Mumbai attacks, the Indian government proposed a new agency, the National Investigative Agency, to create national-level capability to investigate and potentially prosecute similar acts. Also, in response to the Mumbai attacks, the Indian government amended existing laws to strengthen security and law enforcement agencies in fighting terrorism. Two themes that have framed the public debate with respect to the new legislation are states' rights vs. federal power and civil liberties vs. stronger law enforcement powers.

INDIA: NEW ANTI-TERROR LAW FOLLOWING BOMBAY ATTACKS

Keesings World News, Jan. 6, 2009[65]

New anti-terror legislation, drafted in response to the series of attacks in Bombay (Mumbai) on Nov. 26, was approved by the Rajya Sabha (the upper house of the bicameral legislature) on Dec. 18, having been approved by the Lok Sabha (the lower house) the previous day. The Unlawful Activities (Prevention) Act provided new powers for the security services, most controversially the ability to hold suspects for six months without charge. It also made provision for the establishment of a National Investigating Agency responsible for gathering and processing intelligence and investigating terrorism.

Immediate Context

The new anti-terror law was written in response to attacks in Bombay on Nov. 26-29. These attacks were carried out by 10 gunmen who attacked predominantly tourist and Jewish targets. The attackers killed an estimated 183 people and injured many more before all but one of them was killed. One gunman was captured and interrogated by the Indian authorities. The attacks took place over four days, partly due to the slow response of the Indian security forces.

The attackers apparently arrived in Bombay by sea on the evening of Nov. 26. They immediately dispersed around the city to attack a train station, the Taj Mahal and Oberoi Trident hotels, a hospital, a cafe, and the Nariman

---

64. Krishnan, *supra* note 58, at 271-73.
65. *Available at* http://www.keesings.com/breaking_history/asia-pacific/india_new_anti-terror_law_following_bombay_attacks_pub._jan._6,_2009/india_new_anti-terror_law_following_bombay_attacks_-_full_text/.

House Jewish centre. People were killed indiscriminately at all the locations, then hostages were taken at the hotels and the Jewish centre. The Indian security forces surrounded the hotels and the Jewish centre and eventually commandos stormed all three buildings. Several hostages were freed from the hotels but all the hostages in the Jewish centre were killed.

Mumbai has suffered several attacks in the last 10 years, including the train bombing of 2003, other bombings later in 2003 and the 2006 commuter train bombings. The police response to these attacks was widely criticised as insufficient. There was little success in bringing the perpetrators to justice and Pakistan was blamed to a greater or lesser extent in each case.

Reaction and Outlook

The Unlawful Activities (Prevention) Act was passed by the bicameral legislature with the support of both main parties, but was criticised by some smaller parties and by human rights and minority rights groups. Amnesty International said that, while they recognised the duty of the Indian government to provide security, anti-terror laws should not infringe human rights. The Communist Party of India also released a statement affirming its opposition to the legislation on human rights grounds. An earlier anti terrorism act was repealed by the current government because minorities, especially Muslims, felt it was used to unfairly target them. . . .

ISSUES TO CONSIDER

1. What is appropriate legislative response to an act of terrorism?
2. What powers should the legislature grant the executive in times of crisis?
3. Does an attack — regardless of the cost of human life — justify legislation limiting civil and political rights?
4. What are the lessons learned from TADA and POTA?
5. How should the effectiveness of such legislation be weighed and determined?
6. What limits should be placed on the security forces in response to successful terrorist acts?

V. SPAIN

On March 11, 2004, 198 Spaniards were killed and more than 1400 wounded in Madrid when ten bombs exploded in commuter trains, three days prior to national elections. According to most commentators, the objective of the attacks was both to influence the election and to force Spain to withdraw its military forces from Iraq, part of the coalition forces fighting the regime of Saddam Hussein. Following the election, won by the Socialist Party's Luis Rodriguez Zapatero, Spain withdrew from Iraq in spite of strong international political pressure to remain there.

In the following months, Spanish authorities arrested 62 people in connection with the bombing and more than 30 individuals involved in planning additional attacks. According to Spanish sources, some of those arrested had connections to international terrorism, suggesting that not only is Spain a target of international terrorism, but it has, furthermore, become an "entry point to Europe" for terrorists.[66]

Though Islamic fundamentalists carried out the attack, Spaniards have encountered domestic terrorism for years. The Euskadi Ta Askatasuna (Basque Fatherland and Liberty, ETA) has waged a decades-long campaign against the Spanish government in seeking to establish an independent Basque state. The Basques have killed hundreds, intimidated thousands, and forced thousands of Spaniards to live under the threat of violence. Spain's counterterrorism legislation and policy has, over the years, been tailored to the threat posed by ETA (domestic terrorism) rather than to an international/domestic threat.

A. SPANISH DOMESTIC LEGISLATION

Chapter VIII of the Spanish Criminal Code (article 571) defines terrorism as "belonging, acting in the service of or collaborating with armed groups, organizations or groups whose object is to subvert the constitutional order or seriously alter public peace."[67] According to this legislation, mere support—either direct or indirect—of terrorism may lead to prosecution under the law. The low threshold required for liability under the law is reminiscent of the "material support" clause of the PATRIOT Act.[68]

The Spanish model serves as a point of discussion for an additional issue—whether the legislative response to domestic/international terrorism should differ from exclusively domestic terrorism. Over the years, Spain has been criticized for domestic legislation violating human rights regarding ETA.[69] Terrorists in Spain are tried before the Audiencia Nacional (National High Court), created in 1977 with jurisdiction over "crimes committed by persons belonging to armed groups or related to terrorist or rebel elements when the commission of the crime contributes to its activity, and by those who in some way cooperate or collaborate in the acts of these groups or individuals."[70] Since Spain does not have a special antiterrorism law, terrorists are brought to trial in accordance with Spain's Criminal Code.[71]

---

66. Renwick McLean, *Spain Arrested More than 130 Suspects in Islamic Terrorism in '04*, N.Y. Times, Jan. 6, 2005, at A6.
67. Judith Sunderland, Human Rights Watch, *Setting an Example? Counter-Terrorism Measures in Spain* (2005), *available at* http://hrw.org/reports/2005/spain0105/[hereinafter HRW *Counter-Terrorism in Spain*] (last visited July 24, 2007).
68. PATRIOT Act, *supra* note 15, at §805.
69. *See* Tracy Wilkinson, *Spain Could Do Better on Terror Suspects, Group Says; Human Rights Watch Asserts, Among Other Things, That Detainees Need Greater Legal Access*, L.A. Times, Jan. 27, 2005, at A6.
70. HRW *Counter-Terrorism in Spain, supra* note 67.
71. The primary distinction between the treatment of terrorists and that of criminal defendants is that, whereas a non-terrorist must be brought before a judge within 72 hours, a suspected terrorist may be held for up to five days without seeing a judge (an additional 48 hours).

While Article 55 (2) of the Spanish constitution guarantees criminal process, fundamental rights may be suspended in terror cases.[72] Furthermore, according to the Law of Political Parties (Party Act) introduced in 2001, a party that supports terrorism may be outlawed.[73]

ISSUES TO CONSIDER

1. Until recently Spain had been confronted only with domestic terrorism. How does the introduction of international terrorism affect policy and legislation?
2. Is legislation oriented towards domestic terrorism applicable for combating international terrorism?
3. Are Spanish efforts of countering Basque (i.e., domestic) terrorism relevant to countering al Qaeda (i.e., international) terrorism?
4. Is criminal legislation appropriate for countering terrorism?
5. The Spanish response to the train station bombings has been widely criticized for reflecting weakness, if not capitulation; how does that affect policy?

B. SPANISH RESPONSE TO TERRORISM

1. 9/11

According to a Human Rights Watch report at a hearing on human rights in the European Union, Spain after 9/11 applied its existing strict counter-terrorism regime to the investigation, apprehension, and detention of suspected al Qaeda operatives. The climate created by the international campaign against terrorism provided the Spanish authorities with a further pretext to crackdown on Basque separatists and supporters of the pro-independence movement. Spanish authorities were also quick to issue public statements equating stricter controls on immigration with the war against terrorism, contributing to a climate of fear and suspicion toward migrants, asylum seekers, and refugees.

COUNTER-TERRORISM MEASURES AND THE PROHIBITION AGAINST TORTURE AND ILL-TREATMENT

Submission by Human Rights Watch, (Apr. 2003)[74]

Spain's anti-terror laws permit the use of incommunicado detention, secret legal proceedings, and pre-trial detention for up to four years. The proceedings

---

72. Constitución [C.E.] art. 55(2) (Spain).
73. *Id.*
74. *Available at* http://internationalrelationsthirdyear0708.pbworks.com/f/Counter-Terrorism+Measures+and+the+Prohibition+against+Torture+and+Ill-Treatment.pdf/ (last visited Jan. 7, 2011).

governing the detentions of suspected al Qaeda operatives apprehended in Spain in November 2001, July 2002, and January 2003, among others, have been declared secret (causa secreta). The investigating magistrate of the Audiencia Nacional, a special court that oversees terrorist cases, can request *causa secreta* for thirty days, consecutively renewable for the duration of the four-year pre-trial detention period. Secret proceedings bar the defense access to the prosecutor's evidence, except for information contained in the initial detention order. Without access to this evidence, detainees are severely hampered in mounting an adequate defense.

In November 2002, the United Nations Committee Against Torture (CAT) expressed serious concern about incommunicado detention under Spain's criminal laws. A suspect can be held incommunicado for up to five days, without access to an attorney, family notification, services such as access to health care, or contact with the outside world. The CAT concluded that incommunicado detention under these circumstances can facilitate acts of torture and ill-treatment. In Spain, most suspected terrorist detainees are held incommunicado for at least the first forty-eight hours in custody.

In the aftermath of September 11, then Spanish foreign minister Josep Pique told *El País* that "the reinforcement of the fight against illegal immigration is also the reinforcement of the fight against terrorism." Such political rhetoric has been accompanied by increasingly restrictive immigration and asylum policies and practices, [including police harassment in Muslim and Arab migrant communities, which undermine the right to seek asylum and contribute to the creation of a climate hostile toward all migrants in Spain.]

The Party Act adopted in June 2002 enables the state to declare a political party illegal if it fails to respect democratic principles and values. With two exceptions, the legislation is aimed at Batasuna and will not be further addressed.

According to the Party Act, "the government will be able to block financial accounts and operations when it considers that such a step might prevent terrorist activities. The bill authorizes the administration to act not only against terrorist groups, but also against those who support or help them."[75] On June 27, 2002, the Spanish Congress of Deputies passed the LSSICE "Internet Law" which "obliges ISPs to retain traffic logs of their customers for at least one year.

---

75. Rachel Ehrenfeld, *Financing Osama*, FrontPageMagazine.com, Feb. 25, 2005, *available at* http://www.frontpagemag.com/articles/readarticle.asp?ID=17136&p=1 (stating that "Article 9 of the New Party Act, Organic Law 6/2002 of June 27, 2002 stipulates that a political party will be declared illegal if it systematically harms fundamental rights and freedoms by promoting, justifying or exonerating attacks against the right to life and the integrity of the individual, if it foments, facilitates or legitimizes violence, or complements and supports the actions of terrorist organizations").

An opposition amendment bars police or intelligence officials from using such data without court permission."[76]

2. March 2004

The Spanish response to the train bombings must be considered from three different perspectives: criminal law, judicial rulings, and policy regarding withdrawal of Spanish forces from Iraq.

Spain did not enact special or emergency legislation in response to the death of almost 200 innocent civilians. There are a number of possible reasons for the non-response, in and of itself a response: (1) existing legislation was deemed sufficient; (2) Spain did not want to be perceived as pursuing Islamic terrorists; (3) Spanish authorities believe the criminal law paradigm appropriate to countering terrorism and therefore special legislation is superfluous.

In sum, rather than implementing numerous measures intended to grant the law enforcement community additional powers or undertaking vigorous policy initiatives, the Spanish government adopted, in response both to 9/11 and March 2004, a largely passive approach.

In its response to a major terrorism attack on its own soil, Spain differs dramatically from the other surveyed nations whose legislative models have been aggressive. The inconsistency in Spanish policy between domestic and international terrorism is palpable. Spain has responded to long-standing, domestic-based terrorism with resolve politically, legislatively, and operationally, whereas its response to international-based — albeit domestically executed — terrorism has introduced a profoundly different model, one diametrically opposed to the model it previously implemented.

ISSUES TO CONSIDER

1. What national interests are served by seeking to allay the aggressor as Spain did when the government decided to withdraw forces from Iraq?
2. Does allaying the aggressor encourage additional attacks or serve as positive reinforcement for terrorists?
3. Should counterterrorism policy be primarily domestic driven or are international geopolitical ramifications legitimate considerations?
4. What are the fundamental distinctions between exclusively domestic terrorism and internal/external and how do those distinctions affect legal and policy considerations?

---

76. Reporters Without Borders, *The Internet Under Surveillance* 103 (2003), *available at* http://www.rsf.org/IMG/pdf/doc-2236.pdf.

VI. CHINA

A. BACKGROUND

China recognizes over 50 nationalities and ethnic groups; the majority are Han Chinese. The northwest province of Xinjiang—bordering Mongolia, Russia, Afghanistan, Kazakhstan, Kyrgyzstan, Pakistan and India—is unique in its cultural background and challenges. The province is a mix of Han Chinese and Uygher ethnic groups which has lead to extraordinary tensions and outbreaks of violence, including terrorist attacks. Since 1949, periodic unrest in Xinjiang has resulted, in part, from Islamic and Uyghur nationalist movements. Recently, the violence has been influenced by extremism facilitated by external funding and training, particularly Pakistani.

B. STRIKE HARD

The standard Chinese response to the violence described in Chapter 3 has been the "Strike Hard" campaigns. The aim of these periodic campaigns is to reduce crime dramtatically, negate potential terrorist attacks, and restore social order. The campaigns use intelligence information against suspected criminals through swift and severe tactics that process people quickly through the judicial system and punish them harshly. These campaigns serve as reminders of the control government exercises over social, judicial, economic, and political aspects of daily life, particularly when public order is affected. To that end, religious- and nationalist-based unrest in Xinjiang has powerful implications both locally and more broadly: the former because of the recurring violence between Uyghurs and Hans; the latter because other ethnic minorities may feel emboldened.

For those reasons, the campaigns consistently focus their efforts on particular categories of crimes, especially those deemed to pose threats to public order and state security, including potential acts of terrorism. The policy represents aggressive counterterrorism intended to directly strike at religious and nationalist forces perceived as possible sources of unrest.

The government originally launched the Strike Hard campaign in 1996 to combat the rising national crime rate. In most of China, "Strike Hard" was used to combat crime and drug use. In Xinjiang it was implemented to prevent attacks by proactively eliminating terrorist groups and punishing individuals involved with suspected terrorist organizations clearly intending to have a deterrent effect. The campaign included increased surveillance, pressure to report suspected separatists, and expedited judicial procedures and executions.

China labeled the East Turkestan Movement a separatist group, based on religious extremism, and convinced the United States and the United Nations to classify the group as terrorists. Suspected separatists accused of participating in protests, bombings, and assassinations were detainded. In February 1997, an incident that began as a demonstration against Strike Hard turned into a riot with clashes between police and civilians. This was followed by further arrests after three bombs simultaneously exploded on buses in Urumqi.

In 2007, The Chinese police raided a suspected training camp of the East Turkestan Islamic Movement near the border between Afghanistan and Pakistan. Eighteen suspects were killed and seventeen were captured.

ISSUES TO CONSIDER

1. What are the cost-benefits of aggressive counterterrorism?
2. What are the policy implications of identifying a particular ethnic group as endangering state security?
3. What are the limits of deterrence as a policy?
4. When does aggressive counterterrorism have negative repercussions?
5. How important is the court of international opinion?
6. How legitimate is it for a domestic policy to be predicated on an external development (9/11 affecting U.S. policy with respect to the Uyghurs)?
7. What is the relationship between religious extremism and national separatism?

VII. COLOMBIA

The National Front of Colombia was a group of conservative and liberal politicians who sought to reduce the violence spreading across the country in the 1950s and 1960s. They excluded certain dissidents and other political forces from joining the National Front organization. As a result of this exclusion several groups, including the Fuerzas Armadas Revolucionarias de Colombia (FARC), created their own paramilitary groups to combat the National Front. By 1974, FARC had become the largest guerrilla group, in addition to the M-19 and the National Liberation Army (ELN). As such, the creation of the National Front indirectly contributed to the emergence of these guerrilla groups

During the 1970s and 1980s, Colombia became a predominant source of illegal drugs through both production and worldwide trafficking. Guerrilla groups, including ELN and FARC, became actively involved in the drug trade during the 1980s because it provided a major revenue source. As a result of the influx of significant financial resources, both FARC and ELN extended their influence to regions throughout the country through incursions to urban areas where previously they had been relatively inactive.

FARC committed armed assaults, assassinations, bombings, hijackings, kidnappings, as well as drug-related crimes. For example, in 1998, FARC and ELN conducted over 40 attacks countrywide over a two-day period. The attacks were aimed at an extraordinarily wide range of targets including government, military, oil facilities, and private citizens thereby creating a viable threat to national stability and control. The scope of the attacks suggested both significant motivation and resources, not to mention operational capabilities that extended beyond mere region-specific terrorism. The attacks—and threats— were aimed at government institutions across the country. The attacks killed over 275 and an unknown number of wounded. In addition, 30 soldiers and policemen were missing and presumed kidnapped.

Individuals assumed to have either financial resources or to be in positions of political influence were subject to kidnapping for purposes of ransom. Kidnapping victims included the brother of Colombia's president, Americans, diplomatic officials, and peasants who could be convinced to aid FARC or whose families had the money or influence needed by FARC. Kidnapping poses extraordinary challenges to government counterterrorism policy because of the vulnerability of families from whom ransom is demanded. Rather than enabling government to articulate, establish, and implement a cohesive counterterrorism policy, kidnapping—because of family pressure—limits government ability to impose policy in an unencumbered manner.

As a result of this increase in the range, power, and influence of terrorist organizations, the government embarked on a policy largely predicated on attempting to negotiate with terrorists. To that end, in 1998 former President Pastrana gave FARC 51,000 square kilometers in the south-central part of Colombia which FARC used to increase production of illegal drugs, transport military equipment, and negotiate kidnapping ransoms. President Uribe continued to conduct negotiations with terrorist organizations while security forces simultaneously engaged guerilla groups. As a result of this two-headed approached—arguably contradictory—President Uribe's policy resulted in the partial demobilization of the United Self-Defense Forces of Colombia and M-19.

The negotiations have resulted in paramilitary groups relinquishing to the government some of their supplies; in return, the government accepted demands that prison sentences not be imposed, granted almost full immunity against extradition, and allowed the groups to retain a substantial portion of their assets.

The Executive and Legislative branches have both struggled to develop a consistent, effective counterterrorism policy that would have long-term impact. Perhaps, as a result, policy has often been limited to short-term responses instead of long-term strategies. Complicating implementation of more comprehensive strategies has been a reality not faced by the other nations surveyed: a ubiquitous, powerful, and ruthless illegal drug industry and its relationship with various guerilla groups. To that end, illegal drugs have made it difficult to combat paramilitary groups and outside threats, especially as they often overlap and cooperate.

ISSUES TO CONSIDER

1. Given Colombia's unique challenges—the combination of terrorist organizations and the drug trade—is creating a consistent counterterrorism policy realistic?
2. Do the twin realities—drugs and terrorist organizations—lend itself to violations of human rights akin to Russia's conduct in Chechnya?
3. Would China's aggressive (Strike Hard) counterterrorism policy be viable in Colombia?

4. Is Colombia's negotiation policy reflective of Spain's largely non-responsive policy?
5. How does the availability of significant financial resources affect a government's policy?
6. Given the complexity of the historic challenges facing Colombian governments, how is effectiveness best measured?

CHAPTER 5

JUDICIAL REVIEW

I. INTRODUCTION

A critical component of counterterrorism is the role of a nation's judiciary. An unfettered executive, unrestrained by courts and legislatures, is detrimental to liberal democracies attempting to balance national security and individual rights. In examining the role of the judiciary in each of the surveyed nations it is incumbent to understand that different regimes have differing systems. Nevertheless, there is a common thread to this chapter: an examination of the willingness of a nation's judiciary to actively review and, if need be, criticize and intervene in the decisions and actions of the executive branch.

Clearly, executives would prefer to conduct their business without judicial interference; however, what separates liberal democratic regimes from dictatorships is the executive's accountability for its decisions. Whether and how the courts review executive decisions during armed conflict is the principle issue to be analyzed.

ISSUES TO CONSIDER

1. How much should a judiciary defer to the executive?
2. How much deference should courts ascribe to the phrase "national security"?
3. Is judicial review appropriate in time of armed conflict?
4. How much compromising of individual rights should courts tolerate?
5. When should courts intervene?
6. Are courts equipped to intervene and review decisions related to warfare when only the commanders are responsible for the lives of their soldiers?

The seminal court case that articulated the scope of executive power in the United States is based on notice given by the United Steelworkers of America of an impending nationwide strike. Hours before the strike was to begin, President Truman issued Executive Order 10340, directing the Secretary of Commerce to take possession of and operate most of the nation's steel mills. In *Youngstown Sheet & Tube Co. v. Sawyer*, the Supreme Court held that the President did not have the authority to issue such an order. While the executive argued that the "President had 'inherent power' to do what he had done supported by the Constitution, by historical precedent, and by court decisions,"[1] the Supreme Court disagreed. The Court held that "the President's power, if any, to issue the order must stem either from an act of Congress or from the Constitution itself."[2]

Even though the majority held the President did not have the power to issue such an order, the lasting significance of the case is Justice Jackson's concurrence. Justice Jackson analyzed the limits of the President's powers in three different situations.

1. When the President acts pursuant to an express or implied authorization of Congress, his authority is at its maximum, for it includes all that he possesses in his own right plus all that Congress can delegate. In these circumstances, and in these only, may he be said (for what it may be worth), to personify the federal sovereignty. If his act is held unconstitutional under these circumstances, it usually means that the Federal government as an undivided whole lacks power. The strongest of presumptions and the widest latitude of judicial interpretation would support a seizure executed by the President pursuant to an Act of Congress, and the burden of persuasion would rest heavily upon any who might attack it.

2. When the President acts in absence of either a congressional grant or denial of authority, he can only rely upon his own independent powers, but there is a zone of twilight in which he and Congress may have concurrent authority, or in which its distribution is uncertain. Therefore, congressional inertia, indifference or quiescence may sometimes, at least as a practical matter, enable, if not invite, measures on independent presidential responsibility. In this area, any actual test of power is likely to depend on the imperatives of events and contemporary imponderables rather than on abstract theories of law.

3. When the President takes measures incompatible with the expressed or implied will of Congress, his power is at its lowest ebb, for then he can rely only upon his own constitutional powers minus any constitutional powers of Congress over the matter. Courts can sustain exclusive Presidential control in such a case only be disabling the Congress from acting upon the subject. Presidential claim to a power at once so conclusive and preclusive must be scrutinized with caution, for what is at stake is the equilibrium established by our constitutional system.[3]

As a point of reference, it could be argued that the judicial activism advocated both intellectually and in practice by the retired President of the Israel Supreme Court, Aharon Barak, represents one end of the judicial review scale and the position suggested by late Chief Justice Rehnquist represents, if not the extreme other end, then at least an opposing view. The positions

---

1. Youngstown Sheet & Tube Co. v. Sawyer, 343 U.S. 579, 584 (1952).
2. *Id.* at 585.
3. *Id.* at 635-38.

of the Russian, Indian, Spanish, Chinese, and Colombian courts will be examined in the context of the debate between Barak and Rehnquist.

Retired President Barak propounded and implemented judicial activism in his decisions over 15 years.[4] Important for purposes here are Barak's opinions addressing Israel's counterterrorism efforts. Barak articulated his thesis in "A Judge on Judging";[5] Rehnquist in his book *All the Laws But One*.[6] The American experience regarding judicial intervention in counterterrorism is recent, but judicial review of executive decisions during time of war is not. An attempt will be made to compare approaches while examining holdings in *Padilla v. Rumsfeld*,[7] *Hamdi v. Rumsfeld*,[8] *Rasul v. Bush*,[9] and *Boumedienne v. Bush*.[10]

An overriding theme this chapter seeks to address is the proper role of the judiciary in counterterrorism. The word "proper" elicits much debate and little consensus. Some propose that the executive be allowed to make critical command decisions while enclosed in a bubble. Others insist that such an approach is inherently dangerous. Succinctly put, the question becomes whether a supreme court should interfere or intervene in the executive's wartime decision-making or whether the executive should be granted unfettered discretion.

Differences between the seven nations, with respect to the level of judicial review of executive decisions, are best viewed by the following spectrum:

High Involvement ← -- → Low Involvement
Israel   India   Spain   Colombia   Russia   United States   China

Because of the unique nature of the subject, this chapter is organized differently. Prior to a discussion of the seven surveyed nations, Barak's and Rehnquist's opinions are reviewed to illustrate diametrically contrasting perspectives.

A. PRESIDENT BARAK

1. Role of the Court

President Barak's seminal article in the Harvard Law Review, written while sitting as President of the Israel Supreme Court, is a compelling discussion of judicial activism in armed conflict.[11] It advocates active judicial review

---

4. President Barak retired from the Israel Supreme Court in the fall of 2006.
5. Aharon Barak, *A Judge on Judging: The Role of a Supreme Court in a Democracy*, 116 Harv. L. Rev. 16 (2002).
6. William H. Rehnquist, *All the Laws But One: Civil Liberties in Wartime* 225 (1998).
7. Padilla v. Rumsfeld, 352 F.3d 695 (2d Cir. 2003). 542 U.S. 426 (2004).
8. Hamdi v. Rumsfeld, 542 U.S. 507 (2004).
9. Rasul v. Bush, 542 U.S. 466 (2004).
10. Boumedienne v. Bush, 553 U.S. 723 (2008).
11. Barak, *supra* note 5.

against the background of Israel's ongoing struggle with Palestinian terrorism. President Barak's article is a message to the executive that the judiciary will be watching, monitoring, and—if need be—intervening in executive decisions pertaining to armed conflict.

In the article, President Barak discusses the challenges that terrorism presents for democratic countries, arguing that not every effective means is legal.[12] While terrorists adhere to no rules, "a democracy must fight with one hand tied behind its back."[13] Even though a democracy has to fight in this manner, President Barak argues that it still has the upper hand since it preserves the rule of law and respects individual liberties. President Barak argues that these two factors strengthen democracies in fighting terrorism. A democracy is not unlimited or unencumbered in its fight to protect its territory; unlike terrorists, its citizens have rules and laws that must be abided. It is precisely those rules that separate liberal democracies from terrorists. Protecting democracy from "the means the state wants to use to fight terrorism" is necessary in order to preserve democracy.[14]

Should a state resort to illegal means to fight terrorism or disregard its own rule of law, then terrorism has won. A democracy that compromises its values and standards in order to fight terrorists allows the terrorists to undermine the very core of the democracy. Laws are most important in times of war. They were created and developed "precisely so that they will be consulted and obeyed, not ignored" during times of crisis.[15]

According to President Barak, there is a basic tension between components of democracy. Citizens, through their elected representatives, may expect the government to take all steps necessary in fighting terrorism, regardless of their effect on human rights. However, the human rights component of democracy "may encourage protecting the rights of every individual, including the terrorists, even at the cost of undermining the fight against terrorism."[16] Therefore, the executive of a democracy must balance between these fundamentally competing interests so as to protect the rule of law, the essence of democracy. As President Barak wrote, "Terrorism does not justify the neglect of accepted legal norms."[17] The role of the court is to "ensure the constitutionality and legality of the fight,"[18] regardless of whether the decisions of the court are popular with the executive or the public. The independence of the court enables the justices to protect individual rights, regardless of what the public demands.

The role of a justice in protecting democracy and individual human rights is "a much more formidable duty in times of war and terrorism than in times of peace and security."[19] It is during times of war and terrorism that citizens often think it permissible to compromise rights and protections in order to help maintain security. However, justices cannot allow themselves to compromise

---

12. *Id.* at 157.
13. *Id.* at 148.
14. *Id.* at 149.
15. *Id.* at 151.
16. *Id.* at 148.
17. *Id.* at 151.
18. *Id.*
19. *Id.* at 149.

citizens' rights, regardless of whether it is war time or peacetime. Justices cannot have different procedures or standards for wartime without eroding peacetime protections as well. Judicial decisions during times of crisis "remain with the democracy when the threat of terrorism passes . . . entrenched in the case law of the court as a magnet for the development of new and problematic laws."[20]

It is much easier for the executive to change directions or policy, or for the legislature to revoke, amend, or pass new laws to amend existing legislation, than for the judiciary to reverse itself. Mistakes made by the judiciary live on even after they have been overruled. The logic, reasoning, and basis for a decision are recorded in judicial history to be used in the future for other cases whereas overturned executive or legislative actions are generally ignored.[21]

2. President Barak's Theory

President Barak argues that the Israeli Supreme Court's willingness to review executive actions is not improper interference.[22] He sees a crucial distinction between intervening in military considerations and in intervening in equality of treatment questions that may arise from military actions.[23] President Barak sees the role of the Supreme Court not as ruling on the efficiency of security measures for fighting terrorism, but rather as ensuring that the military acts "within the framework of the 'zone of reasonableness'" with regard to its actions and measures.[24]

President Barak believes it is imperative for the judiciary to ensure that executive actions harmonize with principles of democracy; accordingly, they must be evaluated in real time. "The protection of human rights would be bankrupt if, during armed conflict, the courts — consciously or unconsciously — decided to review the executive branch's behavior only after the period of emergency has ended."[25] If a court postpones reviewing executive actions until the period of emergency or time of crisis has passed, then any ruling issued by the court would not contribute to the rule of law. Rights must be protected when the executive seeks to impinge upon them.

Courts must balance between national security interests personified by executive actions and the harm that any action may cause to the rights of individuals. To perform this balancing test, courts must review the actions of the executive at the time that they are taking place. In other words, nations must impose their own limits. "Judicial review of the legality of the war on terrorism may make this war harder in the short term, but it also fortifies and strengthens the people in the long term."[26]

---

20. *Id.*
21. *Id.*
22. *Id.* at 151.
23. *Id.* Barak in discussing the gas mask case from the Gulf War said that the Court was addressing specifically the equality of the distribution of the gas masks, not whether or not the masks should be distributed.
24. *Id.* at 157.
25. *Id.* at 156.
26. *Id.* at 158.

President Barak's theory of "self-imposed restraints" is not an abstraction. It reflects the activist approach adopted by Israel's High Court of Justice. HCJ intervention — what others would define as interference — will be examined later in this chapter by analyzing a number of seminal decisions handed down over the past few years.

B. CHIEF JUSTICE REHNQUIST

Whereas President Barak strongly believes in the responsibility of the Supreme Court to review actions of the executive in a timely fashion, the late Chief Justice Rehnquist's perspective was markedly different. Chief Justice Rehnquist advocated a hands-off approach unlike President Barak's very hands-on theory. In those rare instances where the judiciary does review the legality of executive actions related to armed conflict, Chief Justice Rehnquist believed the examination should wait until the time of crisis has passed.

Chief Justice Rehnquist neither propounded *inter arma silent leges* (in time of war laws are silent), nor did he believe that the law plays the same role in war as in peace. Unlike President Barak, who forcefully argues the judiciary should interpret the laws in the same manner regardless of whether it is a time of war, Chief Justice Rehnquist stated that the laws "will speak with a somewhat different voice" during a time of war.[27]

Distinct from the direction taken by the Israeli High Court under President Barak, the U.S. Supreme Court historically has not interpreted laws uniformly in war and in peace. Chief Justice Rehnquist points out that the Supreme Court traditionally gave the executive branch more leeway during war or crisis, particularly World War II.[28] Though recognizing that "the government's authority to engage in conduct that infringes civil liberty is greatest in time of declared war," Chief Justice Rehnquist argued that the judiciary should not review all executive actions, especially during a crisis.[29]

Even if a court examines the actions of the executive, the timing is critical. Courts have a general reluctance "to decide a case against the government on an issue of national security during a war."[30] While President Barak believes an essential duty of the judiciary is to treat the law equally during war and during peace, Chief Justice Rehnquist argued for recognition of "the human factor that inevitably enters into even the most careful judicial decision."[31] Therefore, he implied postponing decisions until the crisis has passed. As an example, Chief Justice Rehnquist referred to *Ex parte Mitsuye Endo*, in which the Supreme Court voted to uphold civil liberties only near the end of WWII.[32] The Supreme Court decision that Japanese internment was illegal came well after martial law had already ended and American citizens were no longer

---

27. Rehnquist, *supra* note 6.
28. *Id.* at 221.
29. *Id.* at 218.
30. *Id.* at 221.
31. *Id.* at 222.
32. *Id.* at 221 (citing Ex parte Mitsuye Endo, 323 U.S. 283 (1944) (the Supreme Court held that power to protect the war effort from espionage and sabotage did not include the power to detain a loyal citizen)).

living in internment camps.[33] By waiting until after World War II ended to rule on *Endo*, the Supreme Court was ostensibly able to uphold civil liberties but not practically. Chief Justice Rehnquist suggested that it may "actually be desirable to avoid decision on" civil liberties during the war or time of crisis.[34]

The difference between the two approaches is palpable. President Barak advocates and practices active judicial review; the late Chief Justice Rehnquist's approach was much more restrained. They differ not only to the *extent* of judicial review regarding executive actions, but also the *timing* when the judiciary should review. The decisions of their respective courts reflect their differing approaches.

II. UNITED STATES

A. INTRODUCTION

On November 13, 2001, President Bush issued a Presidential Order establishing military commissions for enemy combatants.[35] Over the course of the next four months, three hundred detainees were transported to Guantanamo Bay[36] for purposes of interrogation and hearings before the military commissions. According to Section Four of the Presidential Order, a detainee convicted on any charge could appeal only to the President of the United States or the Secretary of Defense.[37] The significance of this is now clear: the United States government held hundreds of detainees in Guantanamo Bay while denying them independent judicial review both of their status and a determination whether they were a present and continuing danger to the national security of the United States. While it is true that the Supreme Court of the United States does not function as a High Court of Justice (unlike the Israel Supreme Court), the question is whether Chief Justice Rehnquist's philosophy influenced the executive's decisions.[38] When the Chief Justice writes "there

---

33. *Id.* at 221.

34. *Id.* at 222.

35. *Detention, Treatment, and Trial of Certain Non-Citizens in the War Against Terrorism*, 66 Fed. Reg. 57833 (Nov. 16, 2001) [hereinafter *Trial of Certain Non-Citizens*].

36. On January 7, 2002, there were 346 detainees in U.S. custody but the United States refused to comment on the number to be held at Guantanamo Bay. By March 1, 2002, there were 300 known detainees in Guantanamo Bay. Jim Garamone, *Tension Eases at Guantanamo Holding Facility*, Am. Forces Info. Serv., Mar. 1, 2002, http://www.defenselink.mil/news/Mar2002/n03012002_200203012.html (last visited July 22, 2007).

37. *Trial of Certain Non-Citizens*, *supra* note 35 ("submission of the record of the trial, including any conviction or sentence, for review and final decision by" the President or the "Secretary of Defense if so designated by me for that purpose"). *See also* §7(b)(2) ("the individual shall not be privileged to seek any remedy or maintain any proceeding, directly or indirectly, or to have any such remedy or proceeding sought on the individual's behalf, in (i) any court of the United States, or any State thereof, (ii) any court of any foreign nation, or (iii) any international tribunal").

38. According to unconfirmed media reports, President Barak implored the Justices of the U.S. Supreme Court, in particular Chief Justice Rehnquist, to adopt a philosophy of judicial activism. According to these reports, Barak argued that judicial acquiescence in misbegotten executive decisions is more harmful than problematic legislation for legislation can be more easily repealed than the Court would reverse itself.

remains a sense that there is some truth to the maxim *inter arma silent leges* at least in the purely descriptive sense,"[39] the executive is granted broad leeway.

ISSUES TO CONSIDER

1. Are U.S. policy interests advanced by Chief Justice Rehnquist's philosophy of deference to the executive branch during armed conflict?
2. Does the U.S. administration adopt the posture of an "unfettered executive" because it understands that the judicial oversight will be lax at best?
3. Given that the Chief Justice's position had been clearly stated and that Congress was not consulted regarding the establishment of the military commissions, has the concept of checks and balances been seriously weakened?

B. PADILLA v. RUMSFELD

José Padilla sought *habeas corpus* relief against Secretary of Defense Donald Rumsfeld after being detained as an unlawful combatant. While the Supreme Court eventually reversed and remanded the case solely on jurisdictional grounds, the Court of Appeals (see below) analyzed whether the President had the authority to designate someone within the United States an enemy combatant.

PADILLA v. RUMSFELD

352 F.3d 695 (2d Cir. 2003)

We agree that great deference is afforded the President's exercise of his authority as Commander-in-Chief. We also agree that whether a state of armed conflict exists against an enemy to which the laws of war apply is a political question for the President, not the courts. Because we have no authority to do so, we do not address the government's underlying assumption that an undeclared war exists between al Qaeda and the United States. We have no quarrel with the former chief of the Justice Department's Criminal Division, who said:

For [al Qaeda] chose not to violate the law but to attack the law and its institutions directly. Their proclaimed goal, however unrealistic, was to destroy the United States. They used powerful weapons of destructive force and openly declared their willingness to employ even more powerful weapons of mass destruction if they could lay hold of them. They were as serious a threat to the national security of the United States as one could envision.

However, it is a different proposition entirely to argue that the President even in times of grave national security threats or war, whether declared or

---

39. Rehnquist, *supra* note 6, at 221.

undeclared, can lay claim to any of the powers, express or implied, allocated to Congress. The deference due to the Executive in its exercise of its war powers therefore only starts the inquiry; it does not end it. Where the exercise of Commander-in-Chief powers, no matter how well intentioned, is challenged on the ground that it collides with the powers assigned by the Constitution to Congress, a fundamental role exists for the courts. To be sure, when Congress and the President act together in the conduct of war, "it is not for any court to sit in review of the wisdom of their action or substitute its judgment for theirs." But when the Executive acts, even in the conduct of war, in the face of apparent congressional disapproval, challenges to his authority must be examined and resolved by the Article III courts.

These separation of powers concerns are heightened when the Commander-in-Chief's powers are exercised in the domestic sphere. The Supreme Court has long counseled that while the Executive should be "indulge[d] the widest latitude of interpretation to sustain his exclusive function to command the instruments of national force, at least when turned against the outside world for the security of our society," he enjoys "no such indulgence" when "it is turned inward." This is because "the federal power over external affairs [is] in origin and essential character different from that over internal affairs," and "congressional legislation which is to be made effective through negotiation and inquiry within the international field must often accord to the President a degree of discretion and freedom from statutory restriction which would not be admissible were domestic affairs alone involved." But, "Congress, not the Executive, should control utilization of the war power as an instrument of domestic policy." Thus, we do not concern ourselves with the Executive's inherent wartime power, generally, to detain enemy combatants on the battlefield. Rather, we are called on to decide whether the Constitution gives the President the power to detain an American citizen seized in this country until the war with al Qaeda ends.

The government contends that the Constitution authorizes the President to detain Padilla as an enemy combatant as an exercise of inherent executive authority. Padilla contends that, in the absence of express congressional authorization, the President, by his June 9 Order denominating Padilla an enemy combatant, has engaged in the "lawmaking" function entrusted by the Constitution to Congress in violation of the separation of powers. In response, no argument is made that the Constitution expressly grants the President the power to name United States citizens as enemy combatants and order their detention. Rather, the government contends that the Commander-in-Chief Clause implicitly grants the President the power to detain enemy combatants domestically during times of national security crises such as the current conflict with al Qaeda.

As an initial matter, we note that in its explicit vesting of powers in Articles I and II, the Constitution circumscribes and defines the respective functions of the political branches. The Constitution gives Congress the full legislative powers of government and at the same time, gives the President full executive authority and responsibility to "take care" that the laws enacted are faithfully executed. Thus, while the President has the obligation to enforce laws passed by Congress, he does not have the power to legislate.

C. HAMDI v. RUMSFELD

Hamdi was an American citizen captured in Afghanistan during a time of active military hostilities[40] and transferred to Guantanamo Bay. When it was discovered that Hamdi may not have renounced his American citizenship, he was transferred to the Norfolk Naval Station Brig.[41] On his behalf, a petition for writ of *habeas corpus* was filed challenging the legality of the government's decision to detain him on U.S. soil as an enemy combatant. Furthermore, Hamdi demanded that he be provided the opportunity to challenge the government's decision to so define him.[42]

In writing the majority opinion, Justice O'Connor reviewed both international law and constitutional dilemmas. Justice O'Connor's analysis of this question underscores the significantly different approaches of the U.S. Supreme Court and the Israeli High Court. Even when similar conclusions are reached, Justice O'Connor commented that the Constitution "assuredly envisions a role for all three branches when individual liberties are at stake."[43] The real issue, of course, is the particular role of the judiciary: when and how should the judiciary be involved?

In *Hamdi*, the government argued for strong separation of powers in which the judiciary would have very limited ability to review executive actions.[44] Furthermore, the government posited that should the judiciary review the executive, it must do so based on a very deferential standard of review. The government's arguments reflected the view that the Supreme Court should interpret laws differently in times of war and in times of peace.

Justice O'Connor's opinion highlights the tension between national security considerations and individual civil rights. In balancing the state's and petitioner's concerns, the judiciary weighs "'the private interest that will be affected by the official action' against the government's asserted interest, 'including the function involved' and the burdens the government would face in providing greater process."[45] Justice O'Connor's opinion analyzes, step by step, the balancing between national security and "the most elemental of liberty interests — the interest in being free from physical detention by one's own government."[46]

HAMDI v. RUMSFELD

542 U.S. 507, 527-30 (2004)

The government's second argument requires closer consideration. This is the argument that further factual exploration is unwarranted and inappropriate in light of the extraordinary constitutional interests at stake. Under the government's most extreme rendition of this argument, "[r]espect for separation

---

40. Hamdi v. Rumsfeld, 316 F.3d 450, 460 (4th Cir. 2003), *rev'd*, 542 U.S. 507 (2004).
41. *Id.*
42. *Id.*
43. Hamdi v. Rumsfeld, 542 U.S. 507, 536 (2004).
44. *Id.* at 527.
45. *Id.* at 529.
46. *Id.*

of powers and the limited institutional capabilities of courts in matters of military decision-making in connection with an ongoing conflict" ought to eliminate entirely any individual process, restricting the courts to investigating only whether legal authorization exists for the broader detention scheme. At most, the government argues, courts should review its determination that a citizen is an enemy combatant under a very deferential "some evidence" standard. Under this review, a court would assume the accuracy of the government's articulated basis for Hamdi's detention, as set forth in the Mobbs Declaration, and assess only whether that articulated basis was a legitimate one.

In response, Hamdi emphasizes that this Court consistently has recognized that an individual challenging his detention may not be held at the will of the Executive without recourse to some proceeding before a neutral tribunal to determine whether the Executive's asserted justifications for that detention have basis in fact and warrant in law. He argues that the Fourth Circuit inappropriately "ceded power to the Executive during wartime to define the conduct for which a citizen may be detained, judge whether that citizen has engaged in the proscribed conduct, and imprison that citizen indefinitely," and that due process demands that he receive a hearing in which he may challenge the Mobbs Declaration and adduce his own counter evidence. The District Court, agreeing with Hamdi, apparently believed that the appropriate process would approach the process that accompanies a criminal trial. It therefore disapproved of the hearsay nature of the Mobbs Declaration and anticipated quite extensive discovery of various military affairs. Anything less, it concluded, would not be "meaningful judicial review."

Both of these positions highlight legitimate concerns. And both emphasize the tension that often exists between the autonomy that the government asserts is necessary in order to pursue effectively a particular goal and the process that a citizen contends he is due before he is deprived of a constitutional right. The ordinary mechanism that we use for balancing such serious competing interests, and for determining the procedures that are necessary to ensure that a citizen is not "deprived of life, liberty, or property, without due process of law," U.S. Const., Amdt. 5, is the test that we articulated in Mathews v. Eldridge, 424 U.S. 319, 47 L. Ed. 2d 18, 96 S. Ct. 893 (1976). *Mathews* dictates that the process due in any given instance is determined by weighing "the private interest that will be affected by the official action" against the government's asserted interest, "including the function involved" and the burdens the government would face in providing greater process. The *Mathews* calculus then contemplates a judicious balancing of these concerns, through an analysis of "the risk of an erroneous deprivation" of the private interest if the process were reduced and the "probable value, if any, of additional or substitute safeguards." We take each of these steps in turn.

It is beyond question that substantial interests lie on both sides of the scale in this case. Hamdi's "private interest . . . affected by the official action" is the most elemental of liberty interests—the interest in being free from physical detention by one's own government. "In our society liberty is the norm," and detention without trial "is the carefully limited exception." "We have always been careful not to 'minimize the importance and fundamental nature' of the individual's right to liberty," and we will not do so today.

ISSUES TO CONSIDER

1. Should a court write deferentially when holding against the executive?
2. In the context of national security, are tone and style of judicial review as important as content?
3. Should the administration have considered judicial activism prior to establishing Guantanamo and its attendant rules?
4. Did the American judicial history of non-judicial activism in the context of national security give the administration a false sense of security?

As previously discussed, the U.S. Supreme Court has historically been very accommodating to the executive. Indeed, Rehnquist's philosophy clearly states such an approach. In *Hamdi*, Justice O'Connor's tone and style reveal a similar viewpoint, though the decision itself reflects evolution and, potentially, movement towards a more active Court. Justice Stevens' opinion in *Rasul* (see below) is similarly reflective of a more vigorous judiciary. Perhaps the reality of Guantanamo Bay and the treatment of detainees convinced the Court there was no alternative but to restrain the administration.

D. RASUL v. BUSH

In *Rasul v. Bush*, the Supreme Court addressed the following question concerning judicial review: "(w)hether United States' courts lack jurisdiction to consider challenges to the legality of the detention of foreign nationals captured abroad in connection with hostilities and incarcerated at the Guantanamo Bay Naval Base, Cuba."[47] The petitioners were two Australians and twelve Kuwaitis who had been captured in Afghanistan during hostilities with the Taliban and held in military custody at Guantanamo Bay.[48]

In his majority opinion, Justice Stevens held that "what is presently at stake is only whether the federal courts have jurisdiction to determine the legality of the Executive's potentially indefinite detention of individuals."[49] Even though the Court ultimately held against the executive in *Rasul*, it did so narrowly.

Justice Stevens' opinion begins with a brief description of the September 11th attacks on the United States.[50] By including details about the attacks and the damage caused by them, Justice Stevens subtly acknowledges the executive's national security concerns. Unlike Justice O'Connor's direct acknowledgement of the concerns and arguments of the executive, Justice Stevens implies the strength of the executive's argument stating that the President acted pursuant to congressional authorization.[51]

---

47. Rasul v. Bush, *supra* note 9, at 470.
48. *Id.*
49. *Id.* at 485.
50. *Id.* at 470.
51. *Id.*

Justice Stevens explicitly states that the judiciary has the jurisdiction to decide the legality of executive actions. In reaching this decision, Stevens focuses on why the judiciary has jurisdiction without giving undue emphasis to the arguments of the government. His opinion shows more deference to the executive than President Barak would have, yet much less than Justice O'Connor did in *Hamdi*. The tone of Justice Stevens' opinion shows that the Court seems to be moving away from strict interpretation of Chief Justice Rehnquist's philosophy. However, the timing of *Rasul* clearly reflects the late Chief Justice's views on when judicial review should occur.

As discussed earlier, Chief Justice Rehnquist believed that there were times when it was better for the Court to wait to review executive actions. In reference to *Endo*, Rehnquiest wrote that it may "actually be desirable to avoid decision on" civil liberties during the war or time of crisis.[52] Rehnquist's views are, perhaps, best revealed by cases not brought before the Court. Though hundreds of detainees are held at Guantanamo Bay, the Supreme Court has heard very few cases. Chief Justice Rehnquist "believed that the court should reserve its time and effort for cases of national importance that absolutely require its attention."[53]

Unlike the U. S. Supreme Court, which deliberated Guantanamo Bay cases three years after the military commissions were implemented, the Israeli HCJ heard *Marab* while the Israeli Defense Forces was continuing to detain Palestinian terrorists and heard *Physicians for Human Rights* while the conflict was ongoing. Solutions needed to be developed and implemented by the IDF while the Court heard arguments. The U.S. Supreme Court, as highlighted in through both *Rasul* and *Hamdi*, demonstrates reluctance to respond in real time and directly reflects Chief Justice Rehnquist's philosophical approach that certain cases should not be heard during time of crisis. Real-time decisions of the Court in response to ongoing executive action are the essence of robust judicial activism when the executive is engaged in operational counterterrorism.

E. HAMDAN v. RUMSFELD

In *Hamdan v. Rumsfeld*, the Supreme Court signaled to the Bush administration that military procedures[54] were inadequate and demanded a reformulation.[55] Specifically, in discussing the current procedural deficiencies, the Court wrote:

> The commission's procedures . . . provide . . . that an accused and his civilian counsel may be excluded from . . . ever learning what evidence was presented

---

52. Rehnquist, *supra* note 6, at 222.

53. Charles Lane, *The Rehnquist Legacy: 33 Years Turning Back the Court*, Wash. Post, Sept. 5, 2005, at A8.

54. Hearings in the United States Senate, Committee on the Judiciary showed the various interpretations of the impact of the *Hamdan* decision, and the response appropriate from the U.S. Senate. *See House Armed Services Committee Hearing on Standards of Military Commissions and Tribunals*, July 26, 2006, *available at* http://www.publicinternationallaw.org/publications/testimony/MilitaryCommission%20TestimonyHouse%20ArmedServices%20Committe72606.doc. (last visited Oct. 8, 2010).

55. The Court signaled this by stating that the Authorization for the Use of Military Force was not a blank check for the Administration to set up military commissions however they saw fit, but rather, the AUMF was more like the "lowest ebb" of power, akin to *Youngstown Sheet & Tubing Co. v. Sawyer*, requiring further Congressional approval for such commissions.

during any part of the proceeding . . . the presiding officer decides to "close." Grounds for closure include the protection of classified information, the physical safety of participants and witnesses, the protection of intelligence and law enforcement sources, methods, or activities, and "other national security interests." Appointed military defense counsel must be privy to these closed sessions, but may, at the presiding officer's discretion, be forbidden to reveal to the client what took place therein. . . . Moreover, the accused and his civilian counsel may be denied access to classified and other "protected information," so long as the presiding officer concludes that the evidence is "probative."[56]

In further analyzing these deficiencies, the Court held that

even assuming that Hamdan is a dangerous individual who would cause great harm or death to innocent civilians given the opportunity, the Executive nevertheless must comply with the prevailing rule of law in undertaking to try him and subject him to criminal punishment.[57]

In response to *Hamdan*, the United States Congress passed the Military Commissions Act of 2006[58] which expressly eliminated court jurisdiction over all pending and future *habeas* causes of action. While this congressional action addresses some of the Court's concerns in *Hamdan*, it failed to formulate proper interrogation standards. In addition, rather than specifically articulating permissible interrogation methods, the Military Commissions Act granted the Executive authority to interpret the scope and application of Common Article III of the Geneva Convention. The Act's lack of clarity invited of continued violations of detainee rights resulting in the Court's revisiting the issue in *Boumediene v. Bush*.[59]

F. BOUMEDIENE v. BUSH

In *Boumediene v. Bush*, the Supreme Court held in a 5-4 opinion that aliens designated as enemy combatants and detained at Guantanamo Bay have the constitutional privilege of *habeas corpus*.[60] The court also found that §7 of the Military Commissions Act, which limited judicial review of executive determinations of the petitioners' enemy combatant status, did not provide an adequate *habeas* substitute and unconstitutionally suspended the writ of *habeas*. The petitioners argued they possessed a constitutional right to *habeas* review and that the MCA violated the Suspension Clause which prohibits suspension of the writ of *habeas corpus* except during cases of rebellion or invasion when public safety may require it. The government did not claim MCA was a suspension of writ, but instead argued that aliens designated as enemy combatants and detained outside the *de jure* territory of the U.S. do not have

---

56. *Hamdan v. Rumsfeld*, 548 U.S. 557, 734 (2006).
57. *Id.* at 737.
58. 120 Stat. 2600 (Oct. 17, 2006).
59. 553 U.S. 723 (2008).
60. *Id.* at 732.

constitutional rights, and therefore stripping the courts of jurisdiction to hear their *habeas* claims did not violate the Suspension Clause.

The Court noted that the writ was one of the few Constitutional protections of individual liberty prior to the Bill of Rights. The Court also viewed the Suspension Clause under the separation of powers doctrine, and concluded it provides the judiciary with a "time-tested device, the writ, to maintain the delicate balance of governance" among the branches and to prevent "cyclical abuses" made by the legislative or executive branches.[61] The Court determined the Suspension Clause has full effect at Guantanamo, rejecting the government's argument regarding the petitioners' constitutional rights because the U.S. did not assert legal sovereignty over Guantanamo. The Court held that accepting such an argument would create separation of powers problems, by allowing the political branches to govern without restraint: "To hold that the political branches may switch the Constitution on and off at will would lead to a regime where they, not this Court, say what the law is."[62]

The Court found three factors in assessing the reach of the Suspension Clause: (1) citizenship and status of the detainee and the adequacy of the status determination process; (2) the nature of the site where the person is seized and detained; and (3) the practical obstacles inherent to resolving the prisoner's entitlement to the writ. In applying those principles to the facts at hand, the Court noted that the detainees have been held by executive order for the duration of a conflict already one of the longest in American history and although Guantanamo is not technically a part of the U.S., it is under the complete and total control of the U.S. government.[63]

After holding the detainees were entitled to *habeas corpus* review, the Court next addressed whether MCA's jurisdiction stripping was permissible under the Suspension Clause. Because the MCA did not purport to be a formal suspension of the writ, the issue was whether Congress provided an adequate substitute for *habeas corpus*. The Court held that it was clear that by enacting the MCA, Congress intended to create a much more limited procedure than traditional *habeas corpus* review. Although the Court did not want to offer a "comprehensive summary of the requisites for an adequate substitute for habeas corpus," the Court did outline some necessary requirements.[64] "The prisoner is entitled to a meaningful opportunity to demonstrate that he is being held pursuant to 'the erroneous application or interpretation' of relevant law."[65] In addition,

> the habeas court must have the power to order the conditional release of an individual unlawfully detained—though release need not be the exclusive remedy and is not the appropriate one in every case in which the writ is granted.[66]

---

61. *Id.* at 744.
62. *Id.* at 765.
63. *Id.* at 770.
64. *Id.* at 777.
65. *Id.*
66. *Id.*

The Court also stated that depending on the circumstances, additional *habeas* protections may be required. Some additional rights detainees should be granted include the ability to find and present evidence, assistance of counsel, access to government records, information regarding allegations relied upon by the government in the detention, and the ability to confront witnesses, thereby limiting the use of hearsay evidence.

The Court stated that there was significant risk of error in the tribunal's finding of fact, and this risk was too serious to ignore considering that the error will may result in detention for the duration of hostilities that may last more than a generation. The Court held the MCA failed to provide an adequate substitute for *habeas* and as such the writ was unconstitutionally suspended. Therefore, all detainees in Guantanamo have a right to a *habeas corpus* review in federal district courts.

The initial case in which a Circuit court applied the *Boumediene* decision was in *Al-Bihani v. Obama.*[67] In that case, the defendant was a Yemeni citizen held in Guantanamo since 2002. The two issues the court addressed were whether the President can lawfully detain pursuant to an act of Congress and what procedure is due to detainees challenging their detention in *habeas* proceedings. The defendant based his argument on principles of international law arguing that relying on "support" of al Qaeda, as a basis for detention violates international law. According to Al-Bihani, an individual not belonging to a recognized state's military is a civilian who must commit direct hostile acts before they can be lawfully detained. Al-Bihani further argued that the conflict for which he was detained, between the U.S. and Taliban-controlled Afghanistan, officially ended when the Taliban lost control over Afghanistan and therefore he should be released, absent a determination of future dangerousness.

The Court rejected the argument that the U.S. should be bound by international law stating "international laws of war as a whole have not been implemented domestically by Congress and are therefore not a source of authority for U.S. courts."[68] The Court went on to say: "we have no occasion here to quibble over the intricate application of vague treaty provisions and amorphous customary principles."[69] The Court wrote:

> any person subject to a military commission trial is also subject to detention, and that category of persons includes those who are part of forces associated with Al Qaeda or the Taliban or those who purposefully and materially support such forces in hostilities against U.S. Coalition partners.[70]

The Court summarily rejected the defendant's claims that procedures used in his habeas proceedings were inadequate, and therefore the petition for a writ of *habeas corpus* was denied.

---

67. 590 F.3d 866 (2010).
68. *Id.* at 871.
69. *Id.*
70. *Id.* at 872.

JENNIFER K. ELSEA & MICHAEL JOHN GARCIA, JUDICIAL ACTIVITY CONCERNING
ENEMY COMBATANT DETAINEES: MAJOR COURT RULINGS

Congressional Research Service Report for Congress, Apr. 1, 2010[71]

Recent District Court Rulings Concerning Scope of Executive Detention Authority

In the aftermath of the Supreme Court's decision in *Boumediene*, federal *habeas* courts reviewing claims raised by Guantanamo detainees have reached differing conclusions regarding the scope of the Executive's detention authority under the AUMF and the law of war. Judge Richard J. Leon, the first district court judge to rule on this issue post-*Boumediene*, applied the standard employed by the Department of Defense (DOD) in 2004 CSRT proceedings, which authorized the detention of those who were "part of or supporting Taliban or al Qaeda forces, or associated forces that are engaged in hostilities against the United States or its coalition partners . . . [including] any person who has committed a belligerent act or has directly supported hostilities in aid of enemy armed force." More recent rulings by district courts have taken a more limited view of the Executive's detention authority. A few district court judges have held that the Executive has authority to detain persons who were "part of" or "substantially supported" Al Qaeda, the Taliban, or associated forces, so long as those terms are understood to include only those persons who were members of the enemy organizations' *armed forces* at the time of capture. Other judges have held that the Executive has authority under the AUMF and the law of war to detain persons who were "part of" the Taliban, Al Qaeda, or associated forces, but lacks authority to detain nonmembers who provide "support" to such organizations (though such support may be considered when determining whether a detainee was "part of" one of these groups). As discussed *supra*, in *Al-Bihani v. Obama* a three-judge D.C. Circuit panel endorsed the definitional standard used by Judge Leon to assess the Executive's detention authority. It is possible that this issue will be the subject of further litigation, either before the circuit court sitting *en banc* or the Supreme Court.

Several (though not all) district court judges have concluded that an individual's continuing threat to U.S. security is not a relevant consideration in determining whether he may be lawfully detained under the AUMF1 At least one district court judge has expressly held that "the President is authorized to detain [a properly designated enemy belligerent] for the duration of the conflict in Afghanistan, even if [he] poses no threat of returning to the field of battle." However, this conclusion has not been endorsed by every district court judge who has considered the issue.

Al Maqaleh v. Gates, 604 F. Supp. 2d 205 (D.D.C. 2009)

In April 2009, District Court Judge John D. Bates held in *Al Maqaleh v. Gates* that *habeas* may extend to non-Afghan detainees currently held by the United States at the Bagram Theater Internment Facility in Afghanistan, when those detainees had been captured outside of Afghanistan but were transferred to

---

71. *Available at* http://www.fas.org/sgp/crs/natsec/R41156.pdf/.

Bagram for long-term detention as enemy combatants. Judge Bates held that the circumstances surrounding detention of the petitioners in *Al Maqaleh* were "virtually identical to the detainees in *Boumediene*—they are [non-U.S.] citizens who were . . . apprehended in foreign lands far from the United States and brought to yet another country for detention." Applying *Boumediene* as relevant to a determination of the extraterritorial scope of the writ of *habeas corpus*, Judge Bates concluded that the writ extended to three of the four petitioners at issue in *Al Maqaleh*, who were not Afghan citizens.

———————

In May 2010, the D.C. Circuit Court, in *Al-Maqaleh v. Gates*, overturned Judge Bates' decision holding that detainees held in an "active theater of war in a territory under neither the *de facto* nor *de jure* sovereignty of the United States and within the territory of another *de jure* sovereign" are not entitled to *habeas corpus*.[72]

ISSUES TO CONSIDER

1. What are the ramifications of denying detainees the right to *habeas corpus?*
2. What are the dangers of indefinite detention?
3. How does *Al-Maqaleh* impact *Boumediene?*
4. What is the most effective argument for granting detainees *habeas* rights?
5. Does the D.C. Circuit Court decision reflect policy articulated by President Bush in the immediate aftermath of 9/11?
6. Is the D.C. Cirucuit Court decision in accordance with the principles proposed by the late Chief Justice Rehnquist with respect to the role of courts in times of armed conflict?

III. ISRAEL

In developing and implementing a counterterrorism strategy, Israel's policy and decision makers are confronted by the doors of the High Court of Justice (HCJ) that are literally and figuratively open 24/7 to hear petitions of aggrieved Palestinians, or those acting on their behalf. A junior military commander's decision to conduct a particular operation, a senior officer determined to order that a particular geographic area be declared a closed military zone, and a noncommissioned officer's decision not to allow someone to pass through a checkpoint are all petionable in real time to the High Court. The U.S. standard of standing and justiciability are irrelevant; anyone may petition the High Court on behalf of a potentially aggrieved party.

———————

72. 605 F.3d 84, 97-98 (D.C. Cir. 2010).

The principle of judicial activism in Israel is examined by analyzing three petitions filed with the High Court of Justice. The three cases are representative and indicative of the interplay between the executive (which in the West Bank is the IDF); the aggrieved (either a Palestinian who directly petitions or a human rights group petitioning on his behalf); and the Court.

These petitions were filed at the height of Palestinian terrorism and Israeli counterterrorism. The HCJ hearings do not take place in a vacuum; while the Court adjudicates, the IDF is either planning or engaged in military operations against Palestinian terrorists, who similarly are planning their next attack. The decisions have been chosen because they represent three distinct issues brought before the Court.

ISSUES TO CONSIDER

1. What is the legal and policy significance of the phrase "democracies fight terrorism with one arm tied behind their back"?
2. What is the meaning of Barak's argument that the Court's expertise lies in humanitarian law and not military combat?
3. What is the significance of judicial intervention when the issue is presented in real time rather than deferring until the conflict ends?
4. What does the phrase "if executive acts within the 'zone of reasonableness' then there is no basis for intervention" mean?
5. What does the phrase "security considerations are not magic words" mean?

A. MARAB v. IDF COMMANDER IN THE WEST BANK

With the advent of the military operation "Ebb and Flow," the IDF arrested thousands of Palestinians suspected of involvement in terrorism. The operation was a response to a terrorist act that resulted in the deaths of 30 Israelis, many of them elderly, celebrating the Passover meal. The military operation had not been planned thoroughly in advance, and critical non-combat issues were addressed on the fly. As a result, important issues were not considered and left to individual initiative.

One issue not properly planned was where to detain thousands of Palestinians arrested during the operation. As the detention process developed, initial screening of detainees was conducted at brigade headquarters—a process requiring a significant amount of time, sometimes in questionable conditions.

According to Military Order 378, as amended in 1997, a Palestinian may be held for eight days before seeing a judge. When the IDF realized the number of detainees who needed to be processed would result in the Order's violation, the military commander signed Order 1500.[73] According to of this Order, detainees could be held up to eighteen days before seeing a military judge.

---

73. *See* B'tselem, *Operation Defensive Shield: Soldiers' Testimonies, Palestinian Testimonies* 16, *available at* www.btselem.org/Download/200207_Defensive_Shield_Eng.pdf (last visited Oct. 8, 2010).

A petition was filed against this Order by Iad Ashak Mahmud Marab, a detainee.[74] In the petition and oral arguments, counsel argued the Order leads to detention without judicial review and to prolonged mass detention rather than individual review. Counsel claimed the Order was neither preventive nor administrative and violated the principles of proportionality and due process.[75]

The state responded to the petition by arguing that the standard detention law was not suitable for combat situations and that screening of detainees is a time-consuming process. The state argued keeping detainees from meeting with counsel prevents passing of messages that endangers soldiers. The state also argued that the detentions were individualized rather than collective, and they were unique in the context of the special circumstances of armed conflict. In essence, the state argued that its standards were proportional and reasonable.

The Court held that the Order was illegal, ruling that holding individuals for 12 or 18 days without bringing them before a judge conflicted with "fundamentals of both international and Israeli law."[76] The Court also held that judicial review is not separate from detention, but rather is "an integral part of the detention process" and as such cannot legally be separated.[77] The Court's insistence that judicial review is integral to executive detentions reflects President Barak's belief that the judiciary *can* and *must* review executive actions *in real time*.

MARAB v. IDF COMMANDER IN THE WEST BANK

HCJ 3239/02 (2002)

Against this normative background, which demands prompt judicial review of detention orders, the question again arises whether the arrangement established in Order 1500, under which a person may be detained for a period of 18 days without having been brought before a judge, is legal. Similarly, is the arrangement established in Order 1505 legal? This arrangement — which was unaffected by Order 1512 or Order 1518 — provided that a person may be detained for a period of 12 days without having being brought before a judge. In answering these questions, the special circumstances of the detention must be taken into account. "Regular" police detention is not the same as detention carried out "during warfare in the area," Order 1500, or "during anti-terrorism operations," Order 1505. It should not be demanded that the initial investigation be performed under conditions of warfare, nor should it be demanded that a judge accompany the fighting forces. We accept that there is room to postpone the beginning of the investigation, and naturally also the judicial intervention. These may be postponed until after detainees are taken out of the battlefield to a place where the initial investigation and judicial intervention can be carried out properly. Thus, the issue at hand rests upon

---

74. HCJ 3239/02, Marab v. IDF Commander in the West Bank (2002).
75. *Id.* at ¶¶8-10.
76. *Id.* at ¶32.
77. *Id.*

the question: where a detainee is in a detention facility which allows for carrying out the initial investigation, what is the timeframe available to investigators for carrying out the initial investigation without judicial intervention?

In this regard, the respondents claim before us that it was necessary to allow the investigating officials 18 days and after Order 1505, 12 days to carry out "initial screening activities, before the detainee's case is brought before the examination of a judge." This was due to the large number of persons being investigated, and constraints on the number of professional investigators. In their response, the respondents emphasized that "during the warfare operations, thousands of people were apprehended by the IDF forces, under circumstances which raised the suspicion that they were involved in terrorist activities and warfare. The object of Order 1500 was to allow the 'screening' and identification of unlawful combatants who were involved in terrorist activities. This activity was necessary due to the fact that the terrorists had been carrying out their activities in Palestinian populations centers, without bearing any symbols that would identify them as members of combating forces and distinguish them from the civilian population, in utter violation of the laws of warfare." See para. 51 of the response brief from May 15, 2002. The respondents added that it is pointless to bring detainees before a judge, when they have not yet been identified, and the investigative material against them has not yet undergone the necessary processing. This initial investigation, performed prior to bringing the detainee before the judge, is difficult and often demands considerable time. This is due, among other reasons, to "the lack of cooperation on the part of those being investigated and their attempts to hide their identities, their hostility towards the investigating authorities due to nationalistic and ideological views, the inability to predetermine the time and place of the detentions, the fact that most of the investigations are based on confidential intelligence information which cannot be revealed to the person being investigated, and the difficulty of reaching potential witnesses." See para. 62 of the response brief from June 11, 2002.

The respondents thus claim that the investigating authorities must be allowed the time necessary for the completion of the initial investigation. This will, of course, not exceed a period of 18 days, under Order 1500, or 12 days, under Order 1505, as it was amended in Orders 1512 and 1518. In this timeframe, all those detainees against whom there is insufficient evidence will be released. Only those detainees, whose initial investigation has been completed, such that the investigation is ready for judicial examination, will remain in detention.

In our opinion, this approach is in conflict with the fundamentals of both international and Israeli law. This approach is not based on the presumption that investigating authorities should be provided with the minimal time necessary for the completion of the investigation, and that only when such time has passed is there room for judicial review. The accepted approach is that judicial review is an integral part of the detention process. Judicial review is not "external" to the detention. It is an inseparable part of the development of the detention itself. At the basis of this approach lies a constitutional perspective which considers judicial review of detention proceedings essential for the protection of individual liberty. Thus, the detainee need not "appeal" his detention before a judge. Appearing before a judge is an "internal" part of the dentition process. The judge does not ask himself whether a reasonable police officer would have been permitted to carry out the detention. The judge asks himself whether, in his opinion, there are sufficient investigative materials to support the continuation of the detention

Thus, we hold the 18-day detention period without judicial oversight under Order 1500, and the 12-day detention period without judicial oversight under Orders 1505, 1512, and 1518, to be null and void. They will be substituted by a different period, to be set by the respondents. To this end, the respondents should be allowed to consider the matter. Therefore, we hold that this declaration of nullification will be effective six months from the date at which this judgment is given. Compare Tzemach, at 284. We have considered respondents' request to present us with classified information. We are of the opinion that such is neither appropriate nor desirable. We hope that the half-year suspension will allow for the reorganization required by both international and internal law.

ISSUES TO CONSIDER

1. Under what circumstances must detainees be afforded the opportunity to voice complaints before the detaining authority?
2. Detention must not be arbitrary; rather an evidentiary basis should indicate that a particular detainee endangers or may endanger security. How is this possible during operational counterterrorism?
3. In special circumstances is detention possible without judicial intervention? How much time is reasonable for judicial review of the detention process?
4. What is the significance from the perspective of the military commander of such a decision?
5. What effect on combat does the decision have?
6. Is this judicial intervention or judicial interference?
7. Should the Court take into account operational requirements?
8. Should the Court be concerned with how such a decision affects military planning?
9. Is the Court's expertise truly only limited to humanitarian law issues as Barak writes in the article quoted earlier?
10. Is the decision of the Court in line with Barak's theory that democracies fight terrorism with one armed tied behind their back?
11. In a time of combat, when terrorists fight with both hands in front of them, is such judicial activism responsible and reasonable?

B. PHYSICIANS FOR HUMAN RIGHTS v. COMMANDER OF THE IDF FORCES IN THE GAZA STRIP[78]

This case illustrates the Israel Supreme Court's immediate response to petitions filed during combat regarding the IDF's responsibility to honor international humanitarian law obligations. In response to widespread smuggling of arms

---

78. HCJ 4764/04, Physicians for Human Rights v. Commander of the IDF Forces in the Gaza Strip.

and ammunition through an intricate series of tunnels dug between Egypt and the city of Rafah (located in the southern part of the Gaza Strip), the IDF conducted a military operation intended to locate and destroy the tunnels in an effort to weaken terrorist infrastructure.

During the course of the fighting, civilians were injured and the water supply was affected. In addition, complaints were lodged that the IDF was not allowing basic supplies, such as medication, to enter the city. A petition was filed by Physicians for Human Rights, Association for Civil Rights in Israel, The Center for the Defense of the Individual, and B'Tselem, asking the Court to order the IDF to enable critical humanitarian supplies to be received by the local population and to ensure that the water supply be adequate.[79] Similar to *Marab*, the Court heard the case during the course of the armed conflict. The petition was filed on a Thursday, the hearing held the next day. Furthermore, it is important to note that a senior IDF Commander was present in the court-room to respond directly to the Court's questions.

Whether the Court should directly intervene in IDF combat operations while IDF soldiers are at risk must be weighed against the danger to a civilian population similarly at risk—this is the essence of robust judicial activism in times of armed conflict. This dilemma served as the centerpiece of the petition in oral arguments before the Court.

According to the State, the Court should exercise judicial restraint. The state declared the operation's goals were to prevent additional arms smuggling and to destroy terrorist infrastructure. The state also argued that humanitarian measures were taken within the confines of a military operation; furthermore, according to the State, the IDF was attempting to minimize danger to innocent civilians while Palestinian terrorists were using civilians as "human shields."[80]

ISSUES TO CONSIDER

1. Are protections of civilians absolute?
2. How must a military balance between a legitimate combat operation and the obligation to ensure the safety and welfare of civilians?
3. What is the obligation of a military commander to a civilian population during the course of operational counterterrorism?

What does the High Court of Justice review, in the context of combat while attempting to balance national security and individual rights? The Court states it will not rule on the manner in which combat is conducted because that is the responsibility of military commanders when "soldiers' lives are in danger."[81] The decision of whether or not to take military action is not a judicial question. Rather, the sole question before the court is whether the operation meets international humanitarian legal obligations as the Court assumes the operations are a military necessity.[82]

---

79. *Id.* at ¶7.
80. *Id.* at ¶9.
81. *Id.* at ¶16.
82. *Id.* at ¶17.

Physicians for Human Rights v. Commander of the IDF Forces in the Gaza Strip

HCJ 4764/04 (2004)

In general, the judicial review of this Court is exercised ex post facto. A petition is submitted against an action that has already been taken. Occasionally, a significant period of time can elapse between the time the action is taken and before that action is examined by this Court. This, however, is not the case here. Petitioners have not requested that we examine the legal import of military operations that have already concluded. The purpose of this petition is to direct the present actions of the military. This is ex ante judicial review, exercised while military operations are currently underway. This imposes certain constraints on the Court. Of course, petitions that look towards the future are not novel to us. For example, in HCJ 5100/94 Public Committee Against Torture in Israel v. The State of Israel, we examined the legality of guidelines that allowed for the imposition of moderate physical pressure on suspects of an investigation. The purpose of our review there was not to examine actions that had been taken in the past, but to review investigations that were underway at that time. Even so, the current petition is unique in that it asks us to review military operations while they are underway and while IDF soldiers are subject to the dangers inherent to combat. As such, it is appropriate to emphasize that:

> Clearly this Court will take no position regarding the manner in which combat is being conducted. As long as soldiers' lives are in danger, these decisions will be made by the commanders. In the case before us, it was not claimed that the arrangement at which we arrived endangered the lives of soldiers.

The same applies here: humanitarian concerns have been resolved, without endangering the lives of soldiers or the military operations. Subject to this caveat, the situation before us is no different than other situations where this Court has reviewed the legality of military operations.

We do not review the wisdom of the decision to take military action. We review the legality of the military operations. As such, we presume that the operations in Rafah are necessary from a military standpoint. The question before us is only whether these military operations adhere to domestic and international law. The fact that operations are necessary from a military standpoint does not automatically mean that they fulfill legal requirements. Of course, with regard to issues of military concern, we do not stand in the stead of the military commander, and we do not substitute our discretion for his own. That is his expertise. We examine the legal import of his decisions. That is our expertise.

The Future

According to the humanitarian principles of international law, military activities require the following: First, that the rules of conduct be taught to, and that they be internalized by, all combat soldiers, from the Chief of General Staff down to new recruits. See Physicians for Human Rights, at 5. Second, that procedures be drawn up that allow implementation of these rules, and which allow them to be put into practice during combat. An examination of the conduct of the army while fighting in Rafah, as detailed in the petition before us — and we have nothing other than what has been presented to us — indicates significant progress compared to the situation two years ago. See Barake; Physicians for Human Rights and other decisions. This is the case regarding the implementation of the duty to ensure water, medical equipment, medicines, food, evacuation of the wounded, and the burial of the dead. This is also the case regarding the preparation of the army, and the design of procedures that allow humanitarian obligations to be satisfied. The establishment of the Humanitarian Hotline and the District Coordination Office, as well as the assignment of a liaison officer of the Coordination Office to every battalion, greatly aided the implementation of humanitarian principles.

In the framework of our discussion regarding the internalization of humanitarian laws, we emphasize that it is the duty of the military commander not only to prevent the army from harming the lives and dignity of the local residents (the "negative" duty: see supra para. 11). He also has a "positive" duty (para. 11). He must protect the lives and dignity of the local residents. For example, regarding the burial of local residents, the military commander was satisfied that the corpses were transferred to A-Najar Hospital. But this was not enough. He is obligated to do his utmost to ensure that the bodies be brought to a dignified burial according to local custom. He must make prior arrangements in order to ensure there are sufficient supplies of food and water. Damage to the water supply is something that can be anticipated from the outset, and if it cannot be avoided, a solution to this problem must be prearranged. Supplies of medicines, medical equipment and food should also be prepared in advance. Harm to local residents is expected and if, despite every effort to limit this, in the end there will be casualties among residents, this must be prepared for from the outset. Respondent should not rely solely on international and Israeli aid organizations to solve these problems, though their aid is important. The recognition that the basic duty belongs to the military commander must be internalized, and it is his job to adopt different measures from the outset so that he can fulfill his duty on the battlefield.

Additional measures should be adopted so that the established institutional arrangements will be more effective. We were informed that those who called the Humanitarian Hotline had to wait many hours. Col. Mordechai noted several times that some issues should have been referred to him, and not to the Humanitarian Hotline. The lack of information led, on several occasions, to inefficiency in aid efforts by third parties. Thus, for example, a vehicle of Petitioner 1 laden with medical equipment and medicines waited at Erez Crossing while the entrance point was Karni Crossing. However, at Karni Crossing their entrance was again denied, since Israeli doctors were among the passengers in the vehicle, and the army was only prepared to allow the entry of non-Israeli doctors. These issues and others need to be addressed. It is possible that the Humanitarian Hotline needs to be expanded, and there needs to be more effective communication between it and the District Coordination Office and the Coordination Office's liaison officers placed with the combat battalions. It is possible that there is a need, with regard to international and Israeli organizations whose humanitarian involvement is anticipated, to bypass the Humanitarian Hotline and facilitate direct contact with the DCO. It is possible that there is a need to take other measures. This matter is for the respondent to address; it must learn from the events of the day.

With the conclusion of the arguments in the petition, we ordered that the military staff in the area ensure that they solve not only the problems raised by petitioners, but also anticipate new problems that, in the nature of things, will arise in the future. For this reason it has been decided that Col. Mordechai will appoint a senior officer who will remain in direct contact with petitioners. This is the least that should have been done at the time the events were unfolding. The main thing is that it must be done now in order to learn lessons from the episode.

In granting a majority of the petitioners' requests, the Court held all soldiers must learn and internalize rules of conduct, regardless of their rank.[83] The Court also required that "procedures be drawn up that allow implementation of these rules, and which allow them to be put into practice during combat." The Court confirms that the military commander has a duty to prevent his troops from "harming lives and dignity of the local residents."[84]

The above decisions illustrate the unique role of the Israeli HCJ in the context of counterterrorism. Petitions are filed and the Court hears the petitioner almost immediately. In its decisions, the Court adopts a very proactive approach reflecting Barak's jurisprudential philosophy as articulated in the Harvard Law Review article. Does this approach guarantee the state adopts a balanced approach to counterterrorism by enforcing self-imposed restraints or does the Court unnecessarily limit command decision-making by placing itself in the shoes of the commander?

Physicians for Human Rights illustrates Barak's view that real time review is imperative. Barak ordered supplies be brought into the city even though the crisis was ongoing and soldiers were still at risk. The decision both to hear the case and order supplies into Rafah while IDF soldiers were involved in combat reflects a belief that laws should be applied equally in times of war and peace. In this case, the Court demonstrates not only its willingness to review executive actions but also the importance of timing. Timing was literally a matter of life and death as the water supply and humanitarian supplies were crucial to the survival of those living in Rafah.

C. BEIT SOURIK VILLAGE COUNCIL v. THE GOVERNMENT OF ISRAEL AND THE COMMANDER OF THE IDF FORCES IN THE WEST BANK[85]

In developing a counterterrorism strategy, Israel implemented a number of different policies. One that has drawn much attention is construction of the security fence between Israel and the West Bank.

---

83. *Id.* at ¶66.
84. *Id.*
85. HCJ 2056/04, Beit Sourik Village Council v. The Government of Israel and Commander of the IDF Forces in the West Bank [2004] [hereinafter *Beit Sourik*].

The government of Israel decided to build the fence as a means to prevent the infiltration of Palestinian terrorists into Israel. The fence has proven successful; according to available statistics there has been a 90 percent reduction in Palestinian terrorist attacks where the fence has been constructed. The government constructed the fence on the Palestinian side of the Green Line rather than on the Israeli side. According to the government this was done for strategic and topographical reasons because the fence is not a political fence intended to mark the future boundaries between Israel and a future Palestinian state.[86]

In the petition filed, petitioners from the West Bank village of Beit Sourik argued that the fence prevents access to their land; impacts their ability to move freely without excessive bureaucracy; makes use of local water wells almost impossible; greatly hinders access to water for crops; uproots olive trees; injures the livelihood of farmers; does not benefit the local population; and that the real purpose of the fence is annexation of the land for the benefit of the IDF and the Jewish population. Furthermore, the petitioners argued that due process had been violated since military orders regarding the construction of the fence had not been published, denying those injured the right to appeal the decision.

The state in its response to the petition argued that affected landowners were both offered compensation and entitled to appeal to the West Bank military commander against the order to use their land for the fence. Additionally, the state argued the primary purpose of the fence was self-defense, intended to protect Israeli citizens against Palestinian terrorists who could easily infiltrate Israel proper.[87] The state further argued that the measure was a proportional, security-based decision not intended to annex Palestinian lands for political purposes. The state insisted that commanders had balanced national security and individual rights, concluding that the fence reflected a proportional balance.[88] The state did not deny that injury had been incurred by Palestinians, but argued that an effort had been made to minimize the damage.

ISSUES TO CONSIDER

1. How should commanders balance between military necessity (self-defense) and individual rights?
2. What are legitimate security considerations?
3. How is the Court to determine if the means are proportional?
4. What is the proper scope of intervention?
5. How much should the Court press on commanders to find alternatives?

Consider what the court wrote regarding the extent and scope of judicial review and proportionality.

---

86. *Id.* at ¶¶12-15.
87. Israel proper refers to lands not captured in the 1967 six-day war (the West Bank, Gaza Strip, Golan Heights, Sinai Peninsula, and East Jerusalem including the Old City of Jerusalem).
88. *Beit Sourik, supra* note 85, at ¶13.

Beit Sourik Village Council v. The Government of Israel and Commander of the IDF Forces in the West Bank

HCJ 2056/04

Before we examine the proportionality of the route of the separation fence, it is appropriate that we define the character of our examination. Our point of departure is the assumption, which petitioners did not manage to negate, that the government decision to construct the separation fence is motivated by security, and not a political, considerations. As such, we work under the assumption — which the petitioners also did not succeed in negating — that the considerations of the military commander based the route of the fence on military considerations that, to the best of his knowledge, are capable of realizing this security objective. In addition, we assume — and this issue was not even disputed in the case before us — that the military commander is of the opinion that the injury to local inhabitants is proportionate. On the basis of this factual foundation, there are two questions before us. The first question is whether the route of the separation fence, as determined by the military commander, is well-founded from a military standpoint. Is there another route for the separation fence which better achieves the security objective? This constitutes a central component of proportionality. If the chosen route is not well-founded from the military standpoint, then there is no rational connection between the objective which the fence is intended to achieve and the chosen route (the first subtest); if there is a route which better achieves the objective, we must examine whether this alternative route inflicts a lesser injury (the second subtest). The second question is whether the route of the fence is proportionate. Both these questions are important for the examination of proportionality. However, they also raise separate problems regarding the scope of judicial review. My colleague Justice M. Cheshin has correctly noted:

> Different subjects require, in and of themselves, different methods of intervention. Indeed, acts of state and acts of war do not change their character just because they are subject to the review of the judiciary, and the character of the acts, according to the nature of things, imprints its mark on the methods of intervention.

. . . Our answer is that there relationship between the injury to the local inhabitants and the security benefit from the construction of the separation fence along the route, as determined by the military commander, is not proportionate. The route undermines the delicate balance between the obligation of the military commander to preserve security and his obligation to provide for the needs of the local inhabitants. This approach is based on the fact that the route which the military commander established for the security fence — which separates the local inhabitants from their agricultural lands — injures the local inhabitants in a severe and acute way, while violating their rights under humanitarian international law. Here are the facts: more than 13,000 farmers (falahin) are cut off from thousands of dunams of their land and from tens of thousands of trees which are their livelihood, and which are located on the other side of the separation fence. No attempt was made to seek out and provide them with substitute land, despite our oft repeated proposals on that matter.

The separation is not hermetic: the military commander announced that two gates will be constructed, from each of the two villages, to its lands, with a system of licensing. This state of affairs injures the farmers severely, as access to their lands (early in the morning, in the afternoon, and in the evening), will be subject to restrictions inherent to a system of licensing. Such a system will result in long lines for the passage of the farmers themselves; it will make the passage of vehicles (which themselves require licensing and examination) difficult, and will distance the farmer from his lands (since only two daytime gates are planned for the entire length of this segment of the route). As a result, the life of the farmer will change completely in comparison to his previous life. The route of the separation fence severely violates their right of property and their freedom of movement. Their livelihood is severely impaired. The difficult reality of life from which they have suffered (due, for example, to high unemployment in that area) will only become more severe.

These injuries are not proportionate. They can be substantially decreased by an alternate route, either the route presented by the experts of the Council for Peace and Security, or another route set out by the military commander. Such an alternate route exists. It is not a figment of the imagination. It was presented before us. It is based on military control of Jebel Muktam, without "pulling" the separation fence to that mountain. Indeed, one must not forget that, even after the construction of the separation fence, the military commander will continue to control the area east of it. In the opinion of the military commander—which we assume to be correct, as the basis of our review—he will provide less security in that area. However, the security advantage reaped from the route as determined by the military commander, in comparison to the proposed route, does not stand in any reasonable proportion to the injury to the local inhabitants caused by this route. Indeed, the real question in the "relative" examination of the third proportionality subtest is not the choice between constructing a separation fence which brings security but injures the local inhabitants, or not constructing a separation fence, and not injuring the local inhabitants. The real question is whether the security benefit reaped by the acceptance of the military commander's position (that the separation fence should surround Jebel Muktam) is proportionate to the additional injury resulting from his position (with the fence separating local inhabitants from their lands). Our answer to this question is that the military commander's choice of the route of the separation fence is disproportionate. The gap between the security provided by the military commander's approach and the security provided by the alternate route is minute, as compared to the large difference between a fence that separates the local inhabitants from their lands, and a fence which does not separate the two (or which creates a separation which is smaller and possible to live with). Indeed, we accept that security needs are likely to necessitate an injury to the lands of the local inhabitants and to their ability to use them. International humanitarian law on one hand, however, and the basic principles of Israeli administrative law on the other, require making every possible effort to ensure that injury will be proportionate. Where construction of the separation fence demands that inhabitants be separated from their lands, access to these lands must be ensured, in order to minimize the damage to the extent possible.

We have reached the conclusion that the route of the separation fence, which separates the villages of Beit Likia and Beit Anan from the lands which provide the villagers with their livelihood, is not proportionate. This determination affects order Tav/103/03, which applies directly to the territory of the mountain itself, and leads to its annulment. This detention also affects order Tav/104/03 which applies to the route west of it, which turns in towards the village of Beit Likia, in order to reach the mountain. The same goes for the western part of order Tav/84/03, which descends from the mountain in a southeasterly direction. The eastern part of the latter order was not a matter of significant dispute between the parties, but as a result of the annulment of the aforementioned orders, it should be examined anew.

In deciding whether the fence properly balanced security and liberty interests, the Court developed a three-pronged proportionality test for determining legality of state action. According to the Court, the objective must be related to the means (a rational means test); the means used must injure the individual to the least extent possible (least injurious test); and the means used must be of proper proportion to the benefit gained (proportionality test). According to the Court, the state failed to meet this test. Therefore, while holding that the fence is legal, the Court ordered the government to take the necessary steps to reduce the effect on the lives of the Palestinian population by re-contouring the fence.

Subsequently, an additional petition was filed to the HCJ regarding the fence's effect on the residents of the town of Bil'in.[89] The petitioners argued that the fence directly impacts construction of housing projects, access to agricultural lands, and therefore villagers' livelihoods; in addition, the petitioners argued construction of the security fence on Palestinian lands violates public international law. The military commander (respondent) argued the fence, as contoured, is necessary from a security perspective for the purpose of protecting citizens of the State of Israel.

The Court held that security considerations were within the purview of the military commander; however, in applying a proportionality test the Court concluded that the military commander did not sufficiently examine alternatives that would have enabled meeting legitimate security requirements while minimizing harm on the daily life of village residents.

Issues to Consider

1. How does the Court determine whether alternatives have been sufficiently examined?
2. What is the cost of the Court's holding that the commander did not satisfactorily assess harm to Palestinian residents of the village?
3. To whom — according to the Court — does the military commander owe a duty?

---

89. HCJ 8414/05, Yassin v. Israel and Military Commander in the West Bank [2005].

4. Whose interests should the Court hold paramount—Palestinian residents or Israeli citizens?
5. Is the Court not stepping into the military commander's shoes?

IV. RUSSIA

Russia is, in many ways, an emerging democracy. Institutions that were in place during the Soviet period are no longer relevant; the former USSR has been replaced by a number of new nations stretching from Europe to Asia. How the Russian judiciary reacts to counterterrorism is the focal point of this section; to that end, it is useful to review how the courts function.

RUSSIA

Jurist Legal News and Research[90]

I. Law, Courts & Judgments

The Russian judiciary is divided into three branches: The courts of general jurisdiction (including military courts); subordinated to the Supreme Court; the arbitration (commercial) court system under the High Court of Arbitration; and the Constitutional Court (as well as constitutional courts in a number of administrative entities of the Russian Federation). Civil and criminal cases are tried in courts of primary jurisdiction, courts of appeals, and higher courts. The general court system's lowest level is the municipal court, which serves each city or rural district and hears more than 90 percent of all civil and criminal cases. The next level of courts of general jurisdiction is the regional courts. At the highest level is the Supreme Court. Decisions of the lower trial courts can be appealed only to the immediately superior court unless a constitutional issue is involved. The arbitration court system consists of city or regional courts as well as appellate circuit courts subordinated to the High Court of Arbitration. Arbitration courts hear cases involving business disputes between legal entities and between legal entities and the state.

Russia's judiciary and justice system are weak. Numerous matters that are dealt with by administrative authority in European countries remain subject to political influence in Russia. The Constitutional Court was reconvened in March 1995 following its suspension by President Yeltsin in October 1993. The 1993 constitution empowers the court to arbitrate disputes between the executive and legislative branches and between Moscow and the regional and local governments. The court also is authorized to rule on violations of constitutional rights, to examine appeals from various bodies, and to participate in impeachment proceedings against the president. The July 1994 Law on

---

90. *Available at* http://jurist.law.pitt.edu/worldlaw/russia.php.

the Constitutional Court prohibits the court from examining cases on its own initiative and limits the scope of issues the court can hear.

In the past few years, the Russian government has begun to reform the criminal justice system and judicial institutions, including the reintroduction of jury trials in certain criminal cases. Despite these efforts, judges are only beginning to assert their constitutionally mandated independence from other branches of government.

The Duma passed a Criminal Procedure Code and other judicial reforms during its 2001 session. These reforms help make the Russian judicial system more compatible with its Western counterparts and are seen by most as an accomplishment in human rights. The reforms have reintroduced jury trials in certain criminal cases and created a more adversarial system of criminal trials that protect the rights of defendants more adequately. In 2002, the introduction of the new code led to significant reductions in time spent in detention for new detainees, and the number of suspects placed in pretrial detention declined by 30%.

In order to analyze judicial review it is incumbent to understand what the relevant court believes it is reviewing and how that the conflict is defined:

> The Constitutional Court of the Russian Federation in its review of Presidential decrees that authorized the use of military force in Chechnya, while never directly referring to hostilities there as a "non-international armed conflict," none-the-less cited Additional Protocol II as a source of law that should have been applied by parties to the conflict. The Court did not analyze the Protocol, nor did it consider it as applicable law in the judicial review of decrees.[91]

This signifies that the Constitutional Court believes the conflict is not criminal in nature; rather it is a non-international armed conflict. From the perspective of the state, measures available to it in conducting measures to handle the conflict are very different than if the conflict were defined as criminal. However, Russia continues to use its criminal laws and codes with respect to detained, suspected terrorists. The significance of this decision affects the rights and obligations of the state, soldiers, and individuals with whom the state is engaged in combat. How the Constitutional Court applies this definition to the conflict and how the state responds to the Court's decisions are critical aspects of operational counterterrorism.

In an emerging democracy the relationship between the executive and the nascent judiciary is vital; a democracy cannot fully function unless the executive truly respects the judiciary. The two excerpts below offer insight into what the future might hold.

> The Constitutional Court of the Russian Federation was established in 1991 in the wake of the collapse of the Soviet Union. The sources of its authority were the Constitution, which, with its patchwork of amendments, hardly resembled the original text of 1978, and the Law on the Constitutional

---

91. Bakhtiyar Tuzmukhamedov, *Chechnya and the Laws of War*, Crimes of War, October 1999, *available at* http://www.crimesofwar.org/expert/chech-tuzmuk.html (last visited Oct. 8, 2010).

Court of the Russian Socialist Federal Republic of 1991. The Court decided its first case in January 1992. It failed to stay clear of the power struggle between the president and the Parliament that reached its violent climax in the fall of 1993, and was suspended until February 1995.

Currently, the Constitutional Court derives its powers from the Constitution of 1993 and the Federal Constitution Law on the Constitutional Court of the Russian Federation of 1994 (hereafter the Law on the Constitutional Court). It is part of the three-tiered judicial system. But unlike the Supreme Court and the Higher Court of Arbitration that sit at the apex of the pyramids of, respectively, courts of general jurisdiction and courts of arbitration, the Constitutional Court does not rest on a foundation of lower courts. . . .

The first category of cases involves legislative acts passed by public authorities, whether federal or regional, and only public authorities may petition the Court. These cases need not arise from any ongoing dispute. A party with due authority may request an abstract review of a statute.

When confronted with such petitions, the Court shall rule on the constitutionality of federal laws and normative acts issued by the president, or by either chamber of Parliament, or by the Russian government. It may also rule on the constitutionality of constitutions, charters and laws of the component entities of the Russian Federation, as well as on treaties concluded by those entities with the federal authorities and between those entities. Finally, the Court may decide on the conformity with the Constitution of international treaties that have not yet come into force.

The second category comprises cases about jurisdictional disputes between federal authorities, or between federal and regional authorities, or between regional authorities.

The third category consists of cases in which the Constitutional Court is petitioned by private persons or by courts requesting a constitutional review of a law that has been applied or ought to be applied in a particular case.

It is only natural to expect the supreme judicial body of constitutional review to interpret the Constitution; however, unlike the U.S. Supreme Court, the Russian Constitutional Court may deal with it as an abstract question.[92]

The following publicly stated view provides insight into former President Putin's position regarding the role and importance of the Court:

> In assessing the ten-year-long history of the Constitutional Court, Vladimir Putin said "all the Constitutional Court's powers proved necessary." The President explained that the Court protected the constitution, defended people's rights and freedom, and was active in creating and strengthening the legal foundation of the state. Turning to specific features of the legal institution, the President demonstrated that the Constitutional Court, on the one hand, "does not supplant other bodies of power or interfere with their jurisdiction," while, on the other, "it is not dependent on the bodies of power and may influence their activities by its decisions." In this sense, the Constitutional Court "is a higher level of authority, just as an organ of constitutional justice should be."
>
> The Russian president noted that these days, the Constitutional Court enjoys the reputation of a most important and authoritative body. In his view, the fact that representatives of practically all the world courts have

---

92. 94 Am. Soc'y Int'l L. Proc. 166 – ASIL.

come to Moscow, points to the high international prestige of the Constitutional Court of Russia.

When commenting on the quality of the Constitutional Court judges in terms of their responsibility at work, Vladimir Putin stressed that their activities "call for a profound legal knowledge, professional dignity, and occasionally civic courage."

"At the same time," said the President, "the line of development of this most important institution was not a straight one." He admitted that there were repeated attempts to use the court as an arena of political struggle but it was "the principle of independence and non-interference in politics" that won the day.

"Today, this principle is accepted and supported by society and the authorities," said the President proudly. Moreover, "it has been confirmed by the world practice of constitutional justice."[93]

Issues to Consider

1. What is the significance of the conflict's definition in understanding judicial review?
2. How independent can a Court be in an emerging democracy?
3. How attentive must the executive be to the judiciary?
4. What is the proper role of the judiciary in a non-international armed conflict?
5. What is the significance when the Court does not view a conflict as criminal in nature?

A. CONSTITUTIONALITY OF THE CHECHEN SITUATION

The Russian government's actions in the Chechen conflict were addressed by the Constitutional Court in the Judgment of the Constitutional Court of the Russian Federation of 31 July 1995 on the Constitutionality of the Presidential Decrees and Resolutions of the Federal Government Concerning the Situation in Chechnya. The first excerpt below discusses the impact of the majority opinion in the case. Given the extraordinary nature of this opinion, lengthy quotes directly from the dissenting opinions are also provided.

Paola Gaeta, The Armed Conflict of Chechnya Before the Russian Constitutional Court

7 E.J.I.L. 563 (1996)[94]

The constitutionality of four decrees of the central government in the prosecution of the Chechen conflict was challenged in the Russian Constitutional Court by a group of deputies of the State Duma and the Federal Council of the

---

93. Russian President Offers his Evaluation of the Russian Constitutional Court, Nov. 1, 2001, *available at* http://www.cdi.org/russia/johnson/5521-7.cfm (last visited Nov. 28, 2006).
94. *Available at* http://www.ejil.org/pdfs/7/4/1393.pdf/.

Russian Federation (hereinafter RF). Among other things, the applicants argued that two of the decrees at issue, namely those providing for the dispatch of armed forces on the territory of the Chechen Republic, had resulted in a violation of international treaties to which the Russian Federation was a party, and of Article 15, paragraph 4, of the Constitution, by virtue of which both general and conventional international law shall be part of the Russian legal system.

It is not unusual for domestic courts to be called upon to settle cases relating to armed conflict taking place within the territory of a sovereign state. Nevertheless, this decision can be regarded as unique in national case-law, since the Russian Constitutional Court was asked to pronounce upon the lawfulness under international law of *coercive measures by a State against a segment of its own population seeking to secede from the state*. In fact, this could well be the first time a national court has been called upon to scrutinise compliance by a state's armed forces with international rules concerning the protection of civilians and the conduct of hostilities during an armed conflict. . . .

. . . [T]he applicants argued that two decrees of the central authorities were unconstitutional, contending that *they had resulted* in a violation of Article 15 of the Russian Constitution, under which all international law is part of the Russian domestic legal system. The Court had thus been asked, *inter alia*, to verify whether the military action of the Russian armed forces in Chechnya resulted in, or gave rise to, breaches of international humanitarian law.

The Court refrained from dealing with this matter. It stated that an examination of the actions of the Russian armed forces from the point of view of compliance with international law: may not be a subject for consideration by the Constitutional Court of the Russian Federation and ought to be performed by other competent organs.

The Court consequently scrutinised the constitutionality of the decrees by only taking into account their *normative* content and not their *actual* application. The Court found that only one of the challenged acts did not conform to the Russian Constitution, while the other was to be considered in accordance with the Constitution.

Although the Court deemed it inappropriate to pronounce on the question of whether the decrees, as applied by the Russian military authorities, were in conflict with Article 15 of the Constitution, nonetheless it was not unresponsive to the issue of actual compliance with international humanitarian law raised by the applicants.

The Court determined that at the international level the provisions of Protocol II were binding on both parties to the armed conflict and that the actions of the Russian armed forces in the conduct of the Chechen conflict violated Russia's international obligations under Additional Protocol II to the 1949 Geneva Conventions. Nonetheless, the Court sought to excuse this noncompliance because Protocol II had not been incorporated into the Russian legal system. . . .

. . . Another point which deserves to be highlighted is that the Court clearly spelled out that the provisions of Protocol II are binding upon *both* parties to the armed conflict, *i.e.* that the Protocol confers rights and imposes duties also on insurgents.

This statement is all the more important if one considers that, at the Geneva Conference, some States expressed the opposite view, for they were eager to keep rebels at the level of criminals without granting them any international status. This view has also found support in the legal literature.

It is important to [sic] emphasise the determination by the Court that the Russian Parliament had failed to pass legislation to implement Protocol n, and that this failure was one of the grounds—probably even the primary ground—for non-compliance by Russian military authorities with the rules embodied in the Protocol. It is probably true that the enactment of *ad hoc* legislation to implement Protocol II was necessary even if Article 15, paragraph 4, of the Russian Constitution provides that international treaties are part of the Russian domestic legal system: indeed Protocol II [sic] cannot be considered as self-executing in all its provisions. . . .

[The Court's] decision must be commended for the strongly internationalist outlook it reflects. The Court has given pride of place to international law, by taking into account international rules and principles in assessing the constitutionality of the challenged decrees. This approach clearly demonstrates that the Court is fully aware of the close interplay between constitutional and international law. The Court proves to be fully conscious that even the highest bodies of the Russian Federation must comply not only with constitutional provisions, but also with international rules whenever such rules impinge upon the conduct of State organs at home or abroad. Under the principle of the rule of law laid down in the Russian Constitution, the Court emphasized that 'the bodies of power in their activities are bound both by internal and international law.

This laudable approach has manifested itself not only in the various points made by the Court on international law relating directly to the Chechen conflict, but also in two more specific respects. First, the Court has expressly directed the Russian Parliament to implement Protocol II, thus showing how much importance it attaches to actual compliance with that treaty. Secondly, the Court underscored that according to the Russian Constitution and the U.N. Covenant on Civil and Political Rights "victims of any violations, crimes and abuses of power shall be granted efficient remedies in law and compensation for damages caused." In this way the Court has established the applicability of these human rights instruments to remedy at least the most blatant violations of international humanitarian law.

This decision thus clearly demonstrates that the Russian Constitutional Court has become an important institution promoting compliance with international law in the Russian legal system.

In an opinion such as the one described above, the Constitutional Court must define the limits of the phrase "all means at the disposal." The justices' responsibility and the decision's significance are particularly crucial because this was the first case in which these questions were brought before the newly established Court. Determining the limits of state power is the essence of judicial review; doing so while the armed conflict is underway is more reflective of the Israeli model than the late Chief Justice Rehnquist's approach.

A state's obligation to respect international law must be met even if the other side fails to do so. The failure of the Chechens to conduct themselves in accordance with relevant Geneva Convention requirements cannot be used by the Russian government as justification for not respecting those obligations; this point is of major significance in this opinion.

By determining that failure to comply with Geneva Convention provisions cannot be brought before the Court, the judges are clearly expressing the limits of the scope of their judicial review. While the importance of raising that issue can be argued, the decision by the Court is more indicative of the American model rather than the aggressive model propounded by the Israeli High Court of Justice.

The Court ultimately holds that use of the Russian armed forces in the Chechen conflict is a matter to be decided by the legislature rather than by the judiciary. The decision reflects a self-imposed limit on judicial review. Nevertheless, the Constitutional Court directly addressed many of the most important operational questions related to counterterrorism. Furthermore, the Court articulated the position that in the context of separation of powers, the legislature is charged with establishing the guidelines for the conduct of the conflict.

Now consider some of the dissenting opinions in the case.

JUDGMENT OF THE CONSTITUTIONAL COURT OF THE RUSSIAN FEDERATION OF 31 JULY 1995 ON THE CONSTITUTIONALITY OF THE PRESIDENTIAL DECREES AND RESOLUTIONS OF THE FEDERAL GOVERNMENT CONCERNING THE SITUATION IN CHECHNYA

Translation by Federal News Service Group[95]

Summary of the Dissenting Opinions of Six Judges of the Constitutional Court of the Russian Federation

[R]egarding the examination of the constitutionality of: decree No. 2137 of the President of the Russian Federation of 30 November 1994 on measures to restore constitutional legality and law and order in the territory of the Chechen Republic; decree No. 2166 of the President of the Russian Federation of 9 December 1994 on measures to halt the activities of illegal armed formations in the territory of the Chechen Republic and in the zone of the Ossetian-Ingush conflict; order No. 1360 of the Government of the Russian Federation of 9 December 1994 on ensuring the state security and territorial integrity of the Russian Federation, the rule of law, the rights and freedoms of citizens and the disarming of illegal armed formations in the territory of the Chechen Republic and adjacent areas of northern Caucasus; and decree No. 1883 of the President of the Russian Federation of 2 November 1993 on the fundamental provisions of military doctrine of the Russian Federation.

---

95. *Available at* http://www.venice.coe.int/docs/1995/CDL(1995)068add-e.asp/.

Dissenting Opinion of Judge Vitruk

In 1991-94 in the Chechen Republic, which, under Article 65 of the Constitution of the Russian Federation, forms part of the Russian Federation, there did in fact arise an extraordinary situation requiring the central authority to take practical steps, not excluding the use of force, to restore constitutional order in the territory of the Chechen Republic. However, any action by federal authorities must be taken on the basis of and in conformity with the Constitution and the federal laws.

The executive authorities' texts under consideration *viz* decree Nos. 2137 and 2166 and order No. 1360, as well as decree No. 2169 of December 11 on measures to ensure the rule of law, law and order and public safety in the territory of the Chechen Republic form a whole. It is therefore impossible to assess the constitutionality of any one of these texts in isolation.

If the objectives set out in the preambles of the texts are examined independently of the measures they involve, they can be seen to be in conformity with the Constitution of the Russian Federation. They are designed in particular to restore constitutional legality (decree No. 2137), ensure national security, safeguard the rights and freedoms of citizens (decree No. 2166) etc. On the other hand, the measures for which the texts provide in order to attain those goals are a violation of the terms of the Constitution. Their purpose was to establish a special regime that was neither a state of emergency nor a state of war. This regime, which was described by the representative of the President and the Government as a regime for re-establishing the foundations of the constitutional system, constitutional legality and the legal order in the territory of the federal component concerned and which is known in world as "federal intervention," had no basis in Russian constitutional law when the texts in question were issued.

The special regime should have been preceded by the adoption of a federal law on the subject, particularly as regards the use of the armed forces to resolve a constitutional crisis and the curtailment of the rights and freedoms of citizens.

The regime established in the territory of the Chechen Republic has at least two main features. First, it relies heavily on the armed forces of the Ministry of the Interior and the special units of the Federal Security Service and other services, to resolve the conflict between the authorities of the Chechen Republic and the federal authority; this led to a military conflict of a domestic nature. Secondly, it entails a substantial limitation of the rights and freedoms of citizens.

Neither the Constitution nor legislation makes any provision for the special regime established by the presidential and governmental texts, and they lay down no procedural arrangements for establishing such a regime. The references by the representative of the President and the government to the provisions of the laws on security, on defence, on the internal troops of the Ministry of the Interior of the Russian Federation, on the police and on judicial information in the Russian Federation are not legally correct, because these laws do not regulate relations in the situation existing in the territory of a federal component that has declared its sovereignty and its withdrawal from the federation.

The reference to the "Fundamental provisions of military doctrine of the Russian Federation," approved by presidential decree No. 1833, in so far as they provide for the possibility of using the armed forces to resolve domestic conflicts is not correct either, as these provisions are contrary to the Constitution of the Russian Federation and to Article 10 (2) and (3) of the law on defence act. Article 90 (3) of the Constitution stipulates that presidential decrees and orders may not be contrary to the Constitution's terms.

By promulgating decree Nos. 2137, 2166 and 2169, the President exceeded his powers under Articles 83-90 of the Constitution. The President is not free to act as he chooses, because he is required to comply with the Constitution and with federal laws (Article 90 (3) of the Constitution). The President must also observe a principle applicable to all state officials, *viz.* they may do only whatever is provided for by law. (Article 80 (2)) of the Constitution is perfectly clear on this point: the President of the Russian Federation shall adopt measures to protect the country's sovereignty, independence and territorial integrity in accordance with the procedure established by the Constitution of the Russian Federation. The obligation for the President to act within the limits defined by the Constitution is also contained in the oath of loyalty sworn by the President to the people.

The recognition of the existence of presidential powers not enumerated in Articles 83-90, i.e., implicit powers, denotes an illegitimate enlargement of the presidential powers, to the detriment of the powers of the Federal Parliament and the Government. The self-executing nature of the Constitution, as provided for in Article 15 (1) of the Constitution, does not admit of any arbitrary interpretation of these provisions, as that would lead to a violation of other constitutional principles and norms.

By decree No. 2166 the President of the Russian Federation delegated to the Government the powers be considered to be vested in him, i.e., powers concerning the use of "all the means at the state's disposal." This measure is at variance with the Constitution, which establishes the separation of powers between the President as head of state (Art. 80 (1)) and the Government, which exercises executive power in the Russian Federation (Art. 110 (1)).

The presidential decrees under consideration are in contradiction with the hierarchy of constitutional principles, where absolute priority is given to respect for human rights and fundamental freedoms (Art. 2 of the Constitution). According to Article 18 of the Constitution, human rights and freedoms are self-executing. Unfortunately, the orientation of the presidential decrees and governmental orders towards the use of all the means at the State's disposal, without the provision of any safeguards against abuse of such means, together with the absence of any machinery for preventing violations of the rights and freedoms of the peaceable population, has resulted in grave violations of the rights and freedoms of Russian citizens.

From the foregoing I draw the following conclusion. Presidential decree Nos. 2137 and 2166 and governmental order No. 1360 are not in conformity with the Constitution of the Russian Federation, as they violate the constitutional principle of respect for human rights and freedoms laid down in Articles 2, 6 (2), 17 (1) and (2), 18 and 55 of the Constitution, as well as being inconsistent with the Constitution's demarcation of powers, because the promulgation of these texts exceeds the powers of the President and the Government as defined in the Constitution.

Moreover, the procedure employed for the enactment and bringing into force of presidential decree No. 2137 of 30 November 1994 is unconstitutional. Although the decree affects constitutional rights and freedoms, it was not officially published, which is a breach of Article 15 (3) of the Constitution. Furthermore, the procedure for examining the constitutionality of the decree was not completed in accordance with Article 43 (2) of the federal law on the Constitutional Court of the Russian Federation, on the ground that the effects of the decree had ceased to exist by the time the matter was referred to the Court. The governmental order of 9 December 1994 is not in conformity with the Constitution of the Russian Federation as regards the procedure used for its adoption, as it was not adopted by the Government as a collegiate body. . . .

Dissenting Opinion of Judge Ebzeyev

. . . Constitutional responsibility for the execution of a public authority's decision cannot be placed solely on those executing decisions, because the proclamation of the supremacy of rights and freedoms by the Constitution (Article 2) demands that such rights and freedoms be respected both when decisions are being adopted and when they are being executed. Consequently, so-called "excesses of implementation" cannot justify any failure to discharge that obligation.

3. The delegation to the Government of "all the means at the state's disposal" (point 1 of decree No. 2166) disregards the principle of the separation of powers laid down in Article 10 of the Constitution, as not only the constitutional powers of the Government are involved. Furthermore, the "outlawing" (paragraph 2 of the preamble to the said decree) of all anti-constitutional activity means that, from a strictly legal point of view, citizens are deprived of the inherent rights they possess from birth, which is a violation of Articles 17, 18 and 19 of the Constitution.

Whereas governmental order No. 1360 provides for restrictive measures in respect of citizens, it places no limitations either on the actions of state bodies and officials responsible for executing the order or on the use of the armed forces; and it prescribes no guarantees for protecting the civilian population as required by the Protocol Additional to the Geneva Conventions of 12 August 1949, and relating to the Protection of Victims of Non-international Armed Conflicts. Thus there is no observance of commitments deriving from international treaties, which, under Article 15 (4) of the Constitution, form an integral part of the Russian Federation's legal system.

Given the causal links between the said decisions, on the one hand, and the victims and destruction in the Chechen Republic, on the other, it must be concluded that the decisions and the measures for implementing them were incompatible with the requirements of the restoration of the constitutional order; and this confers on those very decisions the character of a violation of the constitutional order of the Russian Federation.

Dissenting Opinion of Judge Zorkin

1. According to the information available to the Constitutional Court, the situation that had arisen in the Chechen Republic should indeed be termed

extraordinary, and on this point I am in full agreement with the Court's decision. But extraordinary situations are not all identical, and they therefore call for the use of different means of response. The very concept "extraordinary situation" does not have any clear legal substance, and the Court did not determine what type of situation had arisen in the Chechen Republic.

To deal with the extraordinary situation in the Chechen Republic, the President resorted to measures that have no basis either in the Constitution or in legislation. This was not the first time that a presidential decree had been issued before the relevant statutory basis has been created.

The Court did not examine the dimension of the events in Chechnya or compare their nature with that of the measures taken. Neither the presence of bands nor the intervention justifies the reference to implicit powers. On the other hand, the circumstance that might have justified it (the organised revolt) was not established by the Court. For that reason, use should have been made of other evidence, based on precise information concerning, in particular, the Security Council's deliberations on the events in Chechnya.

2. By refusing to consider whether the decisions taken were politically expedient, the Court in fact declined to examine their legal nature, because the question of the choice of means not provided for in the Constitution is not only a political issue, but also a legal one. . . .

Dissenting Opinion of Judge Luchin

The essence of this legal opinion can be summarised as follows: the normative texts of the President and the Government of the Russian Federation which are being considered by the Court are not in conformity with the Constitution of the Russian Federation in that as they have no foundation in specific constitutional rules and the allowed the armed forces to be used for the purpose of resolving a domestic conflict, which resulted in illegal curtailment on and massive violation of human rights and freedoms as well as the destruction of the social infrastructure in the territory of the Chechen Republic. . . .

ISSUES TO CONSIDER

1. What issues are the minority opinions focusing on?
2. What is the significance of these issues in the context of the Chechen conflict?
3. What are the limits of judicial intervention?
4. In an emerging democracy, should the judiciary hesitate in criticizing the executive?
5. How are rights of those opposing the State to be determined and defined?

Justice Vitruk states a position whereby the executive's actions in Chechnya are illegal. In the context of determining the extent of judicial review, this approach is more in line with Barak's than with Rehnquist's.

Justice Ebzeyev's approach reflects an understanding of the need to balance, particularly during the course of the conflict. The suggestion that limits should be imposed on the state and that the civilian population must be protected reflects with the opinions of the Israeli High Court of Justice discussed earlier.

Justice Zorkin's addresses one of the most important issues in judicial activism: the need to define the situation. In determining which of the three paradigms — criminal law, POW, or a hybrid version — is relevant to counterterrorism, the executive branch must define the conflict. Otherwise, rights and obligations will be unclear and executive excess a grave possibility.

Justice Zorkin's obvious concern about an unfettered executive was clear. Rather than granting the executive carte blanche in Chechnya, Justice Zorkin demanded boundaries be established thereby limiting counterterrorism measures. Furthermore, the balancing requirement expressed in the High Court of Justice decisions resonates in Justice Zorkin's opinion. The U.S. Supreme Court has yet to articulate clearly the balancing requirement or to set well-defined limits on executive power with respect to counterterrorism.

ISSUES TO CONSIDER

1. What is the significance of both the majority and minority opinions in the above decision?
2. How is the executive to "translate" (implement) the opinions into a reasonable policy?
3. Must judicial opinions serve as a "roadmap" for the executive?
4. What weight must the executive give to judicial criticism, even if it is a dissenting opinion?
5. How is the executive to conduct counterterrorism operations in Chechnya in light of this opinion?

In the majority opinion, the Constitutional Court was sparing in its criticism of the executive branch. The minority opinion is highly critical of the executive branch, far more so than the U.S. Supreme Court when criticizing the executive branch and perhaps more so than the Israeli judiciary. The minority opinions address the most critical aspects of counterterrorism: balancing equally legitimate considerations, defining the conflict, determining the respective parties rights and obligations, and confronting the executive with the consequences of failing to satisfactorily address these issues — severe human rights violations.

B. REGISTRATION

According to press accounts and reports submitted by various human rights groups, the Russian government and certain cities practice "propiska," which literally means "the record of place of residence." In practice it is a system that allows local authorities to deny freedom of movement to certain ethnic groups by requiring a residence permit that restricts both an individual's right to choose his place of residence and to travel within the country.

The practice has been widely implemented against Chechens residing in Moscow. In 1996, the matter was first brought before the Constitutional Court, which ruled that the practice violates the Russian Constitution and is therefore unconstitutional.[96] Though the mayor of Moscow, Yuri Luzhkov, declared he would disregard the Court's ruling, the decision reflects the judiciary's determination to actively review executive counterterrorism measures.

1999 COUNTRY REPORTS ON HUMAN RIGHTS PRACTICES

Bureau of Democracy, Human Rights, and Labor, U.S. Department of
State, Feb. 25, 2000[97]

Mayor Luzhkov signed a resolution in 1996 ordering the deportation of all unregistered persons living in Moscow back to the place where they last were registered to live. Estimates on the number of unregistered persons living in Moscow range from 300,000 to 1.5 million (Moscow has 8.7 million registered residents). Moscow city authorities have released no figures on the number of individuals who have departed "voluntarily" from Moscow but readily admit that some 20,000 to 25,000 annually are deported against their will. This procedure consists of being taken to special shelters, checked for criminal records, then escorted 100 to 150 kilometers out of town. The authorities complain that these deportations are only temporary measures because deportees steadily find their way back to Moscow. At year's end, the resolution was still in effect, and the practice, which police reportedly use to extort money, continues.

In connection with the bomb explosions in August and September, which Moscow officials attributed to terrorists from the Northern Caucasus, Mayor Luzhkov issued an ordinance on September 13 requiring all temporary residents in Moscow since January 1 to reregister within 3 days with the Ministry of Internal Affairs. Reportedly 74,000 temporary residents sought reregistration, of whom approximately 15,500 persons were refused. In order to reregister, residents had to demonstrate a legitimate place of work, payment of city taxes, and a legal place of residence. Moscow authorities also restricted the arrival of new residents to the city and increased road checks and checks in train stations and marketplaces for these new arrivals. Law enforcement officials conducted searches of 26,500 apartments, 180 hotels, 415 guest houses, and 548 nightclubs and cafes. Human rights NGO's claim that authorities detained some 2,000 persons and expelled some 500 from Moscow.

Moscow mayor Luzhkov stated in a March 1998 television interview that he was refusing to implement the Court's decision. He announced that he had instructed the city's police to continue to enforce the old registration regulations.

Luzhkov's actions were clearly illegal, as the Constitution states that the Constitutional Court's rulings are final and mandatory for all state officials. In July 1998, the Supreme Court made a ruling that repealed both temporary and permanent residence permits. Nevertheless, Moscow city authorities have made clear their intention to oppose the ruling and, by the end of 1998, seemed to have persuaded the Federal government that Moscow merits an

96. Noah Rubins, *Recent Development: The Demise and Resurrection of the Propiska: Freedom of Movement in the Russian Federation,* 39 Harv. Int'l L. J. 545 (1998).

97. *Available at* http://www.state.gov/www/global/human_rights/1999_hrp_report/russia.html/.

exception to such decrees. The federal authorities have demonstrated little enthusiasm for enforcing the court rulings. However, the Moscow city regulations have had little if any impact on the numbers of such persons in Moscow.

Despite constitutional rulings, many local governments have been resistant and continue to enact regulations that introduce additional registration requirements. For example, the city of Moscow has shown a high level of inventiveness in circumventing Constitutional Court rulings. Following a February 2, 1998 ruling, the city enacted rules that would not allow officials to refuse citizen registration. However, the new rules retain a feature that ties registration to the size of housing and requires the consent of all those registered in an apartment or house. Basically, as during the Soviet period, only members of the owner's family can move in. Without consent the application would not be considered complete. It would not be refused, nor would it be accepted. Other large cities facing high population influx and migrant pressures retain similar restrictive regimes.

In ruling on the propiska in Moscow, the Constitutional Court held that "in the course of guaranteeing constitutional rights, the legislator must adhere to the demands of Art. 55.2 of the Constitution, which says that no laws denying or belittling human and civil rights and liberties may be issued in the Russian Federation."[98]

The Court also held the following:

[A]ccording to Art. 114 of the Constitution, the federal government ensures the implementation in the Russian Federation of a uniform financial, credit, and monetary policy [and] implements measures to ensure legality and the rights and freedoms of citizens." Regions may not introduce local taxes that violate federal legislation. Under federal law, people should be required to pay only a small, symbolic fee when registering with local authorities as new residents. Instead, the regions were imposing fees of a confiscatory nature. The amount of the registration fees was disproportionate to citizens' real income. In the face of such burdens, the right to freedom of movement and choosing one's place of residence had become an hollow declaration.[99]

The Court went on to hold:

Furthermore, the fact that the fees applied only to the new residents of a particular region constituted real discrimination against citizens based on social origins. Article 19.2 of the Constitution guarantees "the equality of rights and liberties regardless of gender, race, nationality, language, origin, property or employment status, residence, attitude toward religion, convictions, membership of public associations, or any other circumstance." In addition, the article categorically forbids "any restrictions on the rights of citizens based on social, racial, national, linguistic, or religious grounds."[100]

---

98. Konstantin Katanian, *Freedom of Movement in the Russian Federation Today, The Propiska and the Constitutional Court,* 7 East European Const. Rev. 2 (1998).

99. *Id.*

100. *Id.*

In attempting to limit freedom movement of ethnic groups, the local government was acting in violation of the Russian Constitution. The mayor's refusal to respect the holding and to continue the policy presents a major challenge to the Court and the national executive alike.

C. EVOLUTION OF RUSSIA'S COURTS

Currently, the Russian judicial system does not rely on precedents in reaching decisions. However, the Russian Constitutional Court appears to be forging in the direction of using precedents. In January 2010, the Constitutional Court declared that Russia's Higher Arbitrage Court has the right to set precedents that lower arbitrage courts must follow.[101] This decision reflects precedent that might, eventually, extend to the entire Russian legal system. The Constitutional Court also called for an amendment to the legal code in order to ensure compliance with this new decision. "The adoption of a precedent-based legal system would have enormous consequences for Russia. Among the most obvious would be a more level legal field for the courts, prosecutors, and defendants across the entire country and a requirement for better trained and informed lawyers and judges to handle individual cases."[102]

The Russian legal system is changing in other aspects as well. For example, with President Medvedev's support, based on dissatisfaction with the quality of lower courts, the Judiciary is considering introducing courts of appeals that would rehear cases tried in the lower courts. The new system would allow the appeal of all court decisions of a first impression. Specifically, cases would be considered for a second time, reexamining the evidence that was initially rebutted in the first round before reaching a final verdict. After the appeals court reaches its verdict, parties could appeal to what is currently known as "cassation" courts to argue on points of law, not fact (similar to the U.S. court of appeals system).

V. INDIA

A. INTRODUCTION

Given the threats faced by the Indian government, the role of the Indian Supreme Court as a possible "restrainer"[103] presents a great challenge in the context of judicial activism. In considering the Court's role, it is important to recall that India, similar to Israel, was under British rule prior to attaining independence. Just as the Israeli High Court of Justice is rooted in the British

---

101. Paul Goble, *Some Russian Courts Told to Use Precedents to Decide Cases*, Georgian Daily Independent Voice (Jan. 22, 2010), *available at* http://georgiandaily.com/index.php?option=com_content&task=view&id=16590&Itemid=72.

102. *Id.*

103. The phrase is intended in the context of President Barak's concept of "self-imposed restraints."

order nisi, the Indian Public Interest Litigation (PIL) mechanism is similarly based.

Public Interest Litigation is intended to provide the citizen with means to seek redress from the Court regarding a government decision or action.[104] Redress may be sought either directly by the affected individual or on his behalf. The petition requests the government desist from a particular activity; the purpose may be defined as "correcting a wrong."

ISSUES TO CONSIDER

1. The Israeli High Court of Justice has been accused of interfering (rather than intervening) with the executive; does PIL unnecessarily restrict the Indian executive attempting to respond to complex and varied threats?
2. Why should "standing" requirements be loosely applied in PIL?
3. What does it mean in the context of counterterrorism to "correct a wrong"?

DR. ROBERT WINSLOW, INDIA, CRIME AND SOCIETY: A COMPARATIVE
CRIMINOLOGY TOUR OF THE WORLD

http://www-rohan.sdsu.edu/faculty/rwinslow/asia_pacific/india.html

Jurisdiction of the Supreme Court

The Supreme Court has original, appellate and advisory jurisdiction. Its exclusive original jurisdiction extends to any dispute between the Government of India and one or more States or between the Government of India and any State or States on one side and one or more States on the other or between two or more States, if and insofar as the dispute involves any question (whether of law or of fact) on which the existence or extent of a legal right depends. In addition, Article 32 of the Constitution gives an extensive original jurisdiction to the Supreme Court in regard to enforcement of Fundamental Rights. It is empowered to issue directions, orders or writs, including writs in the nature of habeas corpus, mandamus, prohibition, quo warranto and certiorari to enforce them. The Supreme Court has been conferred with power to direct transfer of any civil or criminal case from one State High Court to another State High Court or from a Court subordinate to another State High Court. The Supreme Court, if satisfied that cases involving the same or substantially the same questions of law are pending before it and one or more High Courts or before two or more High Courts and that such questions are substantial questions of general importance, may withdraw a case or cases pending before the High Court or High Courts and

---

104. Public Interest Litigation was an attempt to guarantee fundamental rights and the assurances of the Constitution to all people in reality, not just on paper. Ashok H. Desai & S. Muralidhar, *Public Interest Litigation: Potential and Problems* 159, *in* Supreme But Not Infallible — Essays in Honour of the Supreme Court of India (B.N. Kirpal et al. eds, 2000).

dispose of all such cases itself. Under the Arbitration and Conciliation Act, 1996, International Commercial Arbitration can also be initiated in the Supreme Court. . . .

The judicial system retains substantial legitimacy in the eyes of many Indians despite its politicization since the 1970s. In fact, as illustrated by the rise of social action litigation in the 1980s and 1990s, many Indians turn to the courts to redress grievances with other social and political institutions. It is frequently observed that Indians are highly litigious, which has contributed to a growing backlog of cases. Indeed, the Supreme Court was reported to have more than 150,000 cases pending in 1990, the high courts had some 2 million cases pending, and the lower courts had a substantially greater backlog. Research findings in the early 1990s show that the backlogs at levels below the Supreme Court are the result of delays in the litigation process and the large number of decisions that are appealed and not the result of an increase in the number of new cases filed. Coupled with public perceptions of politicization, the growing inability of the courts to resolve disputes expeditiously threatens to erode the remaining legitimacy of the judicial system. . . .

ISSUES TO CONSIDER

1. Does effective judicial review require timeliness?
2. What is the significance of judicial backlog?
3. If the Court's legitimacy is challenged, what restraints may it impose on the executive?
4. Is effective judicial review possible when a nation like India faces multiple external and internal threats?
5. What are the limits of restraints that a Court should self-impose?
6. Does the executive naturally take advantage of judicial backlog?

While PIL seeks to provide an aggrieved citizen with speedy recourse to government imposition on civil and political rights, the lack of immediacy caused by backlog directly affects the impact of judicial review. India's judicial review model reflects a combination of Barak's and Rehnquist's competing philosophies. PIL is akin in purpose to the HCJ; however, the objective reality of judicial backlog lends itself to the Rehnquist model for PIL is largely predicated on accessibility and judicial independence. Unwarranted delay in scheduling hearings or rendering decisions suggests—whether intentionally or unintentionally—an approach advocated by Rehnquist and by the U.S. Supreme Court in *Endo*.

B. JUDICIAL REVIEW — PUBLIC SAFETY ACT

The Jammu and Kashmir Public Safety Act of 1978 is the main law relating to preventive detention in Jammu and Kashmir and permits administrative detention without trial for a period of up to one year if a person is to be prevented from acting in a manner deemed "prejudicial to the maintenance of public order" or up to two years if their actions are likely to be "prejudicial to the security of the State." The detention orders of the APHC leadership brought under the PSA cited grounds of activities being anti-national, subversive or prejudicial to the security of the state.[105]

The 1978 Act contributed to serious human rights violations. As previously discussed, an unfettered executive unrestrained by an acquiescent judiciary is more prone to violate civil and political rights. In examining Indian judicial activism, the critical query is whether the Court is sufficiently vigilant with respect to the executive's decisions. While PIL seeks to provide the citizen with protection — similar to the Israeli High Court of Justice — the question is whether the Court actually does so.

India: Punitive Use of Preventive Detention Legislation in Jammu and Kashmir

Amnesty International, May 16, 2000[106]

The state government's disregard for court orders quashing detention orders or granting bail is particularly disconcerting as courts are the only resort for anyone seeking legal redress. The function of the judiciary to uphold and protect human rights is undermined in this process. The pattern that has emerged is one of harassment, intimidation and deliberate disregard for the civil and political rights of those who are critical of the government. The government uses preventive detention legislation to silence critics and punish dissent.

. . .

Arbitrary detention in Jammu and Kashmir has a long history. The findings of the Basic Rights Protection Committee under its chairman Justice Farooqi in 1994 are still valid today. It noted the arbitrary detention of people even after their release ordered by designated courts and said that fresh detention orders were served on people immediately after they were shown to have been set free either on court orders or after completing their term of detention. It observed that young men were picked up and held in detention centres "for weeks, months and sometimes even for years before detention orders under the Public Safety Act are served on them; they are booked under the Terrorist and Disruptive Activities (Prevention) Act [TADA] even as they may not be applicable on facts." It said that of a total of 865 of detainees then in Kot Balwal Jail, 560 detainees had "neither been served detention orders under PSA nor booked under TADA."

Similarly a Jammu and Kashmir High Court judge ruling on a public interest petition alleging torture and arbitrary detention, noted in October 1994: "The Police agencies and the administration appear to have thrown to winds the rule of law. All sorts of illegalities are being committed by them and even criminals and terrorists may be ashamed of them. The High Court is replete with such complaints . . . many of which stand substantiated. Hundreds of cases have been brought to my notice where the detenues are

---

105. *India: Abuse of the Public Safety Act in Jammu and Kashmir*, Amnesty International, Apr. 5, 2000, *available at* http://web.amnesty.org/library/Index/ENGASA200132000?open&of=ENG-IND (last visited Oct. 8, 2010).

106. *Available at* http://web.amnesty.org/library/Index/engASA200102000/.

in illegal detention. Despite the strong directions of this court they are not be[ing] released. . . . Scores of cases are pending wherein the detenues have been allegedly done away with after arrest. For years the detenues are languishing in jails/Sub-Jails and interrogation centres without any legal authority. In short, there is a total break down of law and order machinery . . . even this court has been made helpless by the so-called law-enforcing agencies. Nobody bothers to obey orders of this court. . . ."

. . .

When the phased elections in Jammu and Kashmir were almost over, the arrest and detention of almost the entire top leadership of the APHC began. Among the 25 APHC leaders arrested were all the members of the APHC Executive Committee, the highest policy making body of the APHC, except its former chairman, Mirvaiz Moulvi Umar Farooq, who plays an important spiritual role in the state. They were arrested in small groups between 26 August and early November and held in different police stations where criminal complaints were lodged against them; most were transferred from police station to police station or to jails which made it difficult for their families to trace them. At this stage, lawyers had no access to them. Detention orders under the Public Safety Act were served on most of the detainees around 25 September 1999 by the Jammu and Kashmir government, in most cases ordering detention for a period of one or two months.

The detention orders of the APHC leaders stated that since they were likely to obtain bail in connection with these criminal complaints brought against them, and as "you will not refrain from continuing such illegal anti-national and subversive activities in future . . . which are prejudicial to the security of the state . . . as such in order to deter you from continuing such activities your detention under the provisions of the PSA has become imperative."

. . .

Several of the detainees completed their detention period under the PSA on 24 October but were not released. An order from the Government of Jammu and Kashmir merely directed that the detention period in the detention order be omitted; the detention orders remained in force. On 18 November 1999, after several of the detainees in Jodhpur Jail had been presented to the Advisory Board (for composition and functions of the Advisory Board see chapter 4.1), the Home Department of the Government of Jammu and Kashmir confirmed their detention under the PSA and extended the period of their detention to 24 months from the date of arrest, without giving any reason for this extension.

Petitions challenging the detention of the APHC leaders were filed in the Jammu and Kashmir High Court in the first week of October; they challenge their detention on three sets of grounds and aim at the quashing of the detention orders:

- the detention orders suffer from *procedural flaws* as the order of detention and grounds of detention were not communicated to the detainees within the required period; the time of serving the detention order and the grounds of detention were not recorded; supporting material was not given either to the detainees or the detaining authority thus failing to give the detainees the opportunity to make adequate representation to the government; and detainees were not informed if the government approved the detention order within the statutory period;

- and *substantive flaws* as they failed to establish grounds for detention under the PSA; the petitions argue that the orders provided no evidence that the detainee would act in a manner prejudicial to the security of the state in future and that the activities alleged did not fall within the purview of section 8 of the PSA;
- *detention of the APHC leaders in Jodhpur* is unlawful; the detention orders stated that the detainees be lodged in Central Jail Srinagar. The petition also argues that the state legislature cannot make laws with application outside the state, hence the amendment made to section 10 PSA is unconstitutional. . . .

Hearings of the petitions in the Jammu and Kashmir High Court started in December 1999. In February 2000 Amnesty International was informed that the Government of Jammu and Kashmir applied for the petitions to be transferred to the bench of the High Court in Jammu. Amnesty International is not aware of the reasons given for the request of transfer, and a transfer, if granted, may delay further hearings. Meanwhile, the petitions came up for a hearing on 14 March 2000 in the Srinagar bench of the Jammu and Kashmir High Court; the Advocate General sought adjournment till 18 April which was granted by the High Court.

. . .

Noor Mohammad Kalwal, a member of the Jammu and Kashmir Liberation Front (JKLF) was arrested by the Central Reserve Police Force (CRPF) on 8 September 1991; several months later, during which time it is not known if he was charged with any criminal offence, on 27 February 1992, he was served a PSA detention order for one year and lodged in Udhampur subjail. After the expiry of the detention period, he was neither released nor charged with any offence nor produced in any court. On 26 February 1993, he was transferred to the Joint Interrogation Centre at Kot Balwal, Jammu. A petition (387/93) challenging his continued detention was filed but despite his being transferred to subjail Rangreth in Srinagar so he could be produced in court in Srinagar, he was not actually brought before the High Court.

In early 1994, a complaint was brought against Kalwal on two counts under TADA, on both of which the Additional Designated Court, Srinagar granted him bail. When Kalwal was not released, the Designated Court directed police authorities, including the Director General of Police (DIG) to bring the detainee to court. The authorities failed to respond at the first date of hearing in February 1994. On 8 June 1994, police authorities and the Counter Intelligence Kashmir (CIK) moved an application in the court for a new date as, due to non-availability of police escort, the detainee had not been brought to court. On the new date set by the High Court, 14 June 1994, police authorities did not appear nor was the detainee brought to court. The Additional Judge of the Designated Court, Srinagar stated: "It is quite strange that the law executing authorities are not giving due regard to the orders passed by the Court for which the authorities are meant. . . . In this case, not to speak of the execution of the orders by superior officer of the rank of DIG, he has not even cared to send a few lines to this court in respect of compliance with the orders of this court."

It is not known to Amnesty International what happened to Noor Mohammad Kalwal between June 1994 and early 1996 except that he was not released. He was detained under a new PSA detention order (DMS/PSA/415/96) of 26 February 1996 for one year. A petition (107/97) challenging this new detention order was filed in the Jammu and Kashmir High Court which quashed it on 10 November 1997 and ordered his release. He was not released. Instead he was arrested on a charge under TADA which referred to an FIR (No 128/92) registered in 1992 relating to his alleged unlawful possession of a revolver claimed to have been recovered from him at the time of his arrest in 1992—when he had already been in detention for several months, having been arrested in September 1991. The designated TADA court granted bail to Noor Mohammad Kalwal on 17 July 1999. At the time of the bail petition hearing, the prosecution showed the presiding judge a letter from Counter Intelligence Kashmir (CIK) which stated that the detainee should not be released; but in case of release, the CIK should be notified immediately. The prosecution also reportedly showed a letter from CIK to Central Jail Srinagar instructing jail authorities to inform CIK of any imminent releases.

As Noor Mohammad Kalwal was about to be released from Central Jail Srinagar, he was re-arrested at the jail gate by CIK. Two days later he was transferred to Khanyar police station. He was then served another PSA one-year detention order (DMS/BSA/58 dated 30 July 1999, signed by the District Magistrate Srinagar), alleging that he was an "active, dedicated and staunch member of the JKLF," had been involved in crimes including firing on security forces which resulted in the death of a child and activities prejudicial to the security of the state. Noor Mohammad Kalwal has since then been held in Central Jail Srinagar. He was reportedly shifted to Udhampur Jail on 8 February 2000.

. . .

The PSA has been challenged in court mainly on the two grounds given below; neither of these challenges have so far been decided.

The definitions used in the Act including terms in the notion 'acting in a manner prejudicial to the security of the state or the maintenance of public order' are too vague and imprecise to be legally relevant. Kashmir lawyer Syed Tassaduq Hussain in 1999 raised this point in a Social Action Litigation (No.677/99); this petition was admitted in the Jammu and Kashmir High Court but may be sent to a larger bench which could delay the hearing.

The same petition also argues that sections 10 and 11 of the PSA which permit the transfer of a detainee to jails outside the state wrongly ascribes to legislators in the state the power to enact laws having extra-territorial effect. The right to transfer detainees to jails outside the state had already been challenged in the early 1990s by Justice Farooqi. This petition had apparently been transferred to a full bench but had then never been heard and decided. More recently lawyers have also pointed out that all legal changes effected during President's rule in the state (1990 to 1996), including amendments to the PSA, lapsed a year after the elected government took office, unless confirmed by the state legislative assembly. To Amnesty International's knowledge, President's

Act No 3 of 1992 has not been confirmed by the Jammu and Kashmir Legislative Assembly and would appear to be void since October 1997.

The transfer of detainees to distant jails had earlier been stopped on the consideration for the dignity of the detainee. In November 1995, the Jammu and Kashmir High Court had directed that no detainee should be transferred to jails outside the sate in response to a public interest litigation initiated by Jalil Andrabi. He had argued inter alia that detainees have the right to a life with human dignity, to contact family and friends, wear their own clothes and consult and be defended by a lawyer of their own choice. Such conditions are only fulfilled if detainees are held close to their homes.

Dozens of PSA detention orders have been challenged in the High Court over the years. However, to do so is not within the reach of every detainee; it presupposes the detainee's knowledge of this mechanism, actual access to a lawyer by the detainee or his relatives and the financial means to sustain the process of seeking redress. The fact that the detaining authorities may in the public interest withhold facts relevant to detention (section 13(2) PSA) also hampers the detainees' ability to challenge the legality of detention orders.

Hearings of petitions challenging detention orders often take a very long time as the state often fails to respond to court directions to appear and to reply to the petitioners' arguments. As a result petitions are sometimes still pending when detainees have completed their detention. According to the Jammu and Kashmir High Court Bar Association, of some 19,000 habeas corpus petitions filed in detention cases in the past few years, only 2,000 were heard and the rest had become irrelevant ["infructuous" in the terminology of the courts] because of the expiry of the period of detention.

However, some detention orders have been quashed, usually on formal grounds. The following case shows how thoroughly the legal requirements of the PSA are sometimes ignored revealing the intention of the detaining authorities to stifle dissent at any cost. Javed Ahmed Kathwari (21) described as a member of the Hizbul Mujahideen which advocates the accession of Kashmir to Pakistan, was arrested by the CIK Srinagar on 8 January 1995 under TADA in connection with FIR 1/1994 filed in police station CIK, Srinagar, according to which he had been found with arms and ammunition and was alleged to have murdered Sohan Lal Mahra of Gogjibagh in September 1993. As the state anticipated that he would be released on bail, a PSA detention order (DMS/PSA/137/95) for 24 months was issued by the District Magistrate Srinagar on 5 July 1995. He was directed to be detained in subjail Gupkar, Srinagar, as his activities were declared to be "highly prejudicial to the security of the state." The grounds for his detention included that "there is every likelihood that you may get released on bail which will defeat the purpose to deter you from continuing your subversive activities."

Contrary to the magistrate's order, Kathwari was transferred to Sangroor jail outside the state, then to Kot Balwal jail in Jammu. In September 1995, Vijay Kumar Mehra, son of the alleged victim of the detainee, submitted an affidavit in the High Court at Srinagar stating that his father had died a natural death in Amritsar in 1965, i.e. seven years before Kathwari was born.

The expectation that this disclosure would lead to the immediate quashing of the charge and the detention order proved premature. A petition challenging the detention order filed in September 1995 alleged that most of the legal requirements of the PSA had been ignored: the detainee had not been given a detention order, had not been informed of the grounds of detention, or shown relevant material, had not been informed of his right to make representation against his detention, nor had the case been referred to an Advisory Board in the stipulated time, nor had the government confirmed the detention order upon obtaining the opinion of the Advisory Board. Moreover, the detainee had not applied for bail so that the very basis of the detention order was non-existent. On 6 February 1996, the High Court quashed the PSA detention order ordering Kathwari's release while noting that the state "did not care to respond [to the petitioner's arguments] after having been duly served" notice. It had "not followed due course of law in depriving the petitioner of his liberty, guaranteed to him under the constitution." It is not known to Amnesty International if Javed Ahmed Kathwari was in fact released.

In other cases, too, detention orders were issued when the persons concerned were already in detention on a criminal charge in connection with which they had not sought release on bail. In November 1998, the Jammu and Kashmir High Court at Jammu quashed a PSA detention order against Altaf Ahmed Wani issued on 1 October 1997 for a period of 24 months while he was already in detention on the basis of an FIR (65/1997) of 17 August 1997. Justice Sharma said that the detaining authorities had not considered if the detainee had or was likely to move a bail application and as such the detention order lacked any basis.

Only in very rare cases have detainees been awarded compensation for illegal detention when their detention orders were quashed. In August 1997, the Jammu and Kashmir High Court quashed 12 detention orders, ordered the release of those who were detained under these orders and ordered the state to pay Rs. 10,000 to each of the detainees. They were also advised that they could sue the state for damages in a civil court.

4.4. Disregard of the Jammu and Kashmir Government for Court Orders

The quashing of a detention order and a court direction to release a detainee does not necessarily mean that the detainee will in fact be released. Amnesty International is aware of many instances in which court directives have been ignored by state authorities. The pattern of arbitrary detention described in this report, in which detention periods under the PSA are alternated with detention under strings of FIRs in cases for which the accused often obtained bail without ever being released, indicates the intent of the authorities to detain activists critical of the government irrespective of whether courts consider detention legal or not.

The practice of not releasing detainees who completed their detention, whether preventive detention or detention following conviction and sentence, is not new. The Jammu and Kashmir Bar Association on 7 October 1993 filed a petition in the Jammu and Kashmir High Court in which it brought several human rights matters to the attention of the High Court, including inadequate provision of food, drinking water and medical attention in the Joint Interrogation Centres (JIC) Hariniwas and Rangreth in Srinagar. It also said: "there are also a lot of people unlawfully detained at JIC Rangreth, where period of detention has expired and instead of being released, they have been held up for no fault of theirs. People against whom detention orders have been passed by various authorities are also not being shifted to their places of lodgement without any justification. Similarly persons whose interrogation is complete and investigation reports are ready, are also neither being released from JIC Hariniwas nor are they shifted to judicial lockup. The condition of all the detenues lodged at Hariniwas is critical for each one of them is treated inhumanely." It asked the High Court to ensure the release of all detainees languishing in the two joint interrogation centres without any legal justification.

The above highlights the overwhelming problem faced by the Indian Courts engaged in judicial review of the executive during armed conflict. Much like the Israeli model, the judiciary is determined to develop a model enabling immediate judicial review based on accessibility and independence. Dissimilar from the American model, which articulates restraint with respect to *when* to intervene, the Indian model seeks to restrain or, at least, to actively review the executive's actions in real time.

That model, however, is hampered by logistic realities that prevent timely implementation of decisions. Effective judicial review of the executive requires decisions that both mandate restraint and the state's ability and willingness to ensure enforcement. Enforcement of PIL decisions would guarantee not only their relevance but also signal executive respect of the judiciary.

ISSUES TO CONSIDER

1. What are the consequences of an executive that ignores decisions of the judiciary?
2. What judicial measures can be taken to avoid limitless detention of individuals?
3. Can the judiciary compel the release of individuals that the executive refuses to release or to bring before a court?

PHIL HAZLEWOOD, SWIFT JUSTICE SOUGHT IN MUMBAI TERROR CASE

Maktoob News, May 7, 2010[107]

MUMBAI—Calls for swift justice mounted in India on Friday after the lone surviving gunman of the 2008 Mumbai attacks was sentenced to death in a trial praised as a victory for the rule of law.

Pakistani national Mohammed Ajmal Amir Kasab was handed the death penalty on Thursday for waging war on India, mass murder, conspiracy and terrorist acts, nearly 18 months after the attacks that left 166 people dead.

---

107. *Available at* http://business.maktoob.com/20090000467010/Swift_justice_sought_in_Mumbai_terror_case/Article.htm/.

But with predictions that a lengthy, possibly open-ended legal appeal is likely in the high-profile case, government officials said they would push for the execution to be carried out as soon as possible.

"We will try and get the verdict ratified by the high court as early as possible," Ashok Chavan, the chief minister of Maharashtra state, of which Mumbai is the capital, was quoted as saying by the Hindustan Times newspaper.

"We would want Kasab hanged at the earliest. We will ask the Supreme Court to fast-track the hearing of appeal," he added.

Defence Minister A.K. Antony welcomed the verdict and said it sent a message to Pakistan-based insurgents that New Delhi was determined to act against militant groups.

"It has been proved by this judgment (that) if there is a will we can take strong action and we can send a proper message to all criminals and terrorists," Antony told reporters in New Delhi.

"It is a clear message to the terrorists outfits, organisations and groups working there across the border," he said, without naming Pakistan.

The Indian Express meanwhile focused on public reaction to the trial at a special prison court, which on Monday saw Kasab, 22, convicted on nearly all of the 86 charges he faced.

"I am definitely happy that Kasab has been given the death sentence but I also can't help feeling cynical about how long it will take till the sentence is executed," Mumbai tea-seller Mohammed Taufiq Sheikh was quoted as saying.

Sheikh was at the city's main railway station on the night of November 26, 2008 and narrowly avoided being shot as Kasab and an accomplice opened fire and threw grenades at unsuspecting commuters, killing 52.

Dipesh Pandey, whose father was shot and wounded at the station, added: "They have kept Kasab alive for over a year when he and his accomplices wiped out several lives in a few hours that night."

The money spent on keeping the gunman in prison should be spent instead on the families of victims, he added.

Questions about how long Kasab will be kept on death row have have arisen as India has not carried out an execution since 2004 and only two since 1998, while dozens of final clemency appeals to the president are still pending.

They include ones from the killers of former prime minister Rajiv Gandhi, who was assassinated in 1991, and a Kashmiri separatist who attacked India's parliament in 2001.

The Mail Today tabloid said it hoped the appeals process would be as "swift and transparent" as the trial itself, which was completed in just over a year — a rarity in India's notoriously slow-moving justice system.

"The deterrent value of the death penalty will be lost if the appeal process is allowed to linger on for years, if not decades," it said in an editorial.

A letter to The Hindu newspaper said the ultimate penalty "sent out a clear message that terrorism has no place in a civilised community.

"That Mohammed Ajmal Amir Kasab was given legal assistance in an open trial despite his heinous crime underscores the fairness and integrity of our legal system."

The Telegraph reflected a widely-held view in India that Kasab was only "among the lesser minions" in the attacks and that the masterminds in Pakistan were still to be held accountable.

"The latter require as much doggedness from the Indian administration to be brought to book like Kasab. Their conduits within the country too should not go scot-free," it said.

VI. SPAIN

Spain steadfastly defines terrorism as a criminal act and therefore applies the traditional criminal law paradigm to counterterrorism. Since Spain considers terrorism a criminal act, judicial review of counterterrorism measures must be considered in that vein.

ISSUES TO CONSIDER

1. Does application of the traditional criminal law paradigm to counterterrorism suggest limited judicial review?
2. What are the operational limits of using a traditional criminal law paradigm for counterterrorism?
3. What are the benefits of using a traditional criminal law paradigm for pursuing terrorists?
4. What are the similarities and differences between terrorists and criminals?
5. Should there be different measures for terrorists pre-arrest and post-arrest?
6. Should there be special courts and judges that specialize in terrorism cases?

As discussed in Chapter 3, the primary counterterrorism method adopted by the Spanish government in response to the Madrid train bombing is the incommunicado detention of suspected terrorists.

COUNTER-TERRORISM LEGISLATION AND PRACTICE:
A SURVEY OF SELECTED COUNTRIES

Secretary of State, United Kingdom (Oct. 2005)[108]

Spain

94. In terrorist cases, the judge may order that suspects be held incommunicado if they have grounds to believe that knowledge of the suspect's detention would prejudice the investigation. This involves a limitation of detainees' rights in two ways: relatives may not be informed of the detention, and legal assistance is provided by a duty solicitor, not a lawyer of their own choice. All other rights, including habeas corpus, continue to apply. The initial incommunicado order is valid for 72 hours following arrest. It can be prolonged for a

---

108. Dep't of State, *Counter-Terrorism Legislation and Practice: A Survey of Selected Countries* (2005), *available at* http://www.fco.gov.uk/Files/kfile/QS%20Draft%2010%20FINAL1.pdf.

further two days upon the authority of the investigating magistrate. After this period the investigating magistrate must decide whether to commence criminal proceedings.

If so, the investigative magistrate may order preventive detention, at which point the suspect is transferred from police custody to judicial custody (prison). At this point, he may extend the incommunicado period by five days, exceptionally followed by a final period of three days. Thus, it is possible for a person against whom criminal proceedings have begun to be held incommunicado for up to 13 days

95. While the detainee is held incommunicado in police custody, he may be questioned in the presence of the duty solicitor (not a lawyer of his own choosing), who is called in immediately on arrest. The lawyer may advise their client on procedural matters, but may not consult privately with the suspect. A forensic doctor examines the detainee to ensure that they are not physically mistreated and sends a report to the judge. Within the incommunicado period of detention, the suspect is transferred to the judge at the National High Court who has three days in which to hold a judicial interrogation. If the judge thinks there is a case for prosecution, criminal proceedings begin and the suspect is transferred to judicial custody; if not, the detainee is released. The judge must issue a reasoned judgement justifying his decision to begin criminal proceedings and any extension of the incommunicado period. Once in judicial custody, the detainee has the right to be seen by a second court-appointed forensic doctor and continued legal assistance. He may only have access to a lawyer of his own choosing once the incommunicado period has ended.

96. When a person has been charged and held in judicial custody, the period of preventative detention may last two years if the penalty for the offence is imprisonment of three years or more. Where circumstances exist that mean that the matter may not be tried within two years, the court may order one extension of up to a further two years. If the defendant is convicted and the sentence is under appeal, the period of custody may be extended for up to half of the sentence imposed. In practice, therefore, investigating magistrates have up to four years during which they can keep a terrorist suspect in detention and prepare the case for trial, although the defendant must be tried within the four year period.

A. SPANISH JUDICIAL SYSTEM

In Spain, the National High Court hears terrorism cases as part of its criminal docket but the Constitutional Court can return a case to the court where it was originally adjudicated should the Constitutional Court determine that constitutional rights were violated during the course of the proceedings.[109] The National High Court is composed of six investigating judges who examine the cases assigned, gather evidence, and evaluate whether the case should be

---

109. *Spain*, Jurist Legal News & Research, *available at* http://jurist.law.pitt.edu/worldlaw/spain.php (last visited Oct. 8, 2010).

brought to trial, but the Court does not actually try the cases.[110] The most prominent judge in the National High Court is Judge Baltasar Garzon. Judge Garzon indicted Osama bin Laden in 2003[111] and investigates suspected terrorist organizations and activities including suspected al Qaeda cells in Spain.[112]

According to Spanish law, judicial review is limited to a determination of whether there is sufficient basis for continuing the detention of a suspected terrorist. In the event that the judge concludes there is insufficient evidence, the detainee is released. However, should the judge determine otherwise, the detainee will be remanded for further detention. As indicated above, if the detainee has been placed in incommunicado detention, he may not see an attorney of his choosing; rather the attorney is essentially court-appointed. As the judiciary is integrally involved in the decision to hold an individual in incommunicado detention, the concept of judicial review is inherently different than the judicial activism of the other surveyed nations.

ISSUES TO CONSIDER

1. What is the role of the Spanish judiciary in determining the legality of an incommunicado detention?
2. Whose role is it to oppose the imposition of an incommunicado detention?
3. Is incommunicado detention reflective of unfettered prosecutorial discretion without significant judicial review?
4. What standards and criteria are relevant for determining the appropriateness of an incommunicado detention?
5. What branch of government should determine the criteria?
6. What is the proper mechanism for judicial review in such circumstances?

B. MADRID TRAIN BOMBINGS

In the aftermath of the bombing of the Madrid train stations, the Spanish authorities responded by arresting a number of suspects. The following Human Rights Watch report addresses the issue of incommunicado arrests and how the Spanish legal system interprets the significance of this measure.

LIMITATIONS ON CHALLENGING THE LAWFULNESS OF THE DETENTION

Human Rights Watch, Jan. 2005[113]

As of the end of 2004, eighteen people were in jail in Spain in connection with 11-M and forty-one people had been arrested and subsequently released after

---

110. *Profile: Judge Baltasar Garzon*, BBC, Sept. 26, 2005, *available at* http://news.bbc.co.uk/1/hi/world/europe/3085482.stm (last visited Oct. 8, 2010).

111. *Id.*

112. *Judge "Knew Madrid Bombs Not ETA,?"* BBC News, July 15, 2004, *available at* http://news.bbc.co.uk/1/hi/world/europe/3897741.stm (last visited Oct. 8, 2010).

113. *Available at* http://hrw.org/reports/2005/spain0105/7.htm#_Toc93310952/.

varying amounts of time in police custody and prison. The vast majority of the forty-one are on provisional release. A few were simply questioned and released without charge. Rabei Osman el Sayed, an Egyptian who was arrested in Milan on June 7 was extradited to Spain on December 7. He is suspected of master-minding the March 11 attacks. Of the eighteen in pre-trial detention, nine are Moroccans and five are Spaniards, while the remaining four are Syrian, Lebanese, Algerian and Egyptian, respectively; Moroccans account for twenty-two of those detained and subsequently released, while seven Spaniards fall into this category. The twelve Spaniards who have been detained are all suspected of involvement in the theft and/or sale of the explosives used the attacks, or the sale of drugs whose profits were used to finance the attacks.

The detainee, his or her spouse or companion, relatives, and, in the case of minors and incapacitated persons, their legal guardians; the Public Prosecutor; the Defensor del Pueblo; and the competent instructing judge on his own initiative may all file a writ of habeas corpus. The examining magistrate of the district where the detainee is being held is competent to review the petition, except in cases of detention of suspected members of armed groups or terrorists, whose writs of habeas corpus must be reviewed by the Central Instructing Judge, in other words, the same examining magistrate of the Audiencia Nacional who may have ordered the detention in the first place. By contrast, appeals against orders remanding a detainee into pre-trial deten-tion issued by Audiencia Nacional magistrates are reviewed in the first instance by the same examining magistrate but in the second instance by a panel of three judges.

While the letter of the habeas corpus law in Spain appears to be in confor-mity with international standards, the interpretation of the law among legal professionals is so narrow as to render it effectively meaningless. In conversations with Human Rights Watch, the attorney general and high-level representatives of the Ministry of Justice argued that habeas corpus was irrelevant in cases of incommunicado detention because this is a situation in which the arrest and period of detention are under judicial supervision and therefore a priori legal. The criminal defense lawyers consulted similarly stated that they did not consider filing a writ of habeas corpus on behalf of their clients because the detention had been ordered and supervised by a competent judge. One of the 11-M legal aid attorneys said, "Habeas corpus is hardly ever used in Spain. It's absurd . . . it only serves to place [the detainee] at the dis-posal of the judge, and in this case it didn't make sense, all of the time frames were respected."

Human Rights Watch is particularly concerned that the Ombuds Institu-tion (Defensor del Pueblo), though empowered by law to file writs of habeas corpus, does not see it as a useful or even appropriate tool. María Luisa Cava de Llano, First Adjunct of the Defensor del Pueblo, explained that "it is not common because illegal detentions don't happen. In the last four years, we have not submitted any nor have we been asked to do so." When asked if they ever ex officio go to places of detention to verify the conditions or situation of an incommunicado detainee, she said, "It is not our job to disrupt the work of the National Police; in principal we have no reason to believe that a person in incommunicado detention will be mistreated. Our national police and civil guard enjoy prestige among the public and their work is good until it is proven otherwise. Our assumption is that there will not be problems."

Even if there were a broader interpretation of the law and a greater willingness to use this legal tool, there are several practical impediments to incommunicado detainees enjoying the right to habeas corpus. First, they are not informed of this right. The right to challenge the lawfulness of the detention through a writ of habeas corpus is not among the rights that police are obligated to read to detainees at the time of arrest and before the official statement is recorded. It is a fair assumption that many detainees are not aware of this right or of the procedure for exercising it, particularly given that lawyers appear not to regard it as an important right.

Second, the fact that incommunicado detainees do not have the right to notify a person of their choice about the arrest or the place of detention clearly undermines the ability of third parties to file a writ of habeas corpus on their behalf. The CPT, while recognizing that it may be necessary in exceptional cases to deny notification of a third party for brief period of time, has stated that "to deny for up to five days the exercise of [this] right . . . is not justifiable." The CPT takes the position that "a period of a maximum of 48 hours would strike a better balance between the requirements of investigations and the interests of detained persons."

Finally, as detailed above, in most cases the detainee does not see a lawyer until the legally permissible period of incommunicado detention in police custody is almost over. Given that it is the lawyer who is in the best position to counsel the detainee about his various options, including that of filing a writ of habeas corpus, this delay has a direct impact on the detainee's ability to exercise this fundamental right. The European Court of Human Rights has held that "where a detained person has to wait for a period to challenge the lawfulness of his custody, there may be a breach of Article 5(4)." The Court considered that a period of seven days "sits ill with the notion of 'speedily'" under that article. The Human Rights Committee concluded that Article 9(4) of the ICCPR had been breached in a case where the applicant had the theoretical right to file a writ of habeas corpus but had been denied access to counsel throughout his detention.

———————

Many human rights groups, including Amnesty International, have called for Spain to desist from applying incommunicado detention to suspected terrorists.

VII. CHINA

China's counterterrorism strategy is more centralized than almost any other country. The decision of when to arrest, interrogate, and try suspected terrorists largely comes from the central government. The constitution facially provides for an open, fair, and independent judicial system. The reality, however, is vastly different.

China's constitution provides for the creation of several courts: local courts, special courts, and the Supreme Court. Local courts consist of tribunals in counties and administrative districts of cities and are responsible for criminal, civil, and administrative cases. The special courts control military, maritime, and railway cases. The Supreme People's Court is the highest court and has jurisdiction over all of the lower courts. The Supreme People's Court has first hearing rights to criminal and civil cases of national importance and must approve all death penalty cases. The constitution provides for open trials in all cases, except those involving state secrets, privacy, or juveniles.

While seemingly suggesting a transparent court system, the 2008 U.S. Department of State Human Rights report stated suggested otherwise:

> in practice the judiciary was not independent. It received policy guidance from both the government and the [Chinese Communist Party (CCP)], whose leaders used a variety of means to direct courts on verdicts and sentences, particularly in politically sensitive cases. At both the central and local levels, the government and CCP frequently interfered in the judicial system and dictated court decisions. Trial judges decide individual cases under the direction of the adjudication committee in each court. In addition the CCP's law and politics committee, which includes representatives of the police, security services, procuratorate, and courts, had the authority to review and influence court operations at all levels of the judiciary; in some cases the committee altered decisions.[114]

The aftermath of the Xinjiang riots facilitate an examination of the judiciary's actions and its role regarding counterterrorism. While there are almost no records of court decisions in the trials, comparison of an editorial from a Chinese newspaper and an Amnesty International Report highlight differing views regarding the role of the judiciary.

RIGHTFUL PUNISHMENT

China Daily, Oct. 14, 2009[115]

No mercy should be shown to criminals who intentionally take other people's lives, loot property and set fire to shops with a view to disrupting social order. So the death sentences given to six criminals for their part in the July 5 murderous riot in Urumqi are delivery of justice that all people with conscience are expecting

The riot was the most serious and horrible of its kind in the Xinjiang Uygur autonomous region in the last six decades. Altogether 197 innocent people were killed, more than 1,800 injured, and 380 shops and 169 motor vehicles smashed or burned down.

Looking at the crimes these criminals have committed, we can hardly understand how they could be so cruel and heartless. Abdukerim Abduwayit, one of the six, stabbed five people to death and burned down a building, which

114. Bureau of Democracy, Human Rights, and Labor, *2008 Human Rights Report: China* (Feb. 25, 2009), Dep't of State, *available at* http://www.state.gov/g/drl/rls/hrrpt/2008/eap/119037.htm (last visited Oct. 8, 2010).

115. *Available at* http://www.chinadaily.com.cn/opinion/2009-10/14/content_8790353.htm/.

resulted in injuries to several people. Two of the victims were under 18 years. In another case, another of the six criminals set ablaze a grain and oil shop along with others, killing all five of a family, with the eldest victim being 82 years old and youngest just 12.

We don't believe that such criminals will be pardoned in any country with rule of law. Neither do we think that anything other than death penalty can best reflect the will of the general public and the spirit of the rule of law.

It is not easy to investigate the details of a particular case in such a large and complicated riot. But local public security departments and prosecution institutions have been sticking to the principle that there must be strong evidence to incriminate every criminal. More than 1,000 police officers in the city of Urumqi alone and nearly 10,000 more from across the autonomous region have participated in the investigations of the cases, examination of evidence and interrogation of suspects. This speaks volumes to the importance that both the central and local governments attached to the way the cases are handled.

That more than 20 supervisory groups have supervised the entire process of law enforcement such as investigation, interrogation and detention of suspects sends the message that great importance has been attached to strictly following legal procedure in the handling of all cases.

Only when criminals are brought to justice through strict legal procedure can we make sure that right criminals get the right punishment. This principle has obviously been well observed.

Wicked as the criminals are, their rights as defendants are well protected. They have lawyers of their own ethnicity to defend them. They also have the right to defend themselves and the right to provide evidence and every right that a suspect enjoys in court. All the judges and prosecutors are Uygurs since the seven on trial—the remaining one was given life imprisonment, a lesser punishment as he confessed to crimes of murder and robbery, and cooperated with the police—are Uygurs, and Uygur was the language used in the trial. This demonstrates due respect for the rights of those on trial and also how it was made easy for them to exercise their own rights.

We have more to anticipate than just the rightful punishment of the criminals involved in the riot. That is the awareness of more people of all ethnicities that co-existence of all ethnic groups in this country is in the interest of all.

CHINA: HASTY EXECUTIONS HIGHLIGHT UNFAIR XINGIAN TRIALS

Amnesty International, UK, Nov. 10, 2009[116]

The Chinese authorities must ensure all individuals charged with offences during July riots in the Xinjiang Uighur Autonomous Region (XUAR) receive a fair trial and do not face the death penalty, Amnesty International said today.

The China Daily reported today that authorities prosecuted another 20 suspects on Monday, 9 November for offences ranging from murder, arson and robbery linked to the riots.

---

116. *Available at* http://www.amnesty.org.uk/news_details.asp?NewsID=18489/.

Amnesty International believes that statements made by Chinese officials following the unrest made it very difficult for a fair trial to be conducted. Urumqi's Communist Party Secretary stated in a news conference in July that "brutal criminals will be sentenced to death."

The defendants were also denied legal representation of their choice, with judicial authorities in Beijing putting pressure on human rights lawyers not to take up the cases of the accused.

Amnesty International is concerned about the lack of openness and transparency relating to the trials. Public notices about the trials were not issued and no observers were present in court.

Roseann Rife, deputy director of the Asia-Pacific program, said:

> In hastily executing these people after unfair trials, the Chinese authorities are perpetuating some of the very injustices that helped trigger the outburst of violence in the first place.
>
> Given the large number of detentions reported by Chinese officials in connection with the unrest, dozens more trials could take place, possibly leading to more executions. The Chinese government must ensure that the trials are conducted in line with International human rights standards, with transparency and without recourse to death penalty.

The trial follows the execution of eight Uighurs and one Han Chinese person, announced by authorities yesterday. The announcement did not say when the nine were executed but reported that it was after the Supreme People's Court reviewed and approved the sentences.

The nine were among 21 individuals tried and sentenced in October in relation to the July unrest. Another three received suspended death sentences while the rest were sentenced to lengthy prison terms. Their trials lasted less than a day. Their sentences were upheld by the XUAR Higher People's Court on 30 October.

Amnesty International interviewed eyewitnesses following the unrest who accuse the authorities of using excessive force against peaceful protesters including beatings, use of tear gas, and shooting directly into crowds of protesters.

Amnesty International calls on Chinese authorities to examine all acts of violence during the July unrest, including possible excessive use of force on the part of security forces against peaceful Uighur demonstrators.

"A process that fails to openly investigate crimes and acknowledge underlying causes of unrest will only perpetuate tensions and the existing sense of injustice among ethnic minority groups," said Roseann Rife.

ISSUES TO CONSIDER

1. Is judicial review possible in what is largely a centralized governmental system?
2. How does the court carve a niche for itself enabling judicial review?
3. What are the conditions necessary for creating judicial review?
4. What are the practical implications of a regime free of judicial review?

5. How is judicial review to be developed in a largely centralized government structure?
6. How are individual rights protected if there is no judicial review of the executive?

VIII. COLOMBIA

A. INTRODUCTION

Colombia is faced with several challenges in developing counterterrorism strategies, much less developing a process and mechanism for active judicial review of the executive. The judicial system faces threats from paramilitaries, interference from the executive, and a corrupt political and criminal system. Historically, the Colombia courts have been viewed as a weak with very little oversight power over the executive. In 2006, Colombia's Constitutional Court made clarifications to the Justice and Peace Law; paramilitaries who wished to receive reduced sentences must give full and truthful confessions and were penalized for hiding the truth.

B. INVESTIGATION BY THE SUPREME COURT INTO CONGRESS' LINKS TO PARAMILITARIES

According to the Colombian Constitution, members of Congress should be investigated and tried only by the Supreme Court. In 2005, the Supreme Court's criminal chamber launched investigations of members of the Colombian Congress for links to paramilitaries. Previously, reports of cooperation between paramilitary and public officials were received but no claims were investigated. By 2009, 72 members of Congress faced charges, 11 were convicted, 4 acquitted and 25 had resigned in order not to be investigated by the Supreme Court rather by the Attorney-General's Office. The Attorney-General has investigated over 250 similar cases concerning public officials including ministers, governors, mayors, and directors of major state institutions.[117] These prosecutions confirm the extent of infiltration by paramilitary groups in Colombia. However, Human Rights Watch has reported that the executive branch has taken steps to undermine the investigation, including replacing justices on the Court and proposing constitutional amendments that would remove jurisdiction from the Court.

---

117. Office of the United Nations High Commissioner for Human Rights [OHCHR]. Annual Report of the United Nations High Commissioner for Human Rights on the situation of Human Rights in Colombia, ¶55-56, UN Doc. A/HRC.10/32 (Mar. 9. 2009).

BREAKING THE GRIP? OBSTACLES TO JUSTICE FOR PARAMILITARY
MAFIAS IN COLOMBIA

Human Rights Watch (2008)[118]

On September 26, 2007, the Supreme Court indicted Sen. Mario Uribe for conspiring with paramilitaries. The decision was of great significance because of the high profile of Sen. Uribe. Mario Uribe is a second cousin of President Álvaro Uribe and they have a close and longstanding political alliance. The two of them co-founded a branch of the Liberal Party called Sector Democrático in the 1980s. They both ran for Congress in 1986, with Álvaro becoming senator and Mario becoming a representative. When Álvaro Uribe became governor of Antioquia in 1994, Mario was elected to the Senate. Mario's political movement, Colombia Democrática, strongly supported Alvaro's bid for the presidency in 2002. Later, Mario Uribe was a leading proponent of two of Alvaro Uribe's most controversial initiatives in the Congress: the Alternative Penalties Law (a predecessor to the Justice and Peace Law) and the amendment to the Colombian Constitution that allowed Álvaro Uribe's reelection as president in 2006.

Sen. Uribe resigned his Senate seat shortly after the indictment, and so the investigation was transferred to the Office of the Attorney General, where it was assigned to prosecutor Ramiro Marín. On April 21, 2008, Marín ordered Mario Uribe's arrest. Uribe found out about the arrest warrant and fled to the embassy of Costa Rica, where he sought political asylum. The asylum request was denied and on April 22 Mario Uribe was arrested. Human Rights Watch reviewed the prosecutorial resolution ordering Mario Uribe's arrest. The decision was based primarily on the following pieces of evidence, mentioned in the resolution:

First, Salvatore Mancuso testified, first in his Justice and Peace confession and then again before the Supreme Court, that he had met with Mario Uribe on two occasions. During one of those meetings, Mancuso said, Mario Uribe and Eleonora Pineda (a former hairdresser who was running for a seat as a representative in the same region as Mario Uribe, with the backing of the AUC) visited Mancuso in a rural area in the paramilitary-controlled municipality of Tierralta, Córdoba, where Mancuso was hiding due to the criminal convictions and charges pending against him. In his first statement Mancuso said he was not certain of the exact date or order of the meetings; however he later said that the first meeting definitely happened before the 2002 congressional elections. Mancuso said that the meeting had two goals: first, to formalize in front of him a political agreement between Uribe and Pineda by which the two of them would help each other get votes in some areas of Córdoba. According to Mancuso, Sen. Uribe had to have known that Pineda was a candidate of the paramilitaries, as that was why the two of them had gone to Tierralta to visit him. Mancuso added that at the meeting Sen. Uribe committed himself to support the paramilitaries' efforts to initiate negotiations with the government. Mancuso said that the other meeting happened when

118. *Available at* http://www.hrw.org/sites/default/files/reports/colombia1008web.pdf/.

Sen. Uribe once again went to Tierralta to meet with Carlos Castaño; according to Mancuso, because Castaño was busy at the time, he asked Mancuso to meet with Sen. Uribe to once again discuss the negotiations with the government. Sen. Uribe claimed that there was only one meeting and that it was not planned: he said that Eleonora had invited him to lunch with some friends in her house, but she surprised him by instead taking him to Mancuso's ranch. Uribe said that the meeting happened after the 2002 elections. Eleonora Pineda also said the meeting happened after the elections, in 2002, and that she did not initially explain to Mario Uribe that they were going to meet with Mancuso — though she said she did explain it to him as they were on their way. Also, Pineda noted that when they were on their way to meet with Mancuso, at one point she asked Mario Uribe to leave all his escorts and other companions behind for the last stretch of the road trip.

The prosecutor chose to believe Mancuso's version of events over the versions given by Uribe and Pineda. He pointed out that Pineda was close to Mario Uribe, who the prosecutor notes allowed her to join his political movement, even though he obviously knew of her relationship with the paramilitaries. Indeed, starting in 2002 Pineda and Rocio Arias, another congresswoman, were the two most active and open defenders of the paramilitaries' positions in Congress; they have both pled guilty to conspiring with paramilitaries. Yet Mario Uribe, who was the leader of the Colombia Democrática party, allowed both of them to remain within the ranks of the party until February of 2006, when it was reported in the Colombian media that US officials had warned that party leaders who kept politicians linked to paramilitaries in their ranks might have their US visas revoked.

Another factor that might affect Pineda's testimony is fear. On October 5, 2007, shortly after Pineda pled guilty, one of her brothers was killed in the state of Córdoba; according to news reports, members of the military shot him, claiming he was a member of an armed group and had opened fire on them. Pineda's lawyer asserted that her brother's killing was meant to silence Pineda. Also, the prosecutor points out that there is another important piece of evidence against Mario Uribe that tips the scale in favor of Mancuso's version of events: the unusual and very high spike in votes for Mario Uribe in the 2002 elections. Specifically, Sen. Uribe went from getting 3,985 votes in the 1998 elections to nearly triple that amount — 11,136 votes — in the 2002 elections. That's the time when, if Mancuso's version is correct, he presumably would have benefited from the votes that Eleonora Pineda, with paramilitary backing, could have brought him. By the 2006 elections, when he had expelled Eleonora from the party, his votes once again dropped to 3,233.

According to the prosecutor's analysis, the unusual voting patterns are particularly noticeable in the municipalities, such as Montelíbano, Sahagún, and Planeta Rica, where Mancuso had supposedly ordered that people vote for Pineda and Uribe. The prosecutor explains that the paramilitaries apparently divided up the municipalities, ordering that some vote for Uribe and others for another candidate — Miguel de la Espriella — who was also elected to the Senate. Mancuso stated that de la Espriella had been upset with Mancuso for offering some share of his votes to Mario Uribe, but Mancuso calmed him down by assuring him that he would be elected anyway. The prosecutor notes that De la Espriella lost votes in some municipalities in 2002 compared to the 1998 elections—and argues that Mario Uribe got those votes instead.

The prosecutor did not accept Mario Uribe's argument that the spike in votes for him was due to his association with the presidential candidate, Alvaro Uribe, because that argument would not explain the 2006 drop in votes (when Alvaro Uribe was once again running for president, with even higher popularity in the polls). In addition to the allegations about Uribe's dealings with Mancuso in connection with the 2002 elections, the charges against Sen. Uribe are based on allegations that Sen. Uribe sought to work with the paramilitaries to pressure landowners to sell or give him cheap land in 1998. The allegations are based on the testimony of witness Jairo Castillo Peralta, also known as "Pitirri." Castillo is a former paramilitary who operated in the state of Sucre. After leaving the paramilitaries' ranks in the late 1990s, he began providing testimony to prosecutors in several cases. He now has political asylum in Canada and has continued testifying before the Colombian Supreme Court and prosecutors in the parapolitics cases.

Castillo has testified that in 1998 he participated in a meeting with Mario Uribe and landowners, including Olegario Otero Bula, in Sahagun, Cordoba. According to Castillo's testimony, Mario Uribe was seeking "cheap land," and Castillo was ordered to look for such land, determine what people in the region were making payments to the paramilitaries, and seek out the ones—such as Mrs. Luz Marina Zapa—who had not been "paying their quota." . . .

A few months after his arrest, Mario Uribe was once again set free. Deputy Attorney General Guillermo Mendoza Diago granted an appeal Uribe made from the resolution ordering his arrest. In his decision reviewing the arrest order, Mendoza Diago goes over the evidence against Sen. Uribe and reaches the opposite conclusion from that reached by the prosecutor. . . . Based on this analysis, Mendoza Diago concluded that the evidence against Mario Uribe was insufficient to justify his detention and ordered his release.

ISSUES TO CONSIDER

1. What are the obstacles to creating a culture of judicial review?
2. What is the impact of semi-governmental organizations or paramilitaries on exercising restraint of the executive?
3. How does judicial review address questions of corruption?
4. What are the circumstances—political, social, and cultural— facilitating judicial reviews of the executive?
5. How, if judicial review is not fully developed, are restraints imposed on the executive?

IX. CONCLUSION

While it is too early to comment on the U.S. Supreme Court under Justice Roberts, perhaps *Hamdan v. Rumsfeld* and *Boumediene v. Bush* indicate a move toward the Barak model. The Barak model—as articulated in both scholarly writings and court holdings—represents judicial review at its most extreme. Russian judicial review is in its infancy; one of the most important questions is whether the executive branch intends to respect judicial decisions and, if not, what enforcement methods and sanctions the court might have. The cases presented highlight the tension regarding the Chechen conflict. India has introduced Public Interest Litigation as a means of providing the aggrieved individual recourse against the executive. However, the backlog of cases severely hampers the timeliness—and therefore effectiveness—of Indian judicial review. Spain's judicial review is limited to the traditional criminal law paradigm and, in particular, whether incommunicado detentions are lawful. In clear contrast to the other surveyed countries, China has very little judicial review, clearly reflecting the power of the central government. Colombia's judicial review is largely restrained both by historical, institutionalized corruption and the powerful presence of semi-governmental organizations, particularly paramilitaries.

CHAPTER 6

OPERATIONAL COUNTERTERRORISM METHODS

I. INTRODUCTION

This chapter examines and analyzes the surveyed nations' operational counterterrorism methods. The discussion includes an examination of operational considerations, policy implications, and legal dilemmas. Counterterrorism measures must be considered in the context of domestic balancing, international law, judicial activism, intelligence gathering, and interrogation of detainees.

Operational counterterrorism requires, among other attributes, actionable intelligence, operational capability, and an understanding that swift victory is a fiction. In many ways, operational counterterrorism is a never-ending war of attrition comprised of some victories, some defeats; decisions address how and when to act, and against whom. For the purposes of this casebook, operational counterterrorism is defined as:

> The actions of a state, proactive or reactive, intended to kill or injure terrorists and/or to cause serious significant damage to the terrorist's infrastructure.

There is an additional branch to counterterrorism: "soft" counterterrorism which includes economic development, building schools and hospitals, and other direct contributions to developing viable infrastructures. While soft counterterrorism is clearly deserving of attention and discussion, the focus of this chapter (and the book) is operational counterterrorism defined as direct engagement of the suspected terrorist.

One of the most difficult challenges in operational counterterrorism is defining effectiveness. Does killing a particular terrorist indicate success? Should success be defined in a short-term or long-term context, tactically or strategically? Do politics rule the day, meaning that a show of power is the preferred means, as opposed to piecemeal, consistent attacks on identified terrorist targets? Are all individuals involved in the terrorist network legitimate targets? What is the status of terror financiers? After all, money is clearly (along with ideology) the engine that drives terrorist organizations.

These questions — which have no concise or definitive response — serve as the backdrop to the discussion in this chapter. To the mix must be added the requirement that democratic society's conduct operational counterterrorism in accordance both with the rule of law and morality in armed conflict. In developing a viable strategy, decision makers must decide on a course of action that is simultaneously effective and legal.

ISSUES TO CONSIDER

1. At whom are counterterrorist measures aimed?
2. Who are governments attempting to affect?
3. Who is the targeted audience?
4. Are the efforts aimed at the specific terrorist, his or her family, or the community at large?
5. What does deterrence mean and how is it to be implemented?
6. What is collective punishment and how does it differ from individual punishment?
7. Should counterterrorism measures be considered from both the legal and policy perspectives?

II. THE UNITED STATES

A. INTRODUCTION

Since 9/11, the United States has been catching up in the field of counterterrorism. This is most readily apparent in the development and implementation of operational counterterrorism measures. Has the United States clearly articulated a policy that shows foresight, clear principles, and a willingness to alter plans according to lessons learned? Have the Bush and Obama administrations kept their eye on the ball with respect to immediate and potential threats?

In addition, did the Bush administration's response, which included a clear desire to pin the attack on Saddam Hussein, result in critical missteps in the development of an operational counterterrorism policy? By emphasizing a non-existent link between Iraq and bin Laden, did the Bush administration prevent the military from exclusively focusing its efforts and resources on directly engaging al Qaeda? These questions serve as backdrops to a discussion of the United States' post-9/11 operational counterterrorism policies.

B. POST-9/11

America's counterterrorism policy in the immediate aftermath of 9/11 is best analyzed by examining two distinct responses: a broad, generalized response illustrated by Operation Enduring Freedom (OEF) and a specific response reflected by drone attacks, initially implemented by President Bush and subsequently widely applied by President Obama.

On October 7, 2001, the United States attacked Afghanistan in a determined effort to root out bin Laden from the caves where al Qaeda was allegedly hiding.[1]

> Operation Enduring Freedom commenced on Oct. 7, 2001. Early combat operations included a mix of air strikes from land-based B-1, B-2 and B-52 bombers; carrier-based F-14 and F/A-18 fighters; and Tomahawk cruise missiles launched from both U.S. and British ships and submarines.
>
> The initial military objectives of Operation Enduring Freedom, as articulated by President George W. Bush in his Sept. 20th Address to a Joint Session of Congress and his Oct. 7th address to country, include the destruction of terrorist training camps and infrastructure within Afghanistan, the capture of al Qaeda leaders, and the cessation of terrorist activities in Afghanistan.
>
> Secretary of Defense Donald Rumsfeld stated in an Oct. 7th DoD News Briefing that U.S. objectives were to make clear to Taliban leaders that the harboring of terrorists is unacceptable, to acquire intelligence on al Qaeda and Taliban resources, to develop relations with groups opposed to the Taliban, to prevent the use of Afghanistan as a safe haven for terrorists, and to destroy the Taliban military allowing opposition forces to succeed in their struggle. Finally, military force would help facilitate the delivering of humanitarian supplies to the Afghan people.
>
> The British had also defined the goals of their involvement (termed Operation Veritas) in "Her Majesty's Government's Campaign Objectives," dated Oct. 16th. The short term goals of the military action included the capture of Osama bin Laden and other al Qaeda leaders, the prevention of further attacks by al Qaeda, the end of Afghanistan's harboring of terrorists, their training camps and infrastructure, and the removal of Mullah Omar and the Taliban Regime. Long term goals include the end of terrorism, the deterrence of state sponsorship of terrorism, and the reintigration of Afghanistan into the international community.[2]

According to former President Bush, the American campaign was not directed at the citizens of Afghanistan, but rather against the terrorist infrastructure. While the extent of al Qaeda's relationship with the ruling Taliban government prior to September 2001 is a matter of dispute, bin Laden had clearly established northern Afghanistan as a base of operations after the Sudanese government expelled him. Formed in 1994, the Taliban government established control over a chaotic Afghanistan when Kabul was captured from the mujahedeen in 1996. However, only three countries—Pakistan, the

---

1. *Afghanistan Wakes After Night of Intense Bombings*, CNN.com, Oct. 7, 2001, *available at* http://archives.cnn.com/2001/US/10/07/gen.america.under.attack/ (last visited Oct. 8, 2010); *Bin Laden Says He Wasn't Behind Attacks*, CNN.com, Sept. 17, 2001, *available at* http://archives.cnn.com/2001/US/09/16/inv.binladen.denial/ (last visited Oct. 8, 2010); Carl Nolte, *Afghanistan's Ancient Defense; Like Generations Past, Taliban Fighters Finding Refuge Underground*, S.F. Chron., Nov. 7, 2001, at A3.

2. *Operation Enduring Freedom–Afghanistan*, Global Security.org, *available at* http://www.globalsecurity.org/military/ops/enduring-freedom.htm (last visited Oct. 8, 2010).

United Arab Emirates, and Saudi Arabia — recognized the Taliban government. Mullah Omar, the head of the Taliban government, requested that bin Laden keep a low profile in Afghanistan. While bin Laden promised to accede to this request, evidence clearly suggests that Afghanistan served as al Qaeda's operational headquarters for the planning and execution of 9/11.

During the initial military operation which lasted 78 days, the U.S.-led coalition forced al Qaeda to go on the run, initially to western Pakistan (reportedly with the active facilitation of the Pakistani intelligence agency, ISI) and increasingly to Yemen. The coalition also killed approximately 1000 Afghan civilians and dropped 24,000 bombs within the first year. The stated goal of the operation, according to Secretary of Defense Donald Rumsfeld and President Bush, was to "make clear to the Taliban leaders and their supporters that harboring terrorists is unacceptable and carries a price."[3] The articles below reflect the inherent difficulty in operational decision-making, particularly when the mission is broadly and vaguely stated.

COMPLETE 9/11 TIMELINE

Cooperativeresearch.org

Early October 2001: US Launches Attacks on Afghanistan from Pakistani Bases

The US begins using the Shahbaz air force base and other bases in Pakistan in their attacks against Afghanistan. However, because of public Pakistani opposition to US support, the two governments claim the US is there for purely logistical and defensive purposes. Even six months later, the US refuses to confirm it is using the base for offensive operations. Such bases in Pakistan become a link in a chain of US military outposts in Central Asia. Other countries also falsely maintain that such bases are not being used for military operations in Afghanistan despite clear evidence to the contrary.

October 2001: US Military Downplays Importance of Targeting bin Laden

On October 8, 2001, Gen. Tommy Franks, Central Command commander in chief, says of the war in Afghanistan, "We have not said that Osama bin Laden is a target of this effort. What we are about is the destruction of the al-Qaeda network, as well as the . . . Taliban that provide harbor to bin Laden and al-Qaeda." Later in the month, Defense Secretary Donald Rumsfeld makes similar comments, "My attitude is that if [bin Laden] were gone tomorrow, the same problem would exist. He's got a whole bunch of lieutenants who have been trained and they've got bank accounts all over some 50 or 60 countries. Would you want to stop him? Sure. Do we want to stop the rest of his lieutenants?

---

3. *Rumsfeld and Myers Briefing on Enduring Freedom*, News Transcript, Oct. 7, 2001, *available at* http://www.defense.gov/transcripts/transcript.aspx?transcriptid=2011 (last visited Oct. 8, 2010); Jim Garamone, *America Launches Strikes Against Al Qaeda, Taliban*, American Forces Press Service, Oct. 7, 2001, *available at* http://osd.dtic.mil/news/Oct2001/n10072001_200110071.html (last visited Oct. 8, 2010).

You bet. But I don't get up in the morning and say that is the end; the goal and the endpoint of this thing. I think that would be a big mistake." One military expert will later note, "There appears to be a real disconnect between what the US military was engaged in trying to do during the battle for Tora Bora — which was to destroy al-Qaeda and the Taliban — and the earlier rhetoric of President Bush, which had focused on getting bin Laden."

Early October 2001: General Franks Disregards Advice to Open Second Front in Afghanistan

The Washington Post reports in late 2004 that, shortly after Richard Myers officially becomes Joint Chiefs of Staff Chairman on October 1, 2001, he raises doubts about the military plan to topple the Taliban in Afghanistan. General Tommy Franks, the chief of US Central Command, plans a single thrust towards the capital, Kabul, from the north. Myers urges Franks to open a southern front. A brigade of the Army's 10th Mountain Division in Uzbekistan and two Marine Expeditionary Forces in the Arabian Sea are prepared and in position for the role. However, Franks does not position a blocking force to meet any retreating forces. The Washington Post reports, "Some Bush administration officials now acknowledge privately they consider that a costly mistake." Franks later claims that it would have taken too much time to put a force into position and would have antagonized the country's Pashtun majority. Most of al-Qaeda and the Taliban's leaders are eventually able to escape the country. "A high-ranking war planner [later] likened the result to throwing a rock at a nest of bees, then trying to chase them down, one by one, with a net."

Early October-Mid-November, 2001: Air Force Is Repeatedly Denied Permission to Bomb Top al-Qaeda and Taliban Leaders

In mid-November 2001, the Washington Post will report that senior Air Force officials are upset they have missed opportunities to hit top al-Qaeda and Taliban leaders since the start of the bombing of Afghanistan. According to these officials, the Air Force believes it has the leaders in its crosshairs as many as ten times, but they are unable to receive a timely clearance to fire. Cumbersome approval procedures, a concern not to kill civilians, and a power play between the Defense Department and the CIA contribute to the delays. One anonymous Air Force official later says, "We knew we had some of the big boys. The process is so slow that by the time we got the clearances, and everybody had put in their 2 cents, we called it off." The main problem is that commanders in the region have to ask for permission from General Tommy Franks, based in Central Command headquarters in Tampa, Florida, or even Defense Secretary Rumsfeld and other higher-ups. Air Force generals complain to Franks about the delay problem, but never receive a response. For example, at one point in October, a Taliban military convoy is moving north to reinforce front line positions. Targeters consider it an easy mark of clear military value. But permission from Central Command is denied on the suspicion that the target is so obvious that "it might be a trick." In another example, a target is positively identified by real-time imagery from a Predator drone, but Central Command overrides the decision to strike, saying they want a second source of data. An anonymous official calls this request for independent verification of

Predator imagery "kind of ridiculous." The London Times paraphrase officials who claim that, "Attempts to limit collateral damage [serve] merely to prolong the war, and force the Pentagon to insert commandos on the ground to hunt down the same targets." By the end of the war, only one top al-Qaeda leader, Mohammed Atef, is killed in a bombing raid (see November 15, 2001), and no top Taliban leaders are killed.

Furthermore, in analyzing the operational considerations and policy calculations of the Bush administration's decision to attack Afghanistan, there is uncertainty as to whether OEF was a war or a large-sized counterterrorism operation. According to international law, war can be fought only between nation-states. In determining the status of OEF, President Bush's speech before the Congress on September 20, 2001 is instructive:

> The leadership of al Qaeda has great influence in Afghanistan and supports the Taliban regime in controlling most of that country. In Afghanistan, we see al Qaeda's vision for the world.
>
> Afghanistan's people have been brutalized—many are starving and many have fled. Women are not allowed to attend school. You can be jailed for owning a television. Religion can be practiced only as their leaders dictate. A man can be jailed in Afghanistan if his beard is not long enough.
>
> The United States respects the people of Afghanistan—after all, we are currently its largest source of humanitarian aid—but we condemn the Taliban regime. It is not only repressing its own people, it is threatening people everywhere by sponsoring and sheltering and supplying terrorists. By aiding and abetting murder, the Taliban regime is committing murder.
>
> And tonight, the United States of America makes the following demands on the Taliban: Deliver to United States authorities all the leaders of al Qaeda who hide in your land. Release all foreign nationals, including American citizens, you have unjustly imprisoned. Protect foreign journalists, diplomats and aid workers in your country. Close immediately and permanently every terrorist training camp in Afghanistan, and hand over every terrorist, and every person in their support structure, to appropriate authorities. Give the United States full access to terrorist training camps, so we can make sure they are no longer operating.
>
> These demands are not open to negotiation or discussion. The Taliban must act, and act immediately. They will hand over the terrorists, or they will share in their fate.[4]

OEF was defined as an "operation" rather than a war. While the classification may have been political—not declaring war against a state (Afghanistan) whose ruling regime (the Taliban) was not recognized universally and considered illegitimate—from the perspective of international law, the United States was not at war with Afghanistan. As discussed in Chapter 4, the Israel Supreme Court sitting as the High Court of Justice defined the conflict with the Palestinians as "armed conflict short of war." Should the United States have adopted a similar definition, or a variation on that theme, with respect to the American attack on Afghanistan? Do the measures implemented more closely resemble

---

4. *Address to a Joint Session of Congress and the American People*, President Bush, Sept. 20, 2001, *available at* http://www.dhs.gov/xnews/speeches/speech_0016.shtm (last visited Oct. 8, 2010).

operational counterterrorism than war in the classical sense? According to the Israel's HCJ analysis, actions of the coalition forces in Afghanistan would be considered operational counterterrorism, though unconventionally an entire terrorist network located in a sovereign nation was deemed a legitimate target.

OBAMA AFGHANISTAN STRATEGY: MORE TROOPS IN QUICKLY, DRAWDOWN IN 2011

CNN, Dec. 1, 2009[5]

West Point, New York (CNN) — President Obama said Tuesday that the deployment of 30,000 additional U.S. troops to Afghanistan is part of a strategy to reverse the Taliban's momentum and stabilize the country's government.

"There is no imminent threat of the government being overthrown, but the Taliban has gained momentum," Obama said at the U.S. Military Academy. "Al Qaeda has not re-emerged in Afghanistan in the same numbers as before 9/11, but they retain their safe-havens along the border. In his speech Tuesday, Obama said his strategy had three objectives:

- Deny al Qaeda a safe haven
- Reverse the Taliban's momentum and deny it the ability to overthrow Afghanistan's government
- Strengthen Afghanistan's security forces and government

MARC LYNCH, RHETORIC AND REALITY: COUNTERING TERRORISM IN THE AGE OF OBAMA

Center for a New American Security, June 2010[6]

President Barack Obama took office determined to fight terrorist networks such as al Qaeda more effectively by moving away from the most visible symbols and rhetorical framework of former President George W. Bush's "Global War on Terror." The Obama administration seeks to rebuild relations with the Muslim mainstream, marginalize violent extremists and deprive them of popular support, strike hard at terrorist networks and their havens and undermine extremist narratives by restoring American adherence to the rule of law. It seeks to move away from the distorting lens of terrorism in its dealings with the Muslim communities of the world and to define the threat as violent extremism instead of radical Islam.

Though there are significant differences between this strategy and that of the Bush administration in the first half decade after the 9/11 attacks, there is also substantial continuity with the policies and philosophies adopted by the Bush administration in its final two years. The Obama administration built on those efforts, taking advantage of the opportunities offered by a presidential transition and increasing efforts in a range of key areas: engagement, outreach and a rhetorical commitment to restoring the rule of law on the one hand, and

5. *Available at* http://www.cnn.com/2009/POLITICS/12/01/obama.afghanistan/index.html/.
6. *Available at* http://www.cnas.org/files/documents/publications/CNAS_Rhetoric%20and%20Reality_Lynch.pdf/.

on the other, escalated (though not publicly acknowledged) drone strikes and counterterrorism partnerships in the ungoverned spaces where al Qaeda and its affiliated movements thrived.

Despite some potentially serious internal contradictions, this strategy is appropriate and already shows signs of success. While the recent wave of plots against the American homeland demonstrates that al Qaeda and its affiliated movements retain the ability to carry out terrorist acts, these terrorist networks have also faced major setbacks in their bid to attract widespread support and become a mainstream mass movement. They are under growing pressure. The administration's strategy has put the challenges posed by al Qaeda and affiliated movements into proper perspective, both maintaining effective counterterrorism policies and making a major effort to engage with mainstream Muslim populations on issues that matter to them.

Yet success is not assured. Terrorist networks do not necessarily require mass support. Al Qaeda Central, though significantly degraded, continues to survive, operate as a propaganda machine and guide operations. Affiliated movements have taken root, especially in struggling states such as Yemen and Somalia but also in North Africa and beyond. Al Qaeda's narrative retains appeal to a small but committed radicalized base and continues to find outlets on the Internet and in distinct pockets on the margins of mainstream society. Attempted attacks continue to threaten the United States.

While the administration's policy has taken on clearer contours over the last year and a half, it is still easier to say what it is not rather than what it is. President Obama has not yet articulated an effective strategy to the American public. The administration must fill this void. If the strategy cannot be better articulated and a new approach institutionalized in a durable and robust set of institutional commitments and legal authorities, then there is a real risk that it will collapse in the face of challenges or setbacks. Now is the time for the Obama administration to lay out a clearly articulated strategic vision.

ISSUES TO CONSIDER

1. Are large-scale attacks effective?
2. Is individual-specific counterterrorism preferred to group-particular actions?
3. What is the fallout effect from operations such as Operation Enduring Freedom in the context of winning hearts and minds?
4. Does a policy such as OEF suggest actions inconsistent with the principles of a liberal democratic society as articulated by President Aharon Barak in Chapter 5? — pg 99

C. U.S. TARGETED KILLING

1. The Drone Policy

Though Executive Order 12333 forbids American intelligence organizations from assassinating foreign political leaders, the Bush administration actively engaged in drone attacks and the Obama administration has implemented a similar policy in Afghanistan, Pakistan, and Yemen against identified targets, primarily members of the Taliban and al Qaeda.

Following the attack on the USS *Cole* in Yemen on October 12, 2000, which resulted in the deaths of 17 American sailors, the United States conducted a targeted killing of those responsible for the attack. According to media reports, six members of al Qaeda were killed, including one American citizen.[7] When analyzing targeted killings it is important to note that, according to international law, acts of retaliation are illegal. A country may only perform targeted killings if there is reliable, corroborated intelligence information that the action will prevent a future terror attack. With respect to American drone attacks, media reports have never clearly indicated whether those killed intended to carry out additional attacks or if the targeted killing was solely a response to their role in the *Cole* bombing.

> KENNETH ANDERSON, TARGETED KILLING IN
> U.S. COUNTERTERRORISM STRATEGY AND LAW

Brookings Institute Working Paper, May 11, 2009[8]

It is a slight exaggeration to say that Barack Obama is the first president in American history to have run in part on a political platform of targeted killings — but not much of one. "The Bush administration has not acted aggressively enough to go after al Qaeda's leadership," he said. "I would be clear that if Pakistan cannot or will not take out al Qaeda leadership when we have actionable intelligence about their whereabouts, we will act to protect the American people. There can be no safe haven for al Qaeda terrorists who killed thousands of Americans and threaten our homeland today."

Obama did not take long, on assuming office, to begin keeping his promise. On January 23, 2009 a mere three days into his presidency, strikes by Predator drones in the tribal areas of Pakistan destroyed two compounds and killed numerous people, reportedly including a high-value target.4 Strikes continued, even expanded, over the successive months, and administration officials made clear that they had no plans to curtail them — even as they reined in coercive interrogations and announced the closure of Guantánamo Bay.

Obama was right as a candidate and is correct as president to insist on the propriety of targeted killings — that is, the targeting of a specific individual to be killed, increasingly often by means of high technology, remote-controlled

---

7. Doyle McManus, *A U.S. License to Kill; a New Policy Permits the C.I.A. to Assassinate Terrorists, and Officials Say a Yemen Hit Went Perfectly. Others Worry about Next Time*, L.A. Times, Jan. 11, 2003, at A1.

8. *Available at* http://www.brookings.edu/~/media/Files/rc/papers/2009/0511_counter terrorism_anderson/0511_counterterrorism_anderson.pdf/.

Predator drone aircraft wielding missiles from a stand-off position. The strategic logic that presses toward targeted stand-off killing as a necessary, available and technologically advancing part of counterterrorism is overpowering. So too is the moral and humanitarian logic behind its use. Just as crucial programs of Predator-centered targeted killing are underway now in Afghanistan and, with increasing international controversy, Pakistan, over the long term these programs of stand-off targeted killing will be an essential element in United States counterterrorism into the future — and with targets having little or nothing to do with today's iteration of the war on terror.

American domestic law — the law codifying the existence of the CIA and defining its functions — has long accepted implicitly at least some uses of force, including targeted killing, as self-defense toward ends of vital national security that do not necessarily fall within the strict terms of armed conflict in the sense meant by the Geneva Conventions and other international treaties on the conduct of armed conflict.

Targeted killing and the drone policy significantly differ from OEF: coalition air attacks in Afghanistan were intended to destroy the al Qaeda infrastructure while targeted killings and the drone policy reflect attempts to neutralize a specific terrorist identified as presenting a threat. Drone attacks — according to numerous reports — have resulted in significant collateral damage resulting from a combination of faulty intelligence, lack of clearly developed guidelines and criteria defining when the policy can be implemented, and an articulated desire to aggressively engage identified targets.

2. Effectiveness

Governments that fail to determine the effectiveness of a particular course of action will ultimately fail in developing a viable policy. The issue of how to measure effectiveness of a particular policy has been addressed by Edward H. Kaplan, Alex Mintz, Shaul Mishal, and Claudio Samban in an empirical study.[9] If effectiveness is measured as mere response, then any action is effective. However, if policies are intended to meet a well-defined goal, then effectiveness can be determined by analyzing whether the particular goal was achieved. Governments, however, are hesitant to articulate a clearly defined terrorist policy, preferring to address the issue in generalities and clichés.

ISSUES TO CONSIDER

1. Can liberal democracies implement policies that may be borderline legal?
2. Are deliberately murky goals and policies advantageous?

---

9. Edward H. Kaplan, *What Happened to Suicide Bombings in Israel? Insights from a Terror Stock Model*, 28 Studies in Conflict and Terrorism 225 (2005).

3. In developing operational counterterrorism, what is the distinction between a non-state actor and a state actor who provides safe haven to the non-state actor?
4. What are the limits of state power in the context of counterterrorism?
5. Is the twin policy approach adopted by the U.S. reflective of balance between national security and individual rights?
6. Is balancing relevant when taking the fight to the terrorists?

III. ISRAEL

A. INTRODUCTION

Various Israeli governments have tried different policies in response to Palestinian terrorism. In response to the outbreak of the Intifada (1987-1993), administrative detentions and house demolitions were widely used. Following a series of terrorist attacks carried out by Hamas in late 1992, 415 Palestinians were deported to Lebanon for two years. In response to suicide bombings (September 2000 and 2004), targeted killings were implemented and the security fence was constructed. Furthermore, in an effort to deter and prevent family members from providing assistance to those involved in significant terrorist activity, the policy of assigned residence was established and implemented for a limited time. The section below analyzes whether assigned residence respects lawful self-defense.

B. ASSIGNED RESIDENCE

Israel made the decision to implement an assigned residence policy when the intelligence community recognized that family members were actively participating in the terrorist activities of their siblings, spouses, and sons. Unlike deportation, which involves deporting an individual from the West Bank or the Gaza Strip to a foreign nation, assigned residence is the removal of an individual from one area to another area (in the cases to date, assignment was from the Gaza Strip to the West Bank).

The policy's goal was to weaken the base of support and assistance provided to terrorists by their family members. Previously, person-specific counterterrorism was largely, but not exclusively, directed against the particular terrorist (targeted killing, administrative detention, deportation, incarceration). In contrast, the assigned residence policy represented an administrative sanction directed at specific family members.

The High Court of Justice in *Ajuri v. IDF Commander in West Bank* articulated a two-part test regarding assigning residence. The criteria for implementing the policy were the "serious security threat presented by the individual to be assigned" and the significant assistance provided to the terrorist by that individual.[10]

---

10. HCJ 7019/02, Ajuri v. IDF Commander in West Bank [Isr.].

A particular family member would have his residence assigned if intelligence indicated that his sibling or other family member could not conduct terrorism without that individual's aid and person to be assigned presented a threat to state security separate from his family member. The possibility that an individual assigned from the West Bank would become dominant in Gaza-based terrorist groups was deemed unlikely, as the person assigned would lack a power base in the new location.

ISSUES TO CONSIDER

1. What is the "human cost" of assigning the residence of an individual?
2. How far can operational counterterrorism be taken?
3. Is the idea of separating family members a reasonable policy?
4. From the perspective of deterrence, is this a viable policy?
5. What is the effect on the assigned individual?
6. If this is deportation without being called deportation, is the policy a violation of international law?

The Israeli government announced the policy with great fanfare, declaring that it struck at the core of the terrorists' support network.

> One of the measures upon which the Ministerial Committee for National Security decided—all of which within the framework of the Attorney-General's opinion—was assigning the place of residence of family members of suicide bombers or the perpetrators of serious attacks and those sending them from Judaea and Samaria to the Gaza Strip, provided that these family members were themselves involved in the terrorist activity. This measure was adopted because, according to the evaluation of the professionals involved (the army, the General Security Service, the Institute for Intelligence and Special Tasks (the Mossad), and the police), these additional measures might make a significant contribution to the struggle against the wave of terror, resulting in the saving of human life. This contribution is two-fold: first, it can prevent a family member involved in terrorist activity from perpetrating his scheme (the preventative effect); second, it may deter other terrorists who are instructed to act as human bombs or to carry out other terror attacks from perpetrating their schemes (the deterrent effect).[11]

The government further argued that the policy was less harsh than deportation because the individual would still be residing in the territory of the Palestinian authority. After only 15 instances, however, the government stopped the policy as quickly as it was implemented. The policy was so short-lived that it would be empirically and intuitively impossible to discern any possible effect. Nevertheless, the underpinnings of the policy are highly relevant to a study of operational counterterrorism because it targets the terrorists' immediate support system. Even though the policy is no longer in place, it merits closer examination.

Was this by declare legal? Textual. or violations of Right?

---

11. Id.

C. AJURI v. IDF COMMANDER IN WEST BANK

The assigned residence policy, argued before the High Court of Justice, was initially implemented against three individuals: the brother and sister of a one terrorist and the sibling of a second.

Kipah Mahmad Ahmed Ajuri and Abed Amasser Mustafa Ahmed Asida,[12] and Amtassar Muhammed Ahmed Ajuri filed the petitions[13] after a Military Appeals Board upheld the military commander's order to assign the residence of all three. According to the Military Appeals Board, Kipah Ajuri acted as a lookout when terrorists moved explosives while his sister, Amtassar, sewed suicide belts. Abed Asida, according to the Appeals Board, provided his terrorist brother food and clothing, and drove him in his car without knowing of his activities. The petitioners argued that the West Bank and Gaza Strip are separate entities and therefore assigned residence is tantamount to deportation, a violation of Article 49 of the Fourth Geneva Convention.[14] The state based its argument regarding the policy's legality on Article 78 of the Fourth Geneva Convention, which enables an occupying power to assign the residence of an individual for imperative security reasons.

> **Article 78**
> If the Occupying Power considers it necessary, for imperative reasons of security, to take safety measures concerning protected persons, it may, at the most, subject them to assigned residence or to internment. Decisions regarding such assigned residence or internment shall be made according to a regular procedure to be prescribed by the Occupying Power in accordance with the provisions of the present Convention. This procedure shall include the right of appeal for the parties concerned. Appeals shall be decided with the least possible delay. In the event of the decision being upheld, it shall be subject to periodical review, if possible every six months, by a competent body set up by the said Power. Protected persons made subject to assigned residence and thus required to leave their homes shall enjoy the full benefit of Article 39 of the present Convention.[15]

The High Court of Justice reversed the decision with respect to Asida's petition holding that while the petitioner provided assistance to his brother, those actions alone did not satisfy the second part of the test because they did not endanger state security.

> With regard to the first level, it is accepted by all the parties before us — and this is also our opinion — that an essential condition for being able to assign the place of residence of a person under art. 78 of the Fourth Geneva Convention is that the person himself constitutes a danger, and that assigning his place of residence will aid in averting that danger. It follows that the basis for exercising

---

12. HCJ 7015/02, Asida v. IDF Commander in West Bank, IDF Commander in Gaza Strip and Bridget Kessler (Bridget Kessler's daughter was killed in a suicide bombing in Jerusalem. Mrs. Kessler asked and was granted permission by President Barak to address the court.)

13. *Id.*

14. Geneva Convention relative to the Protection of Civilian Persons in Time of War, Aug. 12, 1949, Art. 49, 75 U.N.T.S. 287.

15. Geneva Convention Relative to the Protection of Civilian Persons in Time of War, Aug. 12, 1949, Art. 78, 75 U.N.T.S. 287

the discretion for assigning residence is the consideration of preventing a danger presented by a person whose place of residence is being assigned. The place of residence of an innocent person who does not himself present a danger may not be assigned, merely because assigning his place of residence will deter others. Likewise, one may not assign the place of residence of a person who is not innocent and did carry out acts that harmed security, when in the circumstances of the case he no longer presents any danger. Therefore, if someone carried out terrorist acts, and assigning his residence will reduce the danger that he presents, it is possible to assign his place of residence. One may not assign the place of residence of an innocent family member who did not collaborate with anyone, or of a family member who is not innocent but does not present a danger to the area. This is the case even if assigning the place of residence of a family member may deter other terrorists from carrying out acts of terror. This conclusion is required by the outlook of the Fourth Geneva Convention that regards the measures of internment and assigned residence as the most severe and serious measures that an occupying power may adopt against protected residents.[16]

The commander is obligated to implement the assigned residence policy, with a balanced approach that reflects reasonableness and proportionality. Of the three petitioners, intelligence identified Amtassar Ajuri as the most dangerous. When implementing a counterterrorism strategy, the commander must decide not only which individual poses the greatest threat to state security, but also whether the High Court of Justice (in the context of judicial review) will uphold the decision. The severity of the threat posed by Amtassar Ajuri is clear from the Court's recounting of her activities:

> Amtassar Muhammed Ahmed Ajuri (an unmarried woman aged 34) is the sister of the terrorist Ahmed Ali Ajuri. Much terrorist activity is attributed to the brother, Ahmed Ali Ajuri, including sending suicide bombers with explosive belts, and responsibility, inter alia, for the terrorist attack at the Central Bus Station in Tel-Aviv in which five people were killed and many others were injured. The Appeals Board (chaired by Col. Gordon), in its decision of 12 August 2002, heldlding suicide bombers with explosive belts, — on the basis of privileged material presented to it and responsibility, inter alia, for the terrorist attack at the Central Buyon the basis of testimonies of members of the General Security Service that the petitioner directly and substantially aided the unlawful activity of her brother, which was intended to harm innocent citizens. The Board determined that there was more than a basis for the conclusion that the petitioner knew about the forbidden activity of her brother—including his being wanted by the Israeli security forces and that she knew that her brother was wounded when he was engaged in preparing explosives, and prima facie she also knew that her brother was armed and had hidden in the family apartment an assault rifle. It was also held that the petitioner aided her brother by sewing an explosive belt. The Board pointed out that, on the basis of privileged evidence, which it found "reliable and up-to-date," it transpired that the petitioner indeed aided her brother in his unlawful activity. It held that this was a case of "direct and material aid in the preparation of an explosive belt, and the grave significance and implications of this aid

---

16. *Ajuri, supra* note 10.

were without doubt clear and known [to the petitioner]." Admittedly, the petitioner testified before the Board that she was not involved in anything and did not aid her brother, but the Board rejected this testimony as unreliable. It pointed out that "we found her disingenuous and evasive story totally unreasonable throughout her testimony before us, and it was clear that she wished to distance herself in any way possible from the activity of her brother . . . her disingenuous story left us with a clear impression of someone who has something to hide and this impression combines with the clear and unambiguous information that arises from the privileged material about her involvement in preparing an explosive belt." For these reasons, the appeal of the petitioner to the Appeals Board was denied. It should also be pointed out that in the Respondent's reply in the proceeding before us — which was supported by an affidavit — it was stated that "the petitioner aided her brother in the terrorist activity and, inter alia, sewed for his purposes explosive belts" — explosive belts, and not merely one explosive belt.[17]

Issues to Consider

1. Is assigned residence a form of self-defense?
2. Is the distinction between deportation and assigned residence a fine line?
3. Is the sanction a significant contribution to the commanders' tool box?
4. Was the threat presented by the Ajuri siblings responded to a proportional manner?
5. Why did the High Court of Justice develop a two-part test in determining the policy's legality?
6. What is the appropriate, proportional relationship between a particular counterterrorism measure and severity of the offense?
7. What is the cost of declaring a policy and then quickly abandoning it?

D. TARGETED KILLING

Targeted killing reflects a deliberate decision to order the death of a particular terrorist. It is important to emphasize that an individual will be targeted only if he: (1) presents a serious threat to public order and safety based on criminal evidence or (2) reliable, corroborated intelligence clearly implicates him.[18] Intelligence information is corroborated when it is confirmed by at least two separate, unrelated sources. In addition, for a targeted killing to be lawful no reasonable alternative to eliminating the threat (such as detention) is operationally viable.

According to international law, it is imperative that every effort be made to ensure that collateral damage be limited to a minimum. Accordingly, when

---

17. *Id.*
18. Amos N. Guiora, *Targeted Killing as Active Self-Defense*, 36 Case W. Res. J. Int'l L. 319, 322 (2004).

military commanders plan a targeted killing, they must do their best to avoid injury and damage to innocent civilians.[19]

According to a report in the Jerusalem Post, the IDF has expanded "the list of criteria that need to be met before staging a targeted interception . . . the 'ticking bomb' now refers not only to those on their way to an attack, but those planning and training for one."[20] In September 2004, an Israel Air Force helicopter attacked terrorists training at a terrorist base in Syria. Though the attack was not aimed at a specific terrorist engaged either in planning or executing a specific attack, the raid can be considered an expansion of the targeted killing policy. The attack on the training base, which followed a double suicide bombing in Beer Sheba (a city in southern Israel), was aimed at terrorists in training, without specific knowledge regarding their particular intentions.

1. Israel's Legal Arguments for Targeted Killing

Israel's targeted killing policy was articulated in its response to a petition against the practice filed with the Israel Supreme Court sitting as the High Court of Justice. In *Public Committee Against Torture, Committee for Clean Environment and Human Rights v. The State of Israel*,[21] the state argued that the petition should be denied for the following reasons: (1) The present conflict between Israel and Palestinian terror organizations is defined as "armed conflict short of war";[22] (2) According to the law of armed conflict, terrorists taking part in attacks against civilian or public targets are illegal combatants, not civilians, and are therefore legitimate targets. "Acts of terrorism against a country by non-state sponsored organizations or individuals need to be considered more than just criminal acts. Instead, they should be considered acts of war against the victim nation."[23] In *Israel v. Marwan Barghouti*, the Tel Aviv district court ruled that "terrorists who attack civilians are not 'lawful combatants' entitled to POW status in light of their unlawful activities. . . . Unlawful

---

19. Protocol Additional to the Geneva Conventions of Aug. 12, 1949, and Relating to the Protection of Victims of International Armed Conflicts, June 8, 1977, 1125 U.N.T.S. 3, art. 57.

20. Arieh O'Sullivan, *The Army Redefines the "Ticking Bomb,"* The Jerusalem Post, Sept. 13, 2004, at 2.

21. The opinion, written by just-retired President Aharon Barak, articulates the limits of operational counterterrorism by holding that the targeted killing of known terrorists is legal if done in accordance with international law. This means that the decision and order for a terrorist's targeted killing must be rooted in the principles of proportionality, collateral damage and alternatives. The decision, the last in Barak's corpus of rulings on fighting terrorism, is the final piece in a puzzle of judicially mandated rules for how an army should conduct operational counterterrorism. Rather than engaging in broad, academic discourse, the ruling establishes clear criteria; a checklist of how the state is to make operational considerations. Harming civilians that "take direct part in hostilities," as defined in the decision, "even if the result is death, is permitted, on the condition that there is no other means which harms them less, and on the condition that innocent civilians nearby are not harmed. Harm to the latter must be proportional. That proportionality is determined according to a values-based test, intended to balance between the military advantage and the civilian damage." HCJ 769/02, Public Committee Against Torture v. The State of Israel.

22. *Id.* (This characterization had been previously accepted and adopted by the Supreme Court in a number of decisions.)

23. Frank A. Biggio, *Neutralizing the Threat: Reconsidering Existing Doctrines in the Emerging War on Terrorism*, 34 Case W. Res. J. Int'l L. 1, 4 (2002).

combatants who attack civilians are not entitled to this status." (3) The principle of proportionality must be respected when implementing targeted killing. (4) Targeted killing is used only when the targeted terrorist cannot be arrested using reasonable means and must be in accordance with international principles requiring exhaustion of all reasonable alternatives.

The state also argued that legal scholars who examined the *jus ad bellum* dimensions of terrorism would agree on at least four principles: (1) If it (a state) has suffered an armed attack by terrorist actors, a state is entitled to defend itself forcibly; (2) A victim state's forcible self-defense measures should be timely; (3) A victim state's forcible self-defense measures should be proportionate; (4) A victim state's forcible self-defense measures should be discriminate and taken against targets responsible in some way for the armed attack.

2. Who Are Legitimate Targets?

Determining whether suicide bombers and others involved in terrorist infrastructure are legitimate targets, despite the fact that they are not "soldiers" in the traditional sense of the word, is essential to analyzing whether operation counterterrorism is lawful. Presently, terrorists who take a direct role are viewed as combatants (albeit illegal combatants not entitled, inter alia, to POW status) and therefore legitimate targets. Furthermore, a legitimate target is not limited to the potential suicide bomber who, according to corroborated and reliable intelligence, is on his way to carrying out a suicide bombing. Rather, a legitimate target is identified as any Palestinian who plays a significant role in the suicide bomber infrastructure — that is, "doers" who execute attacks, and "senders" who orchestrate them; in addition, both those responsible for the logistics of an attack and those financing terrorist attacks are increasingly considered legitimate targets though the question of "when" remains unresolved.

ISSUES TO CONSIDER

1. In determining counterterrorism policy, what weight should the state give to the possibility of collateral damage?
2. Should the possibility that innocent civilians will be killed prevent the state from implementing a particular aggressive policy?
3. What should be the chain of command for implementing a targeted killing, and what should be the test for determining necessity?
4. What criteria/guidelines should be established before implementing the policy of targeted killing?
5. Does the principle that combatants die on the battlefield apply also to terrorists killed in a targeted killing?

3. Policy Concerns

To examine counterterrorism is not only to argue the law (particularly in an area considered "gray" by most international law experts), but also to analyze the decision-making process. Accordingly, determining effectiveness of the targeted killing policy is essential.

Israel considers its policy effective for the following reasons: (1) terrorists understand that Israel has been able to penetrate informants into small cells; (2) terrorists have had to change their living and sleeping habits on a regular basis; (3) a significant number of terrorists have been killed.

At the same time, Israel's policy of targeted killings has been highly criticized. Professor Michael Scharf suggests four arguments why the targeted killings may be legal, though the policy "may still be misguided":[24] (1) instances of collateral damage; (2) instances of mistaken identity; (3) cascading threats to the world order; (4) strengthening enemy morale via martyrdom.[25]

ISSUES TO CONSIDER

1. If effectiveness is an elusive term, is arguing "self-defense" sufficient to justify the killing of an individual suspected of involvement in a future terrorist act?
2. In deciding to order the killing of an individual suspected of involvement in a future terrorist act, what criteria should be used for determining operational success?
3. What criteria should be applied in determining when to perform a targeted killing?
4. What is the significance of "freezing" and then "unfreezing" a particular policy?
5. What process is appropriate for the decision to perform a targeted killing and what should be considered before authorizing a specific action?

IV. RUSSIA

A. INTRODUCTION

Russia's operational counterterrorism methods adopted in response to Chechen terrorism are best described as unapologetically hardline. In an interview, Col. Victor Koshelev, Deputy Commander of the Provisional Group of Ministry of Interior Units in the North Caucasus and Chief of the Criminal Militia Service, clearly stated the policy of killing terrorists:

> ... the operation [was] aimed at elimination of wahhabi leader Yunadi Turchaev, who operated in the Chechen capital and in West Chechnya. This time it was the 2nd Kadyrov patrol unit of the Chechen Ministry of the Interior that did a good job. ... Turchaev was a veteran terrorist that hunted security services' staff.[26]

---

24. Michael P. Scharf, *In the Cross Hairs of a Scary Idea*, Wash. Post, Apr. 25, 2004, at B1.
25. *Id.*
26. *Deputy Commander of the Provisional Group of MOI Unites in the North Caucasus and Chief of its Criminal Militia Service Militia Colonel Victor Koshelev Answers Shchit I Mech's Questions*, Ministry of the Interior of Russia, *available at* http://eng.mvdrf.ru/index.php?docid=333 (last visited Oct. 8, 2010).

The U.S. approach to terrorism has been previously described as two-tiered: specific (drone attacks) and general (Operation Enduring Freedom) largely unrestrained by judicial review. The Israeli approach has been marked by tough measures with an understanding that judicial activism acts as a restraint on the executive branch's efforts to develop and implement operational counterterrorism methods. Russia's approach is more reflective of America's, though far less restrained.

B. CHECHEN TERRORISM

Former President Putin's comments, in the aftermath of the Beslan terrorist attack, that Russia "claims its right to carry out pre-emptive military strikes against 'terrorists' 'anywhere in the world' "[27] are a clear articulation of Russia's policy. Col. Koshelev's comments regarding "elimination"[28] leave little doubt as to how President Putin's policy was to be implemented.

ROMAN KUPCHINSKY, ANALYTICAL REPORT

Radio Free Europe/Radio Liberty, Vol. 4, No. 17, Sept. 16, 2004

Terrorism in Russia took on horrifying proportions in August and early September when more than 400 people were killed in four separate incidents in a span of less than two weeks.

The first in the series of terrorist attacks came on 24 August, when two airliners were downed simultaneously hundreds of kilometers apart after flying out of the same Moscow airport.

As Russia was still reeling from the twin attacks that killed 90 passengers, a suicide bomber detonated herself on 31 August outside the entrance to a Moscow subway station, killing 10 and injuring about 50.

Credit for the three attacks—the first two coming in the run-up to presidential elections in Chechnya, and the third just two days after pro-Moscow candidate Alu Alkhanov won the 29 August poll—was taken by a virtually unknown group claiming ties to al Qaeda and calling itself the Islambuli Brigades.

In a message posted on the Internet taking credit for the subway attack, the obscure group stated: "This heroic operation, as we have warned you, is an extension of a wave of support and assistance to the Chechen Muslims. . . .

. . . "The targeting of Russia is only the beginning of a fierce and bloody war in the face of those who have devoted themselves to the eradication of Islam and the murder of its faithful," the message continued. "And this war will serve to dissuade the criminals in the Russian government from killing Muslims and violating the honor of the Muslims in Chechnya, and the rest of the Muslim countries in the region."

---

27. Roberto Fabbri, *Il Giornale*, Sept. 9, 2004, *available at* http://www.globalsecurity.org/wmd/library/news/russia/2004/wwwh40910.htm (last visited Oct. 16, 2006); *see also Russia Offers Reward for Information on Rebels*, MSNBC, Sept. 8, 2004, *available at* http://www.msnbc.msn.com/id/5881958/ (last visited Oct. 16, 2006).

28. *See* Ministry of the Interior of Russia, *supra* note 26.

The attacks and the Islambuli Brigades' messages immediately led many to conclude that if the authenticity of the group's claimed connections and deeds panned out, it could only serve as evidence to prove an argument that Russia has been making for years.

"If one of the terrorist organizations has claimed responsibility for this and it is linked to al Qaeda, that is a fact that confirms the link between certain forces operating on the territory of Chechnya and international terrorism," Putin said condemning the airline bombings.

But just as the Russian government prepared for the next phase of what Defense Minister Sergei Ivanov called "a war where the enemy is invisible and there are no front lines," the fourth and most gruesome of the spate of attacks took place.

The three-day hostage crisis in Beslan, North Ossetia, began when 32 militants stormed a secondary school on 1 September, a day when the school would be filled with students, parents, and teachers assembling for the first day of classes.

The siege would culminate in a bloody and fiery end that would cost the lives of 336 people, including 150 children, prompting President Vladimir Putin to tell the nation on 4 September: "We are dealing with direct intervention of international terrorism against Russia, with a total, cruel and full-scale war in which our compatriots die again and again."

MARSHA LIPMAN, HOW RUSSIA NOURISHES RADICAL ISLAM

Wash. Post, Apr. 5, 2010[29]

... But while the challenge of terrorism cries for long-term, consistent strategy, Russia's system of heavy-handed and unaccountable governance precludes strategic thinking.

In the early 1990s, after the collapse of the Soviet Union, Boris Yeltsin's government responded to armed secessionists in Chechnya by waging a full-scale war. Russia's armed forces were undertrained and undersupplied; horrific atrocities ensued on both sides. The 1996 peace agreement was evidence of Russia's humiliating weakness: A former superpower failed to subdue its own tiny region.

"Peace" in Chechnya entailed frequent kidnappings for ransom, hostage-taking and terrorist attacks. In 1999, a Chechen force invaded the neighboring province of Dagestan, about the same time explosions of apartment buildings in three Russian cities famously took the lives of roughly 300 people.

When Vladimir Putin became president in 2000, his solution was a new war. With it came more atrocities, deeper brutalization and, in Russia at large, growing xenophobia against "those from the Caucasus." This time federal forces defeated the Chechen fighters, but terrorist attacks continued through 2004. The most horrific of these was the seizure of Beslan school where more than 330 hostages, over half of them children, were killed that September.

---

29. *Available   at*   http://www.washingtonpost.com/wp-dyn/content/article/2010/04/04/AR2010040402723.html/.

By the mid-2000s, secession was no longer the issue in Chechnya, but a new problem was building: Militant Islam was on the rise all over the North Caucasus. In the early '90s Islam had still been weak in this traditionally Muslim territory; adults had secular Soviet educations, and the attraction of Russian culture was still strong. But the new generation growing up in the Chechnya devastated by the Russian army, and in neighboring provinces such as Dagestan and Ingushetia, were increasingly influenced by Islamic culture and Islam, not infrequently its radical strains. Clandestine extremist groups called for jihad across the territory of Russia. Training centers for suicide bombers reportedly operate in the North Caucasus.

The Kremlin shifted tactics a few years ago, installing pro-Moscow leaders in these Muslim provinces and reducing the federal government's mission to allocating funds and occasional anti-terrorist operations. It turned a blind eye to subversive attacks, explosions, and assassinations of area police and local administrators, which have become routine in Ingushetia and Dagestan. The central government also ignored the brutal practices local leaders used against Islamic radicals and other criminal or extremist groups. As long as violence was contained within the North Caucasus, the thinking went, the bulk of Russia remained relatively safe. But last week's attacks underscore just how flawed and shortsighted this policy is.

Strains of official rhetoric echo the language of 1999: After the infamous blasts of Moscow apartment buildings, Putin pledged to wipe out terrorists in outhouses. Now he vows "to drag them out of the sewer and into broad daylight." But large-scale use of force is not an option. As happened in the '90s, it is bound to start another vicious circle of punitive measures and extremists' efforts to exact revenge.

Reasonable calls have also been heard. President Dmitry Medvedev spoke last week about the need to create in the North Caucasus "the right kind of modern environment for education, for doing business, for overcoming cronyism . . . and, of course, for confronting corruption." But corruption plagues more than the North Caucasus; it's the texture of the Russian system of governance, which is built on political monopoly and unaccountability. Unless Russia makes systemic reforms, good intentions will not translate into stronger policies.

Issues to Consider

1. Does an aggressive policy characterized by "elimination" suggest a no-holds-barred approach?
2. Does Chechen terrorism justify such an approach?
3. In developing and implementing aggressive operational counterterrorism, does Russia run the risk of antagonizing Chechens who otherwise would not be sympathetic to the terrorists' cause?
4. Does an aggressive policy contribute to the internationalization of terrorism by galvanizing radical Islam to the Chechen cause?
5. What are the long-term costs of an overtly aggressive operational counterterrorism policy?

6. How should we determine the effectiveness of Russia's policy?
7. To be effective does operational counterterrorism necessarily imply human rights violations?

C. POLICY

According to Human Rights Watch, civilian casualties in Chechnya are "attributable to indiscriminate use of force by the federal armed forces . . . in February, 2000 Russian forces executed at least 60 civilians in Aldi and Chernorechiye, suburbs of Groznyy. The perpetrators reportedly raped some of the victims, extorted money, and later set many of the houses on fire to destroy evidence."[30] The 2009 U.S. State Department Report repeatedly states that indiscriminate use of force by government troops in the conflict in the Chechen Republic has resulted in widespread civilian casualties and the displacement of hundreds of thousands of persons.[31]

In addition to allegations of indiscriminate use of force, the Russian military has also been accused in the "disappearances" of many Chechens. In July 2006, the European Court of Human Rights held the Russian Federation responsible for several violations of the European Convention for the Protection of Human rights and Fundamental Freedoms in the disappearance of Khadzhi-Murat Yandiyev, a Chechen civilian.[32]

How are these aggressive tactics actually implemented? By example, Russia's FSB security service has stepped up the pressure on the country's most wanted man (Shamil Basayev) by announcing a $10 million reward for information leading to his "neutralization." A similar reward was offered for former Chechen president Aslan Maskhadov. Both men were eventually killed, although the facts and circumstances surrounding Baseyev's death, including who perpetrated it, remain clouded.[33] This is not the first time that Russia has killed a Chechen leader. Chechnya's first post-Soviet president, Dudayev, was killed by Russian forces in 1996 and his successor, Yandarbiev, died in a car bombing conducted by Russian intelligence.

---

30. *Russia: Country Reports on Human Rights Practices, 2001*, released by the Bureau of Democracy, Human Rights, and Labor, Mar. 4, 2002, *available at* http://www.state.gov/g/drl/rls/hrrpt/2001/eur/8331.htm (last visited Oct. 8, 2010).

31. *Id.*

32. *Russian Federation: First Ruling of the European Court of Human Rights against "Disappearances" in Chechnya*, July 26, 2006, Amnesty International Press Release, available at http://web.amnesty.org/library/Index/ENGEUR460342006?open&of=ENG-RUS (last visited July 21, 2010).

33. *Chechen Rebel Leader Killed*, CNN.COM, Mar. 8, 2005, *available at* http://www.cnn.com/2005/WORLD/europe/03/08/chechnya.rebel.killed/index.html (last visited July 20, 2010). The Russian government also lived up to its promise of $10 million for information leading to Maskhadov's death. *Russia "Paid $10m for Maskhadov,"* CNN.COM, Mar. 15, 2005, *available at* http://www.cnn.com/2005/WORLD/europe/03/15/maskhadov/index.html (last visited July 20, 2010).

D. EFFECTIVENESS AND LEGALITY

The Russian government openly announced its intention to eliminate any individual defined as "public enemy #1." It is unclear whether aggressive operational counterterrorism has deterred Chechen terrorists from carrying out additional terrorist acts. In the aftermath of Maskhadov's killing in March 2005, only two major terrorist attacks occurred in 2005. Nevertheless, in 2009 and 2010 Chechen-based terrorist attacks began to resurface. The decline in terrorist activity between 2005 and 2009 may have been due to Russia's aggressive counterterrorism policies or it may have been a reflection of a tactical decision made by the terrorist organizations.

Regarding the legality of the policy, the same argument Israel makes to defend targeted killing is applicable. Russia argues that aggressive operational counterterrorism has been developed and implemented *in response* to Chechen terrorism, an argument predicated on aggressive self-defense. To meet international law standards, Russian self-defense must be a proportional response; it must be based on reliable, corroborated intelligence; a viable, operational alternative must be lacking; and collateral damage must be minimal. Operational counterterrorism that does not meet this four-part criterion lends itself—wittingly or unwittingly—to accusations that Russian troops in Chechnya are committing human rights violations.

The fine line between aggressive—though arguably legal—operational counterterrorism and death squads separates liberal democratic societies from totalitarian regimes. In a managed democracy such as Russia, "law serves the state and ensures that governors can claim the consent of the governed."[34] The difference between a liberal democracy and a managed democracy is fine; the difference between a managed democracy and a totalitarian regime is very thin. An uncontrolled or overly aggressive policy of elimination is nothing but an indicator of having crossed the line.

ISSUES TO CONSIDER

1. By targeting Chechen leaders, is Russia implementing a policy fundamentally different from the American bombing of Afghanistan?
2. Is a two-tiered counterterrorism policy—attacking *generally* (the bombing of Afghanistan) and *specifically* (targeting specific individuals)—as utilized by the U.S. and Russia more effective than Israel's *target specific* policy?
3. Does the two-tiered approach meet international law standards with respect to minimizing collateral damage, seeking alternatives, assuring proportionality, and attacking only when military necessity dictates?
4. What are the risks in the policy advocated and pursued by Russia?
5. Does Russian operational counterterrorism preclude the meeting of the four-part international law test outlined above?

---

34. *Russia's Week: News and Analysis from Russia and the Former Soviet States*, CDI Russia Weekly #197, Jamestown Foundation, March 13, 2002, Vol. VII, Issue 10, *available at* http://www.cdi.org/russia/197-11.cfm (last visited July 20, 2010).

V. INDIA

A. INTRODUCTION

India's development of an operational counterterrorism policy is more complicated than threats faced by the other surveyed nations. In the aftermath of 9/11, the United States is principally focused on Islamic terrorism; Israel's counterterrorism efforts are almost exclusively directed at Palestinian terrorism; Russia is primarily concerned with Chechnya; Spain in the aftermath of the Madrid train station bombing is primarily concerned with al Qaeda and its local progeny; China is primarily concerned with a Uyghur threat that must be quashed to deter possible separatist ambitions among other ethnic groups; and Colombia faces several complicated, yet distinct from India's, internal threats. The Indian government must navigate three distinct threats: domestic religious tensions involving Hindus, Sikhs, and Muslims; Kashmiri-based terrorism with Pakistani backing; and an external threat posed by Pakistan with whom India has gone to war three times in the past 50 years. It was not by chance that former U.S. President Bill Clinton argued that South Asia is "perhaps the most dangerous place in the world today."[35]

India's operational counterterrorism methods must take into consideration a number of geopolitical realities in the post-9/11 world: (1) America views Pakistan as a lynchpin in the effort to track down bin Laden and other al Qaeda operatives; (2) India is increasingly a major player in the high-tech field; (3) the importance India places on truly being a member of the global village, implying that power has its limits.

B. TERROR THREATS FACED

While historically the principal terrorist threat faced by India is based in Kashmir, major terrorist attacks have occurred primarily—but not exclusively—in Mumbai. Nevertheless, the primary focus of the Indian military in developing and implementing an operational counterterrorism strategy is predicated on responding to events in Kashmir. What is important to note, as has been previously discussed, is that Kashmiri terrorism is not local or indigenous based; rather, according to most reports, Kashmiri terrorists are supported by Pakistan and interlinked with Islamic radical terrorism.

INDIA COMBATS COMPLEX WEB OF PAKISTANI-SUPPORTED TERROR CELLS

The Jewish Institute for National Security Affairs, Oct. 3, 2003[36]

Islamic terrorism in the disputed Kashmir and Jammu regions has been steadily rising in the past few months. In March 2003, 24 Hindus in Kashmir were massacred, including 11 women and two children. In the same month, a

---

35. Terence Hunt, *Security Fears Force Change in Clinton Bangladesh Visit*, Cleveland Plain Dealer, Mar. 20, 2000, at 4A.

36. *Available at* www.jinsa.org.

terrorist attack in Udhampur, a city in the disputed region in northern India, killed 11 policemen and wounded 30. On September 5, 2003, militants shot and killed pro-India politician Mohammad Ismail in Kashmir. Currently, about two dozen armed militant groups claim to be operating inside Indian-administered Kashmir. Most of the groups are part of an alliance known as the United Jihad Council (UJC), which is headquartered in Pakistan-administered Kashmir. Many of the militants were trained in al Qaeda camps in Afghanistan and madrasas, or Muslim seminaries, alongside al Qaeda and Taliban fighters.

There are three main terrorist groups operating in Kashmir: Harakat ul-Mujahedeen, Lashkar-e-Taiba, and Jaish-e-Muhammad. Harakat ul-Mujahedeen, or "Islamic Freedom Fighters' Group," was established in the mid 1980s and was first based in Pakistan. It moved its base to Afghanistan in the 1990s, and today it has as many as several thousand armed militants in Pakistan and Kashmir. The group has also carried out terrorist activities in Burma, Tajikistan, and Bosnia. Lashkar-e-Taiba, or "Army of the Pure," was founded in 1993 and is the military wing of the well-funded Pakistani Islamist organization Markaz-ad-Dawa-wal-Irshad, which recruited volunteers to fight alongside the Taliban. Jaish-e-Muhammad, or "Army of Muhammad," was established in 2000 by a Pakistani cleric named Maulana Masood Azhar. Today, Jaish's membership is estimated at around a few hundred.

Kashmir is no longer the sole operating area target of Islamic separatist terrorists. On August 25, two coordinated bomb blasts killed 52 people and injured another 148 in Mumbai, India's financial capital formerly known as Bombay. Since that day, there have been at least three more incidents involving terrorists and Indian police forces, resulting in over ten people dead.

In the past five years, more than 250 terrorist cells have been discovered and disrupted in India outside Kashmir and Jammu. Hundreds of terrorists are arrested and thousands of kilograms of explosives are seized each year, reported Ajai Sahni, executive director of the New Delhi-based Institute for Conflict Management. In addition, Sahni noted in his article, "A Tide of Terror," which appeared in Outlook India, Sept. 1, 2003, that General Hamid Gul, former Director General of Pakistan's Inter-Services Intelligence (ISI), recently boasted, in private conversations, that this agency had established at least another 300 operational cells across India. Gul also reportedly said that these cells could be activated at any time and had been given the responsibility of recruiting locals sympathetic to the cause.

BRUCE REIDEL, TERRORISM IN INDIA AND THE GLOBAL JIHAD

The Brookings Institution, Nov. 30, 2008[37]

The attacks on multiple targets in downtown Mumbai in late November 2008 is only the latest in a long series of horrific terrorist operations in India. Terrorism in India is a complex phenomenon with numerous perpetrators. The most dangerous terrorist menace comes from groups with intimate

---

37. *Available at* http://www.brookings.edu/articles/2008/1130_india_terrorism_riedel.aspx/.

connections to the global jihadist network centered around Usama bin Laden and al Qaeda and its allies in the Pakistani jihadist culture. While it is too soon to draw firm conclusions about responsibility for the attacks in Mumbai in November 2008, the odds are good that the terrorists and the masterminds behind their plot are connected into the global jihad.

. . . [T]he most dangerous terror menace comes from Kashmiri groups based in Pakistan with long and intimate connections to al Qaeda and bin Laden. The group which has been linked by initial Indian assessments of the Mumbai attack, Lashkar-e Tayiba (literally the army of the pure or righteous), was founded in Afghanistan and Pakistan in the late 1980s and early 1990s by a group of Kashmiri activists with the assistance of the Pakistani intelligence service, the Inter Services Intelligence Directorate or ISI. Usama bin Laden was an early supporter of the group and provided some of the initial funding for its start. The ISI was an enthusiastic supporter of the Kashmiri insurgency and wanted to use asymmetric warfare, i.e. terrorism to undermine Indian control of Kashmir.

The Mumbai attacks displayed a level of sophisticated planning that marks another milestone in the global jihad. Multiple targets within an urban environment, trained and armed killers intent on operating in small teams or alone targeting Americans, Brits, Israelis as well as Indians, careful casing of the targets ahead of the attack and the use of small boats to get close in to the targets are signs of the continuing evolution of terrorist planners. Hotels have long been a favorite target of al Qaeda and its allies from the multiple hotel bombings in Amman by Al Qaeda's Iraq franchise in November 2005 to the attack on the Serena Hotel in Kabul this January and the bombing of the Marriott hotel in Islamabad in September.

ISSUES TO CONSIDER

1. When facing multiple threats, is it possible to develop a counterterrorism strategy that balances rights without violating domestic laws?
2. Should India's counterterrorism methods be restricted to the person-specific approach adopted by Israel or the two-tiered policy adopted by the U.S. and Russia?
3. Are the limits on individual freedom that India's legislation imposes an adequate substitute for operational counterterrorism?
4. In weighing options and their effectiveness, is an aggressive, operational policy (U.S., Russia) more effective than a legislative policy (India)?
5. What is the operational significance of legislation that imposes limits on individual liberty?
6. Given India's geopolitical reality, is operational counterterrorism as exercised by the U.S., Israel, and Russia a viable option?
7. What is the flexibility (or lack of) in developing a counterterrorism policy when a bordering sovereign nation supports a particular terrorist group?
8. What military options does India have given that Pakistan supports Kashmir terror while proclaiming to be America's ally?

C. THE DILEMMA

Eben Kaplan & Jayshree Bajoria, Counterterrorism in India

Council on Foreign Relations, Nov. 27, 2008[38]

. . . Experts say the government's response to terrorist attacks have been episodic; soon after an attack the government appears to take short-term measures. "India lacks a coherent strategic response to terrorism; there is no doctrine (BusinessWeek), and most of our responses are kneejerk," says retired Major General Sheru Thapliyal, who works at the Center for Land Warfare Studies in New Delhi.

Indian security officials usually focus their investigations on the country's Muslim minority following such attacks. India is home to 150 million Muslims, the second largest Muslim population in the world. But a large percentage of them feel disadvantaged and discriminated against by the government and the security forces. . . .

India's counterterrorism measures have often been the subject of appeals by human rights organizations. Deol says Indian officials have a higher tolerance for collateral damage than counterterrorism authorities in many other nations. In an example of such tactics, he says, "Agencies and arms of the state have been accused of turning a blind eye in order to run rival gangs that would be tasked with killing other insurgents, but would also kill innocent people." . . .

Issues to Consider

1. Do the human rights abuses alluded to above reflect a policy or frustration felt by the military and security services whose freedom of action is limited by India's geopolitical realities?
2. What significance should be attached to a counter-infiltration policy rather than counterterrorism operations?
3. If the U.S., Israel, and Russia have clearly articulated operational counterterrorism policies, how would India's policy be defined?
4. If India were to attack terror camps inside Pakistan, would that be akin to the U.S.'s targeted killing in Pakistan? Or would it be construed as a violation of Pakistani sovereignty and therefore an act of war?
5. For India to conduct truly effective operational counterterrorism, is attacking targets inside Pakistan a requirement?
6. If the overwhelming threat India faces is Pakistani-driven, then what internal measures—other than legislation—can India develop?

---

38. *Available at* http://www.cfr.org/publication/11170/counterterrorism_in_india.html.

VI. SPAIN

A. INTRODUCTION

The Spanish government has neither developed nor implemented policy similar to the other surveyed nations. While true that in the aftermath of the Madrid train bombings, eight al Qaeda operatives were killed by Spanish forces and others were arrested, the response to the bombing was limited from an operational perspective.

The initial response was the decision by the newly elected Socialist Government of Jose Luis Rodriguez Zapatero to withdraw Spanish forces from Iraq in spite of strong American opposition to the decision. The decision, which according to many American commentators was capitulatory,[39] seemingly reflected a victory for the terrorist.

ISSUES TO CONSIDER

1. Does the fact that Spain has not been the target of an act of Islamic-based terrorist attack since the train station bombings suggest that the decision to withdraw from Iraq was effective?
2. Though Prime Minister Zapatero had promised the electorate during the campaign to withdraw from Iraq, should the bombings have outweighed the promise?
3. After a reported attempt to assassinate the first President Bush, then President Clinton ordered the nighttime bombing of the Iraqi Intelligence headquarters, an act heavily criticized for being too tepid. What is more effective: a response that causes minimal injury and damage to property, or a conscious decision not to engage terrorists in operational counterterrorism?
4. President Reagan ordered the "strategic re-deployment" of American marines from Lebanon in the aftermath of an attack on barracks that killed 243 marines. According to some students of terrorism, this is a watershed event because terrorists concluded that the United States was a "paper tiger." Could the Spanish decision have a similar long-term effect?

B. COUNTERTERRORISM POLICIES COMPARED

The second response to the bombing was the attempted arrest of suspected al Qaeda terrorists. Nevertheless, unlike the other surveyed nations that actively,

---

39. Leslie Crawford, *Baptism of Ire*, Financial Times Weekend Magazine, July 17, 2004; Marlise Simons, *Spain's New Premier Orders Pullout in Iraq*, Chi. Trib., Apr. 19, 2004. *See Iraq: Spanish Troop Withdrawal a "Blow" to Coalition*, GlobalSecurity.org, Apr. 23, 2004, *available at* http://www.globalsecurity.org/wmd/library/news/iraq/2004/04/wwwh40423.htm (last visited July 21, 2010).

if not aggressively, seek to engage or eliminate terrorists, the Spanish operational counterterrorism policy appears to be predicated on non-engagement. Jonathon Schell's article below discusses the difference between the American and Spanish responses to attacks on their respective soil:

> From the start, the countries' responses differed. In Spain, the attack upon civilians in four Madrid railway stations—killing 191 and wounding some 2,000 people—prompted immediate, huge public demonstrations. Viewed from the United States, where no such response occurred after 9/11, the response at first seemed puzzling: Why demonstrations? Did Spaniards imagine that marches with placards would reach the hearts of people who carry out massacres? On second thought, the logic of the act became apparent: Terrorism is an attack upon civilians, not soldiers; it is meant to strike fear into other civilians. It made sense, then, for civilians, not soldiers, to respond with a clear message: We are not intimidated. Since intimidation is the purpose, the demonstration scored an immediate victory over terrorism. At a stroke, it removed the point of the attack.
>
> Meanwhile, Spanish authorities have been relentless in pursuit of the terrorists. Seventy-nine people are under active suspicion, and of these, 24 are in jail. A Pakistani cell has allegedly been broken up. The Spanish police had also been busy arresting other terrorist suspects—57 are now in prison, awaiting charges—and, according to the police, foiling other possible attacks.
>
> All of this, of course, has differed greatly from the US reaction to 9/11. In the United States, no nationwide public demonstrations occurred; the government took the lead. And it went to war, first in Afghanistan, then in Iraq. The president not only launched the two wars, but set forth a rationale for others. Identifying an "axis of evil" of three governments—Iraq, Iran, and North Korea—that supported terrorists and sought weapons of mass destruction, President Bush has, so far, overthrown only the first of the three.[40]

In analyzing counterterrorism methods developed and implemented by the surveyed nations, Spain clearly stands at an extreme end of the spectrum. The Spanish response has been limited to arrests, an action more reflective of a traditional criminal law paradigm rather than a military or counterterrorist paradigm.

C. CRIMINAL LAW PARADIGM

The following excerpt from a Washington Post report highlights the effect of implementing a criminal law paradigm instead of an operational counterterrorism approach:

> In Madrid, Spanish police arrested more than two dozen people for playing a role in the March 11, 2004, commuter-train explosions that killed 191 people and wounded more than 1,800. Seven other suspects were killed a few weeks later after police surrounded them in a suburb of the capital. Many of those

---

40. Jonathan Schell, *The Atlantic Divide over Fighting Terrorism*, Yale Global, Mar. 16, 2005, *available at* http://yaleglobal.yale.edu/content/atlantic-divide-over-fighting-terrorism (last visited July 14, 2010).

detained were Moroccan immigrants who had lived in Madrid for several years and had records for petty crime, but were not veterans of al Qaeda training camps or considered terrorist threats.

Since then, Spanish investigators have identified two al Qaeda veterans who they think may have helped orchestrate the bombings but whose exact roles remain a mystery. One of them, Amer Azizi, is a Moroccan national who provided military training at camps in Afghanistan and who is also a suspect in the May 16, 2003, suicide bombings in Casablanca, according to Spanish court records.

Another is Mustafa Setmarian Nasar, a native of Syria with Spanish citizenship who is a leading ideologue in radical Islamic circles. The U.S. Justice Department has posted a $5 million reward for Nasar's capture, accusing him of training extremists to concoct chemical weapons.[41]

ISSUES TO CONSIDER

1. Is capitulation in the face of terrorism a valid domestic policy in the present age?
2. Are there long-term policy benefits to a nonaggressive form of counterterrorism?
3. Is the application of the criminal law paradigm appropriate in response to terror attacks such as the train bombing?
4. Does the policy adopted and implemented by Spain encourage additional attacks?
5. Does such a response reflect the globalization of counterterrorism?

VII. CHINA

A. INTRODUCTION

China's operational counterterrorism efforts in Xinjiang largely focus on a strategy of capturing or killing leaders responsible for the riots while addressing root causes; the primary emphasis, however, is on "striking hard" to prevent future attacks.

Operational counterterrorism in China often has two phases: an initial, immediate response to an attack either by the police or military followed by imposition of long-term restrictions on rights and government pressure seeking to influence change from within the attacking group. In the aftermath of an attack, China imposes significant force to minimize potential violence; this is implemented by sending security forces to enforce restrictions, including curfew, intended to ensure public order. The second phase includes limiting information sources, restricting movement within a particular region, and expedited trials for those who allegedly violated the law.

---

41. Craig Whitlock, *Terror Probe Find "the Hands, but Not the Brains," Attackers Often Caught as Masterminds Flee*, Wash. Post Foreign Service, July 11, 2005 at 10, *available at* http://www.washingtonpost.com/wp-dyn/content/article/2005/07/10/AR2005071000987.html? nav=rss_world (last visited July 14, 2010).

ISSUES TO CONSIDER

1. How are limits of a harsh policy defined (if at all) and how is effectiveness defined?
2. What are the dangers of a counterterrorism policy devoid of restraints?
3. Is the court of international opinion a relevant consideration?
4. How — if at all — are proportionality and balance applied in the Chinese paradigm?

B. 2009 XINJIANG RIOTS

The initial response to the riots in Urumqi was to send police to the area to quell the disturbances; it was reported that police opened fire indiscriminately on protesters. In addition, Urumqi was locked-down; as a result, a communications blackout was imposed, text messages were banned, and Internet was shut down for what authorities described as measures essential for regional security.

In the immediate aftermath of the riots, Chinese leaders stated that they would administer severe punishments to people involved in the rioting warning that those guilty of murder would be executed. Within the week, Chinese officials stated that they had arrested over 1000 people; a month later it was unclear how many had been released from prison. Shortly thereafter, China re-implemented the strike hard campaign in Xinjiang; officials claimed they would "root out places where criminals breed, and change the face of public security situation in these areas."[42] In the six months following the riots, China proceeded to implement additional measures to prevent terrorism in the region; however, in the coming months texting was allowed and Internet access gradually restored.

Martin Wayne wrote that China's brutal tactics have worked to turn the society of Xinjiang against the government, marking the approach as remarkably ineffective.[43]

ISSUES TO CONSIDER

1. What is the price of harsh measures?
2. How is effectiveness of a carrot-and-stick approach measured?
3. Is the Chinese policy reflective of tactics (short-term) or strategy (long-term)?
4. How — if at all — are human rights preserved in such a model?
5. What is the impact of limiting communication methods?
6. What are the dangers of the Chinese counterterrorism policy?

---

42. *Xinjiang Police to "Strike Hard,"* BBC NEWS, Nov. 3 2009, http://news.bbc.co.uk/2/hi/asia-pacific/8339367.stm (last visited Feb. 6, 2009).
43. Martin Wayne, China's War on Terrorism 141-42 (2008).

VIII. COLOMBIA

A. INTRODUCTION

In the 1960s and 1970s Marxist guerilla groups — M-19, Revolutionary Armed Forces of Colombia (FARC), National Liberation Army (ELN) — engaged in attacks plunging Colombia into both instability and violence. By the 1980s, Colombia was a major center for drug production and trafficking. In the 1990s, numerous right-wing paramilitary groups formed, which presented an additional threat to the government.

In response to guerilla violence and drug trafficking, President Ayala (1978-1982), imposed a security statute curtailing individual rights, enabling suspected terrorists to be tried in military courts and restricting news coverage. While Ayala earned praise for his successful resolution of an attack (1980) on the Dominican Republic's embassy by M-19, the following year the four primary guerilla organizations increased their attacks on banks and military bases and stepped up their kidnappings (including the kidnapping and death of Ayala's daughter in a failed rescue attempt).

The consequence was a sense that political change was not possible through traditional means, which directly contributed to an increase in the size of paramilitary groups. Accordingly, Colombia decision makers confront three distinct challenges and threats to public order: drug cartels, guerilla groups, and paramilitary organizations. Complicating the dilemma is that the groups represent the political right (paramilitaries) and left (Marxists) alike, combined with the extraordinary violence of the drug cartels. In response to this unique threat — reflecting enormous financial stakes and extraordinary violence — different governments have sought alternative methods including direct negotiation with paramilitaries to resolve the seemingly irresolvable.

The three-pronged threat is exclusively domestic in orientation based on violence motivated by a powerful combination of economic and political forces facilitated by corruption. This complex, multi-dimensional threat is akin to India's challenges with one significant distinction: the multiple threats India faces are largely externally oriented whereas the numerous threats posed to Colombia are exclusively domestic. In addition — and fundamentally distinguishable from the other surveyed countries — Colombia's counterterrorism efforts are significantly impacted by the enormous financial resources available to the drug cartels and the inevitable, resulting corruption.

B. BOJAYÁ MASSACRE

One of the realities of the numerous threats faced by the Colombian government is the violence between competing groups. In 2002, in the town of Bojayá in the Chocó region, 119 innocent civilians — seeking shelter in a church — were killed during a clash between FARC guerillas and paramilitaries. According to various reports, the Colombian military had received previous warning regarding the presence of paramilitaries in the region; however, it failed to take proactive measures to protect the civilian population. Whether this was a result of military incompetence or corruption is unclear.

After the Bojayá Massacre, the Colombian government was pressured in the court of international opinion both by the United Nations and other nation-states. Newly elected President Uribe was called to show a strong response both to terror organizations and paramilitaries that had attacked innocent civilians while passive military forces failed to intervene. Furthermore, human rights organizations, which had been very critical of the military and government, called on the government to prosecute both the perpetrators of the crime and the security forces that had enabled the massacre to occur. In addition, the United States has consistently demanded that the Colombian government proactively engage both the terror organizations and paramilitaries, often in exchange for additional funding from the United States.

To that end, in the aftermath of the massacre the government changed its strategy by pursuing a security policy aimed at strengthening the state's military capacity with the intent to gain control over the country. Simultaneous to this change in policy, the government launched peace talks with terrorist groups reflecting—in many ways—government action devoid of strategic policy and what seemed to be a lurching from event to event.

C. NEGOTIATION

Colombia has a long history of negotiation with terrorism-related groups. While this has been considered a positive act, negotiations often fail as terrorist organizations continue to successfully target innocent civilians. The willingness to negotiate creates the potential for a vicious circle: the government engages in negotiation with a terrorist group only when it becomes powerful enough to be pose a threat at which point the government will seek to negotiate an amnesty agreement freeing the group from responsibility for acts previously committed.

Nevertheless, as a result of negotiations, a number of groups have dissolved. In the late 1980s, the 19th of April Movement (M-19), gave up its weapons, members were pardoned, and the group transitioned into a political party. However, several factions of M-19 refused to become part of the new political party and continued to participate in killings, kidnappings, and bombings. This seems to strengthen the argument that negotiation may have an impact in the short term, but its long-term effectiveness is questionable.

D. FALSE POSITIVES

An additional operational counterterrorism strategy is referred to as "false positives." The military created a rewards system for soldiers who receive vacation or other rewards depending on the number of guerrillas killed. However, this policy ultimately failed because soldiers would attempt to earn rewards without actually proving that a person killed was a member of a terrorist organization. In one instance, victims were lured with false job offers to an area near the Venezuelan border where they were murdered and presented to the army as paramilitaries killed in combat with the soldiers.

Jeremy McDermott, Toxic Fallout of Colombian Scandal

BBC News, June 17, 2010[44]

The toxic fallout of a grisly army scandal continues to spread in Colombia, as more soldiers are arrested over their alleged roles. In recent days another three colonels have been arrested, bringing the total number of military personnel captured to at least 22. The "false positives" scandal has revealed that the army murdered civilians, who were then dressed in rebel uniforms or given guns. They were then presented as guerrillas or paramilitaries killed in combat. These allowed units to fabricate results, and officers to gain promotion. The number of victims is believed to be in the thousands. "The issue of the false positives puts into doubt the doctrine of the security forces with respect to human rights," said Maria Victoria Llorente, director of the think-tank Foundation Idea for Peace. "This puts at risk a prized value for the military: legitimacy."

Demand for Results

By certain measures, the "democratic security" policy of President Alvaro Uribe has been a great success. It has pushed back Marxist rebels from around the cities and deep into their mountain and jungle strongholds. It has demobilised 30,000 members of an illegal right-wing paramilitary army, the United Self Defence Forces of Colombia. It has seen a massive drop in kidnapping and a fall in the murder rate, once among the highest in the world. But Mr Uribe's demand for results has pushed his security forces to the limit—and this appears to have provoked this scandal of the false positives. The scandal broke last October when it was found that poor, young men had been recruited from the slums of Bogota, promised well-paying jobs in the province of Norte de Santander, then murdered in cold blood and presented by the army as having been killed in combat.

The attorney general's office has evidence that 30 young men were murdered in such circumstances, and so far 17 soldiers have been arrested in connection with these extrajudicial killings. However, more examples of false positives are coming to light, spread across the country. Prosecutors now have 900 cases on their books, involving 1,500 victims, with more reports arriving daily. Sixty-seven soldiers have already been found guilty and more than 400 have been arrested and are awaiting trial. A total of 1,177 members of the security forces are currently under investigation linked with cases of extrajudicial killings.

---

44. *Available at* http://news.bbc.co.uk/2/hi/americas/8038399.stm/.

Issues to Consider

1. Do Colombia's complex internal threats present an objective barrier to developing coherent and consistent counterterrorism policies?
2. What does the range of counterterrorism policies, from negotiation to false positives, indicate regarding government decision making?
3. What is the impact of economic factors in developing a counterterrorism policy?
4. Does the range of threats suggest that a strategic policy cannot be articulated and implemented?
5. What is the significance of the court of international opinion?

CHAPTER 7
INTELLIGENCE GATHERING

I. INTRODUCTION

Intelligence is one of the most important counterterrorism tools. Some argue intelligence is *the* most critical issue; without it, operational counterterrorism would literally be "groping in the dark." This chapter focuses on how nations gather, analyze, and utilize intelligence information.

Intelligence is defined as the collection and analysis of information necessary to implement operational counterterrorism. Critical to understanding the significance of intelligence is understanding how governments translate this information into operational measures. Without intelligence information, governments would be unable to "connect the dots" in the best case; in the worst case, governments would be unable to even identify the "dots."

ISSUES TO CONSIDER

1. How does intelligence gathering keep pace with rapidly developing communication technology?
2. Must we distinguish between foreign intelligence and domestic law enforcement?
3. Should the standard for issuing a search warrant be lessened for purposes of intelligence gathering?
4. What are the limits of surveillance?
5. Are reasonable expectations of privacy extended to the Internet?

Intelligence gathering must be specifically tailored to the means by which terrorists and their supporters communicate. To rely on outdated and obsolete methods places governments at a distinct disadvantage. Conversely, unduly infringing on citizens' rights may violate domestic laws specifically legislated to protect against government intrusion. The debate about means is not conducted in a vacuum. Former President Bush criticized the debate over the legality of the administration's wiretapping policy claiming the enemy "listens to the discussion."

II. DEFINING TERMS

Intelligence is gathered primarily from three sources:

(1) human sources (HUMINT) (gathered directly from personal contacts)
(2) signal intelligence (SIGINT) (intercepted communications)
(3) open source information (OSINT) (analysis of publicly available information)

Intelligence is defined as information concerning an enemy or possible enemy.[1] Determining if the information is "actionable" for operational purposes requires that the information meets a four-part test: the intelligence must be **reliable, viable, relevant**, and **corroborated**.

Test Prong	Definition/Use
Reliable	Past experiences show the source to be a dependable provider of correct information; requires discerning whether the information is useful and accurate; demands analysis by the case officer whether the source has an agenda.
Viable	Is it possible that an attack could occur in accordance with the source's information?
Relevant	The information has bearing on upcoming events; consider the time-sensitive and timeliness of the information.
Corroborated	Another source confirms the information in whole or part.

The intelligence community is—in large part—divided into two distinct categories: gathering and analysis. The former gathers the information from the sources listed above while the latter analyzes and translates the information for different audiences, including operators and decision makers.

Intelligence information is the basis for a wide range of counterterrorism measures and sanctions including detention for interrogation, administrative detention, house demolition, assigned residence, drone attacks, and targeted killing. Without intelligence premised on the four-part test above, counterterrorism efforts are nothing more than a "crapshoot" with all the risks the term implies.

While intelligence is at the core of operational counterterrorism, decision makers must develop effective filters before acting on the information, or run the risk of violating civil and political rights. In the detention paradigm, it is particularly essential that decision makers consider the following:

---

1. Merriam Webster Dictionary, http://www.merriam-webster.com/dictionary/intelligence (last visited Mar. 22, 2010).

Factors to Consider when Balancing Source and Detainee Concerns:

Source	Detainee
• Who is the source? • Does the source have an agenda? • Who is the target of the source's information? • What are the risks to the source if the targeted individual is detained? • What are the risks to the source if the intelligence is made public?	• What is the purpose of the potential detention? • What are the risks/cost-benefits if detention is delayed? • What is the nature of the suspicious activity? • What information can the detainee provide? • What is the detention policy? • What are review standards and is detention subject to independent judicial review?

III. UNITED STATES

In the aftermath of 9/11, the question posed was how could the United States not have known of al Qaeda's plans, given that U.S. intelligence agencies had state-of-the-art technology enabling them to intercept conversations worldwide. Despite the available technology, al Qaeda operatives were able to enter the United States, live in the country legally, enroll in and attend flight schools, and implement a well-synchronized terror attack involving 19 terrorists. The plan was not detected even though throughout the summer of 2001 U.S. intelligence agencies consistently heard chatter regarding a possible terror attack.

A. THE 9/11 COMMISSION

The 9/11 Commission was primarily established to investigate how the intelligence community failed to prevent 9/11.[2] The commission's mandate was to provide a "full and complete accounting" of the attacks of 9/11 and recommend how to prevent such attacks in the future.[3]

TESTIMONY OF STEPHEN J. SCHULHOFER BEFORE THE 9/11 COMMISSION ON DOMESTIC INTELLIGENCE-GATHERING

December 8, 2003[4]

An effective intelligence process requires that information be gathered, translated (when necessary), pooled by the relevant agencies, analyzed and then

---

2. *National Commission on Terrorist Attacks Upon the United States, available at* http://www.9-11commission.gov/ (last visited July 21, 2010) [hereafter The 9/11 Commission Report].

3. *Frequently Asked Questions About the 9-11 Commission, available at* http://www.9-11commission.gov/about/faq.htm#q1 (last visited July 21, 2010).

4. *Available at* http://www.tcf.org/list.asp?type=NC&pubid=394 (last visited Mar. 13, 2010).

delivered to those in a position to investigate further or take quick preventive action. Legal rules are largely irrelevant at the stages where our past and current problems have been greatest—translation, analysis, and delivery. Law has posed significant obstacles to the pooling of intelligence, but the obstacles of agency culture, resources, and lines of communication have mattered and still matter much more. Even at the stage of gathering domestic intelligence, the stage where we expect law to govern, capabilities are largely determined by non-legal constraints—technical, budgetary and human resources, the training and priorities of our officers and the organization and cultures of the relevant agencies—all areas where our deficits have been, and continue to be, enormous.

In reaction to the events of September 11th, legal experts, along with most citizens, quickly concluded that we needed immediate steps to strengthen the government's intelligence-gathering authority, steps that, in the conventional cliché, would "shift the balance" between liberty and security. More than two years later, questions centered on legal authority, such as the merits of the U.S. Patriot Act, continue to dominate public discussion of the domestic intelligence function. Yet when the intelligence process suffers from major deficits in resources, personnel, organizational strength, and translation, analytic and delivery capabilities, a preoccupation with questions of legal authority can be misleading and dangerous.

The government's legal powers, prior to September 11th, were very strong, though not perfect. And those imperfections bear little if any of the blame for the failure to prevent September 11th. Rather, severe human, budgetary, and organizational deficits prevented our law enforcement and intelligence agencies from using their strong legal powers effectively. And there is no reason to believe that additional legal authority, in that environment, would have been used to any greater advantage. Though many clear warning signs were in hand, our grave non-legal deficiencies—in organization, staffing levels, technical resources, and priority setting—cost us what chances we had to abort the plot.

Overall, the government currently has amply sufficient legal tools, but it remains sorely lacking in the non-legal capabilities needed to deploy those tools effectively.

Many new measures, though relevant to the counterterrorism effort, are so overbroad that they sacrifice liberty and privacy needlessly and in ways that are likely to prove counterproductive, leaving us both less free and less secure.

Intelligence Gathering Authority Prior to September 11th

Before September 11th, the government possessed far-reaching intelligence-gathering authority, including the electronic surveillance powers conferred by Title III and the still-broader search and surveillance authorities available under FISA. Both statutes had been updated frequently to meet newly identified needs. In particular, FISA authority, primarily concerned with monitoring agents of foreign governments, was made available many years before 9/11 for monitoring individuals (both foreign nationals and US citizens) believed to be associated with international terrorism, even when not associated with any state actor.

Nonetheless, there were weaknesses. Several statutory surveillance authorities had failed to keep pace with new technologies, including cable providers, voice-mail systems and mobile phones. There were many gaps in our powers to trace and neutralize the sources of terrorist financing.

These legal weaknesses were no doubt worth fixing. But it is crucial for the public to understand that they did not play a significant role in our failure to foil the 9/11 attack.

Prior to 9/11, FBI agents and other officials had many items of information that, at least in retrospect, raised bright-red flags about the unfolding plot. Yet, as the Joint Inquiry documented, these alarm bells were repeatedly overlooked or ignored by those who were in a position to take action. Even in the high-risk environment that had been identified in the summer of 2001, there was little to no investigative focus on the would-be hijackers or their accomplices. There was virtually no effort to deploy readily available investigative tools to gather more information about them. Relevant intelligence obtained by CIA and FBI agents typically was not communicated promptly enough (or at all), and when communicated, such intelligence was largely ignored.[5]

According to Prof. Schulhofer, the United States' failure to prevent 9/11 was not the result of a lack of HUMINT or SIGINT. On the contrary, his testimony indicates that the intelligence community had the information necessary to obtain a clear understanding of terrorist aims prior to September 11, 2001. The shortcomings were primarily related to intelligence sharing and analysis, rather than intelligence gathering.

Nevertheless, some officials within the executive branch blamed the U.S. legal system for hindering successful intelligence gathering. It was these hindrances, they argued, that enabled the 9/11 attacks; Attorney General John Ashcroft was particularly vocal in his criticism of government imposed restrictions.

TESTIMONY OF ATTORNEY GENERAL JOHN ASHCROFT BEFORE THE NATIONAL COMMISSION ON TERRORIST ATTACKS UPON THE UNITED STATES

April 13, 2004[6]

But the simple fact of September 11th is this: We did not know an attack was coming because for nearly a decade our government had blinded itself to its enemies. Our agents were isolated by government-imposed walls, handcuffed by government-imposed restrictions and starved for basic information technology.

The old national intelligence system in place on September 11th was destined to fail.

There was a covert action program to capture bin Laden for criminal prosecution, but even this program was crippled by a snarled web of requirements,

---

5. A full transcript of Prof. Schulhofer's Testimony before the 9/11 Commission is available at http://www.tcf.org/list.asp?type=NC&pubid=394 (last visited July 21, 2010).

6. *Available at* http://fl1.findlaw.com/news.findlaw.com/hdocs/docs/terrorism/.ashcroft41304 stmt.pdf (last visited Mar. 13, 2010).

restrictions and regulations that prevented decisive action by our men and women in the field. When they most needed clear, understandable guidance, and our agents and operatives were given instead the language of lawyers. Even if they could have penetrated bin Laden's training camps they would have needed a battery of attorneys to approve the capture. With unclear guidance, our covert action teams' risk of injury may have exceeded the risk to Osama bin Laden.

The single greatest structural cause for the September 11th problem was the wall that segregated or separated criminal investigators and intelligence agents. Government erected this wall, government buttressed this wall and before September 11th, government was blinded by this wall.

The basic architecture for the wall in the 1995 Guidelines was contained in a classified memorandum entitled "Instructions on Separation of Certain Foreign Counterintelligence and Criminal Investigations."[7] The memorandum ordered FBI Director Louis Freeh and others, quote, "We believe that it is prudent to establish a set of instructions that will more clearly separate the counterintelligence investigation from the more limited, but continued criminal investigations.

"These procedures," the memo went on to say, "which go beyond what is legally required, will prevent any risk of creating an unwarranted appearance that FISA is being used to avoid procedural safeguards which would apply in a criminal investigation."

This memorandum laid the foundation for a wall separating the criminal and intelligence investigations, as a matter of fact, established the wall following the 1993 World Trade Center attack, which at the time was the largest international terrorism attack on American soil, the largest prior to September 11th.

The 9/11 Commission disagreed with John Ashcroft; in its final report the Commission stated that the failure to prevent the attacks resulted primarily from the intelligence community's inability to properly understand and analyze the information it heard.[8] The argument that constitutionally based restrictions should be loosened to enhance the U.S. intelligence gathering ability falsely assumes the law had prevented intelligence gathering.

B. PRIVACY AND THE CONSTITUTION

The development of a viable counterterrorism policy requires intelligence gathering; the question in civil democratic society is what costs are legitimate given constitutional and legislative limits on government intrusions of personal privacy.

---

7. Jamie S. Gorelick Office of the Deputy Attorney General, *Instructions on Separation of Certain Foreign Counterintelligence and Criminal Investigations, available at* http://www.au.af.mil/au/awc/awcgate/doj/1995_gorelick_memo.pdf (last visited July 21, 2010).

8. The 9/11 Commission Report, *supra* note 2, at 339-60.

Nowhere has the debate addressing the commensurate means to achieve satisfactory intelligence gathering and an individual's right to privacy been as public as in the United States. The following testimony, given to the 9/11 Commission by Marc Rotenberg, executive director of the Electronic Privacy Information Center, highlights the increasingly critical role technology plays in obtaining intelligence. Rotenberg's testimony also suggests that increased technical abilities can reduce constitutionally granted protections.

> Now, the other key cornerstone to think about in assessing privacy protection in the United States is the Federal Wiretap Act. The wiretap statute was passed in 1968, following perhaps two of the most important privacy cases decided by the United States Supreme Court. One, as indicated above, concerned the use of a tape recorder in a public payphone in the streets of Los Angeles and whether that new investigative method would require the use of a warrant, which is to say judicial approval, or whether law enforcement could be free to use any new form of technology without judicial oversight to gather evidence that could be used in the criminal prosecution.
>
> And the court said quite clearly in Katz v. United States that this new type of technology needs to be subject to Fourth Amendment standards; not that it could not be used or that a prohibition should be established but rather that the traditional Fourth Amendment standards would be required for electronic surveillance. And the following year, in 1968, when the Congress passed the federal wiretap statute, based on *Katz* and the Berger v. New York opinion, it constructed an elaborate regulatory framework imposing significant oversight responsibilities on federal agencies that were using electronic surveillance authority.[9]

In *Katz vs. United States*,[10] the Supreme Court overturned a Court of Appeals decision regarding the legality of government wiretaps on a pay phone used by a suspected gambler. The Supreme Court held that the individual's reasonable expectation of privacy was violated. Using a public phone booth did not constitute a waiver of the individual's right to privacy.

Katz v. United States

389 U.S. 347 (1967)

The Government contends, however, that the activities of its agents in this case should not be tested by Fourth Amendment requirements, for the surveillance technique they employed involved no physical penetration of the telephone booth from which the petitioner placed his calls. It is true that the absence of such penetration was at one time thought to foreclose further Fourth Amendment inquiry. . . . Indeed, we have expressly held that the

---

9. From testimony provided by Marc Rotenberg to the National Commission on Terrorist Attack Upon the United States (9/11 Commission), Dec. 8, 2003. Full text available at: http://www.9-11commission.gov/archive/hearing6/9-11Commission_Hearing_2003-12-08.htm (last visited Mar. 13, 2010).

10. Katz v. United States, 389 U.S. 347 (1967).

Fourth Amendment governs not only the seizure of tangible items, but extends as well to the recording of oral statements, over-heard without any "technical trespass under . . . local property law." Once this much is acknowledged, and once it is recognized that the Fourth Amendment protects people — and not simply "areas" — against unreasonable searches and seizures, it becomes clear that the reach of that Amendment cannot turn upon the presence or absence of a physical intrusion into any given enclosure. . . .

The Government's activities in electronically listening to and recording the petitioner's words violated the privacy upon which he justifiably relied while using the telephone booth and thus constituted a "search and seizure" within the meaning of the Fourth Amendment. The fact that the electronic device employed to achieve that end did not happen to penetrate the wall of the booth can have no constitutional significance.

The question remaining for decision, then, is whether the search and seizure conducted in this case complied with constitutional standards. In that regard, the Government's position is that its agents acted in an entirely defensible manner: They did not begin their electronic surveillance until investigation of the petitioner's activities had established a strong probability that he was using the telephone in question to transmit gambling information to persons in other States, in violation of federal law. Moreover, the surveillance was limited, both in scope and in duration, to the specific purpose of establishing the contents of the petitioner's unlawful telephonic communications. The agents confined their surveillance to the brief periods during which he used the telephone booth, and they took great care to overhear only the conversations of the petitioner himself.

Accepting this account of the Government's actions as accurate, it is clear that this surveillance was so narrowly circumscribed that a duly authorized magistrate, properly notified of the need for such investigation, specifically informed of the basis on which it was to proceed, and clearly apprised of the precise intrusion it would entail, could constitutionally have authorized, with appropriate safeguards, the very limited search and seizure that the Government asserts in fact took place.

Searches conducted without warrants have been held unlawful "notwithstanding facts unquestionably showing probable cause," . . . for the Constitution requires "that the deliberate, impartial judgment of a judicial officer . . . be interposed between the citizen and the police. . . ."

. . . "Over and again this Court has emphasized that the mandate of the [Fourth] Amendment requires adherence to judicial processes," and that searches conducted outside the judicial process, without prior approval by judge or magistrate, are per se unreasonable under the Fourth Amendment subject only to a few specifically established and well-delineated exceptions.

The Government does not question these basic principles. Rather, it urges the creation of a new exception to cover this case. It argues that surveillance of a telephone booth should be exempted from the usual requirement of advance authorization by a magistrate upon a showing of probable cause. We cannot agree. Wherever a man may be, he is entitled to know that he will remain free from unreasonable searches and seizures.

ISSUES TO CONSIDER

1. How should surveillance be conducted?
2. Should the government establish different standards and controls dependent on the method of electronic intelligence gathering (e.g., wiretapping versus computer monitoring)?
3. How should democracies balance effective surveillance with minimizing intrusion?
4. How much intrusion is permissible?
5. How does the government protect the privacy rights of perceived "enemies"?
6. What limits should be set regarding electronic surveillance?
7. When does surveillance impede free speech?
8. What limits, if any, should be set on intelligence gathering?
9. Do Fourth Amendment restrictions apply to terrorism-related intelligence gathering?

C. FISA

The U.S. Congress enacted the Foreign Intelligence Surveillance Act (FISA) in 1978.[11] Its primary purpose was to "secure framework . . . [for] electronic surveillance for foreign intelligence purposes within the context of this Nation's commitment to privacy and individual rights."[12] To achieve these ends, FISA established the Foreign Intelligence Surveillance Court (FISC), a special court with exclusive jurisdiction to hear and grant Foreign Intelligence Surveillance Orders. Much like a grand jury, the only party to FISC is the government; hearings are closed to the public and classified.

According to section 1804 of FISA, gathering foreign intelligence information from a suspected foreign agent must be a significant purpose of the surveillance.[13] Section 1804(a)(7)[14] allows the government to conduct wiretap surveillance of foreign powers or agents of a foreign power. However, section 1804(a)(7) limits surveillance: the conversations cannot involve American citizens; a significant purpose of the surveillance must be to obtain foreign intelligence information; such information cannot reasonably be obtained by normal investigative techniques; and the FISA court must issue a wiretap.[15] According to section 1802,[16] the government may order a wiretap without a warrant provided the FISA court issues a warrant within 72 hours. Between 1978 and 2009, the government submitted 80,625,358 warrant requests;

---

11. Foreign Intelligence Surveillance Act Pub. L. No. 95-511, 92 Stat. 1783 (codified as amended at 50 U.S.C. §§1801-1811, 1821-29, 1841-46, and 1861-62).
12. United States v. Pelton, 835 F.2d 1067, 1074 (4th Cir. 1987).
13. 50 U.S.C. §1801(a)(1)-(6) defines foreign power. 50 U.S.C. 1801(b)(1), (2) (defines agent of a foreign power).
14. 50 U.S.C. §1804 (2006).
15. *Id.*
16. 50 U.S.C. §1802.

81,425,360 were issued.[17] Since 1978, only nine warrant requests have been rejected by the FISA court.

Despite the fact that the Court grants an overwhelming number of warrant requests the Bush administration — in the aftermath of 9/11 — decided to bypass FISA and ordered warrantless wiretaps on phone conversations originating overseas. According to numerous media reports the taps included American citizens,[18] a clear violation of FISA. The excerpt below indicates the potential breadth of the executive branch's surveillance program.

Seymour M. Hersh, Listening In

The New Yorker, May 22, 2006[19]

After the attacks of September 11, 2001, it was clear that the intelligence community needed to get more aggressive and improve its performance. The [Bush] Administration, deciding on a quick fix, returned to the tactic that got intelligence agencies in trouble thirty years ago: intercepting large numbers of electronic communications made by Americans. The NSA's carefully constructed rules were set aside.

[In] December [2005], the Times reported that the NSA was listening in on calls between people in the United States and people in other countries, and . . . USA Today reported that the agency was collecting information on millions of private domestic calls. A security consultant working with a major telecommunications carrier told me that his client set up a top-secret high-speed circuit between its main computer complex and Quantico, Virginia, the site of a government-intelligence computer center. This link provided direct access to the carrier's network core — the critical area of its system, where all its data are stored. "What the companies are doing is worse than turning over records," the consultant said. "They're providing total access to all the data."

"This is not about getting a cardboard box of monthly phone bills in alphabetical order," a former senior intelligence official said. The Administration's goal after September 11th was to find suspected terrorists and target them for capture or, in some cases, air strikes. "The NSA is getting real-time actionable intelligence," the former official said.

The NSA also programmed computers to map the connections between telephone numbers in the United States and suspect numbers abroad, sometimes focusing on a geographic area, rather than on a specific person — for example, a region of Pakistan. Such calls often triggered a process, known as "chaining," in which subsequent calls to and from the American number were

---

17. The number discrepancy is based on modification and withdrawal of some orders. *Electronic Privacy Information Center, Foreign Intelligence Surveillance Act Orders 1979-2005, available at* http://www.epic.org/privacy/wiretap/stats/fisa_stats.html (last visited Mar. 13, 2010).

18. James Bamford, *The Agency that Could be Big Brother*, N.Y. Times, Dec. 25, 2005, *available at* http://www.nytimes.com/2005/12/25/weekinreview/25bamford.html?ei=5088&en=3d099136bc2b2eac&ex=1293166800&partner=rssnyt&emc=rss&pagewanted=print (last visited July 21, 2010).

19. *Available at* http://www.newyorker.com/talk/content/articles/060529ta_talk_hersh (last visited Mar. 13, 2010).

monitored and linked. The way it worked, one high-level Bush Administration intelligence official told me, was for the agency "to take the first number out to two, three, or more levels of separation, and see if one of them comes back" — if, say, someone down the chain was also calling the original, suspect number. As the chain grew longer, more and more Americans inevitably were drawn in.

FISA requires the government to get a warrant from a special court if it wants to eavesdrop on calls made or received by Americans. (It is generally legal for the government to wiretap a call if it is purely foreign.) The legal implications of chaining are less clear. Two people who worked on the NSA call-tracking program told me they believed that, in its early stages, it did not violate the law. "We were not listening to an individual's conversation," a defense contractor said. "We were gathering data on the incidence of calls made to and from his phone by people associated with him and others." Similarly, the Administration intelligence official said that no warrant was needed, because "there's no personal identifier involved, other than the meta-data from a call being placed."

But the point, obviously, was to identify terrorists. "After you hit something, you have to figure out what to do with it," the Administration intelligence official told me. The next step, theoretically, could have been to get a suspect's name and go to the fisa court for a warrant to listen in. One problem, however, was the volume and the ambiguity of the data that had already been generated. ("There's too many calls and not enough judges in the world," the former senior intelligence official said.) The agency would also have had to reveal how far it had gone, and how many Americans were involved. And there was a risk that the court could shut down the program.

Instead, the NSA began, in some cases, to eavesdrop on callers (often using computers to listen for key words) or to investigate them using traditional police methods. A government consultant told me that tens of thousands of Americans had had their calls monitored in one way or the other. "In the old days, you needed probable cause to listen in," the consultant explained. "But you could not listen in to generate probable cause. What they're doing is a violation of the spirit of the law." One CIA officer told me that the Administration, by not approaching the FISA court early on, had made it much harder to go to the court later. . . .

The Bush administration argued that such surveillance was not only necessary, but legal. On December 17, 2005, during his weekly radio address, President Bush defended his authorization of the NSA program.

RADIO ADDRESS OF PRESIDENT GEORGE W. BUSH

The Roosevelt Room, Dec. 17, 2005[20]

In the weeks following the terrorist attacks on our nation, I authorized the National Security Agency, consistent with U.S. law and the Constitution, to

20. *Available at* http://georgewbush-whitehouse.archives.gov/news/releases/2005/12/20051217.html (last visited Mar. 13, 2010).

intercept the international communications of people with known links to al Qaeda and related terrorist organizations. Before we intercept these communications, the government must have information that establishes a clear link to these terrorist networks.

This is a highly classified program that is crucial to our national security. Its purpose is to detect and prevent terrorist attacks against the United States, our friends and allies. Yesterday the existence of this secret program was revealed in media reports, after being improperly provided to news organizations. As a result, our enemies have learned information they should not have, and the unauthorized disclosure of this effort damages our national security and puts our citizens at risk. Revealing classified information is illegal, alerts our enemies, and endangers our country.

As the 9/11 Commission pointed out, it was clear that terrorists inside the United States were communicating with terrorists abroad before the September the 11th attacks, and the commission criticized our nation's inability to uncover links between terrorists here at home and terrorists abroad. Two of the terrorist hijackers who flew a jet into the Pentagon, Nawaf al Hamzi and Khalid al Mihdhar, communicated while they were in the United States to other members of al Qaeda who were overseas. But we didn't know they were here, until it was too late.

The authorization I gave the National Security Agency after September the 11th helped address that problem in a way that is fully consistent with my constitutional responsibilities and authorities. The activities I have authorized make it more likely that killers like these 9/11 hijackers will be identified and located in time. And the activities conducted under this authorization have helped detect and prevent possible terrorist attacks in the United States and abroad.

The activities I authorized are reviewed approximately every 45 days. Each review is based on a fresh intelligence assessment of terrorist threats to the continuity of our government and the threat of catastrophic damage to our homeland. During each assessment, previous activities under the authorization are reviewed. The review includes approval by our nation's top legal officials, including the Attorney General and the Counsel to the President. I have reauthorized this program more than 30 times since the September the 11th attacks, and I intend to do so for as long as our nation faces a continuing threat from al Qaeda and related groups.

On January 27, 2006, amid increasing controversy surrounding the NSA wiretapping program, the White House responded more directly to claims regarding its illegality. The Administration issued a document to journalists entitled *The National Security Agency Program to Detect and Prevent Terrorist Attacks: Myth vs. Reality*,[21] which addressed many of the issues that had

---

21. *The National Security Agency Program to Detect and Prevent Terrorist Attacks: Myth vs. Reality*, Jan. 31, 2006, *available at* http://www.fcnl.org/issues/item.php?item_id=1696& issue_id=80 (last visited Mar. 13, 2010).

come to the forefront of the debate surrounding the President's establishment of the NSA program.

In response to claims that Bush's authorization of the warrantless wiretaps exceeded executive powers, the White House asserted the following points:

- As Commander-in-Chief and Chief Executive, the President has legal authority under the Constitution to authorize the NSA terrorist surveillance program.
- The Constitution makes protecting our Nation from foreign attack the President's most solemn duty and provides him with the legal authority to keep America safe.
- It has long been recognized that the President has inherent authority to conduct warrantless surveillance to gather foreign intelligence even in peacetime. Every federal appellate court to rule on the question has concluded that the President has this authority and that it is consistent with the Constitution.
- Since the Civil War, wiretaps aimed at collecting foreign intelligence have been authorized by Presidents, and the authority to conduct warrantless surveillance for foreign intelligence purposes has been consistently cited and used when necessary.[22]
- The White House document also rejected assertions that the NSA program violated the Fourth Amendment: The Supreme Court has long held that the Fourth Amendment allows warrantless searches where "special needs, beyond the normal need for law enforcement," exist. Foreign intelligence collection, especially in a time of war when catastrophic attacks have already been launched inside the United States, falls within the special needs context.
- As the Foreign Intelligence Surveillance Court of Review has observed, the nature of the "emergency" posed by al Qaeda "takes the matter out of the realm of ordinary crime control."
- The program easily meets the Court's reasonableness test for whether a warrant is required. The NSA activities described by the President are narrow in scope and aim, and the government has an overwhelming interest in detecting and preventing further catastrophic attacks on American soil.[23]

Finally, the White House rejected the argument that warrantless wiretaps violated provisions of FISA:

> The NSA activities come from the very center of the Commander-in-Chief power, and it would raise serious constitutional issues if FISA were read to allow Congress to interfere with the President's well-recognized, inherent constitutional authority. FISA can and should be read to avoid this.[24]

---

22. *Id.*
23. *Id.*
24. *Id.*

ISSUES TO CONSIDER

1. Was bypassing the FISA court justified? Why or why not?
2. What standard did the court apply in issuing the FISA warrants?
3. How do you determine if wiretaps are effective?
4. Does the administration's bypassing of the FISA court suggest that the court will scrutinize future applications more carefully?
5. Does the administration's action suggest short-term gain at the expense of long-term benefit?

D. 9/11 AND THE SEPARATION OF VARIOUS INTELLIGENCE AGENCIES

During the 9/11 Commission hearings, the requirement that evidence from a criminal law investigation be kept separate from intelligence gathering operations was discussed at length. Many cited this so-called "wall" as the fundamental weakness in the United States' counterterrorism strategy arguing that it clearly prevented the government from sharing information obtained in criminal investigations with information obtained through foreign intelligence gathering. The U.S. Dept. of Justice has defined this issue as the "sharing of grand jury investigations with FISA information."[25]

In response to concerns over the wall's perceived obstruction of government intelligence gathering, Congress passed the U.S. PATRIOT Act. Under Sections 202-215 of the PATRIOT Act, investigation of terrorist activities may include both electronic surveillance and search activities.[26] Former Deputy Attorney General Larry Thompson testified before the 9/11 Commission:

> Now, with the help of Congress, we in this country have made great strides toward getting more tools and resources in our efforts to combat terrorism. Many of the new resources or tools are embodied in laws, especially, as the Chairman mentioned, the Patriot Act. I'd like to just mention one provision of the Patriot Act this morning, highlight one provision that I think is extremely important, and that is section 218. Section 218 of the Patriot Act has allowed the FBI and the Department of Justice prosecutors to expand the nature of the

---

25. Former U.S. Deputy Attorney General Larry Thompson stated:

Before the Act was passed, federal law restricted prosecutors' ability to share with the intelligence community information obtained in grand jury testimony or from a criminal wiretap. Evidence about an impending terrorist threat that was presented to a grand jury, for instance, could not be shared with CIA officials. In situations where additional time spent identifying and tracking down terrorists could cost people's lives, this limitation was a significant obstacle to preventing terrorist attacks. Under the new law, law enforcement officers may now share grand jury and wiretap information regarding foreign intelligence with a wide range of federal personnel, including U.S. immigration authorities and members of the intelligence and national defense communities.

Department of Justice Leadership Address, Nov. 8, 2001, *available at* http://www.justice.gov/archive/dag/speeches/2001/110801dagspeechtodojleadership.htm (last visited Oct. 8, 2010).
26. The PATRIOT Act amended the Foreign Intelligence Surveillance Act.

investigation of terrorist activity, especially as it relates to electronic surveillance activities and search activities.

As you know, section 218 provides that FISA investigations, investigations
under the Foreign Intelligence Surveillance Act, can be utilized when foreign
intelligence is a significant purpose of the investigation, as opposed to the old
primary purpose of the investigation. This is a very important distinction and
this is a very important provision.[27]

Stewart A. Baker, former general counsel for the National Security Agency, in
his testimony before the 9/11 Commission, also addressed the intelligence
gathering ability of the United States and the so-called "wall" between traditional law enforcement and the intelligence community.

TESTIMONY OF STEWART A. BAKER AT THE PUBLIC HEARING OF THE NATIONAL COMMISSION ON TERRORIST ATTACKS UPON THE UNITED STATES

Dec. 8, 2003[28]

I'd like to focus on a question that actually Commissioner Ben-Veniste asked or
observed. That we actually had pretty good intelligence about the terrorists in
the lead up to September 11. And I think that's right and what I'd like to focus
on is not September, but August. Because in August the FBI learned that there
were two terrorists whose names we had, who were in the country who were
clearly here to kill Americans.

We had two and a half weeks to find them. They were living openly in San
Diego, they were getting California IDs, they were buying stuff, engaging in
financial transactions, signing rental agreements all in their own name, making reservations on the plane that they would ultimately fly into the Pentagon.
We couldn't find them. That's a terrible failure. And I'd like to explore a little,
from what I can gather, I'm not cleared to review any of this material anymore,
but I have reviewed pretty carefully the public discussions of what happened to
try to explore what went wrong there.

And I think when you look at it closely, it's really a failure of tools and a
failure of rules. The tools problem is the problem we're here to talk about today.
The FBI agent who discovered this and made it his mission to try to find these
guys had some electronic tools, he was able to look in some databases for arrests,
for certain automobile registrations. They hadn't been arrested and they hadn't
been registered in any vehicles. He did not have access to a lot of government
information, so that it took him about a week and a half to figure out what
address one of the terrorists had put on his visa as he entered and then to check
with the hotel that he put down to see if the guy ever stayed there.

He didn't have a computerized access once he got legal authority to go into
either of those databases. So we lost weeks there. Once more, he didn't have

27. National Commission on Terrorist Attacks upon the United States, Public Hearing, Dec. 8,
2003, Larry Thompson, *available at* http://govinfo.library.unt.edu/911/archive/hearing6/9-11
Commission_Hearing_2003-12-08.htm (last visited July 21, 2010).

28. *Available at* http://www.9-11commission.gov/archive/hearing6/9-11Commission_Hearing_
2003-12-08.htm#one (last visited Mar. 12, 2010).

computerized access to any of the records that these guys were generating — not the financial records, not the travel reservation or even some of the California records. So there's clearly a failure of tools. If he could have been able to find those two guys and then check the links that they had to many of the other terrorists — there were direct shared addresses as I remember, links to the people who flew into the south tower and the north tower. We had a chance to stop this. The one chance that I can see in all of the errors that were made where we really could have prevented this if we had the tools to find these guys, and it is a scandal that we don't have them.

So we need that. We need at a minimum an ability to do those searches quickly and efficiently, not just by shoe leather and by calling people which is the method that the FBI has used for a generation. That's just to fight the last war. Obviously the next set of terrorists is not going to be so accommodating as to use their real names. We're going to need other mechanisms and I've listed in my testimony which I've provided about a dozen IT capabilities that our investigators need in order to find these folks and to respond appropriately to crises.

So clearly we need more tools. But I think when you read the story of what went wrong in those two weeks with an eye that is informed by bureaucratic realities and political realities you'll see that there's a problem with the rules as well. It's really — it's heartbreaking to read what this agent said when he asked for the authority to get the assistance of law enforcement — there are a million law enforcement agents in the country, there were three times as many FBI law enforcement agents as intelligence agents, he wanted to get help on that side of the FBI and he was told by FBI headquarters, not on your life. You cannot capitalize, cannot do that because there's a wall between law enforcement and intelligence.

And his response was to say, the American people will not understand this, someone is going to die because of this. Osama bin Laden is the principal beneficiary of the wall that we have built. How can we possibly maintain this? The answer was, we don't like it either, but that's the rule.

Now, I feel strongly about this, obviously, because I was part of building the wall. I was at NSA. I thought the wall responded to an appropriate, reasonable worry — theoretical but real — about civil liberties and privacy and that we could have a wall and still have an effective response to the national security problems that we have. We wrote rules and we thought we had done a fine job of carefully balancing all of those equities. We obviously failed. We failed terribly.

And that failure I think reflects both a desire to constantly add to the protections even against theoretical risks to privacy that we have built into our system, and at the same time, not to spend as much time worrying about whether people will actually be able to do their jobs to protect Americans. Because what finally happened in this case was the rules might just barely have been workable if it were not for the fact that there was a privacy scandal in the FISA Court in 2000 and 2001, in which the court believed it had not been properly informed about contacts across the wall when it was given FISA orders to sign. It ordered a massive review. It threw out one of the principal FBI investigators who appeared before it and I'm guessing, though

I don't know, that disciplinary action and maybe even a perjury indictment was considered for that fellow.

This was so bad that we dropped coverage on terrorism suspects in the United States in early 2001. So al Qaeda is preparing to kill thousands of Americans, we can't even keep up the wiretaps that we have authorized in the past. It's a disaster. And it's a disaster because there was such an intent focus on preventing even the most theoretical privacy abuse. That's the lesson that I would draw from September 11.

I just would say one more thing. I'm very worried that we're going back there, that what we have seen — I gave a speech once, I said, you know, we had two and a half years of serious failures. We had a major failure on September 11. We've had two and a half years to figure out what went wrong, who should be disciplined, and one person has been forced out of government, Admiral Poindexter. And the lesson that you can draw from that is, well, you can screw up pretty badly in protecting the American people, but if you get crossed wires with privacy lobby, you're gone. That is exactly the wrong message to be sending to our FBI and CIA agents.

Issues to Consider

1. What are the limits to the right to privacy?
2. What should be the extent of the sharing of information about U.S. citizens between different intelligence agencies, if any?
3. What measures would most effectively guarantee that law enforcement agencies do not abuse intelligence gathering operations?
4. What constitutional protections exist to prevent undue invasion of privacy and does 9/11 justify waiving otherwise protected rights?

E. INTELLIGENCE POST-9/11

U.S. policy makers recognize the importance of human sources "on the ground" to infiltrate terrorist organizations and provide crucial information otherwise unavailable. The following excerpt illustrates how critical HUMINT can be to the neutralization of terrorist leaders.

Gen. George Casey, the top U.S. commander in Iraq, said the hunt for al-Zarqawi[29] began two weeks ago, and his body was identified by fingerprints and facial recognition.

---

29. On June 7, 2006, U.S. forces in Iraq launched an air strike on a safe house some fifty-five miles north of Baghdad, where al-Zarqawi was hiding. Jordanian by birth, Abu Musab al-Zarqawi transformed himself into a nationless freelance terrorist. Tactically, geographically, and to some extent philosophically, he established a pattern of inconsistency. His flexibility made him all the more fearsome — and all the more difficult to pin down. Despite a bounty of $25 million on his head and vastly increased media attention over the past five years, hard facts about al-Zarqawi's past are few and far between. Hearsay, on the other hand, abounds. As *Foreign Policy* put it, al-Zarqawi's story has become "one of the most powerful and enduring myths of the war on terror." Lee Hudson Teslik, *Profile: Abu Musab al-Zarqawi*, Council on Foreign Relations, June 8, 2006, *available at* http://www.cfr.org/publication/9866/#1 (last visited Mar. 14, 2010).

Casey said an American airstrike targeted "an identified, isolated safe house."

He said tips and intelligence from senior leaders of al-Zarqawi's network led U.S. forces to al-Zarqawi as he was meeting with some of his associates. Casey also said Iraqi police were first on the scene after the airstrike. . . .

Al-Maliki said the Wednesday night airstrike by U.S. forces was based on intelligence reports provided to Iraqi security forces by area residents.

A Jordanian official said the kingdom also provided the U.S. military with information that helped track down al-Zarqawi, who claimed responsibility for a November triple suicide bombing against Amman hotels that killed 60.

The official, who spoke on condition of anonymity because he was addressing intelligence issues, would not elaborate, but Jordan is known to have agents operating in Iraq to hunt down Islamic militants. Some of the information came from Jordan's sources inside Iraq and led the U.S. military to the area of Baqouba, the official said.[30]

ISSUES TO CONSIDER

1. Given the importance of human sources, does the U.S. sufficiently penetrate international terror organizations?
2. Does penetration of domestic terror organizations raise constitutional concerns?
3. What should be the criteria for determining source reliability?
4. What level of source reliability justifies operational counterterrorism based on HUMINT?
5. What are the risks involved in trusting a source?
6. What, if any, constitutional guarantees exist for the potential victim of a source?
7. Should operational counterterrorism decisions be predicated only on SIGNIT, with HUMINT serving as a confirmation?

While the Bush administration suggested the 9/11 attacks could have been prevented if not for legal barriers, the findings of the 9/11 Commission suggest otherwise. Many of the provisions enacted in the PATRIOT Act regarding surveillance and intelligence gathering powers were previously available to federal officials. According to many commentators,[31] the failure was an institutionalized and systemic inability to maximize sophisticated technology available to the intelligence community. Simply put, the United States was unable to make use of the intelligence it had gathered because it lacked the human capability to translate and act on it.

Given that 9/11 is predominantly an intelligence failure, the question is whether lessons have been learned and applied. This is relevant to operational

---

30. *Al Qaeda in Iraq's al-Zarqawi "Terminated,"* MSNBC, June 8, 2006), *available at* http://www.msnbc.msn.com/id/13195017/ (last visited Mar. 14, 2010).

31. *See* Joshua Rovner & Austin Long, *Intelligence Failure and Reform: Evaluating the 9/11 Commission Report,* 14 Breakthroughs 10 (2005). *See also* The Intelligence Community and 9/11: Congressional Hearings and the Status of the Investigation 1/16/03, *available at* http://www.fas.org/irp/crs/RL31650.pdf (last visited July 24, 2010).

counterterrorism both in the United States and abroad. The U.S. drone policy has been characterized by significant collateral damage reflecting, in part, inaccurate intelligence information regarding the presence of innocent civilians. Similarly, the continued struggles of U.S. ground forces in Afghanistan can be attributed, in part, to intelligence gathering/analysis limitations in the complicated Afghan paradigm.

With respect to the attempted Christmas Day bombing (December 2009) on Northwest Airlines Flight 253, much of the blame rests squarely on the shoulders of various airport security procedures (beyond the purview of this book). However, the inability to develop a sophisticated model that would have identified the bomber as an imminent threat and to develop a tracking model that would have facilitated identifying a known threat represents an overwhelming failure of the intelligence community.

ED HORNICK, REPORT ON FAILED CHRISTMAS TERROR ATTACK RELEASED

CNN, Jan. 8, 2010[32]

The government had sufficient information to have potentially disrupted an al Qaeda plot to bomb an airliner on Christmas Day, but failed to identify Umar Farouk AbdulMutallab as a potential bomber, a White House review of the incident shows.

In the end, the six-page report found, it was the inability of the intelligence community to "connect the dots" in putting all the pieces of information and analysis together.

"The intelligence fell through the cracks. This happened in more than one organization," Deputy National Security Adviser John Brennan told reporters after President Obama spoke Thursday.

Information was gathered on a possible al Qaeda plot, according to the report, between mid-October and late December 2009.

"Though all of the information was available to all-source analysts at the CIA and the NCTC [National Counter Terrorism Center] prior to the attempted attack, the dots were never connected, and as a result, the problem appears to be more a component failure to 'connect the dots,' rather than a lack of information sharing," the report said.

Al Qaeda in the Arabian Peninsula, a Yemen-based offshoot of the terrorist network that attacked New York and Washington in 2001, has claimed responsibility for the December 25 plot.

According to the report, U.S. counterterrorism officials had information about AbdulMutallab, al Qaeda threats to Americans "and information about an individual now believed to be Mr. AbdulMutallab and his association with AQAP and its attack planning." But "the dots were never connected"–not because information wasn't shared among U.S. agencies, but because it was "fragmentary and embedded in a large volume of other data."

---

32. *Available at* http://www.cnn.com/2010/POLITICS/01/07/terror.report.findings/index.html/.

Once the threat was discovered, the intelligence community leadership failed to increase resources working on the "full AQAP threat."

The report said the counterterrorism apparatus "failed before December 25 to identify, correlate, and fuse into a coherent story all of the discrete pieces of intelligence" that the U.S. government had in hand about "the emerging terrorist plot."

The report also found there was no mechanism in place to follow leads to their conclusion and to identify this gap ahead of time.

"The overlapping layers of protection within the [counterterrorism] community failed to track this threat in a manner sufficient to ensure all leads were followed and acted upon to conclusion."

There were also a series of human errors which "delayed dissemination of a finished intelligence report and what appears to be incomplete/faulty database searches on Mr. Abdulmutallab's name and identifying information."

Released along with the report was a three-page order from Obama outlining what various agencies need to do to correct the "inherent systemic weaknesses and human errors" the review found.

The departments of State and Homeland Security, the FBI, CIA, National Security Agency, National Counterterrorism Center and the office of the director of national intelligence, as well as the White House national security staff, have been ordered to report back within 30 days.

The report found that the watch-list system is not broken, but "needs to be strengthened and improved."

In addition, a reorganization of the intelligence or "broader counterterrorism community is not required to address problems that surfaced in the review, a fact made clear by countless other successful efforts to the thwart ongoing plots."

The report added that the counterterrorism community failed, "starting with establishing rules and protocols, to assign responsibility and accountability for follow up of high priority threat streams, run down all leads, and track them through to completion."

The U.S. intelligence community possesses the tools necessary to prevent terrorist attacks. There is widespread agreement that information available to the U.S., including HUMINT, SIGINT, and OSINT, was sufficient to prevent 9/11. The challenge facing decision makers is establishing protocol in the years ahead to maximize effective use of available information. The 9/11 Commission addressed many of these issues, encouraging dialogue to answer these difficult questions. But more than dialogue is required to ensure that the United States protects its borders from attacks by terrorists armed with increasing capabilities. While little doubt exists regarding the extraordinary sophistication of the U.S. with respect to signal intelligence, significant doubt remains regarding its human intelligence capabilities.

Intelligence gathering requires innovation and initiative. The constitutional limits on surveillance that *Katz*[33] articulated were not a barrier to

---

33. 389 U.S. 347 (1967).

preventing attacks. The FISA court, as demonstrated by the available statistics, has proven very receptive to government requests for warrants.. As we have discussed, the state of intelligence gathering should not be limited to the viability of wiretapping and other forms of SIGINT. Well-placed human sources can provide states with the invaluable capability of infiltrating cells, and with regards to the U.S. drone policy, can pinpoint targets while minimizing collateral damage.

IV. ISRAEL

A. INTELLIGENCE SOURCES

Israel's counterterrorism intelligence gathering is primarily based on HUMINT and SIGINT.

In Israel, intelligence gathering is largely directed at Palestinians residing in the West Bank and Gaza Strip.[34] Israelis consider intelligence gathering a vital piece in the counterterrorism puzzle; invading the privacy of Palestinian communities and other groups deemed possible "threats to national security" are considered "necessary evils," if they are considered at all.

As discussed in the previous section, much criticism was directed at the Bush administration's NSA wire-tapping program for the perception that it is an unwarranted—if not unconstitutional—measure. According to Israeli Law,[35] wiretaps on phone calls originating from Israel proper must be court-ordered and subject to judicial review. However, the interception of phone conversations originating in the West Bank and Gaza Strip need not be court-ordered. In addition to significant SIGINT abilities, the Israel Security Agency (ISA) has developed a highly sophisticated, effective, and efficient network of Palestinian collaborators. The strength of the Israeli intelligence community is its ability to create and maintain significant HUMINT networks. According to a variety of sources, Palestinians provide their case officers information regarding Palestinian terrorists for any of the following: (1) economic gain (information received is financially remunerated); (2) erasing a criminal record; (3) preventing a terror attack. The network of sources has proven extremely successful in preventing terror attacks.[36] However, collaborators are at great personal risk; Palestinian terrorists killed 1124 suspected collaborators over a six-year period.[37]

---

34. The exceptions to this are the ISA's reported intelligence gathering efforts against Jewish right-wing and left-wing extremists alike in new immigrant and minority communities. None of these will be addressed in this book. In addition, Israel's foreign intelligence gathering efforts will not be discussed.

35. The Secret Monitoring Law, 5739-1979, Laws of the State of Israel, vol. 33, pp. 141-46; *see also* Privacy and Human Rights 2003: Country Reports, Israel, *available at* http://www.privacy international.org/survey/phr2003/countries/israel.htm#ftnref1542 (last visited Oct. 8, 2010).

36. *See* Bethany M. Nikfar, *Families Divided: An Analysis of Israel's Citizenship and entry into Israel Law*, 3 Nw. U. J. Int'l Hum. Rts. 5 (2005); Gabriel Danzig, *In Defense of Collaborators*, The Jerusalem Post, August 28, 2002; Martin Peretz, *"Front Line" in The New Republic Online*, Post Date 9/1/05; Issue Date 9/5/05.

37. *Victims of Palestinian Violence and Terrorism since September 2000, available at* http://www.mfa.gov.il/MFA/Terrorism-+Obstacle+to+Peace/Palestinian+terror+since+2000/Victims+of+Palestinian+Violence+and+Terrorism+sinc.htm (last visited Oct. 8, 2010).

One of the most important issues in intelligence gathering is the source. The ISA depends on sources to provide information. While the case officer is responsible for analyzing the information provided, the service rendered by the informant is literally invaluable. The case officer determines the quality of the intelligence by assessing its reliability and accuracy. Furthermore, the case officer must be convinced that the informant is not giving grudge-based information, intended to pay back an innocent member of the community.

The following article provides a glimpse into the life of an informant.

GERSHOM GORENBERG, THE COLLABORATOR

The Palestinian Human Rights Monitoring Group[38]

M. is Palestinian, but speaks Hebrew with only a hint of his native Arabic. Even when indoors, he wears a pair of wraparound sunglasses pushed to the top of his head, a standard Israeli affectation. He joined Israeli society years ago, without realizing it, when he was recruited by Israel's Shin Bet security service to provide information about other Palestinians. On the surface, he has learned to fit in Israel. But on a deeper level, he is a displaced person, a casualty of a long war. . . . The Shin Bet has been the main agency responsible for gathering intelligence in the West Bank and Gaza Strip since Israel's conquest of those areas in 1967. For security officials, recruiting Palestinian informers is an essential tool. Eighty percent of all attempted terror attacks, according to a spokesman for the Israel Defense Forces, are prevented on the basis of intelligence. Much of it comes from informers.

The S.A.A. refused to let M. answer questions about what information he passed on to Israeli intelligence or how he had gathered it. So before I met with M., I spoke with Roy Politi, who spent several years in the occupied territories as an Israeli Police operative, working closely with Shin Bet.

While the Shin Bet will say nothing about how it conducts its covert battle against terror groups, published (and censored) testimony by ex-officials, along with Palestinian human rights reports, creates an outline of how the agency has recruited and run collaborators over the years. In the best case, the operative who is meeting a prospective informer can provide something the target wants — such as money. One ex-informer, recounting to me his decision to work with the Shin Bet at the beginning of the Israeli occupation, stated bluntly that money was his motive: "I came from hunger. You see bread in front of you. You're not going to take it?" It's often not much bread. Yaakov Perry, who headed the Shin Bet from 1988 to 1995, notes in his autobiography, "Strike First," that payments to informers are necessarily small, lest "sudden riches arouse suspicion."

Another form of payoff has been the Israeli-issued permits needed by residents of the occupied territories — a permit to work or do business in Israel or a "family reunification" permit, allowing a Jordanian-born wife, say, to join her

---

38. *Available at* http://www.nytimes.com/2002/08/18/magazine/18PALESTINIAN.html?pagewanted=print&position=top (last visited Mar. 14, 2010).

husband in the West Bank. In one case Perry describes, a Palestinian man sought a permit for his wife to receive gynecological treatment at the Hadassah Hospital in Jerusalem; Perry, then a young operative, offered to secure the permit if the man would sign up as an informer.

An operative can also play on the rivalries that fragment Palestinian society, exploiting the gaps between "the Dehaishe refugee camp and the people with the big houses next to it," Polity says, "or between Hamas and the secularists." The agent will try to convince the potential Palestinian recruit that by collaborating, he will be doing the right thing for his own people. Indeed, another ex-informer said that he agreed to work with the Shin Bet because he witnessed a bloody grenade attack by Palestinians against Israeli civilians. "If you want to carry out attacks, get soldiers," the man said. "Not the civilians. That's against religion and law."

When M. was recruited in 1987, the era of low-key occupation was coming to a close. Before the year ended, rebellion swept through the West Bank; frustration and humiliation transmogrified into nationalism. To be known as an informer was now deadly—and M. became known.

"I've got no idea how they found it out," he says. But they did, and fear followed. Twice the house of the mukhtar [village elder—EDS.] was torched. Every day, M. says, he heard news of collaborators being hanged in other villages.

Meanwhile, friends who were ex-collaborators told him about the S.A.A. and explained that he could apply to it for help. His application was accepted, and he was given an apartment in a Jewish town and later an Israeli ID card. His wife and children turned down the S.A.A.'s offer to move them to Israel. "The kids are big already, and my wife wouldn't be able to handle it," M. says. "Life is completely different here." M. could not ask his family to cross into a world they didn't know. He was alone.

Under the 1994 Cairo agreement between Israel and the Palestinians and the following year's Oslo II agreement, the Palestinian Authority promised to protect the safety of Palestinians who had worked with Israel in the past. But when the Palestinian leadership arrived from Tunis in 1994, says Gideon Ezra, the former deputy director of Shin Bet and now a Likud politician and the deputy minister of internal security, "the only thing that interested them was who had worked for Israel." So Israel set up the S.A.A., and hundreds of ex-intelligence sources and their families were moved to Israel and given help learning Hebrew, getting jobs and finding new homes. The relocated informers were relieved to be out of danger but were not necessarily happy. "Were you to ask them if they had the chance to do it over, would they collaborate, some of them wouldn't," Ezra reflects. "If they'd known Israel was going to pull out, some of them wouldn't have joined up."

Many more informers, it seems certain, were never exposed and remained in the occupied territories. "The hidden ones stayed to keep on working," Ezra says. Bassem Eid estimates that "tens of thousands" of collaborators were recruited in the years before the Oslo accord. Israeli intelligence veterans suggest that Palestinians exaggerate the numbers but say that the pervasive fear they create makes it harder for terrorists to operate.

With the beginning of the new uprising in September 2000, the Palestinians' hunt for collaborators accelerated. One reason, Eid argues, was Israel's assassination policy. In an effort to end Palestinian violence, Israel has killed key Palestinian activists, often in pinpoint strikes: a helicopter gunship hurling a missile at a wanted man's car, a pay telephone exploding as an Islamic Jihad leader talks on it. Many Palestinians assume the information needed for hits comes from turncoats.

Despite the witch hunt, most Israelis and Palestinians presume that Israel is still gathering information and even recruiting new informers. Against the fear that could dissuade collaborators, there are new pressures to compel Palestinians to work with Israel: deeper poverty and the increased difficulty of moving even from one town to another on roads shut by Israeli checkpoints. Moreover, "People on the Palestinian street have doubts about Arafat," Politi says, and as he sees it, a clever operative should be able to exploit those doubts.

The GSS depends on sources to provide intelligence information. Though the case-officer is responsible for analyzing the information provided, the service rendered by the informant is literally invaluable. The case officer determines the quality of the intelligence information by assessing its reliability and accuracy. Furthermore, the case officer must be convinced that the informant is not giving "grudge-based" information intended to "pay back" an innocent member of the community. In addition to the intelligence received from sources, the GSS and the IDF gather a significant amount of information from intercepted phone conversations originating in the West Bank or the Gaza Strip.

ISSUES TO CONSIDER

1. What reliability standards should be implemented when assessing the quality of intelligence received from informants whose lives are in constant danger as described above?
2. What are the most effective and realistic methods of corroborating the information provided by an informant?
3. What criteria should be established when determining the reliability of a source who has a vested interest in providing information?
4. What safeguards should be implemented for a source-focused intelligence gathering system?
5. Can operational counterterrorism measures be based on uncorroborated intelligence information?
6. Does the fact that terrorist groups have perpetrated attacks despite infiltration by sources suggest inherent limitations of intelligence?
7. Should there be limits on the methods case officers may use in extracting information they know an informant has?

B. RELIABILITY OF SOURCES

For intelligence information to be deemed actionable a source must be considered reliable and the information provided corroborated. In developing the informant network referred to above, the ISA seeks to cross-reference information prior to recommending specific operational missions to IDF commanders.

The criteria for determining source reliability—the essence of the process—has been highly developed in Israel. Sources are classified according to a variety of indexes: quality and accuracy of information previously provided; actionability of information previously provided; whether the informant has a vendetta against the subject of the information; the uniqueness of the information provided (for instance whether the information is commonly known); and the importance of the information.

Conducting operational counterterrorism based on single-source information creates significant risks. Therefore, prior to acting on the available information, the case officer must seek corroborating information. Uncorroborated intelligence presents a significant dilemma: if the information suggests a major terrorism attack, delay in acting may result in innocent civilian deaths. Conversely, undertaking operational counterterrorism missions against an individual falsely identified by a source results, at best, in an unjustified loss of freedom and, at worst, the death of an innocent individual.

This dilemma is at the core of intelligence gathering and operational counterterrorism decision making. The effort to seek corroboration of intelligence information has been a mainstay in Israel's strategy; nevertheless, operational decisions have been made based on single-source information. Though Israeli domestic law does not specifically address source reliability or information corroboration, petitions have been filed before the High Court questioning the reliability of sources. The Court's concern is clear: whether the information available to the ISA justifies a decision to impinge on the freedom of a Palestinian in a non-criminal context.

Issues to Consider

1. If the High Court does not directly question the source, is intelligence reliability largely a matter of "trust me"?
2. What institutional safeguards are required to protect Palestinians named by sources?
3. How—if at all—does the Court analyze source reliability?

After bombing a purported chemical producing factory in the Sudan,[39] then President Clinton largely said "trust me" when asked to submit the evidence justifying the attack. In the follow-up investigation, the intelligence that had been the basis for the President's decision to bomb was found to be incorrect. Was this the only time that executive decisions were based on faulty intelligence?

Since the answer is clearly negative, the challenge facing lawyers, judges, and decision makers is how best to assess both the information and the informant in determining what institutional safeguards should be implemented to

---

39. *See* Jules Lobel, *The Use of Force to Respond to Terrorist Attacks*, 24 Yale J. Int'l L. 537 (1999).

protect the potential target. In the U.S., the arguable safeguard is FISA, though the Bush administration's decision to bypass the court casts doubt on that. In Israel, the High Court of Justice assumes that responsibility.

As evidenced by the above material, intelligence failures are an inevitable aspect of counterterrorism. Unlike other nations, Israel's intelligence failures are not caused by legal restrictions or judicial intervention. Its successes, of which there are many, are directly contributable to the effective convergence of HUMINT and SIGINT.

If no legal barriers exist, how should a nation account for recorded failures? Perhaps the inherent limitations of intelligence gathering are best highlighted by the Israeli model. As discussed earlier, the ISA has penetrated many terrorist cells operating in the Palestinian territories through a well-developed source network in the West Bank and the Gaza Strip. Yet the intelligence community, in spite of the tools at its disposal, is unable to prevent every terrorist attack and has repeatedly misgauged the ability of terrorist organizations. Unlike the Bush administration which sought to bypass existing laws, Israel's legal structure provides the intelligence community with the means necessary but ultimately demonstrates that no counterterrorism operation, no matter how sophisticated the intelligence, can be infallible.

V. RUSSIA

Understanding intelligence gathering in Russia requires understanding the extraordinary power of the Soviet-era KGB.

RUSSIA: INTERNAL SECURITY BEFORE 1991

RussiansAbroad.com[40]

The KGB had been an integral feature of the Soviet state since it was established by Nikita S. Khrushchev (in office 1953-64) in 1954 to replace the People's Commissariat for Internal Affairs (Narodnyy komissariat vnutrennikh del — NKVD), which during its twenty-year existence had conducted the worst of the Stalinist purges. Between 1954 and 1991, the KGB acquired vast monetary and technical resources, a corps of active personnel numbering more than 500,000, and huge archival files containing political information of the highest sensitivity. The KGB often was characterized as a state within a state. The organization was a rigidly hierarchical structure whose chairman was appointed by the Politburo, the supreme executive body of the Communist Party of the Soviet Union ("CPSU"). Key decisions were made by the KGB Collegium, a collective leadership including the agency's top leaders and selected republic and departmental chiefs. The various KGB directorates had responsibilities ranging from suppressing political dissent to guarding borders to conducting propaganda campaigns abroad. At the end of the Soviet period,

---

40. *Available at* http://www.russiansabroad.com/russian_history_364.html (last visited Mar. 14, 2010).

the KGB had five chief directorates, three smaller directorates, and numerous administrative and technical support departments.

In contrast to the United States government, which assigns the functions of domestic counterintelligence and foreign intelligence to separate agencies, the Federal Bureau of Investigation (FBI) and the Central Intelligence Agency (CIA), respectively, the Soviet system combined these functions in a single organization. This practice grew out of the ideology of Soviet governance, which made little distinction between external and domestic political threats, claiming that the latter were always foreign inspired. According to that rationale, the same investigative techniques were appropriate for both foreign espionage agents and Soviet citizens who came under official suspicion. For example, the KGB's Seventh Chief Directorate, whose task was to provide personnel and equipment for surveillance operations, was responsible for surveillance of both foreigners and Soviet citizens.

The KGB's branches in the fourteen non-Russian republics duplicated the structure and operations of the unionwide organization centered in Moscow; KGB offices existed in every subnational jurisdiction and city of the Soviet Union. The KGB's primary internal function was surveillance of the Soviet citizenry, using a vast intelligence apparatus to ensure loyalty to the regime and to suppress all expressions of political opposition. This apparatus served as the eyes and ears of the party leadership, supplying information on all aspects of Soviet society to the Politburo.

A. RUSSIAN INTELLIGENCE TECHNOLOGY

The extent to which Russia utilizes SIGINT is murky, though satellite phone signals have been used to target terrorist leaders' locations. The Russian constitution and various legislations outline the parameters regarding signal intelligence.

PRIVACY INTERNATIONAL, RUSSIAN FEDERATION

Dec. 18, 2007[41]

The Constitution of the Russian Federation recognizes rights of privacy, data protection and secrecy of communications. Article 23 states, "1. Everyone shall have the right to privacy, to personal and family secrets, and to protection of one's honor and good name. 2. Everyone shall have the right to privacy of correspondence, telephone communications, mail, cables and other communications. Any restriction of this right shall be allowed only under an order of a court of law." Article 24 states, "1. It shall be forbidden to gather, store, use and disseminate information on the private life of any person without his/her consent. 2. The bodies of state authority and the bodies of local self-government and the officials thereof shall provide to each citizen access to

---

41. *Available at* http://www.privacyinternational.org/article.shtml?cmd[347]=x-347-559497(last visited Mar. 14, 2010).

any documents and materials directly affecting his/her rights and liberties unless otherwise stipulated under the law." Article 25 states, "The home shall be inviolable. No one shall have the right to enter the home against the will of persons residing in it except in cases stipulated by the federal law or under an order of a court of law."

In 2006, Russia adopted the Law on Personal Data, and the Law on Information, Information Technologies and Protection of Information, which replaced the 1995 Law of Information, Informatization and Protection of Information. Adoption of the Law on Personal Data fulfills Russia's obligation to transpose the Council of Europe Convention for the Protection of Individuals with regard to Automatic Processing of Personal Data into national law. The Law on Personal Data generally protects personal data from being collected and processed illegally and without consent of data subject. However, the law is still far from ideal since it gives wide exemptions to the government. The Law on Personal Data came into force in January 2007, but most of its provisions are still inactive; for example, the law provides for the creation of a data protection authority, but none is operational to date.

The 2003 Communications Law protects secrecy of communications. The tapping of telephone conversations, scrutiny of electronic communications, delay, inspection and seizure of postal mailings and documentary correspondence, receipt of information therein, and other restriction of communications secrets are allowed only with a court order except as otherwise provided by a federal law. The Law on Operational Investigation Activity that regulates surveillance methods used by secret services requires a court-issued warrant. The law was amended in December 1998 by the State Duma. Guarantees for the protection of privacy were emphasized and additional controls imposed on prosecutors. Article 5 of the Law provides that an investigative structure must secure people's privacy. The Law also provides: "If one believes that some actions of bodies conducting operational investigation have infringed on an individual's rights or freedoms, the individual has the right to appeal to a court, a prosecutor, or to a higher body that carries out investigative activities."

The law also provides: "If a person has not been proved guilty during a legally established procedure, then all materials obtained during this operational investigation must be archived for a period of one year and subsequently deleted." However this provision is virtually revoked by the following addition: ". . . unless official interests or justice require otherwise." In December 1999, the law was amended to allow surveillance by the tax police, the Ministry of Internal Affairs, Border Guards, the Kremlin Security Service, the Presidential Security Service, the parliamentary security services and the Foreign Intelligence Service. In 2001, the following provision was added to the Law: "Audio recordings and other materials resulting from interception and wiretapping of the conversation of persons being out of criminal proceedings must be deleted within six months after the wiretapping is over with an appropriate protocol. The judge must be notified three months before materials reflecting the results of operational investigations, implemented on the basis of a court warrant, are deleted." Disclosure of data that affects someone's privacy without his or her consent is legally prohibited unless otherwise stipulated by federal laws. . . .

In 2005, the government, citing concerns about terrorism, approved new regulations for interactions between communication companies and certain government agencies. The new regulations give law enforcement agencies greater access to telephone and cellular phone company clients' personal information and require providers to grant the Ministry of Internal Affairs and Federal Security Service (FSB) 24-hour remote access to their client data-bases. Some experts believed these new rules contradict the Constitution. Given that the authorities have had legal access to these records for 10 years, mobile operator MegaFon's press secretary suggested that the new rules change nothing, and simply make the process "more transparent."

The FSB has conducted phone tapping using the "SORM" system (or "System of Operative Investigative Activities"). In 1998, information about a new SORM-2 system that applies to the Internet was revealed. SORM-2 requires Internet Service Providers (ISPs) to install surveillance devices and high-speed links to local FSB departments, which would allow the FSB to directly access Internet users' communications, although with a warrant requirement. . . .

After the terrorist attack in Moscow of October 2002, the State Duma quickly adopted several amendments to the laws on Mass Media and Terror-ism, banning any distribution of information that could impede anti-terrorist actions. In December 2004, a new concept of the "state of a terrorist emer-gency" was introduced in the State Duma as one counter-terrorism measure. The new regime of a "state of a terrorist emergency" could seriously limit civil rights in case Russian law enforcement bodies receive information about a terrorist act prepared but failed to check this information. In the beginning of 2006, after lengthy discussions, the parliament removed the new proposal from the counterterrorism bill. However, according to the new counterterror-ism law enacted in 2006, Russian secret services can easily wiretap and inter-cept communications during their counter terrorist operations

B. RUSSIA AND HUMINT

Russian intelligence services have traditionally had limited success in penetrating both Chechen society and Chechen terror organizations.

While the KGB was highly regarded for its ability to infiltrate institutions perceived hostile to the Soviet Union, present Russian intelligence efforts to infiltrate Chechnya have largely failed. Commentators assign this failure to the fact that close-knit Chechen society remains a difficult breeding ground for informants. As noted above, intelligence gathering largely depends on the infiltration of sources into specifically identified communities and organiza-tions; Russia's inability to achieve this in Chechnya has negatively affected counterterrorism strategy and tactics.

ISSUES TO CONSIDER

1. Does the inability to infiltrate terror organizations suggest that nations should not conduct counterterrorism?
2. What is the proper relationship between Barak's "self-imposed restraints" and the legitimate need to conduct counterterrorism when

human rights abuses may be inevitable given the lack of specific intelligence information?
3. Can signal intelligence alone provide sufficient basis for counterterrorism operations?

Limited human intelligence gathering capabilities hinder person specific counterterrorism. By contrast to Israel's operational counterterrorism—largely dependent on human intelligence—Russia's difficulty in developing sources within Chechen terror cells limits the military's ability to conduct similar counterterrorism. Nevertheless, Russia has been successful against specific individuals albeit on a limited basis. The targeted killings of Chechen Presidents' Dzhokha Dudayev on April 21, 1996 and Maskhadov on March 8, 2005, were the result of traceable satellite phones rather than improved on the ground intelligence. These successful operations are largely the exception to Russia's intelligence failures.

Arguably, the widely reported human rights abuses by Russian soldiers are a direct result of an inability to specifically identify particular targets. Unlike the Israeli High Court of Justice's judicial activism, the Russian constitutional court does not act as a "restrainer" on military decision makers.

ISSUES TO CONSIDER

1. How much intelligence should be considered sufficient for counterterrorism operations and what criteria should be developed?
2. Given the significant number of human rights violations reported in Chechnya, should Russian decision makers establish criteria for determining when an attack may be warranted?
3. Do attacks such as Beslan warrant "an all-out effort" even if the intelligence picture is not clear?
4. Should the lack of actionable intelligence limit operational counterterrorism measures?
5. What does Russia's limited response to Beslan suggest regarding "the limits of power"?
6. Does Beslan suggest an intelligence failure?
7. How should regimes compensate for a lack of specific actionable intelligence?
8. Are closed-clan cultures penetrable?

C. RUSSIAN SUCCESS

Better intelligence, exemplified by the following incident, enables the Russian forces to successfully execute pinpoint operational counterterrorism. The results are clear and clean—legitimate targets are attacked while minimizing possible human rights violations. The difference between accurate intelligence and an incomplete picture is literally "night and day" from both a tactical and strategic perspective.

FRED BURTON, INTELLIGENCE PAYS OFF IN NALCHICK

Oct. 19, 2005[42]

[T]here is reason to believe that the militants who planned the attacks in Nalchik (an operation that has been claimed by Moscow's arch-enemy, Shamil Basayev) actually were forced into carrying out their operation prematurely, after Russian intelligence got wind of a much larger and more chilling plot — one combining all the most deadly tactics of both Sept. 11 and Beslan.

Russian military contacts and other sources have told us that the events in Nalchik apparently were supposed to be only the first phase of a plan that ultimately was to include flying explosives-laden aircraft into high-profile targets elsewhere in Russia. Though the exact targets have not been confirmed, sources say possible targets included the Kremlin, a military district headquarters and railway hub in Rostov-on-Don, a nuclear plant in the vicinity of Saratov, and a hydroelectric plant or dam on the Volga. Sources also say the militants had a back-up plan that would have involved mining important government buildings and taking hostages — tactics the Chechens have used in other headline-grabbing attacks.

[T]he Nalchik incident fits into wider trend that we have been following in the Chechen/Islamist insurgency for more than a year, and the target sets make sense for what is becoming an increasingly Wahhabist-dominated campaign in Russian territory.

The events on the ground also seem to bear out the sourced intelligence: The militants opened their attack with attempts to seize the airport in Nalchik, where — had they not been beaten back by Russian forces already guarding the target — they would have been able to commandeer the aircraft needed for follow-on operations. The incidents in other parts of the city, which were closely time-coordinated but appear to have involved poorly trained recruits, are believed to have been intended as distractions — drawing attention and Russian security forces away from the strategically crucial airport.

The fact that the follow-on attacks were more or less quickly put down, with (relatively) small loss of life, also fits the notion of a busted operation.

Considering Basayev's claims of responsibility for the Nalchik plot, that clearly seems to have been the intent. Basayev, it must be remembered, is the Chechen commander who has authored many of the most horrific terrorist incidents in Russia. Attacks like those at Beslan and the Moscow theater, and hostage-takings at hospitals and other soft targets typically have resulted in hundreds of deaths at a time — both before and during the bloody responses by Russian security forces. To say that Basayev has a penchant for grand, showy schemes would be something of an understatement.

---

42. *Available at* http://www.petrifiedtruth.com/archives/002726.html (last visited Mar. 14, 2010).

Operationally speaking, that trait seems to undermine his effectiveness as a militant leader—and, in fact, eventually could be his undoing. The fact that that has not yet happened points more toward particular aspects of the political conflict between the Chechen/Islamist insurgents and Moscow than to best practices taught in Terrorism 101.

Under those principles, the most effective forms of attack are those that are simple yet ruthless: They require few resources, and operatives practice airtight "need-to-know" communications. The fewer people who know about a plan—or have access to more details than they need in order to carry out their own part—the less likely the plan is to leak out and be pre-empted. Except for the fact that Basayev has, for the most part, operated in territory where locals have supported at least some aspects of the militant campaign against Russian rule, it is nothing short of amazing that he and his cast of thousands have succeeded to the degree that they have.

But the amount of local support Basayev still is able to command has become something of a question mark, as Chechens themselves have grown weary of the death and destruction in their war. It is said that, partly because of this, Basayev increasingly has surrounded himself with Wahhabi militants—including some Saudi commanders—and is seeking ways to export the campaign from the Muslim-dominated Caucasus republics into Russia proper.

All of this seems logical: Judging from details of the Nalchik plot and others within the past year, Basayev appears intent on mimicking elements of the Sept. 11 attacks—indicating that he at least is studying and learning from al Qaeda, even if he is not intimately linked to it. At the very least, his emerging fixation with air assets is reminiscent of Khalid Sheikh Mohammed—another tactical genius with a penchant for spectacular strikes.

Both the Nalchik operation and the wider plot, had it been carried out, would have mirrored Sept. 11 in other ways as well: Multiple targets, representing a mix of both hard (government installations) and soft (civilian infrastructure) nodes, might have been struck—maximizing the political, economic and sheer terror value of the strikes. The plot shows high degrees of strategic planning and, as a result, could have been designed to inspire audiences in the Muslim world—whether that world is defined to include Russia's Muslim-majority provinces or other regions.

It is important to note here that, though Sept. 11 has become the gold standard for "effective" terrorist attacks, we and others believe that even al Qaeda likely was stunned by its success. The plot was redundant in most aspects: two economic facilities (the World Trade Center towers) and two government facilities (the Pentagon and, it is believed, the Capitol) were targeted, building in a margin of error for planners who likely never expected three of the four aircraft to strike their targets. Similarly, Basayev appears to be hatching redundant plots, so that operations can still be politically and economically effective even if some aspects of the mission fail.

But at Nalchik, almost the entire operation failed before it could get off the ground. The points of failure appear to rest in two areas.

First, there is evidence that Basayev used some and ill-prepared operatives in Nalchik—rather than highly trained and ruthlessly efficient cells, like those that carried out the 9/11 attacks. The assailants acted in groups of five men. Typical al Qaeda operations use four-man cells, in which each member plays a specific and crucial role. Larger cells appear to be the norm in Chechen operations — partly because this allows commanders to play a greater role on the ground, but also perhaps because strikes often include local militants who have been poorly trained. This can be a mixed blessing. For instance, we saw in Beslan would-be suicide bombers who ran away; in Nalchik, some of the fighters — many of whom were well-equipped — fired their weapons while running toward their targets (a tactic very likely to draw return fire and get them killed). The use of larger cells allows for this kind of attrition without endangering the mission, but it also brings into the mix local operatives who have supreme area knowledge — and thus are able to identify launching points and escape routes with lower operational overhead.

Second, and crucially, there was poor operational security in Nalchik. In short, someone snitched, and the op was blown. The snitch could have been someone motivated by the bounties Moscow now is offering for intelligence targeting Chechen commanders, or a mole who has infiltrated the militants' ranks, or perhaps a local parent who overhead a conversation between teenagers — or all of the above. Given the hundreds of people who, according to sources, ultimately would have taken part in the plot, anything is possible. The point is, a lot of people were in the know, and COMSEC — communications security — was next to impossible.

Russian intelligence abilities remain a mixed lot, though Russia has recently shown the ability to develop and utilize sources close to Chechen terrorist leaders. By using tactics similar to Israel — financial renumeration of informants — to gain information that facilitates person-specific counterterrorism, Russia has made significant strides

Acting on a tip from within his own network, police killed Chechen leader Abdul-Khalim Sadulayev during a raid on a hideout in his hometown. Sadulayev had been planning a terror attack in Argun to coincide with the Group of Eight summit of leading industrialized nations in St. Petersburg.

Similarly, Shamil Basayev, the Chechen leader responsible for the Beslan school massacre, was killed by Russian security forces with the help of an informant paid $600,000. Although security forces were very tight-lipped about the circumstances of Basayev's death, it was clear he was betrayed by one of his own men.

ISSUES TO CONSIDER

1. Reliable intelligence information directly contributes to successful, person-specific counterterrorism; when such intelligence does not exist, should governments refrain from acting operationally?
2. The lack of actionable intelligence has undoubtedly resulted in significant human rights abuses and minimal operational success: what should be the baseline for determining that intelligence is actionable?

The killings of the two Chechen leaders suggest a change in the Russian authorities' ability to penetrate the closed-clan culture of Chechnya. These two attacks indicate a policy more akin to the U.S. and Israel's targeted killing policies, rather than an indiscriminate response that previously characterized Russian strategy. Pinpoint counterterrorism meets previously discussed international law principles and suggests greater sensitivity to blowback.

VI. INDIA

This section addresses intelligence gathering in the context of terror coming from Pakistan and the northwestern Indian states of Jammu and Kashmir.

A. KARGIL CONFLICT

In May of 1999, Pakistan crossed the Line of Control (the mutually agreed upon boundary between India and Pakistan) and invaded India in the area commonly referred to as Kargil. The resulting skirmishes, which lasted through the summer, killed 474 Indian military personnel and wounded an additional 1109.[43] The "Kargil Conflict," garnered international attention primarily because of India and Pakistan's mutual nuclear capability. Though concerns of a nuclear standoff never materialized, the conflict brought to the forefront issues surrounding Indian state security. While not an act of terrorism, but an armed attack by a sovereign state, the incident contributed to widespread review and analysis regarding India's intelligence agencies. As India readily admitted in the aftermath of the conflict, the attack came as a total surprise to the Indian government.

In response, India created the Kargil Committee, which released a report addressing how Pakistan was able to move troops into Indian territory without the Indian government's detection. The Committee announced that all government agencies charged with intelligence gathering had failed in their mission.

KARGIL COMMITTEE'S EXECUTIVE SUMMARY, FROM SURPRISE TO RECKONING

Kargil Committee Report, Feb. 25, 2000[44]

It is not widely appreciated in India that the primary responsibility for collecting external intelligence, including that relating to a potential adversary's military deployment, is vested in RAW [Research and Analysis Wing]. The DGMI's capability for intelligence collection is limited. It is essentially restricted to the collection of tactical military intelligence and some amount

---

43. *From Surprise to Reckoning*, Kargil Committee Report, Executive Summary, Feb. 25, 2000, *available at* http://www.fas.org/news/india/2000/25indi1.htm (last visited July 10, 2010).

44. *Available at* http://www.fas.org/news/india/2000/25indi1.htm (last visited Mar. 14, 2010).

of signal intelligence and its main role is to make strategic and tactical military assessments and disseminate them within the Army. Many countries have established separate Defence Intelligence Agencies and generously provided them with resources and equipment to play a substantive role in intelligence collection. For historical reasons, the Indian Armed Forces are not so mandated. Therefore, it is primarily RAW which must provide intelligence about a likely attack, whether across a broad or narrow front. Unfortunately the RAW facility in the Kargil area did not receive adequate attention in terms of staff or technological capability. The station was under Srinagar but reported to Leh which was not focused on Kargil but elsewhere. Hence intelligence collection, coordination and follow up were weak.

The Intelligence Bureau (IB) is meant to collect intelligence within the country and is the premier agency for counter-intelligence. This agency received input on activities in the FCNA region which were considered important enough by the Director, IB to be communicated over his signature on June 2, 1998 to the Prime Minister, Home Minister, Cabinet Secretary, Home Secretary and Director-General Military Operations. This communication was not addressed to the three officials most concerned with this information, namely. Secretary (RAW), who is responsible for external intelligence and had the resources to follow up the leads in the IB report; Chairman JIC, who would have taken such information into account in JIC assessments; and Director-General Military Intelligence. Director, IB stated that he expected the information to filter down to these officials through the official hierarchy. This did not happen in respect of Secretary (RAW) who at that time was also holding additional charge as Chairman, JIC. The Committee feels that a communication of this nature should have been directly addressed to all the officials concerned.

Such lapses, committed at one time or the other by all agencies, came to the notice of the Committee. These illustrate a number of deficiencies in the system. There is need for greater appreciation of the role of intelligence and who needs it most and also more understanding with regard to who must pursue any given lead. It further highlights the need for closer coordination among the intelligence agencies.

The present structure and processes in intelligence gathering and reporting lead to an overload of background and unconfirmed information and inadequately assessed intelligence which requires to be further pursued. There is no institutionalised process whereby RAW, IB, BSF and Army intelligence officials interact periodically at levels below the JIC. This lacuna is perhaps responsible for RAW reporting the presence of one additional unit in Gultari in September 1998 but not following it up with ARC flights on its own initiative. Nor did the Army press RAW specifically for more information on this report. The Army never shared its intelligence with the other agencies or with the JIC. There was no system of Army minorities at different levels from DGMI downwards providing feedback to the Agencies.

There is a general lack of awareness of the critical importance of and the need or assessed intelligence at all levels.

The report determined that the technological weakness of the Indian intelligence community made prevention of conflicts difficult.[45] The committee found serious lapses in the "collection, collation, and assessment of intelligence" that had "no mechanism for tasking the agencies, monitoring their performance, and reviewing their records to evaluate their quality. Nor is there any oversight of the overall functioning of the agencies."[46] In short, the committee perceived that the lack of technology available to recognize the deployment of troops into the Kargil region, coupled with the lack of an organized approach to intelligence gathering within India's government, made prevention of Kargil and future, similar attacks difficult, if not impossible.

ISSUES TO CONSIDER

1. What are the similarities and differences between the Kargil Report and the 9/11 Commission?
2. How does the government address "source intelligence" failure?
3. Is there an effective way to organize the intelligence agencies within the executive branch?
4. If SIGINT is unavailable and HUMINT is limited, what alternative measures can be developed?
5. India is forced to develop counterterrorism strategy in response to the actions of another sovereign; what are the limits of intelligence gathering when the object is a nation rather than a terrorist organization?
6. If Kashmir is disputed territory that both India and Pakistan lay claim to, what is the danger in aggressively developing human intelligence sources?

Similar to 9/11 and the Spanish train station bombings, Pakistan's attack in Kargil highlights failings in India's intelligence gathering and analysis. A 2002 paper addressed the Kargil conflict and echoed the Kargil Committee's discovery of issues endemic to Indian Intelligence Agencies.[47] The paper cited the following problems:

> Lack of control: The Indian situation is characteristic of a highly bureaucratized and politicized outside control and a loose, largely undefined set of rules governing the inner functioning of intelligence agencies. There is no legal, constitutional or legislative control of intelligence in India.
>
> Lack of coordination: Indian intelligence agencies are known to be working at cross-purposes, without any visible lack of coordination.
>
> India's political establishment also focused on heightened terrorist activity in Jammu and Kashmir and thus ruled out major armed incursion. Indian

---

45. *Id.*
46. *Id.* at 26.
47. Surinder Rana & Dr. James J Wirtz, *Kargil Conflict A Systemic and an Intelligence Failure*, Center for Contemporary Conflict (Sept. 2002).

intelligence agencies had continued to direct their efforts based upon prevailing national threat perception in the early 1999, which did not foresee Kargil. Hence, if there was a failure the entire system had failed.[48]

B. MUMBAI TRAIN BOMBING

On July 11, 2006, a series of seven explosions killed at least 174 people on crowded commuter trains and stations in the Indian financial capital of Mumbai. The targets were middle-class business persons, similar to the 9/11 financial sector victims. The bombing of seven trains, during rush hour traffic in Mumbai, also highlighted similar vulnerabilities within Indian intelligence networks. Not only did the act reflect significant SIGINT and HUMINT failings, but India's unfocused response was a direct result of poor intelligence. As the report below indicates, weak intelligence capabilities can frequently result in abuse and frustration in and among the general populace.

> Teams of armed officers continued with their mass round-ups yesterday, with further raids on a number of shanty towns around Bombay. So far they have detained more than 1,300 men, but the police face mounting public criticism at their failure to arrest anyone involved in the terror network that is believed to have been living in India's financial capital for at least three months.[49]

More important, and similar to Russia's historical experience in Chechnya, poor intelligence sends a message to both citizens and terrorists that the state is unable to prevent the attacks.

SUDHA RAMACHANDRAN, INDIA'S SOFT RESPONSE TO THE MUMBAI BOMBINGS

Asia Times, July 19, 2006[50]

The sudden chill that has gripped India-Pakistan relations after the Mumbai blasts has brought back memories of the frostbitten bilateral interaction that followed the terrorist attack on India's parliament building on December 13, 2001. That attack, which was carried out by the Jaish-e-Mohammed, a jihadist outfit that is backed by the Pakistani Inter-Services Intelligence (ISI), pushed India to cut diplomatic ties with Pakistan, as well as sever road, rail and air links with that country. India also deployed its security forces along its border with Pakistan. The two nuclear-armed rivals were on the brink of war; their armed forces were locked in eyeball-to-eyeball confrontation along their border for about 10 months.

This time around, India neither rushed to blame Pakistan for the blasts in Mumbai, nor has it sent its troops to the border as it did in 2001. But a familiar war of words between the two neighbors has been set in motion.

---

48. *Intelligence Failure Led to Kargil*, Feb. 12, 2003, *available at* http://www.rediff.com/news/2003/feb/12kargil.htm (last visited Mar. 14, 2010).

49. Daniel McGrory, *Train Bombers "Funded by British Businessmen,"* Bombay, July 17, 2006, *available at* http://www.timesonline.co.uk/article/0,,3-2273287,00.html (last visited Mar. 14, 2010).

50. *Available at* http://www.atimes.com/atimes/South_Asia/HG19Df03.html (last visited Mar. 14, 2010).

It was Pakistani Prime Minister Khurshid Kasuri's comments to Reuters in Washington in the aftermath of the blasts that provided the immediate spark for the exchange of angry rhetoric. In his remarks, Kasuri seemed to link the blasts with India's failure to resolve disputes with Pakistan. This provoked India to describe as "appalling" Kasuri's linking of terrorist attacks "to the so-called lack of resolution of disputes between India and Pakistan."

Three days after the blasts, Indian Prime Minister Manmohan Singh, while refraining from naming Pakistan, spoke of "terror modules being supported, inspired and instigated by elements across the border."

Few in India believe that Pakistani President General Pervez Musharraf has cracked down seriously on anti-India terrorists. He might have come down on Shi'ite and Sunni sectarian outfits, but such groups as Lashkar-e-Toiba and Jaish-e-Mohammed are allowed to operate openly on Pakistani soil—that is the widely held perception in India. And although infiltration across the Line of Control has fallen steadily since 2001, this is attributed to India's fencing of the LoC rather than any dramatic about-turn in Pakistan's policy of pushing militants into Jammu and Kashmir.

There has been some annoyance in India with the present government's soft approach to tackling terrorism and toward Pakistan. The government's response to terrorist attacks over the past year has been mild. Every terrorist attack that occurred over the past year saw the government issuing a statement that "the peace process will not be affected." While this did not evoke much of a reaction up to now, there are voices now demanding that New Delhi deal with Islamabad more sternly.

Sections within the opposition Bharatiya Janata Party (BJP), which that headed the coalition government during the 2001-02 downturn in India-Pakistan relations, are calling on the government to adopt a "hot pursuit" strategy (where Indian security forces would chase terrorist into their camps in Pakistan) to deal with Pakistan-backed terrorism. Others in the party are saying that they want the peace process, which the BJP-led government started in 2004, to continue but want Islamabad to deliver on its commitments under the agreement. Whether the hawks in the BJP will push for more extreme positions in the coming days remains to be seen.

And then there are those who are looking toward Israel for ideas and inspiration. An editorial in The Pioneer, an English-language daily from Delhi, compares Israel's "tough and unambiguous measures"—the ongoing bombing and blockade of Lebanon to deal with Hezbollah—with the "pusillanimity and squeamishness" of the Indian government. "It is nobody's suggestion that the government should immediately begin bombing terrorist camps across the Line of Control," the editorial says, going on to argue that this, however, is "a compelling and perhaps inevitable option."

B Raman, former head of counterterrorism at India's external intelligence agency, the Research and Analysis Wing (RAW), has called for a return to the pre-1996 policy of "talk, talk, hit, hit" where the political leadership and officials "continued meeting and talking to their Pakistani counterparts, whether there was any useful outcome or not" but "gave a free hand to their intelligence agencies to do whatever they felt was necessary to hurt Pakistan covertly for its use of terrorism against India."

"The time has come," he said, to "talk, talk, bite, bite."

Even strong proponents of the peace process with Pakistan are questioning the benefits of persisting with talks. Noted analyst C Raja Mohan argued: "If Musharraf is not willing or is unable to deliver an end to cross-border terrorism, the [Indian] government can only conclude that it is no longer possible to do business with him."

Sumit Ganguly, director of the India Studies Program at Indiana University in the US, argued that India "should do far more than merely defer the "composite dialogue." Instead, it needs to embark on a relentless campaign to isolate Pakistan diplomatically and to reveal the Musharraf regime's organic ties to the jihadi terror network." He suggested that India "dramatically downgrade its diplomatic presence in Islamabad [and] end all ongoing cultural exchanges." It should launch a "sophisticated, orchestrated and sustained diplomatic campaign on a global basis that uses information available in the public domain to depict the Pakistani state as an incubator of terror."

While hot pursuit and surgical strikes seem robust options that will produce quick results, they might not be as rewarding as hardliners imagine. Those who advocate "tough and unambiguous measures" like those adopted by Israel ignore the fact that these haven't worked to secure Israel against violent attacks. And even if they were successful, such tactics would not work in India's case since India does not enjoy the overwhelming military superiority that Israel does with its neighbors. Besides, India's adoption of such tactics would not have US endorsement that Israel enjoys.

If the threat of military action did not work, would suspending the composite dialogue help? Some analysts are pointing out that suspending or ending the dialogue is not only unlikely to push Pakistan to turn off the terror tap, but also it would undermine the gains India has made from the peace process. The confidence-building measures that are in place today might not have brought a change of heart or attitude in the Pakistan-based terrorist groups or their handlers in the ISI, but they have built a strong constituency for peace among ordinary Pakistanis.

For now, India seems to be keeping its options open. It has deferred the talks, not closed the door on the dialogue option. On Sunday, en route to the Group of Eight summit, Manmohan outlined a strategy that left the option of conditional engagement with Pakistan open even as India mobilized international pressure on Pakistan to stop cross-border terrorism. He reminded the Pakistani government of its commitment made in January 2004 that Pakistani territory would not be utilized for promoting, aiding, abetting and encouraging terrorist acts directed at India and called on the government to back this commitment with action on the ground.

Unlike in 2001-2002, when India rushed to flex its muscles against Pakistan and ended up using all its cards in the beginning, today it seems to be using a calibrated approach. More confused than in 2001, perhaps. And certainly more cautious.

ISSUES TO CONSIDER

1. Is India's intelligence gathering weakness inherently limited by the Pakistani threat?
2. Why should an eternal threat limit domestic intelligence gathering?
3. Is the "wall" referred to in the 9/11 Commission relevant to the Indian experience?

C. 2008 MUMBAI ATTACKS

Arguably, the most significant intelligence failure in India occurred when a handful of armed gunmen rampaged through Mumbai killing approximately 200 people and wounded many more. The following article analyzes the disappointment and anger citizens felt regarding India's government and intelligence services for failing to prevent India's 9/11.

INDIA'S INTELLIGENCE FAILURE

FrontPageMagazine.com, Dec. 9, 2008[51]

As India reels from the bloody aftermath of last month's attacks in Mumbai, the stunned country is asking how a handful of terrorists were able to kill nearly 200, injure scores of others, and pull off what is increasingly being called "India's 9/11." Last week, for instance, tens of thousands of angry Indians took to the streets in demonstrations — not against Lashkar-e-Toiba, the Pakistan-based, Islamic terrorist organization responsible for the attacks, but against their own politicians for not preventing yet another atrocity.

In their sorrow and outrage, many Indians are asking how their government failed, yet again, in its responsibility to protect its people, especially when members of the political class were a target themselves in India's most serious, previous terrorist attack, a 2001 assault on Parliament in New Delhi.

Driving the public furor are revelations that, like in the New Delhi attack, intelligence received before the Mumbai attacks indicated that the city was being targeted and the terrorists would come by sea. According to one Pakistani observer, several "low-profile attacks" were even carried out in different parts of India as rehearsals for the Mumbai assault. Somehow, this critical information, "lost in the system," was never acted upon.

Several theories have been put forward to account for these political and intelligence failures. One is that the Intelligence Bureau, the agency responsible for India's internal security, simply is not large enough to protect a country of 1.1 billion people. Moreover, of the agency's 20,000 employees, only 2,000 are actually engaged in the all-important field work that can be used to uncover terrorist plots before they are carried out. Understaffed and unfocused, India's intelligence services simply lack the capacity to infiltrate terrorist organizations.

---

51. *Available at* http://www.rightsidenews.com/200812092926/global-terrorism/indias-intelligence-failure.html (last visited Mar. 14, 2010).

Intelligence sharing is another problem. India's approximately one dozen intelligence agencies refuse to share information with each other and do not answer to a "central command." Wilson John, a Senior Fellow with Observer Research Foundation in New Delhi and the author of *Karachi: A Terror Capital in the Making*, said that even in the Mumbai attack, all emergency response units were operating in isolation. "There was no one guy in charge, which is why 10 guys were able to hold off hundreds of men deployed from the security forces," said John.

Further hindering the country's counterterrorist efforts is that intelligence lapses are compounded by equipment failures. Consider that the Mumbai terrorists were killed only after the intervention of India's National Security Guards (NSG), a special counter-terrorism unit. Tragically, it took the NSG nine hours to get to Mumbai from New Delhi because its airplane was unavailable. The NSG's equipment, meanwhile, was outdated or simply lacking.

India's police might be expected to step in where its intelligence agencies have fallen short. Instead, there is evidence that the police contribute to India's terrorism problems. In their zeal to arrest Islamic terrorists, they often brutalize innocent, young Muslim men, who then join domestic Muslim terrorist and extremist organizations. A better-trained police, experts say, is vital to India's long-term success against terrorism threats.

The political class is by no means exempt from blame. For instance, the government failed to overhaul the country's domestic security operations after the 2001 New Delhi attack. The main reason, it seems, was cowardice: The Congress Party, whose ruling coalition enjoys support among India's Muslim voters, did not want to alienate a key voting block by enacting tough, anti-terrorism measures. If anything, the Congress Party weakened India's counter-terrorism apparatus, abolishing the 2001 Protection of Terrorism Ordinance backed by the opposition Bharatiya Janata Party (BJP), the Hindu nationalist party.

The BJP is not much better. It protects Hindu extremists and terrorists who have staged attacks against Indian Muslims, thereby aiding the goal of extremists on both sides, and of Islamic terrorists in Pakistan, who hope to reignite communal riots in India that match, or exceed, those that erupted in 1947. To this end, mosques and Hindu temples are being targeted for bombings, as extremists on both sides hope to capitalize on sectarian violence. The BJP is still judged stronger on national security—observers of India's political scene are expecting voters to swing to the BJP in next year's elections as a backlash from the Mumbai attacks. But its reputation has come at the cost of a national consensus that would serve as a bulwark against terrorism, foreign and domestic.

Not all is bleak in India. While the country still has a way to go toward improving its intelligence structure, a crucial first step was made with the recent proposal of a national intelligence oversight committee to gain control of its disjointed network of agencies. India is also considering launching a covert war against the terrorists' camps in Pakistan. Both measures would move the country to an unusual position against terrorism: on the offensive.

In staging the Mumbai attacks, the terrorists had hoped "to stop the heart of India from beating." Not only did they fail in their fanatical ambition, but in spurring much-needed changes in India's security forces, they may have ensured their failure for years to come.

D. INDIA AND THE FUTURE

Indian authorities must develop a multi-focused intelligence gathering infrastructure capable of responding to complex security threats. As discussed, India faces numerous internal and external threats. The development of an intelligence-gathering mechanism capable of responding to these multiple threats demands resources significantly different than those required by the other surveyed nations. India's intelligence gathering efforts must not only be directed towards other sovereign nations, particularly Pakistan, capable of both external and internal (through proxies) attacks, but must also focus on purely domestic threats, including Sikh terrorism, and Muslim-Hindu tensions unrelated to Pakistan and the status of Kashmir.

The transition from human to signal intelligence is a contemporary development in India. As the Kargil Committee recognized, human sources provided the first indication that military forces had crossed into India.[52] What the Committee further concluded is that improved surveillance, particularly through satellite imagery, is necessary for prevention of similar situations.

The increasing emphasis India places on technologically based intelligence gathering includes:

> [S]pecial espionage centres at several places across the country to keep an eye on "terrorists" in Held Kashmir and in India. These centres are in addition to the Intelligence Bureau (IB), Research and Analysis Wing (RAW) and the state intelligence apparatus. Focused to gather information about suspected terrorist activities, the centres have initially been set up at Srinagar, Hyderabad, Guwahati, Mumbai and Kolkata. Personnel of the IB, RAW and some paramilitary forces who have developed expertise in intelligence gathering have been deputed to these centres. The centers will, in fact, work parallel to the existing intelligence apparatus and report directly to a multi-agency centre set up in the IB headquarters here. Their task is to spy on terrorists and gather information that helps prevent terrorist strikes. The Indian Home Ministry, led by Deputy Prime Minister LK Advani, felt that fighting terrorism with guns was not proving sufficient and the intelligence coming through the existing networks was not specific and therefore could not be acted upon quickly. The new centres have been set up with a mandate to pass on their input directly to the Joint Task Force (JTF) set up in New Delhi as part of recommendations by the Kargil Review Committee for strengthening India's intelligence system. The JTF, which draws members from Indian defence forces, paramilitary forces, intelligence agencies and the state police, would examine the input generated by the new centres and promptly take appropriate measures, including alerting the concerned states' police and providing action plans to deal with the problem. The espionage centres are also due to be established in Ahmedabad, Surat, Rajkot and Indore, as the Home Ministry suspects that the banned Students' Islamic Movement of India (SIMI) and other Muslim outfits in those cities could harbour militants. New Delhi chose to disclose the establishment of these centres at a recent meeting of the Parliamentary Consultative Committee, attached to the Home Ministry, to highlight the efforts being made to prevent terrorist attacks.[53]

---

52. "Shepherds" occasionally retained by the Indian government first detected the intrusion.

53. *New Indian Spy Centres in Kashmir to Keep Tabs on Terrorists*, The Daily Times, July 18, 2003, *available at* http://www.jammu-kashmir.com/archives/archives2003/kashmir20030718a.html (last visited Mar. 14, 2010).

Issues to Consider

1. Should different standards for determining invasion of privacy be applied to threats emanating from different sources (international/ Pakistan; domestic/Sikhs; disputed/Kashmir)?
2. What are the similarities and differences between the U.S. response to 9/11 and India's response to Kargil?

Without providing military commanders and decision makers an accurate assessment, intelligence officials have not fulfilled their responsibility. The following demonstrates India's commitment to addressing the technological failures that led to Kargil.

Privacy and Human Rights: Reupulic of India

Privacy International, Dec. 18, 2007[54]

Wiretapping and Surveillance Rules

Wiretapping is regulated under the Telegraph Act of 1885. There have been numerous phone tap scandals in India, resulting in a 1996 decision by the Supreme Court which ruled that wiretaps are a "serious invasion of an individual's privacy" The Supreme Court recognized the fact that the right of privacy is an integral part of the fundamental right to life enshrined under Article 21 of the Constitution. However, the right is only available and enforceable against the state and not against action by private entities. The Court also laid out guidelines for wiretapping by the government. The guidelines define who can tap phones and under what circumstances. Only the Union Home Secretary, or his counterpart in the states, can issue an order for a tap. The government is also required to show that the information sought cannot to be obtained through any other means. The Court mandated the development of a high-level committee to review the legality of each wiretap. Tapped phone calls are not accepted as primary evidence in Indian courts. However, as is the case with most laws in India, there continues to be a gap between the law and its enforcement. According to prominent NGOs, the mail of many NGOs in Delhi and in strife-torn areas continues to be subjected to interception and censorship.

In March 2002 the Indian Parliament, in a rare joint session, passed the Prevention Of Terrorism Act (POTA) over the objections of several Opposition parties and in the face of considerable public criticism. The National Human Rights Commission, an independent government entity, criticized the measure finding that the existing laws were sufficient to combat terrorism The law codifies the Prevention of Terrorism Ordinance that in turn builds on the repealed Terrorists And Disruptive Activities (Prevention) Act (TADA). It gives law enforcement sweeping powers to arrest suspected terrorists, intercept communications, and curtail free expression. Critics argue that the experience of TADA and POTA shows that the power was often misused for political ends

---

54. *Available at* http://www.privacyinternational.org/article.shtml?cmd[347]=x-347-559529 (last visited Mar. 14, 2010).

by authorities and that POTA does little to curb those excesses. Chapter V of POTA deals with the interception of electronic communications, which also creates an audit mechanism that includes some provision for judicial review and parliamentary oversight; however, it remains to be seen how effective such mechanisms will be in practice. In certain high-risk states such as Jammu and Kashmir, search warrants are not required and the government from time to time bans the use of cellular telephones, long distance phones, and cyber-cafes. India's Enforcement Directorate, which investigates foreign exchange and currency violations, searches, interrogates and arrests business professionals, often without a warrant.

On December 13, 2001, the Indian Parliament was attacked by five heavily armed intruders and gun men. A case was duly registered, investigated and prosecuted under the provisions of POTA after it was enacted. The trial court judge convicted the accused persons. On appeal, the New Delhi High Court held that intercepted telephone conversations of the three persons charged under POTA for plotting the attack on the Parliament, were not admissible evidence, although the High Court had previously held that telephone conversations could qualify as admissible evidence under the Indian Evidence Act, the Indian Telegraph Act and the Indian Penal Code, and that it was open for the trial court to consider the intercepts under these laws while deciding the case. The Central Bureau of Investigation appealed against the High Court order and on September 5, 2003 the Supreme Court set the Delhi High Court judgement aside, allowed the appeal and decided that intercepted communications between the accused in the House of Parliament are admissible.

India recognizes it must develop broad-based intelligence gathering abilities. The examples discussed in this section largely draw attention to systemic and institutional weaknesses. How India continues to revamp its intelligence services while coping with legislative restrictions and facing complex threats will significantly affect operational counterterrorism measures in years ahead.

VII. SPAIN

A. REORGANIZATION

The Madrid train bombing exposed overwhelming HUMINT and SIGINT failures. The intelligence gathering and analysis picture in Spain remains unclear.

According to the Spanish Criminal Code, the government "must obtain court approval before searching private property, wiretapping, or interfering with private correspondence."[55] The antiterrorist law gives discretionary

---

55. *Country Reports on Human Rights Practices for 1995, Spain*, U.S. Department of State, *available at* http://dosfan.lib.uic.edu/ERC/democracy/1995_hrp_report/95hrp_report_eur/Spain.html (last visited Oct. 8, 2010).

authority to the Minister of the Interior to act prior to obtaining court approval in "cases of emergency."[56] In spite of statutory authorization to conduct wiretapping surveillance, the Spanish authorities failed to monitor conversations of those involved in planning the train station bombing. Spanish authorities failure to monitor conversations indicated a misperception regarding the desire and ability of Islamic terrorists to commit an attack. Reports, such as the one below, suggest that Spain may be reorganizing the intelligence community's use of SIGINT.

DEFENCE CONCEALS A SATELLITE SPY STATION
IN THE SIERRA OF MADRID

Jan. 28, 2003[57]

Although it seems surprising, telephone taps in Spain were not regulated until roughly a year ago, when the National Intelligence Centre laws were passed. With this new legislation Spanish spies — wary since such scandalous cases as that of the CESID tapping — have to obtain authorisation to interfere in the communications of a Spanish citizen from a High Court judge. But they also have the obligation the spy on and analyse the so-called "signal traffic" of a strategic nature, as has already been mentioned. This means that they can spy on international communications, provided that the taps do not affect Spanish citizens.

Nevertheless, it is surprising to observe how, coinciding with the approval of the NIC laws, the Ministry of Defence created the Armed Forces Intelligence Centre. Oddly, the AFIC is not regulated by any law, nor will it be in the future. Official defence sources confirm that a ministerial order will be published that will simply be limited to specifying the internal organisation of the Centre, but nothing else. Last December, the minister Federico Trillo made a pact regarding the Strategic Defence Review with the PSOE, the Spanish Socialist Party, that envisaged enabling "the process of rationalising the intelligence capabilities of the Defence, Army and Navy Staff, initiated with the creation of the Armed Forces Intelligence Centre."

The same document also mentions that "in order to face up to terrorism coming from beyond our borders, it will be necessary to make use of the capabilities of the Armed Force." Trillo emphasised, before the Congress Defence Committee, that military intelligence will only be orientated towards the cases of "a military threat abroad" and the "theatre of intelligence." However, he also acknowledged that the AFIC will not operate separately from the NIC, since its director Jorge Dezcallar will coordinate its activities. This aspect had already been established in the NIC Act, where it states that one of the missions of its directors is to "maintain and develop (. . .) the collaboration with the information services of the State Security Forces and Bodies and the organs

---

56. *Country Reports on Human Rights Practices 2000*, U.S. Department of State, released by the Bureau of Democracy, Human Rights, and Labor, Feb. 23, 2001, *available at* http://www.state.gov/g/drl/rls/hrrpt/2000/eur/875.htm (last visited Oct. 8, 2010).

57. *Available at* http://cryptome.org/echelon-es.htm (last visited Mar. 14, 2010).

of the civil and military administration that are relevant for intelligence objectives."

But while the NIC is authorised by law to spy on so-called "signal traffic," it is very possible that this institution has delegated the presumed espionage activities that are carried on at the Fresnedillas-Navalagamella base and the Conil chalet to the Army. This is because if a Spanish citizen falls through the "cracks" in the system, albeit by accident, the NIC would be breaking the law that obliges it to obtain prior authorisation to make taps from the High Court. Nevertheless, intelligence sources confirm that the concealed Conil de la Frontera operation continues in the hands of the NIC, that inherited it from the CESID. So, the Spanish intelligence agency could be acting against the the law if it also spies on Spanish citizens from there.

With respect to the alleged tapping carried out at Fresnedillas, the same sources assures us that the installation was never under the control of CESID, but rather was run by the army. This detail would confirm the thesis that CIFAS is currently coordinating the activities that are carried on there. It seems clear that this would be the case because, if military officials are spying on a Spanish citizen, although they may not have intentionally intercepted his communications, nobody would have to give explanations before the courts or before Parliament as a result of this infringement of the fundamental rights to the inviolability of communications.

Years before, CESID had carte blanche to do what it wanted and it did so. It is now very possible that the NIC activities are more controlled thanks to the laws that regulate its functioning. But there is also the AFIC that can be entrusted with doing the "dirty work." Thus, we are in the same position as before, with the sole difference that the intelligence services have changed their name.

ISSUES TO CONSIDER

1. If Spanish authorities view terrorism through the prism of the criminal law paradigm, how can actionable counterterrorism intelligence be gathered?
2. Given Spain's determination that counterterrorism is criminal in nature, how do Spanish intelligence gathering operations differ from those of the United States, Israel, and Russia?

According to reports, Spain has become "the gateway to Europe for North Africans."[58] Successful intelligence gathering by the Spanish authorities will depend upon an ability to infiltrate the immigrant or transient communities that support such attacks. The following excerpt highlights Spain's attempt to control this situation.

---

58. *See* Kathryn Haahr, *Emerging Terrorist Trends in Spain's Moroccan Communities*, 4 Terrorism Monitor, May 4, 2006, *available at* http://www.jamestown.org/single/?no_cache=1&tx_ttnews%5Btt_news%5D=758 (last visited Oct. 8, 2010).

The profile of Melilla, Ceuta and Andalucia, as "hosts" to Islamist terrorist activities, demonstrates the degree to which various terrorist groups have penetrated mainstream Spanish cities and populations. Several significant counterterrorism operations in 2005 (resulting in the arrest of approximately 85 individuals) netted an al Qaeda cell with a nucleus in Andalucia, as well as GSPC members dispersed throughout southern Spain. Of significance, Spanish police arrested a Moroccan national, Bahbah El H. (last name not available) in Nerja, Malaga, who had formerly been the imam of a mosque in Ceuta. It is also important to note that the "first Spanish Taliban," Hamed Abderrahaman Ahmed, was from Ceuta. He spent two years at Guantanamo Bay on suspicions of being an "enemy combatant" allied to al Qaeda.

As a result of the increasing presence of Islamists in the enclaves and Andalucia, Spanish security authorities have deployed counterterrorism agents to Ceuta, Melilla and other cities in southern Spain. As part of their activities, they have stepped up efforts to identify Islamic extremists among the thousands of Spanish Muslims who attend mosques in the two enclaves and Andalucia. According to press reports, the Spanish security services have monitored all of the mosques in Ceuta and Melilla and "analyzed the number of Muslims who attended them, as well as the profile of each of the adherents" (El Mundo, November 24, 2001; El Pueblo de Ceuta, December 20, 2005).

Spanish security officials continue to worry that members of al Qaeda will take advantage of the clandestine immigration pipeline route by inserting terrorists to make their way to either the enclaves or to the Spanish mainland. To this regard, the Directorate General of National police recently advertised 357 posts for anti-terrorist officers to monitor potential Islamists in areas where the presence of Muslim immigrants is well known, such as Melilla, Ceuta, Granada, Malaga and Alicante.[59]

ISSUES TO CONSIDER

1. Much like the challenge Russian authorities face in Chechnya, how can Spanish authorities infiltrate traditionally closed immigrant or transient communities?
2. How should Spain develop a network of sources that provides actionable intelligence?
3. In the aftermath of the Madrid train bombing, are civil liberties more likely to be breached?
4. Does the fact that the perpetrators of the train bombings resided in Spain prior to the attack suggest that Spanish intelligence gathering operations should be significantly different than those implemented in the United States?

Islamic fundamentalists living in Spain carried out the Madrid train bombings. Similar to the London train bombings, the attack on the Glasgow airport, and the plan to simultaneously blow up 13 commercial airline jets on trans-Atlantic routes, the train bombing was not conducted by al Qaeda terrorists

---

59. *Id.*

temporarily living in Spain solely for the purpose of conducting the attack. According to a Spanish government report:

> The group that carried out the 11 March attacks was not linked directly to al Qaeda or any other international terrorist network, although its members claimed to be al Qaeda followers. The group consisted of legal residents of Madrid, mostly of Moroccan origin, who had gradually come to embrace the radical ideology of international jihad, mainly based on information found on radical Islamist websites. They financed their operations through common criminal activities, such as shoplifting, theft and narcotics trading. The material used in the 13 improvised explosive devices was procured within Spain.[60]

B. SPAIN AND HUMINT

Prior to the train station bombing, the Spanish authorities' primary human intelligence gathering was directed towards Basque terrorism. Initially, the Spanish government responded to the train attack on the assumption that ETA was responsible and ignored the possibility that Islamic terrorists were responsible for killing 191 people.

The attack reflects the operational capability of terrorists, both in planning and execution. It also points to a massive intelligence failure similar to 9/11. Analysts failed to predict the train bombings, suggesting a need to develop a network of sources in the relevant communities and to monitor, via electronic surveillance, suspected terrorists planning additional attacks in Spain.

SPAIN PROBED TERROR SUSPECT PRIOR TO MADRID ATTACK

Fox News, March 17, 2004[61]

In Spain, questions already are being asked about whether security agents failed to connect dots that might have enabled them to prevent the terrorists from placing shrapnel-packed bombs on rush-hour trains, killing 191 people.

The investigation into Thursday's attack is focusing on a web of suspected ties to indicted and convicted Islamic radicals that radiate from Zougam, a Moroccan phone salesman. Spanish and Moroccan officials already suspected he was deeply involved in the netherworld of Al Qaeda and its offshoots.

Zougam was arrested with his half brother, Mohamed Chaoui, and another Moroccan, Mohamed Bekkali, just two days after Thursday's bombings.

However, both Zougam and Chaoui caught the attention of Spanish anti-terror Judge Baltasar Garzon as early as 2001, according to an Associated Press review of court documents and a French private investigator with access to Garzon's massive dossier on Al Qaeda operations in Spain.

---

60. *Lessons Learned from Recent Terrorist Attacks: Building National Capabilities and Institutions,* NRC Conference Ljubljana, Slovenia, Chairman's Report, *available at* http://www.nato.int/docu/conf/2005/050727/ (last visited Oct. 8, 2010).

61. *Available at* http://www.foxnews.com/story/0,2933,114405,00.html (last visited Mar. 14, 2010).

But in the fight against terrorists, knowing your enemy doesn't always mean you can stop him from acting. The fruits of globalization—easier travel across borders, quick, cheap and accessible means of communicating—are the same tools terrorists use to slip through cracks.

Mobile phones and e-mail accounts can be used once, then discarded to prevent electronic snooping by intelligence agencies.

Terrorists who need to travel can tap the lucrative black market in forged travel documents.

"They know to create layers and layers of anonymity in the way they communicate," said Magnus Ranstorp, director of the Center for the Study of Terrorism and Political Violence at St. Andrews University in Scotland.

"They are very well versed in staying beneath the intelligence radar screen," he added.

The Madrid bombers appear to have succeeded in keeping their intentions hidden. A U.S. counterterrorism official, speaking on the condition of anonymity, said authorities found no evidence of increased "chatter"— monitored contacts between suspects that might have pointed to a plot—in the days prior to the attack. Similar to the Russian paradigm pre Beslan, Spain has faced extraordinary challenges in penetrating internal (non ETA) terrorism cells.

ISSUES TO CONSIDER

1. What legal and institutional changes should be made in the aftermath of the Spanish intelligence failure?
2. What intelligence gathering lessons can be learned from the experience of other nations?
3. Does an intelligence failure of this magnitude require restructuring existing intelligence mechanisms?
4. Does such an attack justify changing domestic laws?
5. What are the standards necessary to obtain authorization to interfere in the communications of a Spanish citizen from a High Court judge?

VIII. CHINA

In addition to basic intelligence gathering deemed essential for purposes of public order and national security, Chinese intelligence officials target specific domestic groups. In this regard, the Chinese methods are similar to the other surveyed nations. However, in contrast—both philosophically and practically—the Chinese model is based on traditional information gathering methods such as human intelligence and also what has been termed "subtle spying" based on obtaining information a "little bit at a time"[62] from alternative sources.

---

62. Paul Moore, *China's Subtle Spying*, N.Y. Times, Sept. 2, 1999.

In studying China's intelligence methods, the U.S. Commission on China noted that a common tactic used by China was to encourage foreign scientific experts to attend conferences in China as means to gather information. That is, in addition to traditional sources, the Chinese also rely on external sources to provide information contributing to a more complete intelligence picture.

The Ministry of State Security and Military Intelligence Department of the People's Liberation Army primarily gather intelligence. The Ministry of State Security is the civilian intelligence agency with responsibility for foreign and domestic security and intelligence operations. In addition, it has a role in counterintelligence, often engaging in surveillance and suppression of groups considered opposing government policy; these groups include dissidents and ethnic groups.[63] The Ministry of State Security uses the news media as cover, often sending agents abroad as correspondents for state news agencies.

The Military Intelligence Department of the People's Liberation Army is a military organization that collects intelligence on foreign militaries, military doctrine, and weapons systems.[64] It is particularly active in acquiring foreign technology that has military applications. Both the Ministry of State Security and the Military Intelligence Department have affiliated think tanks that portray a public face of the intelligence community.

A. USE OF THE INTERNET FOR INTELLIGENCE

CHINA'S CYBER ACTIVITIES THAT TARGET THE UNITED STATES, AND THE RESULTING IMPACTS ON U.S. NATIONAL SECURITY

Nov. 2009[65]

The Chinese government's lack of transparency in the field of computer network operations makes analysis of the involvement of Chinese state actors challenging at the unclassified level. However, while much about China's government-backed computer network warfare programs remains opaque, military newspapers and professional military journals in China have long expressed professional admiration for perceived U.S. network and electronic warfare capabilities in conflicts such as the 1999 Kosovo campaign and the 2003 invasion of Iraq and have discussed the need to catch up. These journals have engaged in a surprisingly open discussion of the need to develop greater capabilities for computer network operations and have even provided a number of details as to what form these capabilities should assume.

The Chinese government has not publicly issued a strategy or governing concepts for computer network operations such as those contained within *Joint Publication 3–13: Information Operations*, released in 2006 by the U.S. Department of Defense. However, some determined western open-source

---

63. *Open Source Center, An Overview of PRC internal Security Institutions*, Nov. 17, 2007, OSC ID: CPP20071114507001, www.opensource.gov.
64. *Interagency OPSEC Support Staff, Intelligence Threat Handbook* 22 (2004), http://www.fas.org/irp/threat/handbook/front.pdf.
65. *Available at* http://www.uscc.gov/annual_report/2009/chapter2_section_4.pdf (last visited Mar. 14, 2010).

researchers have been able to gain insights into the institutional developments of China's cyber capabilities through studying the debates in these journals.

. . .

"Integrated Network Electronic Warfare"

Analysis of writings from authoritative PLA publications also has revealed the existence of a guiding PLA operational concept titled "Integrated Network Electronic Warfare." Integrated Network Electronic Warfare incorporates elements of computer network operations in tandem with elements of traditional electronic warfare.

Integrated Network Electronic Warfare advocates the employment of traditional electronic warfare operations—such as the jamming of radars and communications systems—in coordination with computer network attack operations. The goal is to create a multispectrum attack on enemy command, control, communications, computers, intelligence, surveillance, and reconnaissance systems in the early stages of conflict, thereby denying the opposing force access to information and communications necessary to move forces and fight in a modern battlespace. As summarized in a 2009 publication, Integrated Network Electronic Warfare would use

> techniques such as electronic jamming, electronic deception and suppression to disrupt information acquisition and information transfer, launching a virus attack or hacking to sabotage information processing and information utilization, and using anti-radiation and other weapons based on new mechanisms to destroy enemy information platforms and information facilities.

While some aspects of Integrated Network Electronic Warfare may remain aspirational for the Chinese military, the PLA takes the concept seriously and views cyberspace, in tandem with the electromagnetic spectrum, as critical arenas of conflict in full spectrum modern warfare. . . . The 2007 revised Outline for Military Training and Evaluation training guidance issued by the PLA General Staff Department directed all branches of the PLA to make training "under complex electromagnetic environments" the core of campaign and tactical training.

In one recent example of such training, in early January 2008 approximately 100 senior-ranking PLA officers from multiple service branches reportedly observed an Integrated Network Electronic Warfare exercise hosted by elements of a group army of the Shenyang Military Region. In the exercise, troops of the defending PLA forces had to fend off attacks from mock aggressor forces employing simulated cyber and electronic attacks. These attacks included a computer virus that sowed confusion by changing logistics requirements, using electrical pulse attacks that destroyed computer motherboards, and jamming communications and radar systems.

Issues to Consider

1. What are the cost-benefits of computer intensive intelligence gathering?
2. Is signal intelligence a substitute for human intelligence?

3. What, if any, limits can be imposed on signal intelligence (with respect to privacy)?
4. Does signal intelligence pose a threat to national sovereignty?
5. Do the methods mentioned by the U.S. Commission on China suggest effective intelligence gathering methods?

B. TARGETING CHINESE DISSIDENT GROUPS

The Office for Foreign Propaganda/State Council Information Office manages sensitive news stories and guides the Chinese media during major events, especially those affecting ethnic minorities and internal violence. The following report from Human Rights Watch discusses the government's influence on sources and how information is obtained.

HUMAN RIGHTS WATCH: CHINA'S FORBIDDEN ZONES

July 6, 2008[66]

Silencing the Sources: Intimidation of Chinese Interviewees

Journalists rely on sources-people who can provide first-hand experience or eyewitness accounts of a particular event or phenomenon-in order to accurately and reliably report the news. Government officials and security forces have traditionally used intimidation and harassment of local sources, which are more easily controlled than foreign journalists, as a means of preventing the dissemination of "sensitive" news through foreign media.

Foreign journalists say that the freedom of movement granted to them by the temporary regulations has increased the number of local sources to which they have access to, but has correspondingly increased the vulnerability of those sources to reprisals from officials, security forces or plainclothes thugs.

Journalists' sources can run serious risks even in relation to fairly innocuous business-related stories. In March, a foreign television news crew did an on-camera interview with an aggrieved former investor in a collapsed pyramid scheme in the northeastern city of Shenyang. The crew learned later that their source was picked out of a meeting of fellow former-investors by uniformed police who beat him so severely he required hospitalization. The source was then briefly put under house arrest following his release from hospital.

A foreign correspondent who, in November 2007, traveled on a government-organized media tour focused on the relocation of local residents adjacent to the Three Gorges Dam project in Hubei province discovered that independent interviews she had conducted brought swift repercussions to one of her local sources. "The next day the interviewee contacted me and said local officials came looking for him and asked why he'd said 'negative things' about the relocation." The source said the officials had detailed

---

66. *Available at* http://www.hrw.org/en/node/62149/section/6 (last visited June 12, 2010).

knowledge of the substance of the previous day's interview, prompting the correspondent to conclude that government officials or security forces had surreptitiously eavesdropped on the conversation. "It's a constant worry to go to talk to [local sources] because some of these local officials can be very vengeful."

Foreign journalists' sources also face risks to their livelihood from vengeful local officials who are displeased with the resulting coverage. A foreign correspondent told Human Rights Watch that a local source working for an international nongovernmental organization focused on poverty relief projects in western China, was subsequently fired from her job as a result of her cooperation with the journalist. The fact that the correspondent had received official permission from the local government to do interviews with staff at the organization and report on their work did not protect the source from reprisal from local government officials who were angered by the source's cooperation with the journalist.

> When I returned to Beijing, I was told by my source that she had been fired because of [local] government pressure [because] it had gotten angry with the [international poverty relief group] and it was [a choice] of either firing her or closing down their [operations]. The problem for me now is that in this case we did ask for [official] permission [for interviews] and it was granted . . . and they told me clearly that regulations allow foreign journalists to interview whomever they want, if the other side consents. But for this woman, [that interview means] she has lost her job.

A local source of another foreign television crew was subjected to severe intimidation by local police in connection with a February 2008 story on environmental pollution. In an effort to protect the source, the television crew went to extreme lengths to remove any links he had to their source by cutting the footage of his on-camera interview and not using any information that could be linked directly to him. Despite those precautions, shortly after the journalists left the area, members of the local Public Security Bureau visited the source and warned him that they would charge him with state subversion if they had evidence that he had provided the journalists with any "sensitive" information. Those threats prompted the source to flee his village twice for weeks at a time. The source has since returned to his home village without any official reprisals, but the incident has caused the correspondent to seriously question the feasibility of "safe" reporting in China.

> Sources aren't secure at all . . . [the authorities] can take out [their revenge] on the people who work for you, who show you the way. Those potential reprisals set the bar for [television] reporting uncomfortably high because it's very hard to assess before you go in whether or not a story is 'worth it' [in terms of risk to sources]. In order for me to do a story, I need to individualize it, to focus on one person who tells a story which can resonate with people, but under the current circumstances I can no longer do that.

Police threats of "subversion" charges against journalists' sources are particularly potent in the wake of the conviction of high-profile human rights activist Hu Jia for "subverting state power" on April 3, 2008. The prosecution's case against Hu included evidence related to interviews he had given to foreign journalists. One veteran foreign correspondent said that the circumstances of Hu's conviction would likely worsen de facto self-censorship among foreign correspondents who don't want to risk putting their sources in danger of criminal prosecution and imprisonment.

For me, this means that if a [journalist] interviews someone, the interview can become evidence in court to charge [the source]. Simply expressing views can be "subversion," so it makes a journalist question, "Do I publish what this person is saying? Or not publish what he says and [therefore] not reflect what's going on in China?"

ISSUES TO CONSIDER

1. What are the risks of targeting one group?
2. Does limiting the media aid or hinder China? How?

IX. COLOMBIA

A. INTRODUCTION

The Administrative Security Department (DAS), has, until recently, been Colombia's main intelligence gathering organization. Created in the early 1950s and reorganized in 1960, it has been responsible for providing security to individuals, police services for the judiciary, and counterintelligence services for both domestic and foreign threats.

B. INTELLIGENCE SCANDAL

In 2008, the Colombia media revealed that DAS had been gathering intelligence on politicians, human rights groups, journalists, clergy, unions, and Supreme Court justices. The operation was revealed when a news magazine obtained an intercept of a phone call between an attorney and the Supreme Court justice investigating President Uribe's supporters' ties to paramilitary death squads. The surveillance consisted of tapping phones, reading emails, watching people's homes, studying their routines, and supplementing information with banking, immigration, and driver's license records. The surveillance focused on individuals and families, even investigating which schools children attended.

The operation's goal was aimed at undermining the activities of individuals perceived to oppose the government. There was no indication that the operation was intended to investigate guerrilla ties or threats to national security.

2009 Human Rights Reports: Colombia

Mar. 11, 2010[67]

The law prohibits such actions; while the government generally respected these prohibitions in practice, there were notable exceptions by some intelligence agencies. The law requires government authorities to obtain a warrant signed by a senior prosecutor to enter a private home without the owner's consent unless the suspect has been caught in hot pursuit, and government authorities generally adhered to these regulations.

Government authorities generally need a judicial order to intercept mail or monitor telephone conversations, even in prisons. However, government intelligence agencies investigating terrorist organizations sometimes monitored telephone conversations without judicial authorization, although evidence obtained in such a manner could not be used in court.

Surveillance by the DAS of high court magistrates, journalists, human rights organizations and activists, opposition leaders, and the Vice Presidency prompted an investigation by the CTI. Press reports indicated DAS surveillance included physical monitoring of individuals and their families, phone and e-mail intercepts, and collection of personal and financial data. A CTI report described a twofold strategy to mount prosecutions against the victims of the surveillance and to disrupt human rights groups' activities through "offensive intelligence." According to a publication released by the National and International Campaign for the Right to Defend Human Rights, examples of DAS harassment included operations involving diverse attacks, setups, and death threats. Former DAS director Jorge Noguera and deputy director Jose Narvaez were under investigation for colluding with paramilitary members to instigate the murders of three unionists, a college professor, and a journalist. The Prosecutor General's Office launched a separate investigation into the wiretapping scandal, and 34 DAS employees were under investigation, 10 of whom, including four directors, were detained. Investigations into the surveillance continued at year's end.

The government continued to use voluntary civilian informants to report terrorist activities and identify terrorists. Some national and international human rights groups criticized this practice as subject to abuse and a threat to privacy and other civil liberties. In the August report of the UN secretary-general on children and armed conflict, the UN called on the government to ensure children were not used for military intelligence purposes, noting this practice puts children at risk of retaliation by illegal armed groups. The FARC publicly justified its February 4 massacre of eight Awa indigenous persons as retaliation for collaboration with the military.

In September 2009, the government announced that the DAS would be dismantled to create a new agency that would focus on intelligence and counter-intelligence involving national security. In an interview the new director, Filipe Munoz, stated that he had been taking steps including stricter controls of

---

67. *Available at* http://www.state.gov/g/drl/rls/hrrpt/2009/wha/136106.htm (last visited Mar. 14, 2010).

wiretaps, firing over 120 people who were involved in the scandal, and promoting a new intelligence law.[68] He stated that had been taken decision that were politically costly and unpopular in order to do the right thing for the country and to limit the expansive power that DAS had gained. He noted "It has been difficult to focus on reforms with so many scandals emerging. Don't forget that since I started, we've not only dealt with illegal wiretaps but also the resurgence of cases of alleged DAS involvement in the deaths of [presidential candidates] Luis Carlos Galan, Carlos Pizarro and Bernardo Jaramillo, even a bomb placed aboard an Avianca airliner. All of which is to remind people that these problems involving DAS and insufficient controls didn't arise yesterday."[69]

ISSUES TO CONSIDER

1. How do scandals impede on intelligence gathering in the future?
2. Would strict rules governing how intelligence is gathered aid or hinder national security and individual rights?
3. What impact is there in targeting individual leaders, or branches of the government, on national security?

---

68. Chris Kraul, *Colombia Spy Chief Works to Clean Up Agency*, L.A. Times, Apr. 22, 2010, *available at* http://articles.latimes.com/2010/apr/22/world/la-fg-colombia-das-qa-20100423 (last visited June 12, 2010).
69. *Id.*

CHAPTER 8

INTERROGATION OF TERRORISTS

I. INTRODUCTION

Custodial detention of terrorism suspects inevitably involves a meeting between the detainee and the interrogator. Both represent a larger entity: the terrorist is usually part of a terrorist organization, the interrogator represents the state. Whether the interrogation setting balances legitimate civil liberties and the state's equally legitimate security needs, either in the immediate aftermath of a terrorist attack or when an intelligence report indicates a detained suspect has information regarding a planned attack, is the focus of this chapter. A variety of guidelines, court decisions, statutes, and international and domestic laws outline the limits of interrogation.

How are interrogators expected to receive critically needed intelligence from suspects who know the rules of the game and understand the interrogator has limited means available with which to extract the information? The interrogator must attempt to gather, quickly and under stressful conditions, important information that may well prevent an attack. Under such circumstances, may the threat of an attack justify exceptions? Perhaps the interrogator's chain of command has suggested—implicitly or explicitly—that bending the rules is acceptable when lives are *potentially* at stake. The circumstances surrounding an interrogation are visceral because it usually takes place in a small, pressure-filled room, soaked with sweat and anxiety.

ISSUES TO CONSIDER

1. Who determines if and whether the situation warrants an exception?
2. What are the criteria for determining the circumstances that justify interrogation methods going beyond the norm?
3. What is, or should be, the norm?

The interrogator determines the focus of the interrogation. The detainee—whether experienced or inexperienced—constantly attempts to determine what the interrogator knows. The detainee must also gauge whether one of his associates (or someone he believed to be an associate) has betrayed him by collaborating with the authorities or by implicating him. If he has been implicated, then his capability to negotiate with the interrogator has been compromised. Since the interrogation — very much like the classic prisoner's dilemma — is largely a guessing game, the interrogator must keep the detainee off guard to elicit the essential information.

Acceptable interrogator methods are essential to this discussion. Whether the seven surveyed nations distinguish between terrorism and the criminal law is relevant to understanding how each nation defines the limits of interrogation. If the relevant paradigm is criminal law, then the detainee is entitled to protections guaranteed within the nation's criminal code. If the detainee is not subject to the criminal law, then a state may conceivably relax restrictions otherwise imposed on the interrogator.

Loosening restrictions may result in significant violations of detainee rights. Furthermore, it does not guarantee that information received is accurate, reliable, and operationally or legally actionable. Incorrect information received in the course of an interrogation not only negatively affects the particular investigation, but, if provided to law enforcement, may contribute to critical misallocation of limited resources. Inaccurate or incorrect information may also lead to wrongful convictions and imprisonment of innocent parties.

These issues are not only the essence of this chapter, but are — in conjunction with intelligence — the heart and soul of counterterrorism. How interrogations are conducted defines societies: whether decision makers and the public adopt an "anything goes" attitude or a "self-imposed restraints" approach is critical to determining how a nation balances competing interests. In the U.S. criminal law paradigm, interrogation limits have been clearly articulated by the Supreme Court. In the Prisoner of War paradigm, Geneva Convention protections extended to the captured soldier exclude the holding of a trial, unless the individual is suspected of having committed a war crime or a crime in captivity. The captured soldier is required to provide his captors only his name, rank, and serial number.

In 1984 the United Nations adopted the Convention Against Torture[1] (CAT); 146 nations are presently signatories, ten are waiting to ratify. With the exception of India, all of the surveyed nations have ratified the CAT. The preamble to the Convention highlights the concern regarding torture:

> **The States Parties to this Convention**
>   Considering that, in accordance with the principles proclaimed in the Charter of the United Nations, recognition of the equal and inalienable rights of all members of the human family is the foundation of freedom, justice and peace in the world,

---

1. Convention Against Torture or Other Cruel, Inhuman, or Degrading Treatment or Punishment, Dec. 10, 1984, 14 U.N.T.S. 85, 23 I.L.M. 1027 (entered into force June 26, 1987), *available at* http://treaties.un.org/Pages/ViewDetails.aspx?src=TREATY&mtdsg_no=IV-9&chapter=4&lang=en (last visited March 18, 2010) [hereinafter Convention Against Torture].

Recognizing that those rights derive from the inherent dignity of the human person,

Considering the obligation of States under the Charter, in particular Article 55, to promote universal respect for, and observance of, human rights and fundamental freedoms,

Having regard to article 5 of the Universal Declaration of Human Rights and article 7 of the International Covenant on Civil and Political Rights, both of which provide that no one may be subjected to torture or to cruel, inhuman or degrading treatment or punishment,

Having regard also to the Declaration on the Protection of All Persons from Being Subjected to Torture and Other Cruel, Inhuman or Degrading Treatment or Punishment, adopted by the General Assembly on 9 December 1975

Desiring to make more effective the struggle against torture and other cruel, inhuman or degrading treatment or punishment throughout the world, have agreed as follows. . . .[2]

II. INTERROGATION: LIMITS AND CONSIDERATIONS

The "ticking time bomb" has been mentioned frequently in the context of terrorism-related interrogations, suggesting the following scenario: a terrorist organization is planning a major attack that, if successful, would result in the deaths of thousands of innocent civilians. According to this scenario, law enforcement officials have detained an individual believed to possess information capable of foiling the plan were he to divulge the necessary information. Some scholars posit such a scenario might serve as justifiable exception to international law and domestic legislation outlawing torture.[3] The argument propounded by Alan Dershowitz[4] suggests that in the context of a ticking time bomb, a judicial warrant should be issued enabling an exception to the prohibition on torture.

While the fact pattern is perhaps feasible from a "Hollywood" perspective, according to professional interrogators the chances of detaining *the one* individual capable of foiling such a plan are literally nil. As will be discussed later, the Israel High Court of Justice criticized the General Security Services' (today, Israel Security Agency) liberal use of the expression "ticking time bomb," which had become a dangerous catch-all phrase.[5] While the phrase was perhaps convenient from the perspective of the intelligence services, the Court believed it inevitably contributed to civil rights violations.

---

2. *Id.*

3. *See* Phillip N.S. Rumney, *Is Coercive Interrogation of Terrorist Suspects Effective: A Response to Bagaric and Clarke*, 40 U.S.F. L. Rev. 479 (2006);).

4. Alan Dershowitz has been the leading advocate of the so-called "torture warrant," whereby a detainee may be tortured under court order in severe circumstances. Similarly, the "ticking time bomb" has been cited as justifying an exception to the no-torture rule. *See* Alan M. Dershowitz, *The Torture Warrant: A Response to Professor Strauss*, 48 N.Y.L. Sch. L. Rev. 275 (2004).

5. H.C. 5100/94, Public Comm. Against Torture in Israel v. State of Israel & General Sec. Serv., ¶16, *available at* http://www.derechos.org/human-rights/mena/doc/torture.html (last visited July 10, 2010).

In determining the limits of interrogation, the efficacy of torture must be examined. That is, does torture work and is it justified from an operational perspective? In analyzing torture and detention it is important to note that the interrogation paradigm is not limited solely to the actual questioning of the interogatee. Rather, interrogation must be understood in its wider context, from the moment the individual is brought to a detention center and the doors are literally and figuratively closed behind him. By example, the U.S. interrogation methods in the aftermath of 9/11 included mistreatment both by prison guards and interrogators: the former captured in the now infamous pictures from Abu Ghraib; the latter in using interrogation measures that included water boarding. For example, Khalid Sheik Mohammed, one of the principal 9/11 planners, was water boarded over 150 times. President Obama's Executive Order (2009) forbade implementation of previously authorized aggressive interrogation measures and eliminated the exception to those techniques carved out for non-military personnel in the 2006 Military Commissions Act.

MICHAEL IGNATIEFF, IF TORTURE WORKS . . .

Prospect Magazine, April 2006[6]

Since no state wants to be seen as torturing suspects but all states want to be able to extract information to protect their citizens, the key question is whether states can use methods of "coercive interrogation" that do not qualify as torture. When the torture convention was ratified by the US Senate in 1994, maintaining a meaningful distinction between coercive but lawful interrogation and outright torture was a central concern. The Senate ratified the convention on the understanding that torture should be reserved for "severe physical or mental pain or suffering" resulting in "prolonged mental harm." Once the war on terror began, the parsing of the convention went still further. In the now notorious memos submitted by the office of legal counsel to the White House in 2002, these definitions were stretched to the point that the threshold for torture "must be equivalent in intensity to the pain accompanying serious physical injury, such as organ failure, impairment of bodily function or even death." Any physical abuse below that standard counted as "coercive interrogation." Some forms of coercive interrogation, the lawyers admitted, might not be torture, but they would still be defined as "inhuman and degrading treatment."

There is thus a conceptual and practical distinction between torture and coercive interrogation. There is a further distinction—at least in theory—between methods of coercive interrogation that are lawful and permissible and those that may be inhuman and degrading. While this distinction exists in theory, most human rights activists would deny that such a distinction can be observed in practice.

6. *Available at* http://www.prospect-magazine.co.uk/article_details.php?id=7374) (last visited 2006 Mar. 18, 2010).

Absolute prohibition, however, is easy. Enforcement is hard, and even rules and punishment for infraction are not enough. The crucial element for enforcement of rules and procedures against abuse of detainees is habeas corpus, the legal requirement of any detaining power in a democracy to produce detainees before a court of law and justify detention to a duly appointed legal authority. As long as the US — or any state, for that matter — has the power to detain at pleasure and in secret, abuse of detainees is inevitable. International pressure, domestic mobilisationmobilization and, finally, congressional legislation are all necessary to stop the practice of "ghost detainees," whose identities remain concealed and who may be held outside the US, inside the US, or in third countries. It should be mandatory that every single detainee held by the US, whether a citizen or not, be publicly known.

Does an outright ban on torture and coercive interrogation meet the test of realism? Would an absolute ban on torture and coercive interrogation using stress and duress so diminish the effectiveness of our intelligence-gathering that it would diminish public safety? It is often said that neither coercive interrogation nor torture is necessary, since entirely lawful interrogation can secure just as effective results. For example, Israeli interrogators have given interviews assuring the Israeli public that physical duress is unnecessary. But we are grasping at straws if we think this is the entire truth. As Posner and others have tartly pointed out, if torture and coercion are both as useless as critics pretend, why are they used so much? While some abuse and outright torture can be attributed to individual sadism, poor supervision and so on, it must be the case that other acts of torture occur because interrogators believe, in good faith, that torture is the only way to extract information in a timely fashion. It must also be the case that if experienced interrogators come to this conclusion, they do so on the basis of experience. The argument that torture and coercion do not work is contradicted by the dire frequency with which both practices occurred.

ISSUES TO CONSIDER

1. In a democracy, who is responsible for determining the limits of interrogation?
2. How should we monitor interrogators?
3. How should the "ticking time bomb" be defined?
4. Should society adopt a "don't know, don't tell" policy with respect to interrogations?
5. What is the acceptable loss of life in the no-torture proposition?
6. Should the criminal law limits of interrogation be applied to counterterrorism?

It is important to understand the universality of this dilemma. While cultural differences exist from country to country and legal regime to legal regime, the basic moral quandary must be addressed by the leadership of each country: what are the limits of interrogation for detainees suspected of involvement in terrorism?

III. UNITED STATES

Reported instances of torture during interrogation in the Abu Ghraib detention facility received much attention:

> Seven members of the U.S. Armed Forces have been convicted . . . for severe violations committed at Abu Ghraib scandal. Graner is the only soldier still imprisoned in connection with the case. The Pentagon cleared four of five top officers overseeing prison policies, and operations of wrongdoing. One brigadier general was relieved of her command and given a written reprimand.[7]

Interrogation policies implemented by the Bush administration violated both the Geneva Convention and U.S. domestic law. In a memo written by Assistant Attorney General Jay S. Bybee to White House General Counsel Alberto Gonzales, Bybee stated that Geneva Convention protections do not pertain to the detainees.[8]

Two independent investigations, the Schlesinger commission and an internal Army review, contain important and disturbing information regarding torture and mistreatment of prisoners in Afghanistan, Iraq, and Guantanamo.[9] While U.S. law forbids torture, the Bybee memo—combined with subsequent statements and actions by the Bush administration—created a climate where basic violations of human rights were acceptable, if not encouraged.

When ratifying CAT, the U.S. Senate made the Convention subject to its own definition of torture:

> [I]n order to constitute torture, an act must be specifically intended to inflict severe physical or mental pain or suffering and that mental pain or suffering refers to prolonged mental harm caused by or resulting from: the intentional infliction or threatened infliction of severe physical pain or suffering; the administration or application, or threatened administration or application, of mind altering substances or other procedures calculated to disrupt profoundly the senses or the personality; the threat of imminent death; or the threat that another person will imminently be subjected to death, severe physical pain or suffering, or the administration or application of mind-altering substances or other procedures calculated to disrupt profoundly the senses or personality.[10]

---

7. Daniel Nasaw, *Report Vindicates Soldiers Prosecuted over Abu Ghraib Abuses, Lawyers Say*, Guardian. Co. UK., Apr. 22, 2009.

8. *See* Memorandum from Jay S. Bybee, Assistant Attorney General, to Alberto R. Gonzales, Counsel to the President and William J. Haynes II, General Counsel for the Department of Defense, Re: Application of Treaties and Laws to al Qaeda and Taliban Detainees (Jan. 22, 2002), *available at* http://www.washingtonpost.com/wp-srv/nation/documents/012202bybee.pdf (last visited Oct. 8, 2010) (on file with author).

9. *See* James Ross, *Hold Officials Responsible*, USA Today, Aug. 27, 2004, *available at* http://www.hrw.org/english/docs/2004/08/27/usdom9275.htm (last visited Oct. 8, 2010).

10. *Quoted in* Sanford Levinson, *Brutal Logic*, Village Voice, May 18, 2004, at 27.

The Bybee memo addressed the relationship between international and domestic law with respect to defining torture in the context of the war on terror.

> You have asked for our Office's views regarding the standards of conduct under the Convention Against Torture and Other Cruel, Inhuman and Degrading Treatment or Punishment as implemented by Sections 2340-2340(A) of Title 18 of the United States Code. As we understand it, this question has arisen in the context of interrogations outside the United States. We conclude below that Section 2340(A) proscribes acts inflicting, and that are specifically intended to inflict, severe pain or suffering, whether mental or physical. Those acts must be of an extreme nature to rise to the level of torture within the meaning of Section 2340(A) and the Convention. We further conclude that certain acts may be cruel, inhuman or degrading but still not produce pain and suffering of the requisite intensity to fall within Section 2340(A)'s proscription against torture. We conclude by examining possible defenses that would negate any claim that certain interrogation methods violate the Statute. . . .
>
> To violate Section 2340 (A) the statute requires that severe pain and suffering must inflicted with specific intent. In order for a defendant to have acted with specific intent, he must expressly intend to achieve the forbidden act. . . .
>
> Here, because Section 2340 requires that the defendant act with the specific intent to inflict severe pain, the infliction of such pain must be the defendant's precise objective. . . . If the defendant acted knowing that severe pain or suffering was reasonably likely to result from his actions, but no more, he would have acted only with general intent.[11]

William J. Haynes, the General Counsel of the Department of Defense, wrote the following regarding interrogation measures:

> Specifically, with regard to Category I techniques, the use of mild and fear related approaches such as yelling at the detainees is not illegal because in order to communicate a threat, three must also exist an intent to injure. . . .
>
> With regard to Category II methods, the use of stress positions such as the proposed standing for four hours, the use of isolation for up to thirty days and interrogation the detainees in an environment other than the standard interrogation booth are all legally permissible so long as no severe physical pain is inflicted and prolonged mental harm intended, and because there is a legitimate governmental objective in obtaining the information necessary that the high value detainees on which these methods would be utilized possess, for the protection of the national security of the United States, its citizens, and allies.
>
> With respect to the Category III advanced counter-resistance strategies, the use of scenarios designed to convince the detainee that death or severely painful consequences are imminent is not illegal for the same aforementioned

---

11. Memorandum for Alberto R. Gonzales *Re: Standards of Conduct for Interrogation under 18 U.S.C. Section 2340-2340(A)*, *available at* http://www.washingtonpost.com/wp-srv/nation/documents/dojinterrogationmemo20020801.pdf (last visited Mar. 20, 2010).

reasons that there is a compelling governmental interest and it is not done intentionally to cause prolonged harm.[12]

While American soldiers were court-martialed for abusing civilians, their actions were clearly the result of government policy. The following report submitted to the United Nations further indicates how U.S. policy shaped and enabled such abuse.

TORTURE BY THE UNITED STATES

The World Organization for Human Rights USA, Jan. 2005[13]

III. Introduction

In particular, through legal memoranda prepared at the highest levels of the U.S. Government, official sanction has been given to carrying out torture for the purpose of detaining and obtaining information from suspected terrorists that presumably might prevent future or imminent acts of terrorism from taking place. Among the specific acts of torture and violations of CAT that have taken place are . . . the following:

- severe physical and psychological abuse of detainees in Abu Ghraib prison in Iraq, and in other detention and interrogation facilities in that country, Afghanistan, and Guantanamo Bay, Cuba;
- "rendition to torture" to other countries for purposes of interrogation of hundreds of individuals suspected of terrorist ties, including at least one known U.S. citizen, Ahmed Abu Ali, who has been detained in Saudi Arabia for over 17 months at the request of the U.S. government, and one Canadian citizen, Maher Arar, who was sent to Syria by the United States for over a year after being detained by U.S. authorities while in transit to his home country of Canada;
- indefinite, arbitrary detention, without a lawful determination of status other than the President's designation of their being "unlawful enemy combatants," of more than 600 detainees in the Guantanamo Bay, Cuba military base;
- execution by torture and other unlawful, extra-judicial means of upwards of 37 detainees being held for interrogation purposes;
- use of unlawfully constituted military tribunals to prosecute suspected terrorists and to keep them detained and subject to interrogation for prolonged periods; and
- maintenance of an undetermined number of "ghost" detainees in secret facilities without charges being filed against them, and without their whereabouts or status being reported to any recognized authorities.

---

12. William J. Haynes II, *Action Memo on Counter-Resistance Strategies, available at* http://www.washingtonpost.com/wp-srv/nation/documents/dodmemos.pdf (last visited Mar. 20, 2010).

13. The Status of Compliance by the U.S. Government with International Convention Against Torture and Other Cruel, Inhuman and Degrading Treatment or Punishment *submitted to* United Nations Committee Against Torture, Jan. 2005, *available at* http://www2.ohchr.org/english/bodies/hrc/docs/ngos/wohr.pdf (last visited Mar. 20, 2010).

Issues to Consider

1. What would be the benefits policy makers would seek to achieve from practices of torture and detainee abuse?
2. How would the effectiveness of this policy be determined?
3. How is the reliability of information received from torture-based interrogation to be assessed?
4. Did 9/11 justify the policy articulated by the memos?
5. What controls should be imposed on guards and interrogators?
6. What is the long-term impact of a torture based interrogation regime?

According to a Council of Foreign Relations report:

Lawrence Shoup, The Council on Foreign Relations Helps Shape Imperial Strategy

The Council on Foreign Relations Debates on Torture, Mar./Apr. 2006[14]

. . . The abuse, torture, and murder at Abu Ghraib and Guantanamo Bay, Cuba ("Gitmo") have been most reported on, but what is most revealing about both locations and the "Salt Pit" U.S. torture center in Afghanistan is the central role of the CIA in all three places. Major General George R. Fay's investigative report on Abu Ghraib pointed out that the CIA was actually in charge of interrogation/torture at that facility and that they "poisoned the atmosphere" there. The "Salt Pit" was a CIA-run camp and the CIA was also very active at Gitmo. Some of their techniques caused deaths, with over 100 detainees dying in U.S. custody over the past several years, most of them murdered by U.S. personnel. Despite these homicides and over 400 criminal investigations of misconduct, only a few low level U.S. soldiers have been tried, convicted, and sentenced to prison terms. The CIA, while most responsible, has been completely exempt from any independent investigations, let alone any real accounting. The chilling fact is that the CIA is entirely above the law.

Many of these CIA torture techniques were codified much earlier in a secret 1963 torture instruction book called KUBARK Counterintelligence Interrogation. These torture techniques have been spread by the CIA throughout the world over the past 40 years, resulting in an epidemic of torture worldwide.

A September 2005 Human Rights Watch report based on interviews with active duty soldiers in the elite 82nd Airborne Division occupying part of Iraq found that military commanders demanded that lower ranking soldiers get intelligence from detainees, without giving guidelines about what was allowed in terms of interrogation techniques. The report found that the torture of detainees at the 82nd Airborne's base in Iraq (called FOB Mercury) took place almost daily from September 2003 to April 2004. It concluded that,

---

14. *Available at* http://www.thirdworldtraveler.com/Foreign_Policy_Institutions/CFR_Debates_Torture.html (last visited Mar. 21, 2010).

since no full scale investigation had taken place and no one had been punished, such torture was probably still continuing today. Detainees captured by the 82nd were held in tents separated from the rest of the base by concertina wire for several days prior to being released or sent to Abu Ghraib. In these tents detainees were tortured to get information under the direction of officers from the military intelligence unit.

A summary of the Human Rights Watch report, based on U.S. soldiers' own testimony, stated that techniques used included: "severe beatings (in one observed incident, a soldier reportedly broke a detainee's leg with a baseball bat), blows and kicks to the face, chest, abdomen, and extremities, and repeated kicks to various parts of the detainees' body; the application of chemical substances to exposed skin and eyes; forced stress positions . . . sometimes to the point of unconsciousness; sleep deprivation; subjecting detainees to extremes of hot and cold; the stacking of detainees into human pyramids; and the withholding of food (beyond crackers) and water." The torture of detainees became so widespread and accepted that it became a means of "stress relief" for soldiers who were welcomed to the tents to beat up or otherwise abuse detainees. If a detainee suffered a broken bone from such beatings, then an army physician's assistant was called in to cover up the beating and agree that the detainee was injured during capture. Military intelligence officers approved of the beatings because they believed that it demoralized the detainees, making it easier to get intelligence from them. Officers and soldiers of the 82nd who wished to behave honorably and tried to report what was happening to superior officers to stop these outrages were told to keep their mouths shut and not risk their careers.

Since investigations about the behavior of other important U.S. military units in Iraq have not been conducted, we do not know if other divisions and units are also guilty of similar torture and abuse of detainees, but it would be surprising if this were not the case, since this problem is epidemic.

In the immediate aftermath of 9/11, the United States defined the "limits of interrogation" extremely broadly. The administration based this policy on the assumption that, other than basic guarantees, detainees are not entitled to Geneva Convention protections. The result was a policy that directly led to the abuses described above.

In the spring of 2009, the most comprehensive accounting of torture during the Bush administration was released by the Obama administration. The Obama administration decided not to prosecute CIA officials for their role in torturing detainees, stating it wanted to move away from a dark and painful chapter in U.S. history.

A. THE SLIPPERY SLOPE OF STANDARDS

International law provisions, particularly the Geneva Conventions, accord detainees certain protections. The Bush administration's initial approach of granting only basic, minimum rights was overwhelmingly discredited by independent observers and subsequently modified by the White House. While al Qaeda operatives are not considered prisoners of war, Part II, Article 13 of the Geneva

Convention relative to the treatment of Prisoners of War guarantees detainees protections:

> Prisoners of war must at all times be humanely treated. Any unlawful act or omission by the Detaining Power causing death or seriously endangering the health of a prisoner of war in its custody is prohibited, and will be regarded as a serious breach of the present Convention. In particular, no prisoner of war may be subjected to physical mutilation or to medical or scientific experiments of any kind which are not justified by the medical, dental or hospital treatment of the prisoner concerned and carried out in his interest.
>
> Likewise, prisoners of war must at all times be protected, particularly against acts of violence or intimidation and against insults and public curiosity.
>
> Measures of reprisal against prisoners of war are prohibited.[15]

In addition, CAT specifically and explicitly prohibits abuses documented above, which would qualify as torture under its definition:

> Any act which by severe pain or suffering, whether physical or mental, is intentionally inflicted on a person for such purposes as obtaining from him or a third person information or a confession . . . or intimidating or coercing . . . when such pain or suffering is inflicted . . . with the consent or acquiescence of a public official . . . it does not include pain or suffering arising only from, inherent in or incidental to lawful sanctions.[16]

In addition, the Army Field Manual 34-52 established clear guidelines for U.S. military personnel:

> U.S. policy expressly prohibits[s] acts of violence or intimidation, including physical or mental torture, threats, insults, or exposure to inhumane treatment as a means of or aid to interrogations. Such illegal acts are not authorized and will not be condoned by the US Army. Acts in violation of these prohibitions are criminal acts punishable under the [Uniform Code of Military Justice].[17]

Despite CAT, existing domestic legislation, and relevant Geneva Convention protections and obligations, the Bush Administration established the following guidelines for the harsh interrogation of detainees.

KENNETH J. LEVIT, THE CIA AND THE TORTURE CONTROVERSY: INTERROGATION AUTHORITIES AND PRACTICES IN THE WAR ON TERROR

1 J. of Nat'l Sec. L. & Pol'y 341 (2005)[18]

Guidelines for Aggressive Interrogations

Which "harsher methods" have been approved? No documents have yet been declassified that show what techniques are used specifically by the CIA, but

---

15. Geneva Convention (III) Relative to the Treatment of Prisoners of War, *opened for signature* Apr. 12, 1949.

16. Convention Against Torture and Other Cruel, Inhuman or Degrading Treatment, or Punishment, *opened for signature* Feb. 4, 1985, art. 1.

17. *Quoted in* David E. Graham, *The Treatment and Interrogation of Prisoners of War and Detainees*, 37 Geo. J. Int'l L. 61 (Fall 2005).

18. *Available at* http://www.mcgeorge.edu/documents/publications/jnslp/05_Levit_Master_c.pdf (last visited Mar. 21, 2010).

one can reasonably assume that the Agency has at least the same range of freedom as that given to the Department of Defense in interrogating unlawful combatants outside the United States. In a Department of Defense memorandum entitled Working Group Report on Detainee Interrogations in the Global War on Terrorism, military officials divided non-routine interrogation techniques into two broad categories. The first category contained 26 techniques, all recommended for approval. These included techniques with names like "Fear Up Harsh," "Rapid Fire," "Dietary Manipulation," "Environmental Manipulation," and "Isolation."

A second set of eight techniques was recommended for approval only "where there is a good basis to believe that the detainee possesses critical intelligence" and where the detainee has been determined to be medically suitable to withstand the technique. The report also calls for an "appropriate specified senior level approval [to be] given for use with any specific detainee" These eight "exceptional" techniques, advanced in the report as legal, are:

> Isolation: Isolating the detainee from other detainees while still complying with basic standards of treatment.
>
> Use of Prolonged Interrogations: The continued use of a series of approaches that extend over a long period of time (e.g., 20 hours per day per interrogation).
>
> Forced Grooming: Forcing a detainee to shave hair or beard. (Force applied with intention to avoid injury. Would not use force that would cause serious injury.)
>
> Prolonged Standing: Lengthy standing in a "normal" position (non-stress). This has been successful, but should never make the detainee exhausted to the point of weakness or collapse. Not enforced by physical restraints. Not to exceed four hours in a 24-hour period.
>
> Sleep Deprivation: Keeping the detainee awake for an extended period of time. (Allowing individual to rest briefly and then awakening him, repeatedly.) Not to exceed 4 days in succession.
>
> Physical Training: Requiring detainees to exercise. . . . Assists in generating compliance and fatiguing the detainees. No enforced compliance.
>
> Face Slap/Stomach Slap: A quick glancing slap to the fleshy part of the cheek or stomach. These techniques are used strictly as shock measures and do not cause pain or injury. They are only effective if used once or twice together. After the second time on a detainee, it will lose the shock effect. Limited to two slaps per application; no more than two applications per interrogation.
>
> Removal of Clothing: Potential removal of all clothing; removal to be done by military police if not agreed to by the subject. Creating a feeling of helplessness and dependence. This technique must be monitored to ensure the environmental conditions are such that this technique does not injure the detainee.
>
> Increasing Anxiety by Use of Aversions: Introducing factors that of themselves create anxiety but do not create terror or mental trauma (e.g., simple presence of dog without directly threatening action). This technique requires the commander to develop specific and detailed safeguards to insure detainee's safety.

In response to the Working Group Report, Defense Secretary Rumsfeld sent a directive to the Commander of the U.S. Southern Command specifically accepting a number of the techniques endorsed in the report, but not the eight exceptional tactics. Rather, the Secretary directed that, in the event that the eight exceptional tactics are warranted, the Commander "should provide [the Secretary], via the Chairman of the Joint Chiefs of Staff, a written request describing the proposed techniques, recommended safeguards, and the rationale for applying it with an identified detainee.

The guidelines just described concern interrogation methods used by the Department of Defense, not necessarily the CIA. One can expect a similar degree of latitude, however, for detainees under the control of the CIA, especially since it appears that the CIA is expected to manage interrogations of senior terrorist leaders.

The 2006 Army Field Manual addressed many of the concerns regarding interrogation measures. Concurrent with the new manual, the Department of Defense issued directive number 2310.01E, regarding the detainee program:

> E4.1.1 All persons captured, detained, interned, or otherwise in control of DoD personnel during the course of military operations will be given humane care and treatment from the moment they fall into the hands of the DoD personnel until release, transfer out of DoD control, or repatriation, including:
>
> E4.1.1.1. Adequate food, drinking water, shelter, clothing, and medical treatment;
>
> E4.1.1.2. Free exercise of religion, consistent with the requirements of detention;
>
> E41.1.3. All detainees will be respected as human beings. They will be protected against threats or acts of violence, including rape, forced prostitution, assault and theft, public curiosity, bodily injuries, and reprisals. They will not be subjected to medical or scientific experiments. They will not be subjected to sensory deprivation. This list is not exclusive.
>
> E41.4 The inhumane treatment of detainees is prohibited and is not justified by the stress of combat or deep provocation.[19]

ISSUES TO CONSIDER

1. What risks did the Bush administration assume when the guidelines for aggressive interrogations were developed and implemented?
2. What is the fallout from developing a policy that violates international and domestic law?
3. Are violations of international and domestic law acceptable in the face of terrorism?
4. Does a major terrorist attack justify waiving the limits of "coercive interrogation"?

---

19. *Definitions, Treatment Policy, and Compliance with Laws of War*, Dep't of Defense, http://news.findlaw.com/hdocs/docs/dod/detainee90506directive11.html (last visited Oct. 8, 2010).

5. What assumptions regarding the efficiency, effectiveness, and efficacy of torture did the Bush administration make?
6. How are questions of morality resolved in the torture scenario?
7. What were the operative advantages attached to the Haynes and Bybee memos?
8. Did actionable intelligence result from this policy advocated by these memos?
9. What are the implications of the Department of Defense Directive being limited only to DoD personnel?

B. CHANGES WITH THE OBAMA ADMINISTRATION

While President Obama articulated an intention to close Guantanamo and end torture practices, as of January 2011, Guantanamo remains open and unsubstantiated press reports suggest harsh interrogation measures are still in effect.

FOON RHEE, OBAMA ORDERS GUANTANAMO BAY CLOSED, BANS TORTURE

The Boston Globe, Jan. 22, 2009[20]

Executive Order requires closure of the Guantanamo detention center no later than one year from the date of the Order. Closure of the facility is the ultimate goal but not the first step. The Order establishes a review process with the goal of disposing of the detainees before closing the facility.

The Order sets up an immediate review to determine whether it is possible to transfer detainees to third countries, consistent with national security. If transfer is not approved, a second review will determine whether prosecution is possible and in what forum. The preference is for prosecution in Article III courts or under the Uniform Code of Military Justice (UCMJ), but military commissions, perhaps with revised authorities, would remain an option. If there are detainees who cannot be transferred or prosecuted, the review will examine the lawful options for dealing with them. The Attorney General will coordinate the review and the Secretaries of Defense, State, and Homeland Security as well as the DNI and the Chairman of the Joint Chiefs of Staff will participate.

The Executive Order directs the Secretary of State to seek international cooperation aimed at achieving the transfers of detainees.

The Order directs the Secretary of Defense to halt military commission proceedings pending the results of the review.

Finally, the Executive Order requires that conditions of confinement at Guantanamo, until its closure, comply with Common Article 3 of the Geneva Conventions and all other applicable laws.

20. *Available at* http://www.boston.com/news/politics/politicalintelligence/2009/01/obama_orders_gu.html/.

Executive Order creates a Special Task Force, co-chaired by the Attorney General and the Secretary of Defense, to conduct a review of detainee policy going forward. The group will consider policy options for apprehension, detention, trial, transfer, or release of detainees. Other Task Force participants include the Secretary of State, the Secretary of Homeland Security, the Director of National Intelligence, the Director of the Central Intelligence Agency, and the Chairman of the Joint Chiefs of Staff. The Special Task Force must submit its report to the President within 180 days.

Executive Order revokes Executive Order 13440 that interpreted Common Article 3 of the Geneva Conventions. It requires that all interrogations of detainees in armed conflict, by any government agency, follow the Army Field Manual interrogation guidelines. The Order also prohibits reliance on any Department of Justice or other legal advice concerning interrogation that was issued between September 11, 2001 and January 20, 2009.

The Order requires all departments and agencies to provide the ICRC access to detainees in a manner consistent with Department of Defense regulations and practice. It also orders the CIA to close all existing detention facilities and prohibits it from operating detention facilities in the future.

Finally, the Order creates a Special Task Force with two missions. The Task Force will conduct a review of the Army Field Manual interrogation guidelines to determine whether different or additional guidance is necessary for the CIA. It will also look at rendition and other policies for transferring individuals to third countries to be sure that our policies and practices comply with all obligations and are sufficient to ensure that individuals do not face torture and cruel treatment if transferred. This Task Force will be led by the Attorney General with the Secretary of Defense and the Director of National Intelligence as co-Vice Chairs.

US: Obama's First Year Record on Counterterrorism Reform Mixed

Human Rights Watch, Jan. 14, 2010[21]

US President Barack Obama has made significant progress in his first year in office toward ending the Bush administration's abusive counterterrorism policies, but he has also made some serious missteps, Human Rights Watch said in a background paper released today. "Counterterrorism and Human Rights: A Report Card on President Obama's First Year," reviews the Obama administration's advances, analyzes its mistakes and urges more meaningful and extensive reforms. "President Obama has done the right thing by ending the CIA's secret prison program and trying to close Guantanamo," said Joanne Mariner, terrorism and counterterrorism director at Human Rights Watch. "Unfortunately, he has also adopted many of the Bush administration's most misguided policies."

Among the administration's key accomplishments, Human Rights Watch cited executive orders to close secret CIA prisons and ban torture and other

---

21. *Available at* http://www.hrw.org/en/news/2010/01/14/us-obama-s-first-year-record-counterterrorism-reform-mixed/.

mistreatment by all US personnel, and its decision to transfer the prosecution of the alleged 9/11 perpetrators from a military commission to a US federal court.

Human Rights Watch singled out the administration's continued reliance on indefinite detention without charge — including in its upcoming plans to transfer some detainees from Guantanamo to a prison in Thomson, Illinois — as being its most serious misstep. "Closing Guantanamo by effectively moving the prison onto US soil won't solve the problem," Mariner said. "The administration needs to prosecute the detainees implicated in crimes, and either repatriate or resettle the rest."

Human Rights Watch said that the administration's record was also marred by its revival of the discredited military commissions to prosecute some defendants; its reluctance to seek accountability for past abuses by US officials; and its efforts to obtain the dismissal of civil cases alleging torture by asserting the state secrets privilege.

Human Rights Watch acknowledged that the Bush administration's legacy of abuse posed daunting challenges, including resolving the cases of the more than 240 prisoners held at Guantanamo when Obama took office. The attempted bombing of a US airliner on December 25, 2009, by a Nigerian man with alleged links to Yemen has exacerbated the difficulty of closing the facility and returning Yemeni detainees to their country.

Human Rights Watch said that Yemenis at Guantanamo should not endure continued detention for a crime carried out without their participation or knowledge. It urged the administration to work with Yemen on a plan for the safe repatriation or resettlement in other countries of the Yemeni detainees who are not subject to criminal prosecution. Human Rights Watch also called on both governments to provide returnees with social and medical services to aid their reintegration and make them less vulnerable to recruitment by militant groups.

In addition, Human Rights Watch criticized the administration's continued reliance on an overbroad understanding of the state secrets doctrine, which has resulted in cases brought by persons alleging to have been tortured being thrown out of court before they can be heard on the merits. By improperly asserting that disclosing information about whether plaintiffs were tortured would damage national security, the Obama administration has barred victims of abuse from seeking redress.

While Human Rights Watch praised the administration for declassifying Bush-era Justice Department memos that provided the legal framework for the use of "enhanced interrogation techniques," as well as for releasing a report from the CIA's Inspector General's office detailing a range of CIA abuses, it criticized Obama's decision to block the release of photographs depicting detainee abuse by US troops.

Human Rights Watch also called on the Obama administration to take more vigorous steps to ensure that senior officials responsible for abusive Bush-era policies are held accountable. It raised concerns that the preliminary review of CIA abuses ordered by Attorney General Eric Holder was focused on so-called "unauthorized" interrogation techniques, and was unlikely to look up the chain of command to the senior-level officials who planned, ordered, and facilitated abuses.

Without the deterrence provided by meaningful accountability, Human Rights Watch said, practices like torture and enforced disappearance will remain available to future administrations as policy options.

"By abolishing secret CIA prisons and banning all use of torture, President Obama took important steps toward setting a new course," Mariner said. "But to renew America's commitment to human rights and US constitutional values, the Obama administration will have to confront the past as well. Only by investigating and prosecuting torture and other crimes against detainees will the US government be understood to have surmounted them."

C. LOOKING FORWARD

The Bush administration's efforts to push the "legal envelope" resulted in serious violations of human and civil rights, well documented abuses that resulted in limited actionable intelligence and potentially irreversible damage to America's foreign policy and image in the Middle East. The White House attempted to redefine the limits of interrogation and to authorize torture from a legal and policy perspective. In a series of memos, White House lawyers authorized illegal interrogation measures, including waterboarding. The actions of interrogators in Abu Ghraib resulted in humiliation, degradation, and ultimately, in at least one case, murder. Against this reality must be weighed questions of effectiveness.

President Obama's Executive Order seeks to re-articulate America's detention regime by applying the Army Field Manual to all American interrogators. To what extent the re-articulation of the interrogation paradigm is successful remains, at present, unclear.

IV. ISRAEL

In the aftermath of the 1967 Six-Day War, Israel occupied the West Bank, the Gaza Strip, the Golan Heights, East Jerusalem, and the Sinai Peninsula. As a result, 392,700 Palestinians living in the West Bank and the Gaza Strip came to live under Israel Defense Forces occupation. Between the years 1967-1987, the occupation was relatively tranquil; the Intifada of 1987-1993, which directly led to the Oslo Peace Process, marked the first time that West Bank and Gaza Strip Palestinians committed widespread terror attacks against the IDF, Jewish settlers living in the territories, and Israelis living in Israel proper.

How Israel responded, and in particular, what interrogation measures were developed and implemented by the General Security Services (GSS) — today know as the Israeli Security Agency (ISA) — is the focus of this section. The ISA is the government agency charged with preventing terrorism in Israel. It does so in a number of different operational manners; one of the most important is the interrogation of Palestinians suspected of involvement in terrorism or believed to have knowledge either of future terrorism acts or of individuals involved in terrorist activity. The ISA director is under the direct control of the Prime Minister and works in close cooperation with the IDF, but is not in the IDF's chain of command.

The following report, written by the Israeli human rights organization B'Tselem, provides an inside look into how ISA (refered to as the GSS) interrogates suspected terrorists.

STANLEY COHEN & DAPHNA GOLAN, THE INTERROGATION OF PALESTINIANS DURING THE INTIFADA: ILL-TREATMENT, "MODERATE PHYSICAL PRESSURE" OR TORTURE ?

B'Tselem — The Israeli Information Center for Human Rights
in the Occupied Territories[22]

The General Security Services ("Shin Bet" or "Shabaq," today called Israel Security Agency) is responsible for security matters and counter-intelligence within Israel and the Occupied Territories. It is directly responsible to the Prime Minister and not subject to any other external control or scrutiny either by a regular Government Ministry or a Knesset Committee. . . .

Article 78 of the Order provides that immediately following arrest, a person may be detained for up to 18 days without coming before a court. This is Stage One. (In East Jerusalem, according to Israeli Law, the period is 48 hours. Our description below concentrates on the Territories.) At the end of this 18 day period, the detainee must be released if he/she has not been charged, unless a judge extends the period. In practice, the Shin Bet (directly or through the police) usually requests this extension and the military judges almost automatically comply. . . .

During this initial period of detention after arrest, the detainee may in theory be interrogated by one of three bodies: (1) military personnel; (2) regular police; or (3) G.S.S. We concentrate on the G.S.S., which is responsible for the bulk of the interrogations of Palestinian suspects both in Israel and the Territories.

G.S.S. interrogation takes place in separate wings or blocks located in detention-centers/prisons which in the Territories are controlled by the I.D.F. or Prison Service and in Israel (in Petah Tikva or the Russian Compound in Jerusalem, for example) by the police. These wings are under the effective control of the G.S.S, Army, police, and prison staff claim that they are not permitted to enter (nor is the International Committee of the Red Cross). In practice (as our research shows) these other bodies do have contact (for example, in escorting the detainee). In legal terms, however, the detainee remains in the formal custody and responsibility of the army or regular Israeli police or prison authority.

The legal provisions for any supervision over G.S.S. interrogations or for dealing with any complaint by detainees (or their lawyers) of any abuses, are not clear. G.S.S. agents do not normally appear in court. After the interrogation, the suspect is handed over to the police investigator who takes down a confession as presented to the court. Requests for extension of detention are

---

22. *Available at* www.btselem.org/Download/199103_Torture_Eng.doc (last visited June 25, 2010).

also made by the police. At this point, there are two main contexts in which complaints about abuses may appear:

First, in the rare cases where signs of ill treatment are visible when the suspect appears in court, a judge might record this in the protocol, but usually only after a formal complaint by the defense attorney. The police or State Prosecutor can justifiably claim no knowledge or responsibility for earlier stages. Military court judges do not normally deal with complaints and refer them to other authorities.

Second, there is the formal procedure known as a "trial within a trial." When the accused's confession during interrogation is the main or only evidence, then a plea of "not guilty" in court is tantamount to alleging that the confession was obtained by improper methods and is therefore invalid and inadmissible as evidence. This calls for conducting a "trial within a trial" on the question of the admissibility of the confession. This forum becomes, in essence, the trial itself dealing with the credibility of the evidence and, by implication, of the G.S.S. Allegations thus can be raised both about the process of interrogation and whether the G.S.S. is telling the truth about its circumstances. . . .

The special status of the G.S.S. can, therefore, lend itself to abuses in the interrogation process that are difficult to control. No law established the G.S.S. in the first place, nor does it have any clear legal authority in which to operate. It relies wholly upon the authority of other agencies — the police, the prison service, the army, the courts — which provide physical space, cooperation and legal cover. It does not have its own hierarchy of supervision or public account-ability. Interrogators are anonymous at all stages, not just in the interrogation itself but in the court. . . .

A. SELF-IMPOSED RESTRAINTS

Over the years, Palestinians interrogated by the ISA have complained of torture; Palestinian, international, and Israeli human rights groups have filed numerous petitions to the High Court of Justice in support of such claims.[23] In response, the ISA consistently denies torturing Palestinian detainees.[24]

The Israeli Supreme Court sitting as the High Court of Justice addresses theses issues in the case below. By imposing limits on interrogation measures, the Court establishes clear guidelines for ISA interrogators.

---

23. Dan Izenberg, *Israle's High Court Eases Way for Palestinians to Sue State*, Jewish Press (Dec. 13, 2006), *available at* http://www.jewishpress.com/page.do/20109/Israel's_High_Court_Eases_Way_For_ Palestinians_To_Sue_State.html (last visited June 25, 2010).

24. B'Tslem, *Torture During Interrogations: Testimony of Palestinian Detainees, Testimony of Inter-rogators*, *available at* http://www.btselem.org/English/Publications/Summaries/199411_Torture_During_Interrogations.asp During_Interrogations.asp (last visited June 25, 2010); B'Tselem, *Absolute Prohibition: the Torutre and Ill-Treatment of Palestinian Detainees*, http://www.btselem.org/English/Publications/Summaries/200705_Utterly_Forbidden.asp (last visited June 25, 2010).

Public Comm. Against Torture in Israel v. State of Israel

HCJ 5100/94 (1994)

This decision opens with a description of the difficult reality in which Israel finds herself security wise. We shall conclude this judgment by re-addressing that harsh reality. We are aware that this decision does not ease dealing with that reality. This is the destiny of democracy, as not all means are acceptable to it, and not all practices employed by its enemies are open before it. Although a democracy must often fight with one hand tied behind its back, it nonetheless has the upper hand. Preserving the Rule of Law and recognition of an individual's liberty constitutes an important component in its understanding of security. At the end of the day, they strengthen its spirit and its strength and allow it to overcome its difficulties. This having been said, there are those who argue that Israel's security problems are too numerous, thereby requiring the authorization to use physical means. If it will nonetheless be decided that it is appropriate for Israel, in light of its security difficulties to sanction physical means in interrogations (and the scope of these means which deviate from the ordinary investigation rules), this is an issue that must be decided by the legislative branch which represents the people. We do not take any stand on this matter at this time. It is there that various considerations must be weighed. The pointed debate must occur there. It is there that the required legislation may be passed, provided, of course, that a law infringing upon a suspect's liberty "befitting the values of the State of Israel," is enacted for a proper purpose, and to an extent no greater than is required. (Article 8 to the Basic Law: Human Dignity and Liberty.)

Deciding these applications weighed heavy on this Court. True, from the legal perspective, the road before us is smooth. We are, however, part of Israeli society. Its problems are known to us and we live its history. We are not isolated in an ivory tower. We live the life of this country. We are aware of the harsh reality of terrorism in which we are, at times, immersed. Our apprehension is that this decision will hamper the ability to properly deal with terrorists and terrorism, disturbs us. We are, however, judges. Our brethren require us to act according to the law. This is equally the standard that we set for ourselves. When we sit to judge, we are being judged. Therefore, we must act according to our purest conscience when we decide the law. The words of the Deputy President of the Supreme Court, Justice Landau, speak well to our purposes:

"We possess proper sources upon which to construct our judgments and have no need, and while judging, are forbidden from, involving our personal views as citizens of this country in our decisions. Still, great is the fear that the Court shall be perceived as though it had abandoned its proper place and descended to the midst of public debate, and that its decision making will be obstructed by one side of the population's uproar and by the other side's absolute and emotional rejection. In that sense, I see myself here as someone whose duty is to decide according to the law in all cases legally brought before the Court. I am strictly bound by this duty. As I am well aware in advance that the public at large will not pay attention to the legal reasoning, but to the end result alone. And that the Court's proper status, as an institution above partisan debates, risks being harmed. What can we do, as this is our function and role as judges."

The Commission of Inquiry pointed to the "difficult dilemma between the imperative need to safeguard the State of Israel's very existence and the lives of its citizens, and preserving its character — that of a country subject to the Rule of Law and holding basic moral values." The Commission rejected an approach suggesting that the actions of security services in the context of fighting terrorism, shall take place in the recesses of the law. The Commission equally rejected the "ways of the hypocrites, who remind us of their adherence to the Rule of Law, while ignoring (being willfully blind) to what is being done in practice." The Commission elected to follow a third route, "the way of Truth and the Rule of Law." In so doing, the Commission of Inquiry outlined the dilemma faced by Israel in a manner both transparent and open to inspection by Israeli society.

Consequently, it is decided that the order nisi be made absolute, as we declare that the GSS does not have the authority to "shake" a man, hold him in the "Shabach" position (which includes the combination of various methods, as mentioned in paragraph 30), force him into a "frog crouch" position and deprive him of sleep in a manner other than that which is inherently required by the interrogation. Likewise, we declare that the "necessity" defence, found in the Penal Law, cannot serve as a basis of authority for the use of these interrogation practices, or for the existence of directives pertaining to GSS investigators, allowing them to employ interrogation practices of this kind. Our decision does not negate the possibility that the "necessity" defence be available to GSS investigators, be within the discretion of the Attorney General, if he decides to prosecute, or if criminal charges are brought against them, as per the Court's discretion.

ISSUES TO CONSIDER

1. What does it mean to enable interrogators to operate in the "twilight zone"?
2. What are the legitimate operational goals of an interrogation?
3. How is "appropriate pressure" operationally defined?
4. How is the "necessity defense" defined and implemented?
5. What are the recommended criteria for determining when the detainee will not cooperate and the interrogation must be stopped?
6. What is the significance — from an interrogation perspective — of denying the detainee the right to meet with an attorney?
7. What criteria should be established for preventing client-attorney meetings?
8. What should be the standard of judicial review for determining whether to prevent a detainee from meeting with an attorney in the context of counterterrorism?

Military commanders and intelligence community officials criticized the decision for curtailing the state's ability to conduct operational counterterrorism. Nevertheless, the former President of the Supreme Court, Aharon Barak, argued that liberal democratic states must have "self-imposed restraints." In the context of interrogations, the significance is clear — measures implemented in the past that violate the detainee's basic rights should not to be used.

How are rights to be protected when interrogators believe that the detainee possesses information vital to an ongoing interrogation or relevant for immediate operational purposes? The High Court's decision in 5100/94 established clear parameters with which interrogators must comply.

Interrogation regulation is, by definition, a nebulous situation, particularly when the relevant interaction takes place in a small room with only two or three people present who have diametrically opposed interests under extremely stressful conditions.

There is little doubt that the High Court of Justice ruling imposes restrictions on the interrogation methods, limiting violations of individual rights. In contrast to the Bush administration's memorandums, which established a legal regime enabling torture, the HCJ opinion articulated an interrogation regime predicated on limits.

B. OPERATION CAST LEAD

The Report of the UN High Commissioner for Human Rights investigated IDF during the Gaza Conflict, including the military action know as Operation Cast Lead, December 2008 to January 2009. During the course of the operation, Palestinian residents of the Gaza Strip were detained and interrogated. The Report details treatment of detained, including reports of shackling, severe beatings, foul conditions, and solitary confinement of detainees. The hypothetical below highlights the dilemma facing interrogators.

OPERATIONAL HYPOTHETICAL

Recently, there has been an increase in significant terror attacks in your country. These attacks have resulted in the deaths 50 innocent civilians in the last month. You have been asked to develop an operational plan to prevent these attacks. According to intelligence reports, the attacks have been carried out both by individuals who previously lived in your country and those who entered specifically for the purpose of carrying out these attacks. A number of individuals (from both categories) have recently been detained, some caught in the act, others based on intelligence information and ongoing interrogations. To that end, the questions below represent operational dilemmas for counter terrorism decision makers.

1. How do you develop a policy that balances the civil rights of the individuals that are attacking you with your interest in preventing additional loss of innocent lives?
2. If you had the option of arresting and detaining a large group, some who attacked you, others who are seemingly innocent would you detain all of them? What would be your criteria for determining who to interrogate?

3. What further interrogation techniques would you authorize to prevent attacks or locate additional terrorists?

HUMAN RIGHTS IN PALESTINE AND OTHER OCCUPIED ARAB TERRITORIES: REPORT OF THE UNITED NATIONS FACT FINDING MISSION ON THE GAZA CONFLICT

A/HRC/12/48. ¶1109-22, Sept. 15, 2009

On the morning of 5 January, shortly after the ground operations began, an estimated 40 Israeli soldiers broke into several homes, including that of AD/01,[25] who described to the Mission how 65 persons, several of whom were holding white flags, were made to assemble in the street. The soldiers separated the men from the women. The men were made to line up against a wall and strip to their underwear. AD/01 indicated that any attempt to resist the soldiers was met with physical force, resulting in injuries.

Approximately 20 minutes later, they were taken into a house owned by Mr. Khalil Misbah Attar, where they were detained for a day, the men still separated from the women. The house had been struck by a number of missiles that morning and was badly damaged. Witnesses indicated to the Mission that the house was at that time being used by the Israeli armed forces as a military base and sniper position.

At around 10 p.m., all of the men were handcuffed behind their backs with plastic restraints and blindfolded. The men, 11 women and at least seven children below the age of 14 were taken on foot to al-Kaklouk located south of the American School, one to two kilometers away. Many of the men remained in their underwear, exposed to the harsh winter weather. Al-Kaklouk is very close to Israeli military artillery and tank positions, and while the detainees were held here at least one tank was engaged in frequent firing.

AD/01 told the Mission that, on arrival at al-Kaklouk, everyone was asked to clamber down into trenches, which had been dug to create a pit surrounded by a wall of sand, about three metres high. There were three such pits, each of which was surrounded by barbed wire. They were estimated to cover about 7,000 square metres ("six or seven *donums*") each. . . . AD/01 described how they were assembled in long single files, rather than massed together, and held in these pits, in the open air and exposed to cold temperatures for three days (till 8 January). Each pit accommodated approximately 20 people. They were forced to sit in stress positions, on their knees and leaning forward keeping their heads down. They were monitored by soldiers and were not allowed to communicate with each other. They had no access to food or water on the first day of their internment, and were given a sip of water and an olive each to eat on the second and third days of their detention (6 and 7 January). They had limited access to toilet facilities. The men had to wait for two to three hours after asking before they were allowed to leave the pits to relieve themselves and sometimes were able to remove their blindfolds for the purpose. A few of them were told to relieve themselves inside the pit, behind a small mount of sand.

---

25. AD/01, and other similar initials, indicate a pseudonym for a witness.

They stated that it was culturally too difficult for the women to seek permission to relieve themselves and they did not ask.

AD/01 states that some tanks were inside the pit with at least one tank positioned at the eastern end. While the people were held there, the tank facing inland each day sporadically fired on the houses along the road opposite the site. . . .

AD/01B and AD/01C recounted that on 8 January, the women and children were released and told to go to Jabaliyah. The men were transferred to military barracks near the northern border, identified as the Izokim Barracks. At the Izokim barracks, the men were detained in pits similar to but smaller than those in al-Kaklouk. They continued to be exposed to the cold temperature, rain and the constant sound of tank movement overhead. The witnesses have described to the Mission the experience of continued and prolonged exposure to the sound of this tank movement as disorienting and creating feelings of futility, isolation, helplessness and abject terror. . . .

The men were held handcuffed and in their underwear in the Izokim barracks overnight. They were questioned intermittently, mostly on details and locations of Qassam rockets, the tunnels and the whereabouts of Hamas parliamentarians. According to statements made to the Mission, they were beaten during the interrogation and threatened with death and being run over by tanks. The Mission notes that the nature and types of questions asked remained the same throughout the interrogations in various detention facilities.

On 9 January, the men were taken to a prison in Israel, indentified by one witness as the Negev prison, where they remained until 12 January. They were detained in one section of the prison, alternating between being held in isolation and in shared cells, and were subjected to harsh interrogation, often by two people dressed in civilian clothes. Interrogation focused on the identification of Hamas tunnels and arms as well as the whereabouts of Gilad Shalit.

AD/01B and AD/01C recounted that they were shackled to a chair with plastic strips and interrogated several times, with AD/01B stating that he was made to strip naked during an interrogation. He was kept in solitary confinement where a soldier would come intermittently during the day, and slam the cell door open and shut, exposing him to extremely cold temperatures. AD/01C stated that during the first interrogation he was verbally threatened and in the subsequent two he was blindfolded and beaten. He was made to stand up and face the wall, following which his face was smashed against the wall several times before he was severely beaten (kicked and punched) on his back and buttocks.

Requests for clothing were denied. During the interrogation the detainees were informed that they were "illegal combatants" and that they had no protection under the Geneva Conventions. They had limited access to food, water and sanitation. Their morning meal was a bottle-cap-sized piece of bread with a drop of marmalade. The evening meal, if provided, consisted of rotting sardines and cheese on mouldy bread.

AD/01C described the experience of being detained, stripped and shackled as one of abandonment, desperation, suffocation and isolation. He continues to experience discomfort where he was beaten and is unable to sit and sleep comfortably.

AD/01C stated that while in Negev prison an additional group arrived. They were kept separately in the second section. The exact number of detainees in the second group is unknown, although AD/01C indicated to the Mission that the second group was smaller.

On 12 January, nine people including the witnesses were blindfolded, handcuffed and transported to the Erez border. AD/01 described to the Mission how they were subjected to harsh interrogation at Erez and made to strip completely. Several hours later they were told to run into Gaza, to look straight ahead and not to look back.

AD/01 states that all 65 detainees from the original group taken from al-Atatra to Israel were eventually released. Some members of his family were detained afterwards, but not in the original group of 65. At the time of writing, three of these remain incarcerated in various detention facilities of the Israel Prison Service. An unknown number remain in prison facing charges of being illegal combatants and members of al-Qassam Brigades. The first hearing was scheduled to be held in August in Israel (exact date not known).

Issues to Consider

1. What are the implications of using harsh interrogation measures during operations?
2. Using the standard of credibility, reliability, veracity, and timeliness of information, how is actionable intelligence received?
3. How does the High Court of Justices decision reflect on the most recent depictions of reported Operation Cast Lead interrogation measures?
4. How does the inability to use torture or other methods impede national security?

Several prisoners were still in detention in August 2009 with approval from Israeli courts.[26]

V. RUSSIA

Interrogation methods in the former Soviet Union were the subject of enormous international concern; the KGB (*Komitet Gosudarstvennoy Bezopasnosti*) was widely accused of regularly violating basic rights of detainees. Accusations were regularly made by former detainees, human rights groups, and other nations condemning KGB interrogation methods. Those interrogated

26. B'Tslem, *Without Trial: Administrative Detention of Palestinians by Israel and the Incarceration of Unlawful Combatants Law*, *available at* http://www.btselem.org/Download/200910_Without_Trial_Eng.pdf (last visited June 10, 2010).

included political dissidents, religious leaders, and enemies of the state; interrogation methods ranged from long-term imprisonment after show-trials to torture and death.

Relevant to this chapter is the question whether individuals suspected of involvement in terrorism are interrogated in accordance with criminal law and granted its protections, or whether they are treated as non-soldier combatants.

With the fall of the Berlin Wall in 1989 and the collapse of the Soviet Union in 1992, the international human rights community expressed hope — if not optimism — that interrogation methods of the new Russian government would significantly differ from that of the former Communist regime.

A. RUSSIA'S CRIMINAL CODE

While no single provision of the Russian Criminal Code specifically addresses the interrogation limits of terrorist suspects, Article 205 defines the crime of terrorism:

Article 205. Terrorism

1. Terrorism, that is, the perpetration of an explosion, arson, or any other action endangering the lives of people, causing sizable property damage, or entailing other socially dangerous consequences, if these actions have been committed for the purpose of violating public security, frightening the population, or exerting influence on decision-making by governmental bodies, and also the threat of committing said actions for the same ends, shall be punishable by deprivation of liberty for a term of five to ten years.

2. The same deeds committed:

    a) by a group of persons in a preliminary conspiracy;

    b) repeatedly;

    c) with the use of firearms shall be punishable by deprivation of liberty for a term of eight to fifteen years.

3. Deeds stipulated in the first or second part of this Article, if they have been committed by an organized group or have involved by negligence the death of a person, or any other grave consequences, and also are associated with infringement on objects of the use of atomic energy or with the use of nuclear materials, radioactive substances or sources of radioactive radiation, shall be punishable by deprivation of liberty for a term of 10 to 20 years.

Note: A person who has taken part in the preparation of an act of terrorism shall be released from criminal responsibility if he facilitated the prevention of the act of terrorism by timely warning governmental bodies, or by any other method, unless the actions of this person contain a different corpus delicti.[27]

Article 302 defines the limits of interrogation within this criminal framework.

Article 302. Compulsion to Give Evidence

1. Compulsion to give evidence used with regard to a subject, defendant, victim, or witness, or coercion of an expert to make a report through the

---

27. A full copy of the Russian Criminal Code is available at http://www.russian-criminal-code.com (last visited Mar. 21, 2010).

application of threats, blackmail, or other illegal actions, by an investigator or a person conducting inquests, shall be punishable by deprivation of liberty for a term of up to three years.

2. The same act, joined with the use of violence, mockery, or torture, shall be punishable by deprivation of liberty for term of two to eight years.

Do these limits indicate that individual terrorist suspects are interrogated in accordance with the criminal law paradigm? Furthermore, does this paradigm guarantee protection of individual rights? The following 2007 United Nations Committee Against Torture report delineates general protections afforded criminals under Russian Federation laws.

UNITED NATIONS, REPORT OF THE COMMITTEE AGAINST TORTURE

Apr. 30-May 18, 2007[28]

The Committee welcomes the following positive developments: The entry into force between 1 July 2002 and 1 January 2004 of the new Code of Criminal Procedure adopted in December 2001, which, inter alia, introduces jury trials, stricter limits on detention and interrogation.

The Committee is concerned about the areas set out below: While noting the State party's assertion that all acts that may be described as "torture" within the meaning of article 1 of the Convention are punishable in the Russian Federation, the definition of the term "torture" as contained in the annotation to article 117 of the Criminal Code does not fully reflect all elements of the definition in article 1 of the Convention which includes the involvement of a public official or other person acting in an official capacity in inflicting, instigating, consenting to or acquiescing to torture. The definition, moreover, does not address act aimed at coercing a third person as torture. Laws and practices that obstruct access to lawyers and relatives of suspects and accused persons, thus providing insufficient safeguards for detainees, include: Internal regulations of temporary facilities i.e. IVS (temporary police detention) and SIZOs (pretrial establishments), failure of the courts to order investigations into allegations that evidence has been obtained through torture, as well as reported reprisals against defence lawyers alleging that their client has been tortured or otherwise ill-treated, and which appear to facilitate torture and ill-treatment. The Committee is concerned at: The particularly numerous, ongoing and consistent allegations of acts of torture and other cruel, inhuman or degrading treatment or punishment committed by law enforcement personnel, including in police custody; The law enforcement promotion system based on the number of crimes solved, which appears to create conditions that promote the use of torture and ill-treatment with a view to obtaining confessions; The Committee is further concerned at: Continuing reports of hazing in the military (*dedovshchina*) as well as of torture and other cruel, inhuman or degrading treatment or punishment in the armed forces, conducted by or with the consent, acquiescence or approval of officers or other personnel,

---

28. *Available at* http://books.google.com/books (last visited Mar. 20, 2010).

notwithstanding the State party's reported intention to develop an action plan to prevent hazing in the armed forces; Documented reports that victims who lodge complaints are subjected to further reprisals and abuse and that there is no system of protection for witnesses of such acts; Hundreds of reports that investigations are inadequate or absent, and that despite thousands of officers charged with such offences, that there is widespread impunity.

The Committee is concerned at: The absence of training to detect signs of torture and ill-treatment for medical personnel in general and for personnel at temporary police detention facilities, in particular; While the Code of Criminal Procedure states that evidence obtained by torture shall be inadmissible, in practice there appear to be no instruction to the courts to rule that the evidence is inadmissible, or to order an immediate, impartial and effective investigation.

The Committee is concerned at: Reliable reports of unofficial places of detention in the North Caucasus and the allegations that those detained in such facilities face torture or cruel, inhuman or degrading treatment; Numerous, ongoing and consistent allegations that abductions and enforced disappearances in the Chechen Republic, in particular during anti-terrorist operations, are inflicted by or at the instigation or with the consent or acquiescence of public officials or other persons acting in official capacities and the failure to investigate and punish the perpetrators; The federal law "On counteracting terrorism" signed on 6 March 2006 fails to explicitly outline the applicability of the safeguards for detainees in the Code of Criminal Procedure to counter-terrorist operations. . . .

While Russia ratified the CAT, reports suggest torture is implemented by Russian authorities. The following excerpt, prepared by a consortium of Russian and American Human Rights Organizations, addresses the issue of torture.

RUSSIAN NGO SHADOW REPORT ON THE OBSERVANCE OF THE CONVENTION AGAINST TORTURE AND OTHER CRUEL, INHUMAN OR DEGRADING TREATMENT OR PUNISHMENT BY THE RUSSIAN FEDERATION FOR THE PERIOD FROM 2001 TO 2006

Public Verdict, 2006[29]

[T]he definition of torture given in the note to Art. 117 of the Criminal Code fails to include a key element of torture, cruel and degrading punishment, i.e. direct or indirect involvement of a public official. Moreover, the provision introducing a definition of torture is located in a section of the Code dealing with crimes against life and health, rather than official crime. As a result, it applies only to acts committed by private individuals. Crimes committed by public officials in their official capacity are punished under

---

29. *Available at* http://eng.publicverdict.ru/topics/library/16291106.html (last visited Jan. 7, 2011).

specific provisions dealing with official crimes, rather than general criminal provisions which currently include Art. 117. This fact is proven by par. 31 of Russia's 4th Periodic Report quoting statistics of prosecutions for official crimes, where you will not find any sentences under Art. 117.

Secondly, a list of purposes qualifying ill-treatment as torture is narrower in the note to Art. 117 of the Criminal Code than in Art. 1 of the Convention. The Convention mentions such purposes as obtaining information or a confession from the victim or a third person, punishing or intimidating the victim or a third person, and discrimination, whereas the definition in Art. 117 of the Russian Criminal Code does not define ill-treatment of the victim in order to coerce a third person as torture. Moreover, the note to Art. 117 fails to mention purposes such as intimidation or discrimination.

Not only is the definition of torture in domestic criminal law inconsistent with some of the standards established by the Convention, we also need to note that neither the Criminal Code nor any other domestic act gives a definition of cruel and degrading treatment.

However, the lack of definitions of torture, cruel and degrading treatment in the criminal law does not mean that criminal prosecution of public officials who use torture is impossible in Russia. They can be prosecuted under Art. 286 and 302 of the Criminal Code.

Art. 302 of the Code establishes criminal liability for coercion for the purpose of obtaining evidence, including the use of torture. The definition of torture given in the note to Art. 117 of the Criminal Code is used for the purposes of Art. 302.

The Federal Law of 8 October 2003 also amended the text of Art. 302 of the Criminal Code. In its former version, Art. 302 came close to the definition of torture given in Art. 1 of the Convention, but contained substantial limitations. Firstly, Art. 302 only applied to investigators acting in official capacity, whereas torture can be used by police detectives — also to obtain evidence or confession. In addition, Art. 302 in its old version punished for the use of torture against a specific individual (suspect, accused, victim, witness, expert) with a specific purpose, namely to coerce a suspect, accused, victim or witness into giving evidence or to force a certain opinion from an expert. The use of torture and ill-treatment against persons without a formal status in the proceedings with the purpose of obtaining information about a crime or its traces, and the use of torture for other purposes than those stated in Art. 302, were not punishable.

The new version of Art. 302 expands the range of subjects liable under Art. 302 through a phrase "as well as another person, with consent or acquiescence of the investigator." In this case, it is unclear who is liable for the crime — the agent committing the torture or the investigator consenting to, or encouraging it — or both. Secondly, it remains unclear how authorities should qualify torture committed by a public official, but without the investigator's consent or acquiescence; torture unrelated to obtaining evidence or expert opinion, and torture used by public officials outside the context of criminal investigation. No answers to these questions have emerged from investigatory and judicial practice, as Art. 302 of the Criminal Code has had a very limited application. It can be seen, in particular, from Art. 4 of Russia's 4th Periodic Report lacking statistics of prosecutions under Art. 302.

Given that torture, cruel and degrading treatment are prohibited by the Russian Constitution and a number of federal laws, public officials who use torture can be prosecuted for abuse of power (Art. 286 of the Criminal Code). In practice, Art. 286 is the one applied most often for criminal prosecution of public authorities guilty of torture.

However, the criminal law qualification of torture, cruel and degrading punishment as abuse of power hinders the fulfillment of obligations under the Convention. Firstly, the general wording of Art. 286 does not give public officials a clear and unambiguous signal that torture and cruel treatment are prohibited and criminalized. Secondly, Art. 286 of the Code applies to other types of abuse of power, as well as torture. As a result, relevant government authorities that collect statistics on abuse of power in general do not have specific statistics on torture, cruel and degrading punishment. It deprives government of any possibility of assessing the actual incidence of torture and planning effective prevention. In particular, par. 34 of Russia's 4th Periodic Report quotes judicial statistics of prosecutions for abuse of power under part 3 Art. 286 of the Criminal

Code (abuse of power involving the use of violence, weapons or methods of restraint, causing serious harm). They fail to indicate, however, in how many cases the perpetrators were prosecuted specifically for torture.

As noted above, Art. 286 of the Criminal Code, normally applied to punish officials guilty of torture, is also applied in other cases of official abuse of power. It creates a situation where law enforcement authorities and judges perceive torture as something no more dangerous to society than any other type of official abuse of power, not necessarily involving violence. As a result, sentencing for torture, cruel and degrading treatment is just as severe—and at times less severe—than punishment for other types of official misconduct.

ISSUES TO CONSIDER

1. Does Russian legislation impose restraints on interrogators?
2. What is the impact of a lack of definitions with respect to the rule of law in the context of interrogations?
3. How are detainees to be protected if torture is not unequivocally defined?
4. Are self-imposed limits possible in this paradigm?
5. What protections are extended to a detainee in accordance with Russian legislation?
6. Are judicial holdings more effective protections than legislation?

B. TORTURE IN CHECHNYA

Nowhere is the issue of torture in Russia more relevant than the conflict between Russian forces and Chechens.

Chechnya: No Means to Live

World Organisation Against Torture, Jan. 2004[30]

Although the practice of torture is massively widespread in Chechnya, law-enforcement agencies make no effort to curb this practice; worse they deny torture even takes place. For example, there are commands issued by the Commander of the United Group of Forces in the Northern Caucasus, specifically no. 145 in 2001 and No. 80 in 2002, which are intended to prevent massive violations of human rights. There is also the order from the Prosecutor General, No. 46 of 2001, enumerating various violations and crimes. None of these orders contain any mention of torture. The very existence of these orders has been prompted by the fact of mass violations of human rights, which has drawn complaints not only from Chechen civilians and human rights groups, and has been covered by domestic and foreign journalists, but even the official representative of human rights and the pro-Moscow Chechen leadership have admitted human rights violations are widespread. Nevertheless, there has been evasion regarding the issue of torture.

We cannot rule out the possible existence of disciplinary action, that soldiers have been reprimanded regarding torture or mistreatment of detainees. However, in cases where there was a reprimand, there was not punishment, and the reprimand was in fact for "allowing a leak of information."

With a lack of even a concept of the prohibition of torture in the charters, regulations, and instructions operating in the Interior Ministry, the army, and other government law-enforcement agencies, the possibility and the conditions for torture can be conveyed under the guise of "tactical methods," used "during the course of work," in direct communications with colleagues. Moreover, in secret and internal instructions there is a regulation allowing the application of the so-called "forced interrogation," which is a term signifying torture used to a captured enemy under conditions of combat, above all when on the territory controlled by the enemy.

As indicated by the report below written by OMCT, the World Organisation Against Torture, generalized fear of torture permeates many aspects of life in Chechnya.

> There is an enormous amount of documentation attesting to the widespread nature of torture in Chechnya, but at the same time, many stories have not been heard because the victims of torture are also frequently disappeared. The dead bodies of persons who have been detained frequently show traces of torture. Common forms of torture include severe beatings, extensive use of electro-shock, including electro-shock to the genitals, and mutilation such as cutting off the victim's ear. Victims of torture, like all residents of Chechnya, are afraid to go to the hospital for treatment because of frequent military searches of hospitals. In the face of the horrors faced by Chechen people on a daily basis, the Russian government has been claiming that the situation in Chechnya is "normalised." In March 2003, a constitutional referendum was

---

30. *Available at* http://www.omct.org/files/2004/05/2321/chechnya_eng.pdf (last visited Mar. 20, 2010).

organised, which approved a constitution establishing Chechnya as an autonomous Republic within the Russian Federation. However, the legitimacy of the referendum has been seriously doubted. Although violence perpetrated by Russian state agents appeared to decrease immediately before the referendum, once the vote had taken place, the Russian armed forces and other state agents committed human rights abuses with renewed force.[31]

In November of 2006, Human Rights Watch released its report entitled *Widespread Torture in the Chechen Republic Human Rights Watch Briefing Paper for the 37th Session UN Committee Against Torture* regarding the use of torture in Chechnya by Russian and Chechen security forces.

TORTURE BY PERSONNEL OF THE SECOND OPERATIONAL INVESTIGATIVE BUREAU (ORB-2)

Human Rights Watch[32]

ORB-2 was established in 2002 and formally charged with detecting, preventing and suppressing actions by organized criminal groups.

Human Rights Watch interviewed several dozen people who were detained and tortured at ORB-2 premises between 2004 and 2006, as well as their relatives and lawyers; they consistently told of ORB-2 personnel coercing confessions under brutal ill-treatment and torture; denying detainees access to lawyers of their choice; preventing medical documentation of signs of torture by denying access to doctors and keeping detainees in custody until the signs of torture fade and, if suspects sought to renounce their coerced confessions after they were transferred to remand custody, subjecting them to further ill-treatment as punishment and to force them to stand by the original statements.

In cases we researched, ORB-2 personnel seized persons, usually young males, from their homes, places of work, or the streets without identifying themselves or providing a warrant or any explanation. They then brought the detainees to the ORB-2 temporary detention facility and immediately started interrogating them.

In almost all cases, the detention was officially registered only after several days. During this time detainees' families had no information on their relatives' whereabouts, and the ORB-2 personnel interrogated the detainees in the absence of a lawyer, or with the participation of a lawyer appointed by ORB-2 personnel. According to the interviewees, the appointed lawyers ignored their complaints about torture — although they saw the torture marks on their clients' bodies — and instead encouraged them to accept the charges.

During interrogations, ORB-2 personnel subjected the detainees to severe beatings, torture with electric shocks, suffocation, and threats or imitation of sexual violence. Most interviewees told Human Rights Watch that during

---

31. Position Paper of the World Organisation Against Torture, 2004 United Nations Commission on Human Rights 60th Session, *available at* http://www.omct.org/pdf/PP04.pdf (last visited June 26, 2010).

32. *Available at* http://hrw.org/backgrounder/eca/chechnya1106/2.htm#_Toc150776963 (last visited July 21, 2010).

these interrogations, which lasted for many hours, they were forced to confess to serious crimes, such as multiple murders or terrorist attacks, as well as to name other people allegedly involved with the rebel movement. In some cases, the confession had been prepared beforehand by the interrogators and contained exact dates, places, and identities of the victims. In other cases, the detainees themselves had to "choose" a crime and invent details that the interrogators would then record.

Once the confession was obtained and signed, the detainee was kept in the ORB-2 temporary detention facility for several days or sometimes weeks to allow any signs of torture, such as bruises or burns, to fade. The investigators would then transfer the accused to the remand prison (SIZO-1) in Grozny, where they stayed until and during trial.

———————

The report above suggests not much is new with respect to Russian interrogation methods. Similar to Soviet-era accounts, Russian interrogators subject Chechen detainees to torture and other basic violations of civil and political rights. According to applicable legislation, terror suspects are subject to the traditional criminal law paradigm. However, available reports indicate a torture-based paradigm has been consistently implemented and imposed in contravention to both international and domestic law.

The critical question is whether these interrogation methods directly or indirectly contribute to Russia's operational counterterrorism efforts. The answer is not clear.

ISSUES TO CONSIDER

1. In determining effectiveness, what benefits has Russia accrued from the policy of torturing detainees?
2. What is the significance of "fabricated criminal charges"?
3. What advantages can be gained from compelling detainees to sign confessions?
4. Are interrogations that employ torture a reasonable response to terrorism?
5. Does torture suggest a weakness on the part of the Russian authorities?

VI. INDIA

This section analyzes how Indian police officials interrogate those arrested in the aftermath of terrorist attacks. The limits of lawful interrogation in India have been statutorily regulated in a number of legislative acts; however, a discussion of India's interrogation policies cannot be divorced from geopolitical realities. As discussed throughout the casebook, India is confronted with three separate, yet connected, terrorist threats: internal, internal-external, and external. To that end, the government's flexibility in conducting operational counterterrorism is restricted. What needs to be examined is whether those limitations extend to the interrogation setting.

A. INTRODUCTION

The following excerpt, penned by R.K. Abichandani, a judge on the High Court of Gujarat, demonstrates the legal limits of interrogation under Indian law. Furthermore, it hints at the challenges Indian authorities face when balancing the rule of law with the requirement to adequately protect the state and its citizens.

R.K. ABICHANDANI, CUSTODIAL DIGNITY

High Court of Gujarat[33]

The arrest of a person suspected of crime does not warrant any physical violence on the person or his torture. But, when the captive exercises his fundamental right to silence against self-incrimination (Art. 20(3)) during his interrogation, the police often abuse their authority by use of criminal force to extort information. The tyrannical way of custodial interrogation that exposes the suspect to the risk of abuse of his person or dignity has prompted the Supreme Court to ordain that interrogation should not be accompanied with torture or use of "third degree" methods. (Kartar Singh v. State of Punjab, (1994) 3 SCC 569.) The constitution as well as the statutory laws condemn the conduct of any official in extorting a confession or information under compulsion by using any third degree methods. A confession to police officer cannot be proved as against a person accused of any offence (Sec. 25 Evidence Act) and confession caused by threats from a person in authority in order to avoid any evil of a temporal nature would be irrelevant in criminal proceedings as, inter alia, provided in Sec. 24 of the Evidence Act. Sections 330 and 331 of the Indian Penal Code provide for punishment to one who voluntarily caused hurt or grievous hurt to extort the confession or any information which may lead to detection of an offence or misconduct. The expression "life or personal liberty" in Article 21 includes a guarantee against torture and assault even by the State and its functionaries to a person who is taken in custody and no sovereign immunity can be pleaded against the liability of the State arising due to such criminal use of force over the captive person. As held by the Supreme Court in D.K. Basu v. State of W.B. (1997) 1 SCC 416 "custodial torture" is a naked violation of human dignity and a degradation which destroys, to a very large extent, human personality. It is a calculated assault on human dignity and whenever human dignity is wounded, civilization takes a step backwards — flag of humanity must on each such occasion fly half-mast. The convicts, undertrials, detenues and other persons in custody cannot be denied the precious right of the right to live with human dignity included in the expression "life or personal liberty," except according to the

---

33. *Available at* http://gujarathighcourt.nic.in/Articles/custodialdignity.htm (last visited Mar. 21, 2010).

procedure established by law by placing such reasonable restrictions as are permitted by law. Any form of torture or cruel, inhuman or degrading treatment would fall within the inhibition of Art. 21, whether it occurs during investigation, interrogation or otherwise. Using any form of torture for extracting any kind of information would neither be right nor just nor fair and would therefore offend Art. 21. A crime-suspect can indeed be subjected to a sustained and scientific interrogation in accordance with law but he cannot be tortured or subjected to third-degree methods or eliminated with a view to elicit information, extract confession or derive knowledge about his accomplices, weapons etc. "State terrorism" is no answer to combat terrorism.

ISSUES TO CONSIDER

1. Does the constant threat of terrorism mean that India *should* have relaxed protections for terrorist suspects?
2. Should the various protections provided to terrorist suspects in India differ depending on the type of terror they are accused of?
3. Indian law proscribes use of the "third degree." Is this position tenable or has Indian law curtailed investigatory techniques so extensively that the authorities have no choice but to break the law?

B. REPORTS OF CUSTODIAL ABUSE

Human rights organizations have repeatedly claimed that detainees in Indian custody have been regularly subjected to torture. The complaints focus on detainees arrested on suspicion of involvement in criminal and terrorism offenses alike; to that end, terrorism-related torture allegations have particularly emphasized interrogations in Jammu and Kashmir.

COUNTRY REPORT ON HUMAN RIGHTS PRACTICES 2009—INDIA

U.S. Department of State, March 2010[34]

The law prohibits torture and generally does not allow authorities to admit coerced confessions in court; NGOs and citizens alleged that authorities used torture to extort money, as summary punishment and to coerce confessions. In some instances authorities used the confessions as evidentiary support for death sentences.

The ACHR stated the following in its June report Torture in India 2009: "Torture in police custody remains a widespread and systematic practice in India. They also noted the lack of an effective system of independent monitoring of all places of detention facilitates torture."

NGOs asserted that custodial torture was common in Tamil Nadu, and credible sources claimed police stations in Punjab, Andhra Pradesh, Haryana,

34. *Available at* http://www.state.gov/g/drl/rls/hrrpt/2009/sca/136087.htm (last visited Mar. 21, 2010).

and Chandigarh used torture to obtain desired testimony. The Asian Human Rights Committee claimed police used torture and assault in Kerala and Gujarat as a means of criminal investigation.

NGOs claimed the NHRC underestimated the number of rapes, including custodial rapes, that police committed. Some rapes may have gone unreported due to the victims' feelings of shame and fears of retribution.

On May 29, doctors confirmed that Assiya Jan and her sister-in-law Neelofer had been raped prior to being killed in the Shopian district of Jammu and Kashmir (see section 1.a.), although a subsequent postmortem examination ordered by the CBI in September refuted those findings.

On June 2, a Dalit woman alleged that four Madhya Pradesh police officers gang-raped her while she was in custody in Betul district. The officers claimed the woman was making a false accusation to escape her arrest for harassing her daughter-in-law for dowry. At year's end a government of Madhya Pradesh internal probe committee continued to investigate the allegation.

An investigation continued into the February 2008 case in which two commandos from the Haryana police allegedly raped a woman after pulling her out of a moving rickshaw.

––––––––––––––

India's legislative and judicial branches are cognizant of the delicate balance required to conduct lawful and effective counterterrorism. Much of their focus has emphasized the requirement to carefully consider the legitimacy — and therefore, admissibility — of a suspect's custodial confession.

SOLIL PAUL, COUNTER-TERRORISM LAWS: THE SUPREME COURT ON CONFESSIONS

South Asia Terrorism Portal[35]

. . . It must also be clear that such presumption against the validity of custodial confessions stands rebutted only in extreme and grave times; only when existing laws fail to effectively tackle or successfully address pressing dangers to society and the nation. Even under such extraordinary circumstances, this is not to argue that custodial confessions be treated on par with non-custodial confessions, but rather, to acknowledge the 'suspect' nature of the former, and ensure that stringent safeguards be made an intrinsic part of the scheme of such laws, and that such safeguards be scrupulously observed so as to prevent the possibility of the extortion of any false confession.

These circumstances and the need for such safeguards have been clearly recognised and the Supreme Court in the POTA Case, noted:

> Parliament has explored the possibility of employing the existing laws to tackle terrorism and arrived at the conclusion that the laws are not capable. It is also clear to Parliament that terrorism is not a usual law and order problem.

––––––––––––––

35. *Available at* http://www.satp.org/satporgtp/publication/faultlines/volume16/Article2.htm (last visited Mar. 21, 2010).

Nevertheless, the Court emphasised, in the same breath, the need to balance the security concerns of the nation with well-established values of the civilized world, and warned:

> The protection and promotion of human rights under the rule of law is essential in the prevention of terrorism . . . If human rights are violated in the process of combating terrorism, it will be self-defeating. Terrorism often thrives where human rights are violated, which adds to the need to strengthen action to combat violations of human rights . . . The lack of hope for justice provides breeding grounds for terrorism . . . In all cases, the fight against terrorism must be respectful to the human rights.

This brings us to the crucial question: what safeguards does the law enact?

As already stated, the first and foremost precondition for any valid confession is mandated by Article 20(3) of the Constitution: "No person accused of any offence shall be compelled to be a witness against himself." In addition, Section 24 of the Evidence Act specifically bars confessions that may be the result of any inducement, threat or promise, from the courts' consideration. Thus any confession, be it custodial or non-custodial, to be accepted by a court of law, should not be "compelled," in other words, must be "voluntary." This means that counterterrorism laws have to primarily safeguard the voluntary nature of a confession and see to it that no form of compulsion is used against the accused while extracting a confession.

What would 'voluntary' mean or encompass in this context? The Supreme Court in Defender Pal Singh, after referring to a few legal dictionaries and cases clarified:

> the crux of making a statement voluntary is, what is intentional, intended, unimpelled by other influences, acting on ones own will, through his own conscience.

While upholding the constitutionality of Section 15, TADA Act, in Kartar Singh, the Supreme Court had enumerated specific guidelines

> to ensure that the confession obtained in the pre-indictment interrogation by a police officer . . . is not tainted with any vice but is in strict conformity with the well recognized and accepted aesthetic (sic) principles and fundamental fairness.

ISSUES TO CONSIDER

1. Does the threat of confessions obtained through torture justify the presumption that all custodial confessions are invalid?
2. Should torture utilized to obtain information from suspects be punished differently than sadistic torture?
3. Does India's long history of terrorism mean that aggressive counterterrorism methods should be viewed favorably?

C. INTERROGATIONS IN RESPONSE TO TERRORIST ATTACKS

As discussed above, India's interrogation methods and policies have been oft-criticized. The Indian Judiciary and Parliament have attempted to address

these concerns by limiting the use of confessions and other inculpatory statements made by individuals during interrogation. Yet, questions persist both
with respect to the extent to which authorities respect these limitations and
the effectiveness of existing interrogation methods.

In the aftermath of terror attacks, India has actively implemented the
practice of narcoanalysis. Whether the method — evidentially not adopted
in the other surveyed countries — is effective remains unclear. Adoption suggests an effort to develop alternative interrogation measures.

PRAVEEN SWAMI, FACTS, FICTION OR THE FOG OF DRUGS?

The Hindu, Oct. 18, 2006[36]

Much of the Mumbai Police's account has emerged from narcoanalysis of key
suspects — a practice its proponents have marketed as a humane, scientific
and, above all, reliable alternative to extracting confessions through old-
fashioned torture.

Mumbai Police officials say they succeeded in seeing through the multiple
veils of deceit and denial behind which key suspects hid the truth about the
bombings by using hypnosis-inducing drugs. At a September 30 press conference, Mumbai Police commissioner M.N. Roy said the investigation "relied
heavily on scientific procedures like narco-analysis tests." It was only after psychiatrists at the National Institute of Mental Health and Neurological Sciences
conducted tests on the suspects, Mr. Roy said, that "the pieces fell in place."

Ever since similar tests on stamp paper scam accused Abdul Karim Telgi
yielded a vast mass of information on his purported high-level facilitators,
both courts and criminal investigators have come to have an increasing
faith in hypnosis-inducing drugs. However, a mass of scientific literature
and practitioner accounts exists to dispute this deepening consensus.

Experts seem to agree that the outpourings produced by hypnosis-inducing
truth drugs such as sodium pentothal and sodium amytal often fall short of the
truth. In a recent paper prepared for the Andhra Pradesh Police's Criminal Investigation Department, Superintendent of Police M. Sivananda Reddy pointed to
the "baffling mixture of truth and fantasy in drug-induced output." By disrupting suspects' defences, Mr. Reddy noted, drugs "may sometimes be helpful in
interrogation, but even under the best conditions they will elicit an output
which is partially contaminated by deception [and] fantasy." At best, they "provide rapid access to information that is psychiatrically useful but of doubtful
validity as empirical truth."

Mr. Reddy observed that the United States' 9th Circuit Court of Appeals, in
the case of *United States v. Solomon*, after a comprehensive examination of the
issue, had concluded, "narco-analysis does not produce reasonably reliable
statements." "The almost total absence of controlled experimental studies of

---

36. *Available at* http://www.hindu.com/2006/10/18/stories/2006101801331200.htm (last
visited Mar. 22, 2010).

'truth drugs' and the spotty and anecdotal nature of psychiatric and police evidence," he concluded, "require that extrapolations to intelligence operations be made with care."

Psychiatrists involved in narco-analysis have long been clear about the limitations of the science. As early as 1954, American psychiatrist John McDonald noted that suspects subjected to narcoanalysis sometimes confessed to crimes they could not have committed — or continued to practise deceit. Dr. McDonald pointed, in his presentation to the American Psychiatric Association, to cases where suspects confessed to crimes which it could be proven they had not committed. "It is clear from these accounts," Dr. McDonald observed, "that narcoanalysis is often unsuccessful in eliciting the truth."

While defending the utility of narcoanalysis under specific circumstances, Dr. McDonald flatly stated that it could neither be used to "determine the truthfulness of a statement made to the police" nor to "obtain confessions from suspects." Noting that police officers, not trained psychiatrists, conducted much of the questioning, Dr. McDonald argued that standard questioning techniques were "unrewarding and to be deplored in narcoanalysis." This was because the "highly suggestible state of the drugged person may give rise to false or misleading answers especially when the questions are improperly phrased." In Dr. McDonald's view, psychiatrists called on to participate in such exercises "should on ethical grounds refuse to perform narcoanalysis."

Proponents of the use of psychiatric technology for criminal investigation note, with justification, that both truth-seeking science and its administration have been refined in recent years. Brain fingerprinting, for example, matches evidence from crime scene with information stored in the human mind. Sounds, words or images from a crime scene — information that investigators take care to first confirm would be known only to perpetrators — are shown to suspects. Then, the suspects' P-300 brain wave responses are measured to determine whether their memories contain this information.

All of this points to the need to assess the evidence so far available on the Mumbai bombings with great care. Some of what has emerged from suspects' statements seems liberally laced with fantasy. For example, key suspect Faisal Sheikh told interrogators that one member of his cell received instructions from the "ISI chief" to assassinate the former Deputy Prime Minister, L.K. Advani. To anyone even remotely familiar with the workings of covert services, it seems unlikely that the then Director-General of the ISI, Lieutenant-General Ehsan-ul-Haq, would have met with a low-level agent to discuss such plans. Another suspect, CNN-IBN television recently reported, claimed to have seen top al Qaeda operative Mohammad Atta while training in Pakistan — a disclosure that would have been sensational were it not for the fact that the terrorist died during the New York terror bombings of 2001.

Several points of detail also need clarification. Suspects, for example, have told the Mumbai Police that a Pakistani national fabricated the devices used in the bombing — a somewhat mystifying act, since the suspects themselves are stated to have received training in Pakistan. Finally, why so many Pakistani nationals were despatched to carry out the strikes when local Lashkar cadre were available needs to be explained.

It is possible the Mumbai Police do have answers to these and other questions—answers they wish to disclose in a court of law, rather than to journalists. As things stand, though, it is hard to see just what this evidence might be. Key suspects such as top Maharashtra Lashkar-e-Taiba organisers Rahil Sheikh and Zabiuddin Ansari are thought to have fled the country, while Pakistan has made clear it will not allow Indian interrogators to question the terrorist group's top leadership. Neither the Intelligence Bureau nor the Research and Analysis Wing is likely to allow intercepted communications between the bombers and their bosses in Pakistan to be produced in a court of law, for fear of disclosing India's technical capabilities—and limitations. As such, providing a coherent account of the command-level planning and execution of the Mumbai bombings could prove difficult.

Nevertheless, the use of techniques such as narcoanalysis has not prevented complaints of abuse filed against interrogators, as suggested by the followig excerpt.

Anupam Dasgupta, India's Secret Torture Chambers

The Week, July 14, 2009[37]

Little Terrorist, as the intelligence sleuths came to call him, turned out to be a hard nut to crack. No amount of torture would work on 20-year-old Mohammed Issa, who was picked up from Delhi on February 5, 2006. The Delhi Police believed that he had a hotline to Lashkar-e-Toiba deputy chief Zaki-ur-Rehman Lakhwi, who later masterminded the 26/11 attack on Mumbai. At a secret detention centre in Delhi, the police and intelligence officers tried every single torture method in their arsenal-from electric shock to sleep deprivation-to make Issa sing. He stuck to his original line: that he had come from Nepal to visit a relative in Delhi. Only, they refused believe him.

According to the police, the youth from Uttar Pradesh, who had moved to Nepal in 2000 along with his family after his father, Irfan Ahmed, was accused in a terrorism case, returned to India to set up Lashkar modules in the national capital. More than six months after he was picked up, the police announced his arrest on August 14. He has since been shifted to the Tihar jail. His lawyer N.D. Pancholi said Issa was kept in illegal custody for months. If not, let the police say where he was between February 5 and August 15, he challenged.

Issa could have been detained in any of Delhi's joint interrogation centres, used by the police and intelligence agencies to extract precious information from the detainees using methods frowned upon by the law. As one top police officer told THE WEEK in the course of our investigation, these torture chambers spread across the country are our "precious assets". They are our own little Guantanamo Bays or Gitmos (where the US tortures terror suspects from Afghanistan and elsewhere for information).

---

37. *Available at* http://sanhati.com/articles/1660/ (last visited Jan. 7, 2011).

Not many admit their existence, because doing so could result in human rights activists knocking at their doors and bad press for the smartly dressed intelligence men. It is a murky and dangerous world, according to K.S. Subramanian, Tripura's former director-general of police, who has also served in the Intelligence Bureau. "Such sites exist and are being used to detain and interrogate suspected terrorists and it has been going on for a long time," he told THE WEEK. "Even senior police officers are reluctant to talk about the system." So are people who have been to these virtual hells that officially do not exist.

THE WEEK has identified 15 such secret interrogation centres-three each in Mumbai, Delhi, Gujarat and Jammu and Kashmir, two in Kolkata and one in Assam. (One detention centre that is shared by all security and law enforcement agencies is in Palanpur, Gujarat.) Their locations have been arrived at after speaking to serving and retired top officers who had helped set up some of these facilities. Those who have spent time in these places had no idea where they are. They were taken blindfolded and were allowed no visitors. The only faces they got to see were those of the interrogators, day in and day out.

The biggest of the three detention centres in Mumbai, the Aarey Colony facility in Goregaon, has four rooms. The Anti-Terrorism Squad questioned Saeed Khan (name changed), one of the accused in the Malegaon blasts of September 2006, here. He was served food at irregular intervals (led to temporary disorientation) and was denied sleep. Another secret detention centre maintained in the city by the ATS at Kalachowky has a sound-proof room. Sohail Shaikh, accused in the July 2006 train bombings, was held here for close to two months. "He was kept in isolation for days together," said an officer. "He crumbled after being subjected to hostile sessions. Intentional infliction of suffering does not always yield immediate results. Sometimes you have to wait for many days for the detainee to break. It is a tedious process." The smallest of the three facilities at Chembur has just two rooms.

Parvez Ahmed Radoo, 30, of Baramulla district in Kashmir, was illegally detained in Delhi for over a month for allegedly trying to plot mass murder in the national capital on behalf of the Jaish-e-Mohammed. The Delhi Police's chargesheet says he was arrested from the Azadpur fruit market in Delhi on October 14, 2006. But according to Parvez's flight itinerary, he travelled from Srinagar to Delhi on September 12 on SpiceJet flight 850. The flight landed at Delhi airport at 12.10 p.m. He had to catch another flight at 1.30 p.m. (SpiceJet flight 217) to Pune, where, according to his parents, he was going to pursue his Ph.D. But he never boarded the Pune flight as he disappeared from the Delhi airport.

Parvez wrote an open letter from the Tihar jail, where he is currently held, in which he said he was arrested from the airport on September 12 and kept in custody for a month. Apparently, he was first taken to the Lodhi Colony police station and then to an apartment in Dwarka, where electrodes were attached to his genitals and power was switched on. (Delhi's secret detention centres are located at Dwarka in south-west Delhi, the Inter-state Cell of the Crime Branch in Chanakyapuri in central Delhi, and the Lodhi Colony police station in south Delhi.)

"After my arrest on September 12, I was taken to Pune, where I was shown pictures of many Kashmiri boys," Parvez said in the letter. "They wanted me to identify them. As I didn't know any one of them, they brought me to Delhi again and threw me into the torture chamber of Lodhi Road [sic] police station. They took off my clothes and started beating me like an animal, so ruthlessly that my feet and fingers started bleeding. I was later forced to clean the blood-stained floor with my underwear. They gave me electric shocks and stretched my legs to extreme limits, resulting in internal haemorrhage. I started passing blood with my urine and stool. Later I was shifted to one flat near Delhi airport [he later identified the place as Dwarka]. From the adjacent flats, voices of crying and screaming had been coming, indicating presence of other persons being tortured."

Throughout his detention, wrote Parvez, he was asked to lie to his parents that everything was fine. In the letter he also gave the mobile number from which the calls were made—9960565152. His family is trying to collect the call site details of the number to prove his illegal detention. Delhi-based journalist Iftikhar Geelani, who spent nine days in the Lodhi Colony police station after his arrest in 2002 on spying charges, is yet to get over the traumatic experience. "There are lock-ups with such low ceilings that a person will not be able to stand," he said. "There is an interrogation centre within the police station where people are brutally tortured with cables, and some are completely undressed and abused. They also have a facility to raise the temperature of the cell to a point where it is unbearable and then suddenly bring it down to freezing cold."

Assistant Commissioner Rajan Bhagat, spokesman for the Delhi Police, denied the existence of such facilities. "Nobody ever asked me the question [about secret detention centres]," he said. "We don't operate any such facility in our police stations." But Maloy Krishna Dhar, former joint director of the IB, confirmed the existence of secret detention centres in Delhi and other parts of the country. He was convinced that detention outside the police station and torture are an inevitable part of the war on terrorism. "Now I would never dream of doing the things I did when I was in charge," said Dhar. "But security agencies need such facilities." Interrogating suspected terrorists at secret detention centres, he said, is the most effective way to gather intelligence. "If you produce a suspect before court, he will never give you anything after that," he said. In other words, once you record the arrest you are within the realm of the law and you have to acknowledge the rights of the accused-arrested and contend with his lawyer.

An officer who worked in one of the detention centres admitted that extreme physical and psychological torture, based loosely on the regime in Guantanamo Bay, is used to extract information from the detainees. It includes assault on the senses (pounding the ear with loud and disturbing music) and sleep deprivation, keeping prisoners naked to degrade and humiliate them, and forcibly administering drugs through the rectum to further break down their dignity. "The interrogators isolate key operatives so that the interrogator is the only person they see each day," he said. "In extreme cases we use pethidine injections. It will make a person crazy."

Molvi Iqbal from Uttar Pradesh, a suspected member of the Harkat-ul-Jihadi-Islami who is currently lodged in Tihar, was held at a secret detention centre for two months according to his relatives. They alleged that during interrogation a chip was implanted under his skin so that his movements could be tracked if he tried to escape. "He fears that the chip is still inside his skin," said one of his relatives. "That has shattered him."

Kolkata has its own Gitmos in Bhabani Bhawan, now the headquarters of the Criminal Investigation Department, and the Alipore Retreat in Tollygunj, a bungalow that is said to have 20 rooms. They were bursting at the seams at the height of the Naxalite movement, but are more or less quiet now. "A large number of innocent people, as well as suspected terrorists, have disappeared after being taken to such secret detention centres," said Kirity Roy, a Kolkata-based human rights lawyer. "Their bodies would later be found, if at all, in the fields."

That was how militancy was tackled, first in Punjab and then in Kashmir. Today no secret prison exists in Kashmir officially after the notorious Papa-2 interrogation centre was closed down. But secret torture cells thrive across the state. The most notorious ones are the Cargo Special Operation Group (SOG) camp in Haftchinar area in Srinagar and Humhama in Budgam district. Then there are the joint interrogation centres in Khanabal area of Anantnag district and Talab Tillo and Poonch areas in Jammu region. Detentions at JICs could last months. Lawyers in Kashmir have filed 15,000 petitions since 1990 seeking the whereabouts of the detainees and the charges against them without avail.

The most recent victim of the torture regime was Manzoor Ahmed Beigh, 40, who was picked by the SOG from Alucha Bagh area in Srinagar on May 18. His family alleged that he was chained up, hung upside down from the ceiling and ruthlessly beaten up. He died the same night. Following public outrage, the officer in charge of the camp was dismissed from the service in June.

Maqbool Sahil, a Srinagar-based photojournalist who was held at Hariniwas interrogation centre for 15 days, says it is a miracle that he is alive today. "If you tell them [interrogators] you are innocent, they will torture you so ruthlessly that you will break down and confess to anything," he says. Human rights organisations are understandably concerned. Navaz Kotwal, coordinator of the Commonwealth Human Rights Initiative, said that there should be an open debate on the illegal detention centres. "The US had a debate on the Gitmos. Our government should come forward and respond to these allegations," she said.

No one wants to compromise the nation's safety, but the torture becomes unbearable, and questionable, when innocent people like the 14-year-old boy Irfan suffer (see box on page 30). The security of the country and its people is important and terrorism should be crushed at all cost. But the largest democracy in the world should also ensure that human rights are not violated.

Dhar defended the secret prison system, arguing that the successful defence of the country required that the security establishment be empowered to hold and interrogate suspected terrorists for as long as necessary and without restrictions imposed by the legal system. "The primary mission of the agencies is to save the nation both by overt and covert means from any terrorist threat," he said. "But to keep the programme secret is a horrible burden."

ISSUES TO CONSIDER

1. Does a suspect subjected to narcoanalysis give information voluntarily?
2. Should investigators, relying on traditional methods that fail to turn up useful evidence, be allowed to utilize techniques of questionable reliability in hope that evidence will come to light?
3. Is it accurate to assume that individuals investigated for a crime will naturally make allegations that investigators abused them?
4. In a country as religiously divided as India, would it be more effective to have interrogators only question people who practice the same faith?
5. How does the Indian interrogation paradigm compare to the U.S., Israeli, and Russian models?
6. What circumstances, if any, justify enhanced interrogation techniques?

In the aftermath of the 2008 Mumbai attacks one gunman was captured alive. During his public trial he has made the following claims regarding his interrogation:

> The Accused gunman in last year's bloody siege of Mumbai retracted his detailed confession Friday, saying police tortured him into admitting his role in the attacks that left 166 people dead. Mohammed Ajmal Kasab, 21, who is being tried in a special court—and was photographed carrying an assault rifle during the attack on Mumbai's main train station—told the judge he came to Mumbai as a tourist and was arrested 20 days before the siege began. On the day the attacks started, Kasab said, police took him from his cell because he resembled one of the gunmen, shot him to make it look like he had been involved in the violence and re-arrested him. Friday's statement was not the first reversal from Kasab. In February, he told a judge he wanted to attack India in order to free the divided region of Kashmir where Muslim militants are fighting for independence. He later recanted that statement, saying it was obtained under duress. It was unclear what impact Kasab's statement would have on the case, and the prosecution brushed it off. "All the while, I expected that Kasab was about to take a U-turn in the case," said Ujjwal Nikam, the prosecutor. "He is a military-trained commando. It's not going to affect our case."
>
> In July, Kasab, who could face the death penalty if convicted, surprised the court when he suddenly confessed, saying he would rather be hanged in this world than face "God's punishment" in the next. In his confession, he spoke of spraying gunfire into the crowd at the train station and described in detail a network of training camps and safe houses across Pakistan, revealing the names of four men he said were his handlers. The photo of Kasab casually walking through the station with his rifle has become the enduring image of the attacks. But Kasab said police tortured him into falsely confessing. The assault 13 months ago lasted nearly three days and paralyzed India's commercial hub. During the attacks, 10 young men armed with assault rifles stormed two luxury hotels, a Jewish center and the train station. Nine of the gunmen were killed, leaving only Kasab, who was wounded in a shootout with police, authorities said. He told the court Friday he was initially arrested last year after wandering around

Mumbai late at night looking for a place to stay, and his Pakistani citizenship aroused suspicion.[38]

Although the defendant alleges torture, it is unclear at this time whether any abuses occurred during his interrogation, or whether he is simply fabricating the story.

ISSUES TO CONSIDER

1. If the claims of the accused gunman are correct, how does the Indian interrogation paradigm compare to the U.S., Israeli, and models?
2. Does the complexity of India's threats affect the interrogation model and methods implemented?
3. What circumstances, if any, justify enhanced interrogation techniques?

Much like Russia and Spain, India utilizes a criminal law model to classify terrorists. Promulgation and subsequent repeal of statutes reflect the realities of India's dilemma: aggressive counterterrorism tempered by internal and external considerations alike. Indian authorities may continue to develop alternative interrogation methods such as narcoanalysis or may implement enhanced measures — if not torture — as claimed in the aftermath of recent, significant terrorist attacks. What interrogation measures are implemented depends on the attack's severity, circumstances, and what group or nation stands behind the attack.

VII. SPAIN

As discussed in earlier chapters, Spain did not modify its existing criminal law paradigm in response to the Madrid train bombings. Rather, Spain responded to the attack as if it were a non-terrorist criminal act. This, however, does not guarantee that authorities did not use more aggressive interrogations methods.

According to the Spanish criminal code, Spain does not have specific anti-terrorism laws, rather treating terrorism as an aggravated form of a crime. According to Spain's penal code, a terrorist offense is committed if the purpose of the act is to "subvert the constitutional order or seriously public peace."[39] However, Spain does deviate from its standard procedural laws when dealing with suspected terrorists.

Human rights organizations have accused Spanish law enforcement authorities of subjecting detainees to interrogations that violate international law norms and conventions. Complaints have addressed the interrogations of

---

38. Associated Press, *Mumbai Gunman Recants Confession, Alleges Torture*, USA Today, Dec. 18, 2009, *available at* http://www.usatoday.com/news/world/2009-12-18-mumbai-gunman-recant_N.htm.

39. *Setting an Example? Counter-Terrorism Measures in Spain*, Human Rights Watch, Vol. 17, No. 1(D), Jan. 2005, *available at* http://hrw.org/reports/2005/spain0105/spain0105.pdf (last visited Oct. 8, 2010).

Spanish citizens suspected of involvement in ETA and other criminal activity. Detainee's held incommunicado, primarily ETA suspects, report they were tortured or ill-treated by Civil Guards or police officers. The European Court of Human Rights examined the case of 15 Catalans suspected of being sympathizers of a Catalan independence movement: "The Catalans alleged they had been subjected to physical and mental torture and inhuman and degrading treatment on their arrest and in custody in Catalonia and at the Civil Guard headquarters in Madrid in mid-1992."[40] Amnesty International also reported that a group of journalists who had been arrested were held incommunicado.[41] After being released, several of the detainees said they had been tortured by asphyxiation with a plastic bag, exhausting physical exercises, threats, and simulated execution.

Human Rights Watch has also issued critical reports about the custodial interrogation practices of Spanish authorities.[42] Following the 2004 Madrid train bombings, Human Rights Watch reported the following:

> Human Rights Watch gathered testimonies about the experience of nine 11-M (March 11, 2004 train bombings, referenced hereinafter as 11-M) suspects. Of these, two were held for five days before the official police statement was taken; five were held for four days; and the remaining two were held for two days. One suspect was held for nearly ninety-six hours before his statement was taken. In almost all cases, the lawyer was notified the same day the statement was to be taken; he or she was only told the detainee's name, and the time and place of the proceeding.
>
> The three 11-M defendants with whom Human Rights Watch spoke recounted that they had been questioned by police during the incommunicado period without the presence of their lawyer. Defendant X said he was illegally questioned nightly without a lawyer present, sometimes two or three times a night, for the four nights he spent in police custody. Defendants Y and Z both said they were each questioned once by the police during their incommunicado period. The girlfriend of a fourth defendant told Human Rights Watch that he had been interrogated every day while in police custody.[43]

Human Rights Watch has further expressed concern that Spain's incommunicado detention policy creates conditions that facilitate the commission of torture or other forms of mistreatment of suspects in custody.[44] The need for medical examinations of suspects in custody has been recommended as a safeguard against torture or mistreatment while in custody.

> Under Spanish law, all detainees in police custody have the right to an examination by a forensic doctor. As described above, the November 2003 reform of the LEC [Spain's Code of Criminal Procedure] added the right of incommunicado detainees to request a second forensic examination. This reform, however, falls short of compliance with the CPT [European Committee for the

---

40. *Id.*
41. *Id.*
42. *Id.*
43. *Id. at* 32-33.
44. *Id.* at 34.

Prevention of Torture] and the Human Rights Committee's recommendations, as it still does not allow the detainee to be examined by a doctor of his or her own choice.[45]

According to Spanish law, those suspected of committing a crime have the right to be informed immediately, in an understandable manner, of his or her rights and the grounds for the arrest (Art. 520(2)). All detainees have the right to choose a lawyer and to request that the lawyer be present during any interrogations (Art. 520(2)(c)). "Detention in police custody should last 'no longer than the time strictly necessary to carry out the investigations aimed at establishing the facts'; the detainee must be released or brought before a judicial authority within seventy-two hours" (Art. 520(1)).[46] While incommunicado detention is allowed by law, the following must be addressed: whether according to Spanish law a detainee may be tortured or whether there are clear restrictions and guidelines delineating the limits of coercive interrogation. Furthermore, what branch of government guarantees that security and law enforcement officials will not violate statutory restrictions?

The concern expressed by Human Rights Watch over Spain's current anti-terrorism practices led to a series of recommended changes to Spanish policies. The central concerns pertain to the failure of Spain's Criminal Code and Code of Procedure to provide adequate safeguards against ill-treatment while suspected terrorists were in detention. The group has urged the Spanish government to ensure adequate safeguards for detainees in police custody by undertaking the following measures:

- All reports of ill-treatment during police custody should be fully investigated. Judges must act promptly to ascertain the veracity of all allegations of mistreatment that come to their attention, even when the forensic medical examinations do not reveal any physical abuse.
- The National Police and Civil Guard should ensure that all suspects in custody are treated with dignity. Measures designed to protect the physical integrity of suspects and others in the detention facility should be limited to those strictly necessary. In particular, the practice of holding suspects and presenting them in court without shoes should be abolished.
- Independent observers, including accredited nongovernmental and international organizations, should be allowed access to police stations to verify the material and physical conditions of detainees.

The Constitutional Court of Spain seeks to ensure that the recommendations of NGOs such as Human Rights Watch are duly implemented. As the supreme interpreter of the Spanish Constitution, the Court is responsible for the protection of fundamental rights and therefore has jurisdiction to hear individual appeals for protection against violations committed by any public power.

45. *Id.*
46. *Id.*

While Spain has been widely criticized for its treatment of ETA suspects, international concern has not been raised regarding interrogations conducted in the aftermath of the train station bombing. This seems to indicate that the Spanish authorities have not adopted more stringent interrogation methods used by the other surveyed nations.

ISSUES TO CONSIDER

1. In the context of terrorism interrogations, which branch of government is best suited for establishing guidelines for interrogators?
2. Is it appropriate that the courts or legislatures curtail the executive?
3. If the criminal law paradigm is implemented against terrorists, what should be the limits of interrogation?
4. What is the significance of domestic — rather than foreign-based terrorism — when developing an interrogation model?
5. Does the decision not to re-articulate the interrogation model after the Madrid train bombings suggest a "business as usual" approach?

VIII. CHINA

A. INTRODUCTION

In recent years, the issue of torture in China has become a subject of public concern and debate, particularly after several prominent wrongful-conviction cases came to light in 2005. The growing willingness of officials to acknowledge that Chinese scholars and journalists have been tortured in is a significant step forward. Chinese scholars and journalists are increasingly publishing detailed critiques of the criminal justice system, addressing issues including weak investigations, a lack of professionalism in the police, and confessions extorted by torture. Chinese officials and analysts have characterized torture as "widespread," "deeply entrenched," a "stubborn illness," and a "malignant tumor" that "is difficult to stop" in practice, with forced confessions characterized as "common in many places in China because the police are often under great pressure from above to solve criminal cases."[47]

The government's willingness to acknowledge the pervasiveness of torture was confirmed when the Supreme People's Procuratorate (SPP) published *The Crime of Tortured Confession (Xingxun Bigong Zui)* in late 1997, which included China's first publicly released official statistics on criminal cases of torture-based confession. According the report, there was an average of 364 cases

---

47. *Return of "Murdered Wife" calls China's Judicial System in Question, China View*, Apr. 5, 2005, http://news.xinhuanet.com/english/2005-04/05/content_2789158.htm (last visited Aug. 23, 2010).

per year between 1979 and 1989, upward of 400 cases per year in the 1990s, and 241 persons had been tortured to death over the two-year period of 1993-1994.

In light of this, the government has undertaken a number of measures to directly address torture as an interrogation measure. In August 2003, the Minister of Public Security, Zhou Yongkang, issued a set of unified regulations on law enforcement procedures for public security institutions entitled "Regulations on the Procedures for Handling Administrative Cases" which included procedures that defined police powers; imposed time limits for confiscation of property, investigations, and examination of suspects; and articulated legal means for gathering evidence.

In 2004, the Ministry of Public Security issued regulations prohibiting the use of torture and threats to gain confessions and initiated a nationwide campaign to improve criminal investigation capacity. In the same year, the SPP launched a nationwide campaign to crack down on officials who abuse their powers. The SPP announced in 2005 that eliminating interrogation through torture was a priority of its work agenda and instructed procurators that torture-based confessions cannot justify formal approval of arrests and that prosecutors must eliminate illegally obtained evidence.

In addition to initiatives at the central level, several promising similar initiatives have occurred regionally. The Zhejiang provincial Public Security Department issued regulations regarding forced confessions stating that local police chiefs will be expected to resign in any district where there are more than two cases of forced confessions resulting in injuries, miscarriages of justice, or public order problems. In mid-April 2005, Sichuan law enforcement and judicial authorities issued a joint opinion prohibiting use of illegally obtained evidence, and required courts to exclude coerced statements and confessions if police cannot provide a rational explanation of the alleged coercion or refuse to investigate allegations of abuse. Furthermore, the Hubei provincial procuratorate, high court, justice department, public security bureau, and State security bureau issued regulations on criminal evidence, including the prohibition of testimonies acquired through torture-based confessions.

Practical measures to combat torture have included introducing measures to eliminate torture including audio and video recording in interrogation rooms, strengthening representation during the investigative and pretrial phase of the criminal process by placing lawyers on a 24-hour basis in pilot police stations, designing interrogation rooms that separate suspects from interrogators, and placing resident procurators in places of detention and near public security bureaus to supervise law enforcement personnel.

The UN Special Rapporteur has observed positive developments at the legislative level, including the planned reform of several laws relevant to the criminal procedure, intended to bring Chinese legislation into greater conformity with international norms, particularly the fair trial standards contained in the International Covenant on Civil and Political Rights (ICCPR) that China signed in 1998 and is preparing to ratify. The Special Rapporteur suggests that China might endeavor to increase transparency regarding the number of death sentences, as well as to consider legislation that would allow direct petitioning to the SPC in cases where individuals claim relief by lower courts, particularly in cases involving the use of torture and access to counsel.

B. CHINA AND GUANTANAMO

In 2002, the United States welcomed foreign interrogators from several countries including China, Libya, Jordan, Uzbekistan, and Tunisia to aid in interrogations of prisoners at Guantanamo.

FOREIGN INTERROGATORS IN GUANTANAMO BAY CENTER FOR
CONSTITUTIONAL RIGHTS

Center for Constitutional Rights[48]

The U.S. allowed Chinese officials access to the Uighurs in Guantánamo as a diplomatic concession. China's human rights record is egregious, and Uighurs are one of the most persecuted groups in China. All of the Uighur prisoners are believed to have been interrogated by Chinese security forces while in Guantánamo.

Numerous Uighur prisoners in Guantánamo, including Ali Thabid, Bahtiyar Mahnut, Sabir Osman, and Huzaifa Parhat, were told by Chinese interrogators that they would be killed or imprisoned if the U.S. returned them to China. One Chinese interrogator even told prisoner Adel Abdul Hakim that he was "lucky" to be in Guantánamo because in a Chinese jail, he would be "finished." Uighur prisoner Abdusemet was threatened and deprived of sleep and food by Chinese interrogators.

Chinese officials told another prisoner that the Defense Department has given the Chinese information the prisoner had previously provided to U.S. interrogators about himself and his family, violating specific promises by U.S. interrogators that they would not provide this information to the Chinese. The Chinese also attempted to photograph this prisoner during his interrogation, and when he resisted, U.S. soldiers forcibly restrained him and held his head so that the Chinese could clearly photograph his face.

The U.S. government has consistently exploited the Uighurs' fear of torture and death at the hands of the Chinese. Prisoner Adel Noori reports that around January 2004, CIA or Defense Department officials threatened to send him to China unless he cooperated and spied on other non-Uighur prisoners in Guantánamo. When he refused, he was punished severely. Mr. Abdusemet also stated that an American who identified himself as a White House representative specifically threatened to send Mr. Abdusemet to China if he did not cooperate.

---

48. *Available at* http://ccrjustice.org/files/Foreign%20Interrogators%20in%20Guantanamo%20 Bay_1.pdf (last visited Mar. 21, 2010).

Testimony of Jason Pinney Before the House Committee on Foreign Affairs, Subcommitte on International Organizations, Human Rights, and Oversight

Chinese Interrogation vs. Congressional Oversight: The Uighurs
at Guantanamo, July 16, 2009[49]

In September of 2002, our country permitted a delegation from the People's Republic of China to travel to Guantanamo and interrogate all twenty-two Uighurs held at the prison. Prior to the interrogations, the Americans "softened up" the men by denying them sleep and in some cases food. Our government also provided the Chinese interrogators with copies of the Uighurs' files, including detailed information on their families, despite previous assurances to the men that their information would not be shared with their Chinese oppressors. The men were left alone with the Chinese in an interrogation room for several hours. No member of the US military was present.

Many of our clients have said that these interrogations were the hardest thing they had to endure during their seven years at Guantanamo. The Chinese made threats against family, and against the men themselves. Each of the Uighurs was told that he would be sent back to China and imprisoned, or worse. The men were petrified of what would happen to themselves and their family members if the Chinese carried out on their threats. They were also subjected to stress techniques such as forced sitting for many hours in a cold room, bound and shackled. Some of this mistreatment appears to have been administered at the instruction of the Chinese.

All of this would not be possible without the support and cooperation of the United States. Military personnel went as far as forcefully holding up my clients' heads by the hair and beard so that the Chinese could take their picture. Statements from our clients' Combatant Status Review Tribunal ("CSRT") transcripts exemplify the Uighur experiences at the hands of Communist Chinese interrogators. Remarkably, these CSRT statements were all made in response to direct questions from tribunal panel members. Sometimes, it was the first question that was asked. It appears that some military officers were concerned that the Chinese were allowed to interrogate the men.

- Salahidin Abdulahat (now in Bermuda) described to his Combatant Status Review Tribunal ("CSRT") panel how he was forcibly interrogated, threatened, and deprived of sleep and food by the Chinese delegation. Furthermore, he described how "there was on American person . . . representing the president's house" who threatened to send him back to China if he did not cooperate with the delegation. He said that the Chinese "took our picture forcefully and recorded our voices and threatened to hit us and do other things." He pleaded with his CSRT panel "to not let those things happen again to us [because] it would hurt us really bad."

---

49. *Available at* http://foreignaffairs.house.gov/111/pin071609.pdf (last visited Jan. 7, 2011).

- Sabir Osman (still in Guantanamo) echoed these remarks. He said that the Chinese made threats against him, and told him that the American government had already agreed to turn him over to China. He also described a conversation with an MP in which "[t]he MP came in and said that they had orders from higher up and we have to hold you by your neck and they will take your picture."
- Ablikim Turahun (now in Bermuda) said that he was told if he agreed to return to China he would only be in prison for three to four years. The Chinese baited him by telling him that he could be with his family afterwards. Mr. Turahun knew the risks of believing the Chinese. He chose to stay in Guantanamo.
- Adel Abdul Hakim (now in Sweden) was told that he was "lucky" to be in Guantanamo; if they took him back to a Chinese jail, he would be "finished." Most of the Uighurs refused to cooperate with the Chinese interrogators. As punishment, the Americans put all but two of them in solitary confinement for up to twenty days. No light, no air, no human contact.

CHAPTER 9

DEFINING TERRORIST STATUS AND RIGHTS

I. INTRODUCTION

Much uncertainty remains regarding one of the seminal issues in terrorism: how to determine the rights and status of suspected terrorists and the appropriate judicial forum for trying suspected terrorists. Doing so requires, in part, resolving whether the terrorist defendant has the right to confront his accuser.

By example, in the context of American criminal and constitutional law, the Sixth Amendment guarantees a defendant the right to "be confronted with the witnesses against him." Granting that right to terrorist-defendants potentially requires exposing both intelligence information and the means and methods by which it was received. However, the larger question—which shall be discussed in this chapter—is whether terrorists should be accorded the same rights as criminals or whether terrorism is a separate paradigm. The question is not abstract; the answer dictates what rights are to be extended to individuals defined as suspected terrorists.

How the paradigm is defined determines before what court of law—if at all—a suspected terrorist is brought. That is, if terrorism is defined as war then terrorists are treated as prisoners of war; if terrorism is viewed in accordance with the criminal law paradigm then suspected terrorists shall be accorded the same rights as traditional criminals and if neither category is appropriate then an alternative paradigm needs to be articulated.

ISSUES TO CONSIDER

1. Should terrorists be granted trials?
2. What should be the guiding principle in determining what judicial regime is appropriate for trying terrorists?
3. In determining which alternative regime to implement, what considerations and interests should be taken into account?
4. What issues and rights are at stake?
5. Should terrorists be granted the same rights as criminal defendants?

> 6. Should terrorists be treated as prisoners of war, who may not be brought to trial unless they are accused of having committed a war crime or of committing a crime in captivity?

II. UNITED STATES

A. MILITARY COMMISSIONS

In the aftermath of 9/11, the Bush administration concluded that Article III courts were inappropriate for trying terrorists and those who provided terrorist safe harbor.[1] Administration official argued that an alternate judicial regime was required to fight terrorism effectively. Accordingly, President Bush issued an Executive Order establishing military commissions.

DETENTION, TREATMENT, AND TRIAL OF CERTAIN NON-CITIZENS IN THE WAR AGAINST TERRORISM

Military Order §1(a), November 13, 2001, 66 Fed. Reg. 57,833 (Nov. 16, 2001)

By the authority vested in me as President and as Commander in Chief of the Armed Forces of the United States by the Constitution and the laws of the United States of America, including the Authorization for Use of Military Force Joint Resolution (Public Law 107-40, 115 Stat. 224) and sections 821 and 836 of title 10, United States Code, it is hereby ordered as follows:

Section 1. Findings

(a) International terrorists, including members of al Qaida, have carried out attacks on United States diplomatic and military personnel and facilities abroad and on citizens and property within the United States on a scale that has created a state of armed conflict that requires the use of the United States Armed Forces.

(b) In light of grave acts of terrorism and threats of terrorism, including the terrorist attacks on September 11, 2001, on the headquarters of the United States Department of Defense in the national capital region, on the World Trade Center in New York, and on civilian aircraft such as in Pennsylvania, I proclaimed a national emergency on September 14, 2001 (Proc. 7463, Declaration of National Emergency by Reason of Certain Terrorist Attacks).

(c) Individuals acting alone and in concert involved in international terrorism possess both the capability and the intention to undertake further terrorist attacks against the United States that, if

---

1. Article III courts, defined by Article III of the U.S. Constitution, constitute the Supreme Court of the United States and the remaining courts of the judicial branch. Congress can vest these courts with jurisdiction to hear certain cases involving disputes between citizens of different states or countries.

not detected and prevented, will cause mass deaths, mass injuries, and massive destruction of property, and may place at risk the continuity of the operations of the United States Government.

(d) The ability of the United States to protect the United States and its citizens, and to help its allies and other cooperating nations protect their nations and their citizens, from such further terrorist attacks depends in significant part upon using the United States Armed Forces to identify terrorists and those who support them, to disrupt their activities, and to eliminate their ability to conduct or support such attacks.

(e) To protect the United States and its citizens, and for the effective conduct of military operations and prevention of terrorist attacks, it is necessary for individuals subject to this order pursuant to section 2 hereof to be detained, and, when tried, to be tried for violations of the laws of war and other applicable laws by military tribunals.

(f) Given the danger to the safety of the United States and the nature of international terrorism, and to the extent provided by and under this order, I find consistent with section 836 of title 10, United States Code, that it is not practicable to apply in military commissions under this order the principles of law and the rules of evidence generally recognized in the trial of criminal cases in the United States district courts.

(g) Having fully considered the magnitude of the potential deaths, injuries, and property destruction that would result from potential acts of terrorism against the United States, and the probability that such acts will occur, I have determined that an extraordinary emergency exists for national defense purposes, that this emergency constitutes an urgent and compelling government interest, and that issuance of this order is necessary to meet the emergency. . . .

Sec. 3. Detention Authority of the Secretary of Defense. Any individual subject to this order shall be —

(a) detained at an appropriate location designated by the Secretary of Defense outside or within the United States. . . .

Sec. 4. Authority of the Secretary of Defense Regarding Trials of Individuals Subject to this Order.

(a) Any individual subject to this order shall, when tried, be tried by military commission for any and all offenses triable by military commission that such individual is alleged to have committed, and may be punished in accordance with the penalties provided under applicable law, including life imprisonment or death. . . .

(c) Orders and regulations issued under subsection (b) of this section shall include, but not be limited to, rules for the conduct of the proceedings of military commissions, including pretrial, trial, and post-trial procedures, modes of proof, issuance of process, and qualifications of attorneys, which shall at a minimum provide for —

(1) military commissions to sit at any time and any place, consistent with such guidance regarding time and place as the Secretary of Defense may provide;

(2) a full and fair trial, with the military commission sitting as the triers of both fact and law;

(3) admission of such evidence as would, in the opinion of the presiding officer of the military commission (or instead, if any other member of the commission so requests at the time the presiding officer renders that opinion, the opinion of the commission rendered at that time by a majority of the commission), have probative value to a reasonable person;

(4) in a manner consistent with the protection of information classified or classifiable under Executive Order 12958 of April 17, 1995, as amended, or any successor Executive Order, protected by statute or rule from unauthorized disclosure, or otherwise protected by law, (A) the handling of, admission into evidence of, and access to materials and information, and (B) the conduct, closure of, and access to proceedings;

(5) conduct of the prosecution by one or more attorneys designated by the Secretary of Defense and conduct of the defense by attorneys for the individual subject to this order;

(6) conviction only upon the concurrence of two-thirds of the members of the commission present at the time of the vote, a majority being present;

(7) sentencing only upon the concurrence of two-thirds of the members of the commission present at the time of the vote, a majority being present; and

(8) submission of the record of the trial, including any conviction or sentence, for review and final decision by me or by the Secretary of Defense if so designated by me for that purpose.

When establishing the military commissions, the administration relied on the Supreme Court's holding in *Quirin*,[2] where the Court used three different terms (illegal combatant, enemy belligerent, enemy combatant) to refer to captured Germans. While the Court upheld President Roosevelt's decision to bring the German saboteurs before a military tribunal, the Court did not resolve the larger, far more crucial issue of defining the saboteurs. The Court stated that "we have no occasion now to define with meticulous care the ultimate boundaries of the jurisdiction of military tribunals to try persons according to the law of war."[3] In attempting to determine the *Quirin* Court's working definition for any one of those interchangeably applied terms, it was assumed that the Court was referring to an individual engaged in combat with the United States who for whatever reason, was not a soldier as commonly understood.

The appellants in *Quirin* were German soldiers who lost their status when they *purposefully* discarded their uniforms. Unlike terrorists, who do not belong

---

2. Ex parte Quirin, 317 U.S. 1 (1942).
3. *Id.* at 46, 63.

to a regular army, the Court seemingly applied this "working definition" to individuals who, by all accounts, had been soldiers but as a result of their actions lost their status. In doing so, they enabled the Court to hold they were not soldiers when captured thus not entitled to prisoner of war status.

By relying on *Quirin*, the Bush administration established an alternative judicial regime established to try individuals because of an assumed involvement in 9/11. This alternative judicial regime was premised on two foundations: (1) the detainees were not prisoners of war and therefore could be brought to trial; and (2) the detainees were not entitled to traditional Article III protections afforded to defendants in the criminal law paradigm.

According to administration officials who testified before Congress, the fundamental purpose of the Presidential Order was to bring "justice to persons charged with offenses under the laws of armed conflict"[4] and to "target a narrow class of individuals — terrorists."[5]

ISSUES TO CONSIDER

1. Was the administration correct in asserting that Article III courts are not appropriate for trying the detainees?
2. What rights guaranteed to criminal law defendants were perceived as threatening to the administration's counterterrorism efforts?
3. What alternatives to Article III courts could the administration have developed without creating a new legal regime?
4. What were the policy considerations in developing the military commissions?
5. What were the operational considerations in developing the military commissions?
6. In determining which paradigm is applicable to counterterrorism, what factors need to be balanced?
7. Are the rights of the defendant paramount or does combating terrorism justify adjusting the rights traditionally accorded to defendants?
8. Is denying the defendant the right to confront an accuser indicative of a "slippery slope"?
9. How much can the criminal law process be altered in the context of counterterrorism?
10. Can the state risk introducing evidence in accordance with the rules of evidence?

Not everyone agreed with the Bush administration's rationale for establishing the military commissions. Criticism centered on the lack of an independent judiciary, the lack of an appeals process, the lack of a sentencing

---

4. Testimony of The Honorable Michael Chertoff, Assistant Attorney General, Criminal Division, U.S. Dep't of Justice, Nov. 28, 2001, *Department of Justice Oversight: Preserving Our Freedoms While Defending Against Terrorism, available at* http://scholarship.law.georgetown.edu/cgi/viewcontent.cgi?article=1095&context=cong (last visited Oct. 8, 2010).

5. *Id.* (Testimony of The Honorable John Ashcroft, Attorney General, U.S. Dept. of Justice).

regime known to the detainee, the process by which counsel was assigned, and the ability of the prosecutor to submit classified evidence to the court that the defendant would not be entitled to review. The backlash suggested that determining the appropriate forum for trying suspected terrorists required closer examination of two related questions: what is the appropriate definition of those engaged in terrorism and what rights should they be granted?

JOAN FITZPATRICK, MILITARY COMMISSIONS: JURISDICTION OF MILITARY
COMMISSIONS AND THE AMBIGUOUS WAR ON TERRORISM

96 A.J.I.L. 345 (2002)

Have the attacks of September 11 resulted in a shift from metaphorical war/actual crime control to actual armed conflict? The suggestion that international terrorists pose a criminal threat is met with impatience in some quarters, as if it somehow diminishes the magnitude of the events of September 11. Terrorist crimes arguably differ from other transnational crimes, in that they are politically motivated and pose a threat to national security. However, in democratic societies, crimes against national security — espionage, for example — are not generally handled by military commissions. The Military Order of November 13 appears to rest on a perception that the current terrorist emergency is legally of a warlike character, and not simply a danger to national security or suitable grounds for military involvement in law enforcement.

The order refers generally to individuals and groups involved in international terrorism, and to the necessity for the United States Armed Forces to respond to their threats, to subject suspected terrorists to military detention and trial, and to depart from "the principles of law and the rules of evidence generally recognized in the trial of criminal cases in the United States district courts" because of the "danger to the safety of the United States and the nature of international terrorism." Trial may be for violations of any "applicable laws."

If the war on terrorism is now to be conceived of as an international armed conflict, it is one of startling breadth, innumerable "combatants," and indefinite duration. The United States considers a wide variety of groups to be engaged in international terrorism, as reflected in the lists of foreign terrorist organizations adopted by the secretary of state. These groups include Aum Shinrikyo, Basque Fatherland and Liberty, the Kurdistan Workers' Party, the Liberation Tigers of Tamil Eelam, the Real IRA, and the Shining Path. The U.S. military provides support to some governments engaged in internal armed conflicts against listed groups, notably the Revolutionary Armed Forces of Colombia and the Abu Sayyaf Group in the Philippines. This war on terrorism will endure until all these groups, and others similar to them, are eradicated.

The criminal law process guarantees the accused, and subsequently the defendant, the following protections: (1) a presumption of innocence until proven guilty; (2) evidence is submitted in an open court of law; (3) the right to confront witnesses; (4) the right to remain silent; (5) right to appeal to an independent judiciary; and the (6) right to trial by a jury of peers. Perhaps the most important right granted by the criminal law process is the defendant's right to confront his accusers, thereby enabling cross-examination in open court. However, since counterterrorism is based on intelligence, the prosecution would be obligated to make intelligence sources available for cross-examination. The risk is extraordinarily significant—and potentially life-threatening—for sources who testify.

Adopting a paradigm that does not guarantee the defendant the right to confront witnesses enables the prosecution to base a case, either in whole or in part, on intelligence information. As an example—albeit one that was criticized by the Supreme Court in *Hamdi v. Rumsfeld*[6]—the United States attempted to introduce intelligence information via the Mobbs Declaration.[7]

> On remand, the Government filed a response and a motion to dismiss the petition. It attached to its response a declaration from one Michael Mobbs (hereinafter "Mobbs Declaration"), who identified himself as Special Advisor to the Under Secretary of Defense for Policy. Mobbs indicated that in this position, he has been "substantially involved with matters related to the detention of enemy combatants in the current war against the al Qaeda terrorists and those who support and harbor them (including the Taliban)." He expressed his "familiar[ity]" with Department of Defense and United States military policies and procedures applicable to the detention, control, and transfer of al Qaeda and Taliban personnel, and declared that "[b]ased upon my review of relevant records and reports, I am also familiar with the facts and circumstances related to the capture of . . . Hamdi and his detention by U.S. military forces."
>
> Mobbs then set forth what remains the sole evidentiary support that the Government has provided to the courts for Hamdi's detention. The declaration states that Hamdi "traveled to Afghanistan" in July or August 2001, and that he thereafter "affiliated with a Taliban military unit and received weapons training." It asserts that Hamdi "remained with his Taliban unit following the attacks of September 11" and that, during the time when Northern Alliance forces were "engaged in battle with the Taliban," "Hamdi's Taliban unit surrendered" to those forces, after which he "surrender[ed] his Kalishnikov assault rifle" to them. The Mobbs Declaration also states that, because al Qaeda and the Taliban "were and are hostile forces engaged in armed conflict with the armed forces of the United States," "individuals associated with" those groups "were and continue to be enemy combatants." Mobbs states that Hamdi was labeled an enemy combatant "[b]ased upon his interviews and in light of his association with the Taliban." According to the declaration, a series of "U.S. military screening team[s]" determined that Hamdi met "the criteria for enemy combatants," and "a subsequent interview of Hamdi has confirmed that he

---

6. Hamdi v. Rumsfeld, 504 U.S. 507 (2004).

7. The Mobbs Declaration is a statement supplied by a Department of Defense official, summarizing the intelligence information known to the authorities regarding the activities of a particular defendant. The material is used in detention hearings. In Israel, the classified information presented to the Judge regarding a defendant was previously referred to as "negative security material" and reflected the known intelligence based on HUMINT and SIGINT alike. The material was used for a variety of criminal law and administrative sanctions. The primary issue is the reliability of the source(s) and whether the material is corroborated.

surrendered and gave his firearm to Northern Alliance forces, which supports his classification as an enemy combatant."[8]

In a series of memos, the Bush administration clearly articulated a position that those detained in the war on terrorism were not guaranteed Geneva Convention rights. Though the memos were later "corrected," the administration's initial response posited that the detainees were not entitled to full Geneva Convention protections; in other words, the administration determined they were not soldiers and therefore could be brought to trial.

According to the Geneva Convention,[9] captured soldiers must be returned to their home state upon the cessation of hostilities. Unlike war, where culmination is marked by an agreement between the warring states, cessation of hostilities is difficult to foresee. The lack of a foreseeable, agreed upon end to the conflict directly affects the detainees' present and future status.

Unlike criminals, whose date of release is determined either by judge or jury in their presence, enemy combatants, as defined by the Bush administration, are held in a black hole. In large part, this policy has been adopted by the Obama administration.

ISSUES TO CONSIDER

1. Under what circumstance is indefinite detention justifiable?
2. What are the dangers emanating from indefinite detention?
3. How does the state determine if the individual in indefinite detention represents a continued threat to the nation's security?
4. How much of a threat does the individual have to present in order to remain in indefinite detention and what is the benchmark?
5. What government agency should be responsible for reviewing the status of the detainee? Should there be an independent review?
6. What act must an individual commit in order to be the recipient of these significantly reduced rights? Who decides?

B. THE PRESIDENTIAL ORDER

In November 2001, President Bush issued a Presidential Order that did not clearly define the term "enemy combatant." According to Section 2 of the Order, the following individuals will be brought before the military commissions:

> (a) The term "individual subject to this order" shall mean any individual who is not a United States citizen with respect to whom I determine from time to time in writing that:
> > (1) there is reason to believe that such individual, at the relevant times,
> > > (i) is or was a member of the organization known as al Qaeda;

---

8. *See Hamdi, supra* note 6, *at* 513.
9. Geneva Convention Relative to the Treatment of Prisoners of War art. 118, Aug. 12, 1949, 6 U.S.T 3316, 75 U.N.T.S. 135.

(ii) has engaged in, aided or abetted, or conspired to commit, acts of international terrorism, or acts in preparation therefore, that have caused, threaten to cause, or have as their aim to cause, injury to or adverse effects on the United States, its citizens, national security, foreign policy, or economy;

(iii) has knowingly harbored one or more individuals described in subparagraphs (i) or (ii) of subsection 2(a)(1) of this order.[10]

According to the above, an enemy combatant may be defined as any individual, who *in any way, shape, or form* came in contact with any member of al Qaeda during any period of time with the intent of causing harm, *in the broadest definition of harm*, to the United States. An enemy combatant, as defined in the Presidential Order, is an individual who need not necessarily have been involved in an act of terrorism in the present; it is sufficient to have provided assistance in the past, even if minimal. Furthermore, the minimal degree required is not defined, leaving significant grounds for liberal interpretation in determining whether an individual is an enemy combatant.

ISSUES TO CONSIDER

1. Is a broad definition of "enemy combatant" effective?
2. What are the risks of such a definition?
3. Does casting a wide net contribute to combating terrorism?
4. Should terrorists who have different positions/responsibilities be differentiated?
5. What level of intelligence needs to be submitted to determine if an individual is an enemy combatant?
6. What are criteria for determining whether an individual is an enemy combatant?

RANDY JAMES, A BRIEF HISTORY OF MILITARY COMMISSIONS

Time, May 18, 2009[11]

Expressions of shock and betrayal flowed from human rights groups against President Barack Obama last week after it was announced that some Guantanamo Bay terror suspects would continue to be tried by military commissions rather than conventional federal courts. "President Obama is backtracking dangerously on his reform agenda," warned Human Rights Watch director Kenneth Roth. The head of the American Civil Liberties Union, Anthony Romero, called Obama's announcement "absurd," adding, "These tribunals have no place in our democracy."

---

10. *Id.*
11. *Available at* http://www.time.com/time/nation/article/0,8599,1899131,00.html (last visited Jan. 7, 2011).

President Bush established the secretive commissions to try accused terrorists two months after the Sept. 11 attacks, though only three defendants have been prosecuted amid legal challenges and repeated setbacks in the U.S. Supreme Court. Obama explicitly criticized the commissions during the presidential campaign and suspended their use on his second day in office, the same day he ordered the Guantanamo Bay detention facility closed within the year. But privately White House officials worried about winning conventional convictions against some "high-value" defendants, including accused Sept. 11 mastermind Khalid Sheikh Mohammed. (The standard for admitting evidence is more rigorous in civilian court, and some confessed terrorists were not first told of their right against self-incrimination, which could bar their confessions from court.) Of the 240 detainees at Gitmo, 13 have been referred to military commissions for trial.

In a statement announcing his reversal, President Obama stressed the reconfigured commissions will increase legal protections for defendants, such as barring information obtained through brutal interrogations and limiting the use of hearsay evidence. "This is the best way to protect our country, while upholding our deeply held values," Obama said on May 15. Many Republicans and some Democrats applauded the move, insisting that some terror suspects are simply too dangerous to be tried in open court with the full protections afforded American citizens. "I give them great credit for coming to their senses," said David Rivkin, a former Reagan administration lawyer. . . .

Defendants are offered fewer legal protections in military commissions than civilian courts, such as the right to public proceedings and a trial by jury. Military officers serve as judges and jurors (in cases that call for a jury) and the right to an appeal is not guaranteed. Unlike courts martial, which are mainly concerned with violations of the Uniform Code of Military Justice by U.S. servicemembers, modern military commissions are generally intended to try foreign combatants accused of violating the laws of war. As it is with many war powers, the Constitution is vague about the scope of military commissions; legal wrangling over the extent of the commissions' authority goes back more than a century. In 1866, the Supreme Court said a military commission could not try an Indiana lawyer accused of agitating for the Confederacy, ruling that citizens must be tried in civilian courts when they're open and accessible. But in 1942, the court upheld President Roosevelt's tribunals for the eight accused German saboteurs in the failed scheme known as Operation Pastorius. More recently the court slapped down the Bush Administration's planned commissions in three separate cases, ruling among other things that only Congress can establish the tribunals; that some protections of the Geneva Conventions must extend to prisoners; and that the prisoners' right to habeas corpus cannot be suspended. Obama's decision to revive the commissions virtually ensures those battles will draw on.

The next article highlights a lack of clarity within the federal judicial system regarding detention of suspected terrorists and rights they are to be granted.

CHARLIE SAVAGE, PUSH ON TO CLARIFY RIGHTS FOR DETAINEES

Boston Globe, May 31, 2005, at A6

In what would be the first major effort by a Republican to get the GOP-led Congress to establish U.S. detention law, Senate Judiciary Committee Chairman Arlen Specter, Republican of Pennsylvania, has scheduled a hearing in June to launch his effort to create clear due process rules for suspected terrorists who are being held without trial. . . .

Federal district judges have reached conflicting decisions on how to handle those lawsuits, including whether detainees have a right to see classified evidence against them. To clarify matters and treat all cases uniformly, Specter is proposing that all detention lawsuits be heard in a secret federal court that now exists only to oversee national security-related surveillance by the government.

Judiciary Committee aides said Specter also plans to review problems that have plagued the military commissions Bush established to try detainees on criminal charges. The commissions were shut down by a federal judge last fall on the grounds that they violated the Geneva Conventions.

But several detainee advocates were cautious about Specter's idea of granting exclusive jurisdiction over detention cases to the so-called "FISA Court"—named after the federal Foreign Intelligence Surveillance Act, which allows special wiretap warrants to be used against suspected foreign agents. . . .

In June 2004, the Supreme Court ruled, 6 to 3, that Congress implicitly empowered Bush to indefinitely hold suspected "enemy combatants" without trial when it authorized the use of military force against the perpetrators of the Sept. 11 terrorist attacks in New York and Washington. But the court also ruled that detainees were entitled to greater safeguards than they had received.

In response, the military set up hearings in which three officers reviewed the cases of each Guantanamo detainee to see if they should be held as enemy combatants. But detainees were not given a lawyer and could not see all the evidence against them.

Two federal judges have come to opposite conclusions about whether the military's hearings met the standards the Supreme Court established last year. That issue is now before an appeals court.

The above underscores the very problem the Court failed to clarify in *Quirin*: who qualifies as an enemy combatant? Justice Stevens's dissent in *Rumsfeld v. Padilla*[12] addresses this issue:

Whether respondent is entitled to immediate release is a question that reasonable jurists may answer in different ways. There is, however, only one possible answer to the question whether he is entitled to a hearing on the justification for his detention.

---

12. Rumsfeld v. Padilla, 542 U.S. 426 (2004) (Stevens, J., dissenting).

At stake in this case is nothing less than the essence of a free society. Even more important than the method of selecting the people's rulers and their successors is the character of the constraints imposed on the Executive by the rule of law. Unconstrained Executive detention for the purpose of investigating and preventing subversive activity is the hallmark of the Star Chamber. Access to counsel for the purpose of protecting the citizen from official mistakes and mistreatment is the hallmark of due process.

Executive detention of subversive citizens, like detention of enemy soldiers to keep them off the battlefield, may sometimes be justified to prevent persons from launching or becoming missiles of destruction. It may not, however, be justified by the naked interest in using unlawful procedures to extract information. Incommunicado detention for months on end is such a procedure. Whether the information so procured is more or less reliable than that acquired by more extreme forms of torture is of no consequence. For if this Nation is to remain true to the ideals symbolized by its flag, it must not wield the tools of tyrants even to resist an assault by the forces of tyranny.[13]

The need to develop standards for determining *when* and *why* an individual may be detained is ultimately more significant than *how*. For a nation to determine that an individual is deprived of rights fundamental to the criminal law process places a heavy burden on the state.

The Supreme Court addressed the issue of the military commissions and enemy combatants in *Hamdan*:

The commission's procedures . . . provide . . . that an accused and his civilian counsel may be excluded from, and precluded from, ever learning what evidence was presented during any part of the proceeding . . . the presiding officer decides to "close." Grounds for closure include the protection of classified information, the physical safety of participants and witnesses, the protection of intelligence and law enforcement sources, methods, or activities, and "other national security interests." Appointed military defense counsel must be privy to these closed sessions, but may, at the presiding officer's discretion, be forbidden to reveal to the client what took place therein. Another striking feature is that the rules governing Hamdan's commission permit the admission of any evidence that, in the presiding officer's opinion, would have probative value to a reasonable person. Moreover, the accused and his civilian counsel may be denied access to classified and other "protected information," so long as the presiding officer concludes that the evidence is "probative" and that its admission without the accused's knowledge would not result in the denial of a full and fair trial.[14]

In further evaluating the procedures for the military commissions, the Court held that: "Even assuming that Hamdan is a dangerous individual who would cause great harm or death to innocent civilians given the opportunity, the Executive nevertheless must comply with the prevailing rule of law in undertaking to try him and subject him to criminal punishment."[15]

---

13. *Id.*
14. Hamdan v. Rumsfeld, 548 U.S. 557, 560 (2006).
15. *Id.* at 563.

Issues to Consider

1. What standards of proof are applicable when determining who is an enemy combatant?
2. How engaged must the individual be in order to be classified an enemy combatant?
3. Is a time limit appropriate in determining when the individual was last engaged?
4. What mechanisms enable the suspected terrorist to state his case?

"Actively engaged" is defined as follows: participating in the planning of an attack, providing harbor to those committing the attack, ensuring the availability of financial resources, providing significant logistical support, or actually performing the act. These form the essence of terrorism. In rejecting the government's argument regarding Hamdi's right to challenge his detention, the Supreme Court held as follows:

> We therefore hold that a citizen-detainee seeking to challenge his classification as an enemy combatant must receive notice of the factual basis for his classification, and a fair opportunity to rebut the Government's factual assertions before a neutral decisionmaker. "For more than a century the central meaning of procedural due process has been clear: 'Parties whose rights are to be affected are entitled to be heard; and in order that they may enjoy that right they must first be notified.' It is equally fundamental that the right to notice and an opportunity to be heard must be granted at a meaningful time and in a meaningful manner." These essential constitutional promises may not be eroded.
>
> At the same time, the exigencies of the circumstances may demand that, aside from these core elements, enemy combatant proceedings may be tailored to alleviate their uncommon potential to burden the Executive at a time of ongoing military conflict. Hearsay, for example, may need to be accepted as the most reliable available evidence from the Government in such a proceeding. Likewise, the Constitution would not be offended by a presumption in favor of the Government's evidence, so long as that presumption remained a rebuttable one and fair opportunity for rebuttal were provided.[16]

Amos N. Guiora, American Counterterrorism: The Triangle of Detention, Interrogation and Trial

Magna Carta Institute's Symposium, Towards a Global Legal Counter-Terrorism Model: Transatlantic Perspectives, 2010

The Obama Administration has an extraordinarily full plate of demanding decisions. With respect to counterterrorism, the President must address core issues and resolve long simmering dilemmas. While examining the actions of the Bush Administration is important, resolving existing conundrums is essential. In that vein, as these lines are being written, the Administration announced on November 13, 2009 that it would prosecute Khalid Shaikh

---

16. Hamdi v. Rumsfeld, 504 U.S. 507 (2004).

Mohammed, the self-described mastermind of the Sept. 11 attacks, in a Manhattan federal courtroom, a decision that ignited a sharp political debate but took a step toward resolving one of the most pressing terrorism detention issues. The decision, announced by Attorney General Eric H. Holder Jr., could mean one of the highest-profile and highest-security terrorism trials in history would be set just blocks from where hijackers for Al Qaeda destroyed the World Trade Center, killing nearly 3,000 people. Mr. Holder said he would instruct prosecutors to seek death sentences for Mr. Mohammed and four accused Sept. 11 co-conspirators who would be tried alongside him. But while the civilian system would handle those cases, he said five other detainees would be prosecuted before a military commission. Mr. Holder said he was confident that the men would be convicted, and other administration officials said they had ample legal authority to keep classified information secret. They also suggested that they could continue to detain anyone deemed to be a combatant under Congress's authorization to use military force against Al Qaeda. . . .

Similarly, terrorists are distinct from soldiers; the latter are part of the nation-state's military whereas the former belong to non-state entities. According to the Geneva Conventions, a soldier must meet a four part test: conduct himself in accordance with the laws of war, carry his weapon openly, wear readily visible insignia and belong to a chain of command. Of those four, the only relevant criterion to terrorism is a hierarchy that some terrorist organizations have created. Clearly, terrorists—in the main—do not carry their weapons openly (e.g., suicide bombers) nor wear readily distinguishable apparel that distinguishes them from the civilian population. Most importantly, terrorists deliberately target innocent civilians in a willful effort to advance their cause. Whereas soldiers are trained to distinguish between innocent civilians and combatants, terrorists do not distinguish between categories of potential targets. In essence, while soldiers are taught to kill but not to be killers, terrorists do not burden themselves with such hair splitting.

III. ISRAEL

Israel has historically applied a two-track approach to Palestinians suspected of having committed acts of terrorism. Following the June 1967 Six Day War, the Israel Defense Forces established military courts in the West Bank and the Gaza Strip for the purpose of trying Palestinians suspected of committing acts of terrorism.

Military judges are appointed by military commanders who have command responsibility over the West Bank and the Gaza Strip; military prosecutors are similarly appointed. Palestinians are represented before the courts by civilian defense attorneys, Palestinians and Israelis alike.

Palestinians brought before the Court are initially interrogated by the Israel Security Agency (ISA), and afterwards by the Israel police. The charge sheet, based either on the individual's confession or testimony of others, is submitted to the Court by the military prosecutor; the case is heard by a panel consisting of either one or three judges depending on the severity of the charges. The trial is conducted according to Rules of Criminal Procedure and Evidence akin to those in Israeli civilian courts. If convicted, the defendant may appeal to the Military Court of Appeals; the prosecution may appeal if the Court has acquitted the defendant.

The second track that Israel has implemented is administrative detention. Administrative detentions, unlike the criminal process, are not punitive. Rather, an individual is detained if available intelligence indicates the individual is involved in the preparation of a *future* attack and the information gathered cannot be made public both because of a need to protect the informant and the means used to gather the information. In such instances, a senior IDF Commander will sign an administrative detention order upon receipt of a recommendation from the ISA and a legal opinion from an IDF Legal Advisor. The legal opinion will analyze the intelligence information and attempt to gauge whether the High Court of Justice will deny a petition should the detainee file one.

Administrative detentions are codified in article 85 of the Defense Emergency Regulations Act (1945). The maximum detention period is for renewable six-month periods, subject to independent judicial review. There is no statutorily determined time period limiting the number of detentions. Renewability requires demonstrating the detainee continues to present a viable security threat. In the overwhelming majority of cases, the basis for extension of the initial detention order is the *same* intelligence that had served as the basis for the military commander's initial decision.

ISSUES TO CONSIDER

1. When does intelligence information become too far removed to justify continued detention?
2. How significant must the information be in order to justify both the initial detention and its extension?
3. How great of a threat must the individual continue to present for the information to still be valid?
4. From the state's perspective what are the advantages of administrative detention compared to criminal prosecution?
5. What is the significance of Israel's two-track approach in the context of determining the rights and status of the detainee?

Administrative detention has been heavily criticized[17] for a number of reasons. The criticism has primarily concentrated on two critical issues: the detainee's inability to confront his accuser and the resulting "fishing expedition" his lawyer is required to conduct. However, unlike the initial

---

17. *See, e.g.,* Orna Ben-Naftali & Sean S. Gleichgevitch, *Missing in Legal Action: Lebanese Hostages in Israel,* 41 Harv. Int'l L.J. 185 (2000), Eitan Barak, *With the Cover of Darkness: Ten Years of Games with Human Beings as "Bargaining Chips" and the Supreme Court,* 8 PLILIM 77, 80-81 (1999) (Heb.).

U.S. Military Commission mechanism established by the Presidential Order, the Military Commander's decision regarding the administrative detention of an individual is subject to independent judicial review by the High Court of Justice.[18]

A. TRIALS OF DETAINEES

Trials can take place in either of two different venues: civilian courts or IDF military courts distinct from a court martial, which only tries soldiers.

An overwhelming majority of Palestinians accused of terrorist acts are tried in the Military Court, even if the act was committed in Israel proper (pre-1967 borders). The primary reason for this is substantive: if the act was planned in the West Bank, the participants reside in the West Bank, and the terrorist activities occur primarily in the West Bank, Military Courts are deemed to have jurisdiction over the matter.

The judicial trial process is similar to the U.S. criminal system (there is no jury); to that end, the defendant is innocent until proven guilty, the state submits a charge sheet, and similar to courts in large U.S. cities, over 90 percent of defendants plead out.

Akin to the constitutionally guaranteed right to confront the accuser in the United States, secret intelligence information cannot be submitted to the court for purpose of conviction. However, it can be the basis for a suspect's initial detention and remand extension. In Israel, a suspect who has been arrested must be brought before a judge within 24 hours. In the West Bank, as amended in 1997, a Palestinian can be held for up to eight days without seeing a judge.[19]

ISSUES TO CONSIDER

1. Should there be a term limit for administrative detentions?
2. What is the appropriate process for determining what classified information should be made available to the detainee?
3. After an individual has been administratively detained, what should be the process for evaluating if the criminal law process can be utilized?
4. Does a two-track approach achieve the goals of protecting the state and guaranteeing basic rights to the detainee?
5. What are the advantages of defining the detainee as an enemy combatant as compared to a criminal?
6. What safeguards need to be institutionalized to ensure that the enemy combatant is guaranteed basic rights?

---

18. HCJ 5784/03, Salama v. IDF Commander in Judea and Samaria; HCJ 3239/02, Marab v. IDF Commander in the West Bank.

19. Military Order 378. In Israel, according to section 9.3.3 of the penal code a detainee must be brought before a judge with 24 hours.

B. APPLICATION

On April 14, 2002, the Israel Defense Forces arrested Marwan Barghouti in Ramallah. Barghouti, who was the head of the Tanzim, a militant wing of Arafat's Fatah organization in the West Bank, challenged the jurisdiction of the Court to try his case arguing:

1. The authority of the State of Israel to try Palestinians who attack Israelis was negated upon the signing of the Oslo Accords.
2. The rules of international law reject Israel's right to try the Defendant, since he is a freedom fighter opposing occupation. All forms of opposition have been defined as legitimate, including the use of violent force. If such a fighter is apprehended, he is to be defined as a prisoner of war and not as a criminal.
3. The Defendant was kidnapped from Ramallah by IDF soldiers contrary to the Oslo Accords and international law.
4. The Defendant holds immunity negating the right of the State of Israel to put him on trial.
5. The indictment is political and constitutes an indictment against the entire Palestinian people.[20]

Though Barghouti was a resident of the West Bank, a politically based decision was made to bring him to trial in an Israeli civilian court rather than in the West Bank Military Court. Barghouti was brought to trial before an Israeli civilian court; Judge Zvi Gurfinkel's holding is equally applicable either to a military or civilian court for it clearly articulates the status and rights of a detainee arrested and tried before a court of law in the context of "armed conflict short of war."

STATE OF ISRAEL V. MARWAN BARGHOUTI

Ruling by Judge Zvi Gurfinkel, Dec. 12, 2002
District Court of Tel Aviv and Jaffa Criminal Case No. 092134/02

The Defendant claims that he is to be considered a prisoner of war, and, accordingly, the Occupying Power is forbidden to prosecute him under criminal law.

The Defendant is not to be considered a prisoner of war.

Terrorists who attack a civilian population do not fall within the framework of "lawful combatants" entitled to the status of "prisoners of war," since they do not meet the conditions, in accordance with international law, that a lawful combatant is required to meet. The heads of the Palestinian terror organizations, of whom the Defendant is one, systematically violate the rules of war.

International law distinguishes between two groups of combatants who undertake hostile actions against the State of Israel.

---

20. State of Israel v. Marwan Barghouti, Ruling by Judge Zvi Gurfinkel, Dec. 12, 2002, *available at* http://www.mfa.gov.il/MFA/MFAArchive/2000_2009/2002/12/State%20of%20Israel%20vs%20Marwan%20Barghouti-%20Ruling%20by%20Jud (last visited Oct. 8, 2010).

The first group of elements that undertake hostile actions against the State comprises persons who are part of regular armies that engage in combative actions against the State of Israel in accordance with the rules of war.

Combatants who act within the framework of this group and are apprehended receive the status of prisoners of war. Prisoners of war are not prosecuted in accordance with criminal law for their participation in combative actions, provided that they acted in accordance with the rules of war. If, however, they acted contrary to the rules of war, they may be prosecuted on account of war crimes.

In order for a combatant to be recognized as prisoner of war, he must meet four cumulative conditions as established in the Third Geneva Convention of 1949 (Article 4(2)):

> The first condition is the presence of a commander responsible for his subordinates.
> The second condition is the presence of a fixed distinguishing sign that may be identified from a distance.
> The third condition is that combatants must carry their weapons openly.
> The fourth condition is that the actions undertaken must be in accordance with the rules and customs of law.

Regarding the Defendant, three of the four conditions are not met.

The field staff, commanders and perpetrators of actions did not bear a fixed distinguishing sign, and accordingly could not be identified from a distance.

The weapon they carried was not overt — on the contrary. The explosives were placed in belts carried by the perpetrators on their bodies, under their clothes, and the weapons were concealed until the moment when they were suddenly revealed at the place of the attack.

The acts of resistance were not managed in accordance with the rules of war, which prohibit injury to civilians; rather, the combat was directed against civilians, including women and children, passengers on buses, shoppers in markets, persons walking in the streets of the city, persons sitting in cafes and eating in restaurants, passengers in cars and pedestrians. None of these are actions that are undertaken by army combatants; these are acts of mass murder against civilians, women, men and children who are not engaged in combat and are not armed, on their way to schools, homes and places of work, while walking, eating or engaging in recreation.

The conditions established in international law in the above-mentioned Geneva Convention must be met cumulatively, and since three of the four conditions were not met, it must be determined that the Defendant is not a legal combatant, and accordingly is not a prisoner of war. Rather, he engaged in acts of murder against persons who are not party to combative actions, causing mass injury to civilians in their places of residence and gathering.

The second group of combatants identified by international law is referred to as "unlawful combatants." This group comprises the members of terrorist organizations and enemy forces that take part in acts of terror and hostility against Israelis and Israel, but who, in apprehension, are not entitled to the status of prisoners of war.

International law distinguishes, by way of a central and fundamental value, between combatants and civilians. One of the most important goals of the rules of war is to ensure that those injured during war shall be solely enemy combatants, while the civilian population shall be afforded protection and shall not be injured.

In order to implement this distinction, great importance is attached to the ability to distinguish between a combatant and a civilian during combat.

In his book, Dinstein notes that "if combatants can disappear within a civilian public, any civilian within that public will be considered a combatant and will suffer the consequences accruing therefrom." In his opinion, this is the central reason for the distinction between lawful combatants, who act in accordance with the rules of law, and unlawful combatants, who do not wear uniforms, or do not carry their weapon openly or who attack civilians. In so doing, they blur the distinction between combatant and civilian, and also endanger the population among whom they operate.

Accordingly, international law negates the right of unlawful combatants to enjoy the status of prisoners of war.

Regarding these combatants, Dinstein notes: "These unlawful combatants may be prosecuted and punished with the full severity of the law. The protection of the rules of law is denied to them, and accordingly they are subject to the usual criminal sanctions in national law. The unlawful combatant is prosecuted on account of a usual offense before the national court."

This distinction by international law between lawful and unlawful combatants is based on a very large number of documents, and in addition is anchored in international practice and employed by other armies around the world, such as the US army and the German army.

As stated above, the Defendant is an unlawful combatant and may be prosecuted under criminal law for deliberate injury to innocent civilians.

Moreover, even if we assume that the Defendant is a (lawful) combatant — and it is evident that he is not — the deliberate injury of innocent civilians is considered a violation of the rules of war in accordance with international law, and he may be prosecuted under criminal law for war crimes. The jurisdictional authority in such a case is granted to the state in whose territory the offense is committed.

In his book Dinstein further notes that in the case of an unlawful combatant who is also a war criminal, the apprehending power has the choice of prosecuting him for a normal criminal offense — murder, in the case of the Defendant — or for an offense relating to the violation of the rules of law, such as injury to civilians.

The Defendant attempts to seize on the Geneva Convention in order to argue that the State of Israel does not have the authority to try him as an unlawful combatant for the offenses of murder. However, consistent regard for the Geneva Convention reveals that a combatant is forbidden to attack civilian targets and civilians. Moreover, Article 48 of the Complementary Protocol of the Geneva Convention from 1949 states that constant caution must be undertaken when managing military operations in order to avoid injury to civilians.

The Defendant's actions, as well as the actions of the field commanders subordinate to him, and those actually executing the attacks, were undertaken against a civilian population within the territories of the State of Israel and within the territories of Judea and Samaria. The actions were perpetrated among a civilian population, which was used as a hiding place and as cover for planning, organizing and executing the acts of terror and killing.

The central objective of the actions of the Defendant and his subordinates is to injure and murder innocent Israeli citizens who are present in an area in which no combat is taking place. These are civilians who were pursuing an ordinary way of life, like any other person, in an area populated by an innocent civilian population that does not constitute a part of the array of combatants.

This policy of terror, the goal of which was to injure as many civilians as possible, is utterly prohibited under international law. The rules of law note the obligation to exercise maximum caution in order to prevent injury to civilians.

The Defendant's method of combat is, in the clearest possible manner, contrary to the most basic rules of law, and accordingly he is not entitled to enjoy the protections afforded under international law to combatants who act in accordance with the rules of war.

We have seen that there is no impediment in terms of the rules of law to the prosecution of the Defendant in accordance with criminal law in the State of Israel.

ISSUES TO CONSIDER

1. Does Judge Gurfinkel's holding articulate the most effective judicial regime for balancing the rights of the individual with the legitimate rights of the state?
2. Does Judge Gurfinkel's opinion suggest any restrictions or limitations on a detainee's rights in the context of a judicial process?
3. How does Judge Gurfinkel's opinion compare with Justice O'Connor's in *Hamdi?*
4. Does Judge Gurfinkel adequately and sufficiently address Barghouti's rights?
5. In comparing and contrasting the judicial regimes available in Israel, does the court adequately protect the defendant's rights?

The Israeli two-track approach—criminal trials and administrative detentions—is subject to robust judicial review. In determining which option is appropriate for a particular detainee, judicial oversight exercised by the High Court of Justice is a significant factor in the executive's decision-making process. The two-tiered approach is intended to protect a number of different constituencies: the defendant, the public, and the intelligence source.

IV. RUSSIA

In analyzing what paradigm Russia implements, two questions are relevant: how is the conflict defined and how does that definition impact public debate and legislation? While the Constitutional Court in the Constitutionality of the Presidential Decrees and the Resolutions of the Federal Government concerning the Situation in Chechnya,[21] never expressly used the term "non-international armed conflict," it did state that Geneva Convention Additional Protocol II should have been applied by the parties.[22]

According to a U.S. State Department report in 2003:

> Russia passed several new antiterrorism laws, began implementing previously passed legislation, and facilitated effective interdiction of terrorist finance flows by becoming a full member of the Financial Action Task Force (FATF). In February, the Russian Supreme Court issued an official government list of 15 terrorist organizations, the first of its kind in Russia and an important step toward implementation of counterterrorism statutes. Following the promulgation of the list, the 15 organizations were prohibited from engaging in any financial activities.[23]

Nevertheless, according to the Russian penal code, terrorists are considered criminals, subject to a specific category within the criminal justice system.

> The Russian Criminal Code categorizes the following offenses as criminal: terrorism, hostage-taking, hijacking of an aircraft, sea vessel, or train, organization of an illegal armed unit, attempts on the life of a State or public figure, and attacks on person or agencies enjoying international protection.
>
> The Code provides that serious criminal offences are pre-meditated actions for which the maximum punishment does not exceed 10 years, imprisonment. Particularly serious pre-meditated actions carry a maximum punishment of ten years' imprisonment or more. The Russian Criminal Code states that the punishment for "terrorism" is imprisonment for a period of from 5 to 10 years, for a period of from 8 to 15 years in cases with aggravating circumstances and for a period of from 10 to 20 years in cases with especially aggravating circumstances.
>
> Russian legislation establishes increased liability for recruiting and training of terrorists and the financing of terrorist activities and organizations. Pursuant to the Criminal Code of the Russian Federation, persons who recruit, train or finance terrorists may be considered accessories to a criminal offence and prosecuted. Inducing a person to commit a terrorist offence (by recruiting the person) constitutes incitement and the perpetrator is held liable under the Criminal Code. If a person has facilitated the commission of a terrorist offence by means of advice, directions, the provision of information, that person may be considered an accomplice to the offence. The liability of such a person is stipulated in the relevant article of the special section of the Criminal Code.[24]

21. Judgment of the Constitutional Court of the Russian Federation of July 31, 1995 on the Constitutionality of the Presidential Decrees and the Resolutions of the Federal Government concerning the Situation in Chechnya.

22. Sobraniye Zakonodatelstva Rossiyskoy Federatsii # 33, Art.3424, 14 August 1995; Bakhtiyar Tuzmukhamedov, *Chechnya and the Laws of War*, Crimes of War, Oct. 1999, http://www.crimesofwar.org/expert/chech-tuzmuk.html (last visited Oct. 8, 2010).

23. *Available at* http://www.globalsecurity.org/security/library/report/2004/pgt_2003/pgt_2003_31621pf.htm.

24. National Laws and Measures for Counter-Terrorism and Regulation of Biology, Depaul University, College of Law, *available at* http://www.law.depaul.edu/centers_Institutes/ihrli/downloads/managing_terrorisms_consequences.pdf (last visited Oct. 8, 2010).

A Chechen, Islan Mukaev, was sentenced in a Daghestan Court to a 25-year prison term for allegedly participating in the execution of six captured Russian soldiers. In May 2005, one of the participants in the Beslan school massacre was prosecuted in Vladikavkaz, the North Ossetian capital. The defendant, Nur-Pashi Kulayev, was charged with nine crimes, including terrorism, murder, and banditry. According to press accounts, one of his two attorneys had only been practicing law for two weeks prior to being appointed by the State.[25]

> Prosecutors Gnl Nikolai Shepel and Maria Semisynova sought life imprisonment on behalf of 1343 plaintiffs. The trial judge is Tamerlan Aguzarov, and Kulayev is defended by Umar Sikoyev and Albert Pliyev, the latter of which had only practised law for 2 weeks prior to being appointed by the state. His defence lies in the claim that he was one of the recruited Chechnyans who were told they would be attacking a military checkpoint, and had no foreknowledge their target was the Beslan school; he was reportedly among several of the militants who argued in favour of capturing the local Beslan police station instead. While no witnesses have claimed he shot any of the victims, several have testified that he ran around the gymnasium shouting curses and threatening to shoot various hostages with his assault rifle — though Kulayev testifies that he was only given the firearm to carry because his leaders didn't want any of their weapons left lying around where hostages could seize them.
>
> He has testified that Polkovnik smashed his cellphone in rage, stating that Russian forces were unwilling to negotiate, and that the bloodbath started when Russian snipers killed two hostage-takers that were carrying detonators for the explosives strung around the gymnasium. Polkovnik then shot three of the militants including the two female suicide bombers who had objected to the scholastic target, detonating their bombs. Nur-Pashi was supposed to be shot himself, by his brother Khan on orders from Polkovnik, but Khan refused.[26]

In June 2004, the Federation Council approved amendments to the Criminal Code that established maximum sentences for terrorism-related crimes. There was an unsuccessful attempt to change the punishment system after Beslan: in January 2005, the State Duma rejected amendments enabling punishment of terrorists' relatives.

ISSUES TO CONSIDER

1. Is the criminalization of terrorism the appropriate response to the Chechen conflict?
2. Do criminal courts offer the most effective response to terrorists committing acts such as those committed at Beslan and the Moscow opera?
3. Would the Israeli two-track approach be applicable to Russia?

---

25. Douglas Birch, *Admitted Militant Goes on Trial in Russian School Hostage Case,* The Baltimore Sun, at 10A (May 18, 2005).

26. http://en.wikipedia.org/wiki/Nur-Pashi_Kulayev.

Implementation of methods extending beyond the criminal law paradigm suggests recognition that the traditional approach is ineffective. The United States, post-9/11, instituted the military commissions as an alternative paradigm that was widely criticized; the Israeli approach—particularly administrative detention policy—is considered a serious violation of detainee's rights because the right to confront the accuser is denied.

In spite of particularly violent terrorist attacks, the Russian approach has been to consistently categorize terrorists as criminals rather than as "enemy combatants." In spite of this, it has been documented Russian forces have *not* treated Chechen terrorists as criminals in the zone of combat.[27] Accordingly, the question of whether Russia considers Chechens engaged in combat with Russian forces criminals, enemy combatants, or terrorists requires a multiple response.

Once caught, a Chechen fighter is brought to trial similar to a traditional criminal and is subject to the relevant sections of the Russian penal code. As described above, the criminal law process includes a prosecutor, defense attorney, judge, and the right to confront the accuser.

However, unlike criminal defendants suspected of having committed a serious crime, Chechen terrorists are subjected to human rights violations in combat. The Russian approach is similar to the American and Israeli approach of engaging terrorism in the zone of combat. However, it is dissimilar from the American approach, as articulated by the military commissions, in that the terrorist defendant is provided a full criminal process that more closely resembles the Israeli criminal law approach, as distinct from the administrative detention model.

UNITED DEPARTMENT OF STATE: 2009 HUMAN RIGHTS REPORT: RUSSIA

Burueau of Democracy, Human Rights, and Labor, Mar. 11, 2009[28]

Trial Procedures

Trials typically are conducted before a judge without a jury (bench trials). The defendant is presumed innocent. The defense is not required to present evidence and is given an opportunity to cross-examine witnesses and call defense witnesses. Defendants who are in custody during the trial are confined to a caged area and must consult with their attorneys through the bars. Defendants have the right of appeal.

---

27. *See Worse Than a War*, Human Rights Watch Backgrounders, March 2005, *available at* http://hrw.org/backgrounder/eca/chechnya0305/ (last visited Oct. 8, 2010); *Russia*, Human Rights Watch, Human Rights Overview, Jan. 2006, *available at* http://hrw.org/wr2k6/pdf/russia.pdf (last visited Oct. 8, 2010); *Briefing—Torture, "Disappearances" and Alleged Unfair Trials in Russia's North Caucasus*, Amnesty International, Sept. 30, 2005, *available at* http://web.amnesty.org/library/index/engeur460392005 (last visited Oct. 8, 2010); *Violations Continue, No Justice in Sight*, Amnesty International, July 1, 2005, *available at* http://web.amnesty.org/library/index/engeur460292005 (last visited Oct. 8, 2010).

28. *Available at* http://www.state.gov/g/drl/rls/hrrpt/2009/eur/136054.htm (last vistited Jan. 7, 2011).

The law provides for the use of jury trials for a limited category of "especially grave" crimes, such as murder, in higher-level regional courts.

During the year the ECHR on multiple occasions found the country in violation of provisions of the European Convention on Human Rights with regard to trial procedures. In 2008, the latest year for which statistics were available, the court found 159 violations by the country involving the right to a fair trial and 20 violations involving proceedings that exceeded a "reasonable" length of time.

There has been a trend to further limit the use of jury trials. In December 2008 the State Duma enacted, and the president signed, a law providing that certain crimes, including terrorism, espionage, hostage taking, and mass disorder, would be heard by panels of three judges rather than by juries. Supporters of the legislation justified it on the grounds of the war on terrorism and juries' alleged incompetence to judge cases involving terrorism, espionage, and state security. They also alleged that clan relations in the North Caucasus made it impossible to empanel objective juries there. Although the competence of jury trial participants, including advocates for both parties and to some extent judges, remained a serious concern to domestic and international observers, critics described the legislation as a violation of the constitution and a major step backwards in the protection of individual liberties.

No further action was taken during the year on a draft law introduced in the State Duma in December 2008 that would substantially expand the definitions of espionage and treason. The draft law caused serious concern among some lawyers, human rights activists, and government officials who claimed that, if enacted, the law would provide virtually unfettered discretion to security forces to charge almost anyone who had any contact with foreign governments or international organizations or persons with treason. In February, after consulting with the newly reconstituted Presidential Council on Human Rights, President Medvedev announced that the draft law would be revised to reflect these concerns. The law had not been discussed further by year's end.

Issues to Consider

1. Does the Russian mixed approach suggest that in reality the Chechen fighter is considered an enemy combatant?
2. What is the significance/benefit to the state of a mixed approach?
3. If the terrorist can be engaged in combat and similarly be subject to a full criminal trial, is it accurate to describe him as a criminal?
4. Would the establishment of military tribunals, such as Guantanamo, improve Russia's counterterrorism efforts?
5. Does the terrorist benefit from the criminal law process and the guaranteeing of rights that are not incorporated in the enemy combatant paradigm?
6. Does an avowed policy of defeating terrorism suggest that the enemy is defined as an enemy combatant and not as a criminal?

V. INDIA

For most of its history, India has applied the criminal law paradigm rather than developing or implementing an enemy combatant paradigm.

On March 26, 2002, however, the Indian parliament passed the Prevention of Terrorism Act (POTA). POTA, which replaced the Terrorist and Disruptive Activities (Prevention) Act (TADA), articulated a new Indian approach regarding the terrorist paradigm. The question is whether the Special Terror Courts established by POTA were an attempt to develop a hybrid system similar to Israel's administrative detention or akin to U.S. policy post-9/11.

THE PREVENTION OF TERRORISM ACT, 2002

March 28, 2002, Act No. 15 of 2002, Chapter 4[29]

The POTA Special Courts

(1) The Central Government or a State Government may, by notification in the Official Gazette, constitute one or more Special Courts for such area or areas, or for such case or class or group of cases, as may be specified in the notification.

(2) Where a notification constituting a Special Court for any area or areas or for any case or class or group of cases is issued by the Central Government under sub-section (1), and a notification constituting a Special Court for the same area or areas or for the same case or class or group of cases has also been issued by the State Government under that sub-section, the Special Court constituted by the Central Government, whether the notification constituting such Court is issued before or after the issue of the notification constituting the Special Court by the State Government, shall have, and the Special Court constituted by the State Government shall not have, jurisdiction to try any offence committed in that area or areas or, as the case may be, the case or class or group of cases and all cases pending before any Special Court constituted by the State Government shall stand transferred to the Special Court constituted by the Central Government.

(3) Where any question arises as to the jurisdiction of any Special Court, it shall be referred to the Central Government whose decision in the matter shall be final.

(4) A Special Court shall be presided over by a judge to be appointed by the Central Government or, as the case may be, the State Government, with the concurrence of the Chief Justice of the High Court.

(5) The Central Government or, as the case may be, the State Government may also appoint, with the concurrence of the Chief Justice of the High Court, additional judges to exercise jurisdiction of a Special Court.

---

29. *Available at* http://www.satp.org/satporgtp/countries/india/document/actandordinances/POTA.htm#4 (last visited Apr. 4, 2010).

(6) A person shall not be qualified for appointment as a judge or an additional judge of a Special Court unless he is, immediately before such appointment, a sessions judge or an additional sessions judge in any State.

(7) For the removal of doubts, it is hereby provided that the attainment, by a person appointed as a judge or an additional judge of a Special Court, of the age of superannuation under the rules applicable to him in the service to which he belongs, shall not affect his continuance as such judge or additional judge.

(8) Where any additional judge or additional judges is or are appointed in a Special Court, the judge of the Special Court may, from time to time, by general or special order, in writing, provide for the distribution of business of the Special Court among all judges including himself and the additional judge or additional judges and also for the disposal of urgent business in the event of his absence or the absence of any additional judge. . . .

25. Jurisdiction of Special Courts

(1) Notwithstanding anything contained in the Code, every offence punishable under any provision of this Act shall be triable only by the Special Court within whose local jurisdiction it was committed or, as the case may be, by the Special Court constituted for trying such offence under section 23.

(2) If, having regard to the exigencies of the situation prevailing in a State, —

(a) it is not possible to have a fair, impartial or speedy trial; or

(b) it is not feasible to have the trial without occasioning the breach of peace or grave risk to the safety of the accused, the witnesses, the Public Prosecutor and a judge of the Special Court or any of them; or

(c) it is not otherwise in the interests of justice, the Supreme Court may transfer any case pending before a Special Court to any other Special Court within that State or in any other State and the High Court may transfer any case pending before a Special Court situated in that State to any other Special Court within the State.

(3) The Supreme Court or the High Court, as the case may be, may act under this section either on the application of the Central Government or a party interested and any such application shall be made by motion, which shall, except when the applicant is the Attorney-General of India, be supported by an affidavit or affirmation.

26. Power of Special Courts with Respect to Other Offences

(1) When trying any offence, a Special Court may also try any other offence with which the accused may, under the Code, be charged at the same trial if the offence is connected with such other offence.

(2) If, in the course of any trial under this Act of any offence, it is found that the accused person has committed any other offence under this Act or under any other law, the Special Court may convict such person of such other offence and pass any sentence or award punishment authorised by this Act or such rule or, as the case may be, under such other law.

27. Power to Direct for Samples, etc.

(1) When a police officer investigating a case requests the Court of a Chief Judicial Magistrate or the Court of a Chief Metropolitan Magistrate in writing for obtaining samples of handwriting, finger-prints, foot-prints, photographs, blood, saliva, semen, hair, voice of any accused person, reasonably suspected to be involved in the commission of an offence under this Act, it shall be lawful for the Court of a Chief Judicial Magistrate or the Court of a Chief Metropolitan Magistrate to direct that such samples be given by the accused person to the police officer either through a medical practitioner or otherwise, as the case may be.

(2) If any accused person refuses to give samples as provided in sub-section (1), the Court shall draw adverse inference against the accused. . . .

29. Procedure and Powers of Special Courts

(1) Subject to the provisions of section 50, a Special Court may take cognizance of any offence, without the accused being committed to it for trial, upon receiving a complaint of facts that constitute such offence or upon a police report of such facts.

(2) Where an offence triable by a Special Court is punishable with imprisonment for a term not exceeding three years or with fine or with both, the Special Court may, notwithstanding anything contained in sub-section (1) of section 260 or section 262 of the Code, try the offence in a summary way in accordance with the procedure prescribed in the Code and the provisions of sections 263 to 265 of the Code, shall so far as may be, apply to such trial:

Provided that when, in the course of a summary trial under this sub-section, it appears to the Special Court that the nature of the case is such that it is undesirable to try it in a summary way, the Special Court shall recall any witnesses who may have been examined and proceed to re-hear the case in the manner provided by the provisions of the Code for the trial of such offence and the said provisions shall apply to and in relation to a Special Court as they apply to and in relation to a Magistrate:

Provided further that in the case of any conviction in a summary trial under this section, it shall be lawful for a Special Court to pass a sentence of imprisonment for a term not exceeding one year and with fine which may extend to rupees five lakh.

(3) Subject to the other provisions of this Act, a Special Court shall, for the purpose of trial of any offence, have all the powers of a Court of Session and shall try such offence as if it were a Court of Session so far as may be in accordance with the procedure prescribed in the Code for the trial before a Court of Session.

(4) Subject to the other provisions of this Act, every case transferred to a Special Court under section 25 shall be dealt with as if such case had been transferred under section 406 of the Code to such Special Court.

(5) Notwithstanding anything contained in the Code, but subject to the provisions of section 299 of the Code, a Special Court may, if it thinks fit and for reasons to be recorded by it, proceed with the trial in the absence of the accused or his pleader and record the evidence of any witness, subject to the right of the accused to recall the witness for cross-examination. . . .

31. Trial by Special Courts to Have Precedence

The trial under this Act of any offence by a Special Court shall have precedence over the trial of any other case against the accused in any other court (not being a Special Court) and shall be concluded in preference to the trial of such other case and accordingly the trial of such other case shall remain in abeyance.

32. Certain Confessions Made to Police Officers to Be Taken into Consideration

(1) Notwithstanding anything in the Code or in the Indian Evidence Act, 1872 (1 of 1872), but subject to the provisions of this section, a confession made by a person before a police officer not lower in rank than a Superintendent of Police and recorded by such police officer either in writing or on any mechanical or electronic device like cassettes, tapes or sound tracks from out of which sound or images can be reproduced, shall be admissible in the trial of such person for an offence under this Act or the rules made thereunder.

(2) A police officer shall, before recording any confession made by a person under sub-section (1), explain to such person in writing that he is not bound to make a confession and that if he does so, it may be used against him: Provided that where such person prefers to remain silent, the police officer shall not compel or induce him to make any confession.

(3) The confession shall be recorded in an atmosphere free from threat or inducement and shall be in the same language in which the person makes it.

(4) The person from whom a confession has been recorded under sub-section (1), shall be produced before the Court of a Chief Metropolitan Magistrate or the Court of a Chief Judicial Magistrate along with the original statement of confession, written or recorded on mechanical or electronic device within forty-eight hours.

(5) The Chief Metropolitan Magistrate or the Chief Judicial Magistrate, shall, record the statement, if any, made by the person so produced and get his signature or thumb impression and if there is any complaint of torture, such person shall be directed to be produced for medical examination before a Medical Officer not lower in rank than an Assistant Civil Surgeon and thereafter, he shall be sent to judicial custody.

33. Power to Transfer Cases to Regular Courts

Where, after taking cognizance of any offence, a Special Court is of the opinion that the offence is not triable by it, it shall, notwithstanding that it has no jurisdiction to try such offence, transfer the case for the trial of such offence to any court having jurisdiction under the Code and the Court to which the case is transferred may proceed with the trial of the offence as if it had taken cognizance of the offence.

34. Appeal

(1) Notwithstanding anything contained in the Code, an appeal shall lie from any judgment, sentence or order, not being an interlocutory order, of a Special Court to the High Court both on facts and on law.

Explanation. — For the purposes of this section, "High Court" means a High Court within whose jurisdiction, a Special Court which passed the judgment, sentence or order, is situated.

(2) Every appeal under sub-section (1) shall be heard by a bench of two Judges of the High Court.

(3) Except as aforesaid, no appeal or revision shall lie to any court from any judgment, sentence or order including an interlocutory order of a Special Court.

(4) Notwithstanding anything contained in sub-section (3) of section 378 of the Code, an appeal shall lie to the High Court against an order of the Special Court granting or refusing bail.

(5) Every appeal under this section shall be preferred within a period of thirty days from the date of the judgment, sentence or order appealed from: Provided that the High Court may entertain an appeal after the expiry of the said period of thirty days if it is satisfied that the appellant had sufficient cause for not preferring the appeal within the period of thirty days.

POTA was heavily criticized. On September 17, 2004, it was announced that the Act would be repealed.[30]

SACHIN MEHTA, REPEAL OF POTA — JUSTIFIED

LegalServiceIndia.com[31]

The developments after the enactment of the POTA, including the responses received by the POTA review committee show that the POTA is worse then TADA. POTA provides for criminal liability for mere association or communication with suspected terrorists without the possession of criminal intent (Section 3(5) of the POTA). Section 4 of POTA is similar to Section 5 of TADA in laying out a legal presumption that if a person is found in unauthorized possession of arms in a notified area, he/she is automatically linked with terrorist activity. Section 48(2) provides for the option of pre-trial police detention for up to 180 days. As under the TADA, where 98% of the cases never reached the trial stage, this Section 48(2) could also be misused by the police by keeping an accused for long periods of detention without charge or trial. Special courts for trials are established under POTA which are given the discretion to hold trials in non-public places, like prisons, and to withhold trial records from public scrutiny, thus preventing the independent monitoring of special court sessions. Section 32 provides that confessions made to police officers are to be admissible in trial, which has increased the possibility of coercion and torture in securing confessions.

The provisions contained under the POTA were mostly contained in existing laws, except those, which were contained in the Criminal Procedure Code, the Indian Penal Code, the Evidence Act or the Constitution of India. The Act

---

30. Human Rights Watch: Human Rights News, *India: POTA Repeal a Step Forward for Human Rights: Government Should Dismiss All POTA Cases* (Sept. 22, 2004), *available at* http://hrw.org/english/docs/2004/09/22/india9370.htm (last visited Oct. 8, 2010).

31. *Available at* http://www.legalservicesindia.com/articles/pota.htm (last visited Oct. 8, 2010).

effectively undermines the fundamental tenet of the criminal justice system by putting the burden of proof on the accused. But the Act also had some provisions, which were not attacked for being against human rights. These provisions stated that Confessions must be recorded within 48 hours before a magistrate, who will send the accused for a medical examination if there is a complaint of torture. Further a legal representative of the accused can be present for part of the interrogation. Moreover police officers can be prosecuted for abusing their authority. The POTA also provided that victims could be paid compensation.

In addition, fault was found with POTA for discarding "the fundamental right of [the] accused to due process and [a] presumption of innocence. Persons arrested under POTA could be held for 30 days before authorities had to produce them in a special court of law."[32] POTA also allowed for the admission of evidence that would otherwise not be allowed in a criminal trial.

The Supreme Court has convicted and sentenced to life three Jamait-ul-Mujahidin militants, including Ashiq Hussain Faktoo, who were acquitted by a Jammu TADA court of the charge of killing human rights activist H.N Wanchoo in 1992. Allowing an appeal filed by the CBI against their acquittal, a Bench of Mr. Justice S.N. Variva and Mr. Justice B.N. Agrawal took a diametrically opposite view on the admissibility of the evidence in the case based solely on the confessional statements of the three militants recorded under Section 15 of TADA. The TADA court had rejected the evidence on four counts. Firstly, the police official concerned did not ask the accused whether they were making the confessional statements voluntarily. Secondly, the CBI SP did not tell the accused that the confessional statement could be used against them as evidence. Thirdly, the statements were recorded in Hindi which was not the official language of the court and lastly, the SP did not ask the accused whether they wanted to add or subtract anything from their confessional statements. After going through the confessional statements of the three accused, the Supreme Court was of the opinion that all procedures, which the TADA court thought were not followed, were actually scrupulously followed.[33]

ISSUES TO CONSIDER

1. Do the multiple threats faced by India lend themselves to the adoption of the criminal law model?
2. Would the implementation of either the American or Israeli dual approach satisfactorily protect the rights of Indian detainees?
3. What policy considerations justify adopting a judicial regime that minimizes detainee rights?

---

32. Kranti Kumara, *Repeal of India's Draconian Anti-Terrorism Law*, Nov. 27, 2004, *available at* http://www.wsws.org/articles/2004/nov2004/ind-n27.shtml (last visited Oct. 8, 2010).

33. *3 JuM Ultras Get Life Term for Murder*, The Tribune (Chandigarh, India), Feb. 3, 2003, *available at* http://www.tribuneindia.com/2003/20030203/nation.htm#4 (last visited Oct. 8, 2010).

The Russian approach perhaps most closely resembles the Indian approach — the detained terrorist is defined as a criminal and once in custody is guaranteed full rights in accordance with the criminal law paradigm.

POTA's repeal suggests that the Indian government responded to international criticism of draconian powers granted to state authorities. These powers enabled the state to implement measures extending beyond the traditional criminal law paradigm. The measures were reflective of a hybrid system that included aspects of the criminal law paradigm incorporating special measures directly affecting the rights of the individual detainee. The hybrid paradigm implemented by India for a short period of time has, in essence, been replaced by the traditional criminal law paradigm.

Whether India will maintain the criminal law paradigm is unclear. For example, after the Mumbai train bombing of 2006, 19 suspects were brought to trial before a special court, rather than regularly constituted courts.

Issues to Consider

1. Do special courts suggest that the defendant is more of an enemy combatant than a criminal defendant?
2. Are special courts sufficiently able to ensure the rights of a criminal defendant?
3. Does the convening of a special court suggest the adoption of an Israeli or American dual-track approach, or an alternative model?
4. Does a special court suggest a speedier trial at the expense of judicial caution and detainee rights?
5. What rights will be most susceptible to violations if a regular criminal law court does not hear the trial?

VI. SPAIN

Spain views terrorism as a criminal matter whereby terrorists are tried in courts of law established in accordance with the Spanish penal code. In addition, "(U)nder Spanish law, terrorism is classified as a crime that can be prosecuted even if it is alleged to have been committed in another country."[34]

DR. MARÍA TERESA FERNÁNDEZ SÁNCHEZ,
FACULDAD DE DERECHO, WORLD LAW: SPAIN

Universidad de Salamanca, Feb. 15, 2001[35]

Crimes of terrorism are outlined in the second section of the Spanish Penal Code, (Chapter V, Title XII, Book II). Title XII explicitly refers to crimes against

---

34. Chris Johnston, *9/11 Terror Suspects on Trial in Spain*, Times Online, Apr. 22, 2005, *available at* http://www.timesonline.co.uk/article/0,,3-1580871,00.html (last visited July 20, 2010).

35. *Available at* http://jurist.law.pitt.edu/world/spaincor3.htm (last visited Apr. 4, 2010).

the "public order," however a clear definition of this concept of "public order" is not included in the Code itself. "Public order" is generally understood as the normal working of public and private institutions, and thought to be about maintaining the internal peace and free development of the fundamental rights and freedoms of citizens. In fact, "public order" consists of maintaining the conditions essential for social coexistence in a peaceful environment, while remaining within the democratic framework established by the Spanish Constitution.

Articles 571 of the Penal Code defines the objective elements of the crimes of terrorism, including arson and destruction. These actions appear separately in another part of the Penal Code; they are considered as crimes of terrorism only when other elements are present. Those additional elements are that the author of the crime must belong to, act in the name of, or collaborate with armed bands, organizations or groups whose goal is to disturb the constitutional order or the public peace.

Art. 572 of the Spanish Penal Code penalizes any individual who acts against the life, health or freedom of any person when the author of the crime is linked with an armed or terrorist organization. This requirement is essential as well in the regulation accompanying art. 574—a residue regulation that penalizes any crime that is not described expressly in the Penal Code but which has the same conditions and the same goals as the rest of the crimes of terrorism.

It is important to realize that when speaking about belonging to, acting in the name of, or collaborating with an armed or terrorist group it is understood that a direct relationship has to exist between the author of the crime and the armed group or terrorist organization. The Spanish Supreme Court recognizes an "armed group" as an association concentrating on armed action from which permanent links are born. Hierarchy and discipline are important to armed groups, whose actions are usually numerous and unpredictable, and who attack with suitable instruments of violence provided by their criminal organization (STS, 2nd hall, 25-1 and 27-5-1988).

When the criminal act causes the death of a person, the sanctions outlined in the Penal Code for crimes of terrorism can reach a maximum of 30 years of prison. For terrorist acts consisting of arson and destruction, the sanctions range from 15 to 20 years in prison. When a person is seriously injured, the sanction is also 15 to 20 years. When an injury is minor, or the actor who belongs to the armed group threatens, coerces or illegally detains another person, the sanction ranges from 10 to 15 years of prison. These prison terms can be even longer if the terrorist actions are directed against government officials, including: The local, regional or national Government; The regional or national Parliament; The Consejo General del Poder Judicial or the Supreme Court; and The Army, State Security Forces, and regional and local police.

The Spanish legislature also penalizes other sorts of terrorist actions, as illustrated in Penal Code art. 573. A group may be penalized if they maintain an arsenal of weapons, munitions, and substances or devices which are explosive, inflammable, incendiary or asphyxiating (including components of any of these weapons). Along with using or placing these elements, actors are also penalized for manufacturing, dealing, transporting, or providing of any these substances, instruments or devices. The sanction for any of these actions is a prison term extending from 6 to 10 years. Art. 573 also provides that the actors must belong to an armed group or terrorist organization.

The legislature has additionally realized that a terrorist group cannot act without a good infrastructure and, above all, without substantial economic resources. Therefore "crimes of terrorism" include attempts to steal property with the goal of obtaining funds to aid terrorist groups. This crime is described in art. 575 of the Penal Code, in which the legislature describes the sanctions for crimes against property. Sanctions for crimes against property are increased when the crime is classified as a crime of terrorism.

The legislature has also anticipated the "crime of collaborating with an armed group" (art. 576 Penal Code). A "crime of collaboration with an armed group" generally means every act of surveillance over persons, goods or installations. Also included are: To construct, arrange, use or cease logging or depots; To hide or transport persons who have a link with the armed group or terrorist organization; To organise or assist in training; and, in general, any other method of collaboration, help or cooperation with these groups and with their activities. The crime of collaboration with an armed group carries a penalty of 5 to 10 years in prison and includes fines. This sanction can be increased when the collaboration risks the life, health, freedom or property of the affected persons, and should their actions result in an actual injury, the law classifies the persons who collaborate as authors of the crime.

Article 577 of the Penal Code, concerning acts designed to disturb the constitutional order and the public peace, is somewhat peculiar. The perpetrator of such acts does not necessarily have to act as a member of an armed group or a terrorist organization. In fact, if one person commits a crime (such as homicide, personal injury, destruction, arson, illegal detention, threats, coercion, or maintaining an arsenal) but doesn't belong to an armed or terrorist group, he or she will be punished not as a terrorist but with the standard sanction for these crimes. However, the higher penalty will be increased by one-half because of the goal of the perpetrator, bringing it closer to the sanction imposed for crimes of terrorism.

The Spanish Penal Code penalizes preparatory acts — such as provocation, conspiracy and proposition — only in exceptional cases. These exceptional cases may be found in art. 578, where the preparatory acts are sanctioned when the perpetrator prepares to commit crimes of terrorism as defined in the Spanish Penal Code. The sanction is minor compared to the rest of the sanctions for a crime of terrorism. There is one special preparatory act: the apology. It consists of either directly addressing a large group of persons, or by using a subversive medium that includes ideas or doctrines that exalt the crime and its author. It has proven very difficult to apply this law in an actual case.

In art. 579 of the Spanish Penal Code, the legislature gives Judges and Courts the discretion to reduce the sanction for any of the crimes of terrorism. This exceptional treatment is conditioned upon the terrorist voluntarily giving up his criminal activities and presenting himself to the authorities to confess his crimes. Furthermore, he has to collaborate with the authorities to impede new crime and to assist them in obtaining evidence used to capture other criminals, as well as to hinder the development of armed or terrorist groups with whom he was affiliated.

Finally, as a response to the aggravating history of backsliding in enforcement of the previous Spanish Penal Code, the legislature has taken preventative measures: art. 580 of the Penal Code provides that the rulings and convictions handed down by a foreign Judge or Court in relation to crimes of terrorism will be considered equal to the conviction dictated by a Spanish Judge or Court and duly enforced.

Cándido Conde-Pumpido Tourón, Justice of the Supreme Court of Spain clearly articulates the Spanish approach; terrorists are criminals and the existing Spanish criminal justice system is the appropriate judicial regime for bringing terrorists to justice.

Cándido Conde-Pumpido Tourón, Judicial Response to Terrorism: National Venues, The Spanish Model

10th International Judicial Conference in Strasbourg from 23 to 24 May[36]

. . . Terrorism does not constitute a form of war in the strictest sense, but rather a form of crime, whilst possessing specific characteristics which set it apart from ordinary crime. As political insurrections or coups d'etats, it is a threat to society: its intention is to change the existing political situation through violence. It is the terrorists who present their crimes as methods of war, whilst directing their attacks against civilian victims. It is the role of democratic governments, in their fight against terrorism, to decide whether they can accept this claim or whether they prefer to treat terrorists as perpetrators of a specific kind of crime.

In Spain, the fight against terrorism is not undertaken in a bellicose way, but as a specific chapter in the fight against crime, independent of the political problems it poses and which cannot be left to one side. This is why criminal law and the courts are essential instruments in the fight against terrorism.

2. In our country, an indictment on terrorist offences comes under the jurisdiction of the Assize Court, called the Audiencia Nacional, a specialised body of jurisdiction, based in Madrid, whose jurisdiction covers all offences committed throughout the whole of the national territory. It is an ordinary court, a civil tribunal made up of professional judges, members of the judiciary, appointed by the Judicial Service Commission in compliance with predetermined legal criteria, who are irremovable and answerable only to the law. The tribunal is independent from the executive and, hence, the government exerts no influence upon it whatsoever. In no circumstances are such prosecutions left to ordinary juries, given the risks involved.

---

36. *Available at* http://www.coe.int/T/E/Com/Files/Ministerial-Conferences/2002-judicial/Panel1_C%C3%A1ndidoCondePumpidoTour%C3%B3n.asp (last visited July 20, 2010).

There are fundamentally three advantages of this specific jurisdiction: (1) centralisation, the criteria can thus be unified and some distance be taken from the place of the conflict; (2) specialisation, enabling a more in-depth knowledge of the problems surrounding the prosecution of terrorist acts and improving efficacy and (3) security, which can be stepped up as protection is concentrated around one single site and a limited number of judges.

The judicial investigation of terrorist trials is carried out by the central investigative tribunals which are also specialised bodies based in Madrid with jurisdiction over the whole of Spain. They are responsible for directing and supervising the police investigation, gathering evidence in preparation for the judgment and authorising methods to counterterrorism which may restrict fundamental freedoms such as, for example, searches of places of residence and telephone tapping.

The judicial investigation also enjoys a clear advantage compared to other regimes: depositions, made with every guarantee of confidentiality before the judge and in the presence of the defence lawyers, can be used as evidence for the judgment in cases where the witnesses are unable to appear in court as they have died, are abroad or in an unknown location, as quite frequently happens in complex trials dealing with terrorism or organised crime.

The decision handed down by the tribunal of the Audencia Nacional is subject to appeal in the Supreme Court in the same conditions as any other ruling, whereas appeals on points of law come under the criminal chamber, of which I am a member, with no specialisation.

3. The procedural rules are basically the same as in ordinary prosecutions, respecting the guarantee of the right to a defence and the principle of the presumption off innocence. The rules of evidence are identical.

Until 1988, there was special legislation in place but since then (LO 4/1988 of 25 May), matters linked to terrorism are dealt with by the Penal Code and the ordinary Criminal Procedural Code. This does not imply that we are no longer according terrorism the special treatment it deserves, as the law is the most precious tool of a state based on the rule of law in facing up to the manifestations of crime; as terrorist behaviour is a very specific form of crime, it is necessary to apply the law in order to establish specific investigative means or ways in which to preserve evidence.

The respect of constitutional guarantees is not incompatible with efficacy and this is possible if the penal and procedural instruments are adapted in the best way possible to the challenges thrown up by the fight against terrorism.

ISSUES TO CONSIDER

1. Is a modified criminal law process more effective than a hybrid paradigm?
2. Does the Spanish system better preserve basic rights of a detainee than the Israeli two-track approach?
3. Does the Spanish system facilitate the development of an enemy combatant paradigm?
4. How would the U.S. Supreme Court rule on the Spanish approach?

VII. CHINA

Similar to the other surveyed nations, China has adopted the criminal law paradigm regarding terrorism-related crimes defined as endangering national and public security. To that end, terrorism has been incorporated into the criminal code thereby defining terrorism as criminal acts. In 2005, China amended the criminal code to include punishment for terrorism and financing terrorism in explicit terms.

According to Article 120 of the Chinese criminal code:

> Whoever forms or leads a terrorist organization shall be sentenced to fixed-term imprisonment of not less than 10 years or life imprisonment; persons who actively participate in a terrorist organization shall be sentenced to fixed-term imprisonment of not less than 3 years but not more than 10 years; other participants shall be sentenced to fixed-term imprisonment of not more than 3 years, criminal detention, public surveillance or deprivation of political rights
>
> Whoever commits the crime in the preceding paragraph and also commits murder, explosion, or kidnapping is to be punished according to the regulations for punishing multiple crimes.[37]

Article 120(a) specifies that financing a terrorist organization be punished as a crime:

> Whoever provides funds to any terrorist organization or individual who engages in terrorism shall be sentenced to fixed-term imprisonment of not more than five years, criminal detention, public surveillance or deprivation of political rights, and shall also be fined; if the circumstances are serious, he shall be sentenced to fixed-term imprisonment of not less than five years, and he shall also be fined or his property shall be confiscated.
>
> Where a unit commits the crime mentioned in the preceding paragraph, it shall be fined, and the persons who are directly in charge and the other persons who are directly responsible for the offence shall be punished in accordance with the provisions of the preceding paragraph.

ISSUES TO CONSIDER

1. Given the nature of the threat China faces, is the criminal law paradigm appropriate?
2. What are the cost-benefits in applying the criminal law paradigm to a country the size of China?
3. Do the threats China faces more closely resemble Israel, Russia, or India (regardless of size)?
4. Given the complexity of Chinese society, would a two-track approach not be more realistic and effective?
5. Does the possibility that Uyghurs benefit from external influence (Pakistan) affect what model is adopted (akin to India-Pakistan)?

---

37. Chinese Criminal Code art. 120.

6. Does the criminal law paradigm lock the state into one model when flexibility — given circumstances — might be more beneficial to the state?

COMBATING MONEY LAUNDERING AND TERRORIST FINANCING IN CHINA

Speech of Deputy Governor Xiang Junbo, Sept. 25, 2005[38]

Money laundering is always accompanied by criminal activities generating economic gains and to our society, the damage is obvious. Money laundering not only destroys the fairness and equality principle of market economy, disturbs orderly competition, damages reputations and normal operations of financial institutions, threatens the soundness and safety of financial systems, but also becomes the source of corruption and erodes the social fundamental institutions. To be more troublesome, money laundering and terrorist financing have interlaced with each other and threatened global security. A series of terrorist attacks in the last four years have already rung the alarm bell. Money laundering and terrorist financing have already threatened and challenged seriously the human society, sustainable development in the 21st century.

II. China has established comparative complete legal system in anti-money laundering and terrorist financing in line with the fundamental principle of "ruling by law."

Article 120(I) and Article 190 of the current *Criminal Law* in China defined terrorist financing and money-laundering crime as criminal acts. Money-laundering crime in China has its special features. First, on the basis of the defined money-laundering crime act, both natural person and legal person are treated as the criminal offenders; second, punishment of money-laundering crime also cover laundering illegal gains from oversea upstream criminal acts; third, although there are only four different upstream criminal acts, there are totally 27 different crimes within them, including smuggling, trafficking, production of narcotic drugs and illegal possession of psychotropic substances, illegal cultivation of drug plants, organizing, leading and participating in mafias, weapon and ammunition smuggling, counterfeit currency smuggling, cultural relic smuggling, precious metal and jewelry smuggling, organizing, leading or participating in terrorist organizations etc; fourth, criminal punishments of money laundering include maximum 10 year imprisonment, detention, property confiscation and criminal fines.

Given the centrality of money laundering and financing to terrorism, defining the offense as a crime is instructive regarding how China addresses the

---

38. *Available at* http://www.pbc.gov.cn/english/showaccdoc.asp?col=6500&id=84 (last visited Apr. 4, 2010).

paradigm question. Rather than creating a unique — or alternative — category and model for terrorism and terrorists, Chinese decision makers have adopted and implemented an exclusive criminal law paradigm in response to existing threats that are largely confined to specific regions and have, too date, not expanded into the larger population. Therein lies the rub: should both the nature and locations of terrorism change — by example, Uyghur riots outside of Xinxiang — then the question will be whether the paradigm will also change.

VIII. COLOMBIA

In 2003, Colombia enacted an antiterrorism law. According to the law, the armed forces are allowed to arrest, interrogate, and detain suspects for up to 36 hours and may search homes and obtain intelligence information without a warrant or any judicial oversight. The New Code of Criminal Procedure allows criminal judges in specialized circuits to try an individual who, during an armed conflict, either carries out or conducts indiscriminate or excessive acts. These acts, according to the Code, include targeting a civilian population or threatening the population for purposes of intimidation. The perpetrator, if found guilty, will be sentenced for 15 to 25 years, fined, and banned from exercising any public right for 15 to 20 years. Below are the specific articles from this Code that pertain to terrorism.

NEW CODE OF CRIMINAL PROCEDURE OF COLOMBIA

Articles 144, 182, 343, 345, and 348

Article 144. Acts of terrorism.
Any person who, on the occasion of or in the course of, an armed conflict, engages in, or orders the commission of, indiscriminate or excessive attacks or makes the civilian population a target of attacks, reprisals or acts or threats of violence with the principal objective of terrorizing the civilian population, shall be liable, by that act alone, to a term of imprisonment of between fifteen (15) and twenty-five (25) years, a fine of between two thousand (2,000) and forty thousand (40,000) times the minimum statutory monthly wage, and loss of rights and public functions for a period of between fifteen (15) and twenty (20) years.

Article 182 of the Penal Code provides for a term of imprisonment of between one and two years for anyone who forces another person to do, condone or fail to do anything, a penalty that will be increased by between one third and one half (article 183) when the objective pursued by the perpetrator is of a terrorist nature.

Article 343. Terrorism.
Any person who provokes or maintains the population, or a segment of the population, in a state of anxiety or terror through acts that endanger the lives, physical integrity or the freedom of the persons or buildings or means of

communication, transport, processing or conveyance of fluids or motive power, making use of means capable of causing destruction, shall be liable to a term of imprisonment of between ten (10) and fifteen (15) years and a fine of between one thousand (1,000) and ten thousand times the minimum statutory monthly wage, without prejudice to the penalty to which he or she is liable for the other offences committed in connection with such conduct.

If the state of anxiety or terror is caused by a telephone call, a magnetic tape, a video, a cassette or an anonymous letter, the punishment shall be from between two (2) and five (5) years and a fine of between one hundred (100) and five hundred (500) times the minimum statutory monthly wage.

Article 345. Management of resources linked to terrorist activities.
Any person who manages money or assets linked to terrorist activities shall be liable to a term of imprisonment of between six (6) and twelve (12) years and a fine of between two hundred (200) and ten thousand (10,000) times the minimum statutory monthly wage.

Article 348. Instigation to commit an offence.
Any person who publicly and directly incites another person or persons to commit a specific offence or type of offence shall be liable to a fine.

If the act is engaged in for the purpose of committing the crimes of genocide, enforced disappearance, extortive kidnapping, torture, forcible displacement or homicide or for terrorist purposes, the penalty shall be a term of imprisonment of between five (5) and ten (10) years and a fine of between five hundred (500) and one thousand (1,000) times the minimum statutory monthly wage.

In response to the Code's enactment, criticism focused particularly on the broad powers granted to the government and the drastically reduced rights of the individual.

RIGHTS COLOMBIA: ACTIVISTS SAY NEW TERRORISM LAW WILL CURB RIGHTS

Inter Press Service, Dec. 24, 2003

Colombia's new anti-terrorism law will undermine what little progress has been made towards preventing forced disappearances of people by the armed forces, and will weaken the independence of the courts and due process, according to human rights activists.

Rocío Bautista, president of the Association of Relatives of the Detained and Disappeared (ASFADDES), told IPS that the anti-terrorism legislation passed this month by Congress constitutes "a grave setback in terms of legislation on forced disappearance."

In 2000, after 12 years of efforts by human rights groups and the families of the disappeared, Congress finally passed law 589, which classifies forced disappearance as a criminal offence and creates mechanisms for its prevention and eradication — achievements that will be weakened by the new law, said Bautista.

Under the anti-terrorism law approved by the Senate on Dec. 10, the armed forces will be able to arrest people for up to 36 hours, search homes, and spy on private communications without a legal warrant or judicial oversight.

The new legislation also foresees the creation of a new registry containing private information on all Colombians, to which military authorities will have access. In addition, the armed forces will be given police powers, including the authority to interrogate suspects.

Bautista said the new law was passed against the recommendations of international human rights bodies, which expressed their opposition to the granting of police powers to the military.

On Nov. 18, the United Nations Committee Against Torture called on the Colombian government of right-wing President Alvaro Uribe to reconsider the possibility of adopting measures that would grant judicial police functions to the military and allow lengthy interrogations and arrests of suspects without a legal order or judicial oversight.

The Committee Against Torture, tasked with preventing the practices prohibited by the Convention Against Torture, of which Colombia is a signatory, set a one-year deadline for the state to report on compliance with its recommendation.

According to ASFADDES, the new law could fuel an increase in forced disappearances, and will limit, "in a grave manner, the mechanisms and guarantees in place for victims and their families."

The problem, says the human rights group, is that "the very same state agents that could be involved in alleged human rights abuses will be in charge of carrying out the investigations, and collecting and handling evidence."

ASFADDES reports that 6,340 cases of forced disappearance were committed, mainly by members of the armed forces, between 1979 and May 2003.

Gustavo Gallón, president of the Colombian Commission of Jurists (CCJ), said the enactment of the new law is disturbing at a time when "the polarisation has reached the extent that the Colombian government is stigmatising not only ordinary people opposed to its policies," but leading international authorities on human rights as well.

Gallón was specifically referring to an incident that occurred earlier this year, when then-defence minister Marta Ramírez said U.N. Special Representative to Colombia James LeMoyne had "defended the terrorists."

That remark came after Lemoyne told reporters that "the backbone of the FARC (Revolutionary Armed Forces of Colombia — the main guerrilla group) consists of between 1,000 and 1,500 ideologically committed men and women who have been fighting for 15 to 20 years."

The CCJ has documented a number of arbitrary detentions of human rights defenders, trade unionists and other social activists.

According to the CCJ, the common denominator in such cases is that despite the joint efforts of the security forces and the office of the public prosecutor, no evidence is found against the detainees to press charges, nor is there any sign of a serious judicial investigation of their cases.

Furthermore, many of the arrests are carried out with the participation of hooded individuals who point to the people to be detained, and on many opportunities the detainees are released shortly after being hauled in, due to a lack of evidence of any wrongdoing or crime.

The cases documented include a number of raids conducted on Aug. 21 in the town of Saravena in the northeastern province of Arauca by members of the security forces and people from the office of the public prosecutor, who were accompanied by two hooded individuals.

"The operation included raids of the offices of social organisations, trade unions and human rights groups, and of the homes of several people. A total of 42 people were arrested that day," states a CCJ report.

Those arrested included 14 trade unionists, five community activists, two teachers, three health workers, a human rights defender, a public employee, and one minor.

A report by the London-based rights watchdog Amnesty International said that six days after the arrests, 14 of the 42 detainees had been released, while the remaining 28 were still in prison.

Activist Juan Carlos Celis, with the Corporation Movement for Life, a group that forms part of the Network of Initiatives for Peace and Against War, an umbrella organisation that links around 30 peace groups, was arbitrarily detained by the police in Bogota on Dec. 11, 2002 and tortured.

Celis was described by the police as "the brains behind the wave of terrorism" expanding in the city. He was arrested as part of a series of operations carried out on the basis of information furnished by the government's network of civilian informants, who provide "intelligence" in exchange for money.

According to Amnesty International, the police "raided his home without a search warrant and without the presence of the appropriate judicial authorities. Juan Celis was beaten and subjected to electric shocks to force him to confess responsibility for crimes of terrorism."

The CCJ said members of a committee made up of representatives of civil society set up to discuss official human rights policy with the government has asked the office of the vice-president for information on Celis's case, but has not yet received any response. The activist remains in prison.

The representative in Colombia of the United Nations High Commissioner for Human Rights (UNHCHR), Michael Fruhling, said last Friday that the government and Congress had approved the new anti-terrorism law against the opinion of the office he heads in Colombia.

Fruhling said many aspects of the new legislation invade the privacy of citizens and amount to an abuse of basic human rights.

He also said that giving the military judicial police powers was in violation of international human rights treaties signed by Colombia, and would debilitate the independence of the judiciary.

But Carlos Franco, director of President Uribe's human rights programme, said that "no human rights convention prohibits granting judicial police functions to the security forces."

In Colombia, legislation that involves constitutional reform or fundamental human rights must be approved by the Constitutional Court of

Colombia before becoming law. In August 2004, the Constitutional Court declared the anti-terrorism law unconstitutional due to procedural irregularities that occurred during the approval of the law by the Colombian Congress.[39]

IX. CONCLUSION

The United States, in the immediate aftermath of 9/11, defined suspected terrorists as enemy combatants thereby enabling their detention in Guantanamo Bay, Abu Ghraib, and so-called "black sites." The enemy combatant paradigm created by the United States allowed for violations of the Geneva Conventions. Such a model has not been adopted—or if adopted then subsequently revised—by the other surveyed nations.

While the Obama administration has articulated an intention to adopt a different approach both terminologically and substantively, it remains to be seen what policy will actually be developed and implemented. Russia and China have adopted a criminal law paradigm with respect to suspected terrorists, However, that paradigm has not been applied to operational counterterrorism. India has largely implemented a criminal law paradigm though a special court has been created and suspected terrorists have been brought to trial before that forum. Spain has consistently adhered to a criminal law paradigm, only extending the time a detainee can be held in incommunicado detention. Israel has created a twin-track approach—criminal trial and administrative detention—thereby granting the state broader detention powers based both on criminal law and administrative sanctions. Colombia, in response to multiple threats (akin to India) has implemented a paradigm that enables the state to bring suspected terrorists to trial before not regularly constituted courts.

---

39. Ludqig De Braeckleleer, *Privacy of Communications in Colombia,* OhMyNews, http://english.ohmynews.com/ArticleView/article_view.asp?menu=A11100&no=382113&rel_no=1&back_url= (last visited Aug. 23, 2010); Sentencia C-818-04 sobre inexequibilidad del Acto Legislativo No. 02 de 2003.

10

WHERE TO TRY TERRORISTS?

I. INTRODUCTION

There are four viable forums for trying suspected terrorists: domestic criminal courts, military commissions, domestic national security courts, and international courts. Criminal courts are predicated on existing domestic, judicial regimes while military commissions and national security courts represent alternative domestic judicial regimes especially created to address a specific threat, terrorism. As discussed earlier, some nations try suspected terrorists exclusively before existing criminal courts while others implement a two-track system that utilizes both domestic courts and military commissions. The United States and Israel utilize a two-track approach providing decision makers the flexibility to determine which judicial regime is most appropriate for a specific defendant. National security courts represent a "hybrid" model, trying only suspected terrorists while providing defendants greater rights than existing military commissions without extending the full panoply of rights guaranteed by domestic courts. No terrorist has, to date, been brought to trial before an international court.

Deciding which judicial forum is relevant depends on defining the status of the particular detainee. If a terrorist-defendant is defined as a traditional criminal, then he is entitled to full rights and protections guaranteed by the criminal law paradigm. However, if terrorists are not defined as criminals, then existing laws may not be applicable because certain rights inherent to the criminal law paradigm may be withheld from the terrorist-defendant.

To try a terrorist in an international court would signify the internationalization of counterterrorism. Rather than each surveyed nation bringing defendants to trial before a domestic court, an individual accused of terrorism would be brought to trial before an international tribunal. Such a court could be a treaty-based terror court or a tribunal[1] similar to the International Criminal Court or a combination of domestic and international courts.

---

1. William Carmines has put forth such a recommendation, along with a 50-page treaty. The ITT idea, generally speaking, would be a treaty-based tribunal formed by like-minded nations

This chapter analyzes the three domestic alternatives through the lens of the U.S. judicial system. Nevertheless, the options — existing domestic courts, military commissions, and specially constituted national security courts — are relevant to the other surveyed countries and can, therefore, be applied by analogy. To that end, unlike previous chapters which have emphasized a comparative, global perspective, this chapter will focus on the United States while addressing an issue relevant to the other six nations. A treaty-based terror court is analyzed by examining the ramifications of an international approach to counterterrorism.

ISSUES TO CONSIDER

1. What is the most appropriate role for the courts?
2. What legal regime guarantees rights and protections for the defendant while protecting society's interests?
3. What criminal law punishment theory is most relevant to terrorism?
4. What is the fundamental purpose in bringing terrorists to trial?

Accused terrorists have been brought to trial before domestic courts (U.S., Israel, Russia, India, Spain, Colombia, and China), military commissions and military courts (U.S. and Israel), and special terrorism courts (India and Colombia). If the right to confront the accuser is preserved and otherwise guaranteed rights are similarly protected, then special courts need not be established. Conversely, if the full panoply of rights guaranteed by the criminal law process is not extended to terrorists but the right to trial is protected, then alternative judicial regimes, including national security courts, are viable options.

II. DOMESTIC JUDICIAL REGIMES

A. ARTICLE III COURTS

One of the primary considerations in determining where to try a suspected terrorist is ascertaining whether a particular judicial forum facilitates balancing legitimate national security considerations with equally legitimate individual rights. The essay below articulates specific reasons why Article III courts may not be the appropriate forum for post-9/11 detainees.

---

united to combat international terrorism by trying international terrorists. It gives the ITT jurisdiction to try international terror suspects detained by member states. That is, once a party to this treaty, a member state should not try a suspected terrorist in a domestic court. In fact, once the suspect is arrested and detained on international terror charges (including, but not limited to, the actual use of terrorist activity, as well as threat, financing and, harboring of such terrorists), the suspect then, within 7 days unless an extension applies, must be transferred to the ITT's Administrative Counsel for further detention, pre-trial hearings, interrogation, and potential prosecution.

Walid Phares, Moussaoui: Wrong Court, Wrong Debate?

Foundation for Defense of Democracies, May 4, 2006[2]

Should we be surprised by the watershed debate following Zacarias Moussaoui's trial ending? Not really. The jury rendering of its recommendation is not unusual throughout the American legal war with Terrorism: For the five years court struggle to try al Qaida members and other terrorists in the U.S. legal structure hasn't been working. After the classroom, America's court room is too alien to the conflict. In short Moussaoui's case is not the only one to display a systemic crisis, all other cases did and will continue to do. My take on it, as an analyst of past and future terror wars, can be simplified: The terrorists are processed in the wrong courts and our debate on this legal process is the wrong debate.

Let me be clear from the beginning: The issue I am raising is not about the death sentence or life in prison sentencing. That part should have been the last stage in the debate: The one that seals the sentencing logic, not the discussion that makes the debate. The *Moussaoui* trial is not about the principle of common criminal sentencing per se; it is about criminalizing Terrorism and its root ideologies. Here are few points that make my analytical case:

1. Zacarias Moussaoui's personal life is not a main factor in determining this particular mass crime, but one of the factors that could lower the punishment, if incriminated. If he had a bad childhood or other negative factors that affected his clarity of thinking, it should be considered as elements of clemency in the case of extreme sentencing, but not the foundations of the case evaluation. For 9/11 and the war it was part of, was not a personal vendetta by M. Moussaoui against the U.S. Government, but an al Qaida genocidal war against the American people. This and other similar cases aren't a private affair between individuals — with some bad luck — and U.S. policies with consequences on national security. By his own admitting, M Moussaoui is a member, call him Jihadist or not, of a Terrorist organization. He shouldn't be tried in a U.S. Court system designed to process common crimes instead of war crimes.

2. The victims of September 11, 2001 weren't selected by al Qaida, or even by the perpetrators—including Moussaoui—personally. The men, women and children massacred throughout that day of infamy are the targets of a Terror war on America not vandalism on two towers in New York and a large building in Washington. Terrorism could have targeted other high rises and objectives in different cities. The matter is not an individual vendetta between Moussaoui and the 3,000 persons Mohammed Atta and his Jihadists have killed. America was targeted as a nation for the purpose of genocide. As a massacred collectivity, the victims of 9/11 belong to the nation not to their relatives. As individuals

---

2. *Available at* http://www.defenddemocracy.org/index.php?option=com_content&task=view&id=11782128&Itemid=102 (last visited July 20, 2010).

the victims are profoundly mourned by all Americans and above all by their survivors. So who tried al Qaida on behalf of the nation?

3. Moussaoui is part of machinery larger than himself. In the 9/11 planning process, he is not a sole mechanism acting individually. He was executing orders by al Qaida and had the intention of carrying them out. He is a nucleus that fell behind, in a wider cell that moved forward. His relation to the massacre is not pragmatic but mechanical. Hence the judicial process of finding out if he caused or not, the process of specific deaths of 9/11 is not the issue: For he has openly admitted, and it was proven, that he was part of the machinery put in place to perpetrate the massacre. That he slipped, failed or missed his opportunity is only one fact within a greater reality: his commitment to achieve the mass-killing and his participation in a chain of event that led to it, even if he didn't walk through the last part of the horror.

4. More seriously is the current system ability to process the Terror cases: Per my own experience and open documents available, most of the players in a current court room setting are often unable to absorb the density of the confrontation. The Jury, made of ordinary citizens, generally do not comprehend the ideology of the Jihadists, hence can't make a strategically educated decision, not on the sentencing process but on the essence of the war crime at hand. U.S. Judges are highly capable of controlling the procedure in their court rooms but haven't been enabled by the system to try a war with Jihadi terror, if not specialized in Salafism, Khumeinism and other movements' strategies, thinking process or even tactics. Prosecutors as well are thrown into battles of ideas beyond their basic training. In the *Moussaoui* case, the jury asked for a dictionary, refused by the judge. The question deserves an answer.

5. As for the defense lawyers, and I was one in the past, in the absence of specialized courts, they would twist history and geopolitics to achieve a legitimate goal: win their case. But instead of focusing on proving the innocence of their clients and distancing him/her from the enemy, they tend to defend the ideology of their client, putting themselves in the wrong side of the war their nation is victim of.

These above five facts and many more to develop in the future constitute the basis of U.S. failure in the courts processing of Jihadism-related Terror cases. What is needed for future successes is the following:

a. That Congress identifies the ideologies of the Terrorists. In the heels of many congressional hearings which already produced significant bipartisan consensus, as well as in several speeches by the President since last September, the country not so far from identifying the missing link. Simply speaking: educate the jury, the judges, the prosecutors and the defense attorneys, as to who is the enemy and what is its ideology. The rest should flow as American justice at its best, impartial and fair.

b. As in France and Spain, train "Counter-Terrorism Judges." From Paris to Madrid, these bright specialized men and women have all the tools they need to decide on procedures deemed appropriate to prosecute and ultimately try the Terrorists at war with democracies. A similar training could provide the Justice Department with "Counter Terrorism Prosecutors." In a sum, all players in the court room must at some point be acquainted with what they will have to reflect on, in Terrorism cases.

Moussaoui feels he won all the way, even if he got life in prison. He played the martyrdom card till his audience nauseated. He then played his personal life card till he obtained the mitigating factor. He played it tight, close, and smartly. His colleagues brought down towers five years ago, but Moussaoui administered another type of strikes against his foes: Defeating them through their own system.

What the court room in Virginia missed in its trial of the decade was the factory that produced Moussaoui's mind. A life sentence is not necessarily a bad choice in democracies, or the wrong message to send when needed, if the nation the jury came from is enabled to cast a death sentence on the ideologies of hatred.

Issues to Consider

1. What is the cost of allowing a terrorist-defendant to manipulate a trial?
2. Should a judge provide more leniency to a terrorist-defendant than to a criminal-defendant regarding courtroom conduct?
3. Are jury trials appropriate for terrorist-defendants? Should existing judicial regimes be adhered to regardless of the circumstances?
4. How should self-representation be addressed?
5. Is the dilemma regarding which forum is appropriate for terrorist-defendants primarily legal or political?
6. What should be the factors in determining whether the pre-existing judicial paradigm is effective and appropriate?
7. How should the effectiveness of an alternative paradigm be judged?

B. UNITED STATES MILITARY COMMISSIONS

President Bush's November 2001 Presidential Order, known as Detention, Treatment, and Trial of Certain Non-Citizens in the War Against Terrorism, established military commissions for the express purpose of trying individuals suspected of involvement in terrorism. Premised on a belief that the existing civilian judicial paradigm was insufficient with respect to the threat posed by terrorism, the administration chose to eschew Article III courts.

With respect to the debate surrounding the establishment of the military commissions, Professor Linda Dickinson's interpretation of the administration's motives is particularly insightful:

> Despite the availability of legal arguments, however, those supporting the Administration's actions have justified them primarily in the language of policy. They have made clear that they view law—at least the typical legal protections afforded defendants in criminal trials—to be a nuisance

(or, worse, a danger) in the context of fighting terrorism. They contend that the normal principles governing adjudication of criminal responsibility ought to be suspended for several reasons. First, such trials take a long time and cost a great deal of money. Thus, they argue that trials of untold numbers of terrorists in civilian courts would be inefficient. Second, civilian trials would present risks to civilian judges and jurors, who might be targeted by terrorists in retaliation for their decisions. Third, they argue that there is no need to protect rights of people who are, after all, international terrorists. For example, they contend that it is ludicrous to suggest that we should have read al Qaeda members their Miranda rights before apprehending them in the caves at Tora Bora. Fourth, the evidence available to convict terrorists does not necessarily fit the strict evidentiary requirements, such as the chain of custody requirement or the hearsay rule, applicable in civilian courts. Indeed, much of the evidence is secret, we are told, and could compromise national security if it came to light in a public trial. Furthermore, public trials are subject to capture by grandstanding defendants who might use the process to air their views and thereby undermine the fight against terrorism. Fifth, it is alleged that indefinite secret detentions and military commissions give the government, and in particular the Executive branch, needed control over the process. In short, the view is that we cannot afford much law here. Stern measures are needed for violent times.[3]

In the aftermath of the Order's issuance, the Department of Defense issued rules, procedures, and instructions heavily favoring the prosecution regarding rules of evidence, burden of proof, right to counsel, admissibility of classified information, right to confront the accuser, preponderance of the evidence required for conviction, sentencing guidelines, and flexibility with respect to what crimes the defendant may be charged. In establishing the commissions, the administration circumvented constitutional guarantees and privileges articulated in Article III; that baselines articulating what cases are suitable for prosecution were not developed is telling.[4]

The following excerpt highlights criticisms of the military commissions; the comments are relevant to the commission and other judicial regimes created for the singular purpose of trying terrorist-defendants.

JENNIFER TRAHAN, TRYING A BIN LADEN AND OTHERS:
EVALUATING THE OPTIONS FOR TERRORIST TRIALS

24 Hous. J Int'l L. 475 (2002)

Absence of Standard Trial Procedures

Aside from questioning the legality of using military commissions, another issue is whether, as a policy matter, the circumstances justify subjecting foreign defendants accused of terrorism to trials lacking certain safeguards provided in federal district courts (or, for that matter, most likely in trials before international tribunals). Military commission trials will (a) not afford the

---

3. Laura A. Dickinson, *Using Legal Process to Fight Terrorism: Detentions, Military Commissions, International Tribunals, and the Rule of Law*, 75 S. Cal. L. Rev. 1407 (2002).

4. Private correspondence with senior official; e-mail on record with author.

accused a jury trial; (b) not be governed by the Federal Rules of Evidence; (c) not be open to the public in certain circumstances; (d) not require unanimous support for convictions, except for death sentences; and (e) not permit appellate review to an independent court.

. . . While using military commissioners in place of jurors to hear cases before a military commission has been upheld as constitutional, the replacement of the jury seems unnecessary in terrorism trials. The United States may have at least two reasons not to use jurors: (a) concerns with juror safety and (b) concerns that juries may inappropriately acquit. Neither argument is persuasive. While security would obviously need to be stringent for a jury trial of suspected al Qaeda terrorists, similar trials have successfully occurred in the past, and the United States apparently is willing to try Zacarias Moussaoui in federal district court. Although fears of additional terrorism are legitimate, they should not drive U.S. decisions regarding the administration of justice. Moreover, it is unclear that terrorism concerns would be greater for a federal court trial as opposed to a trial by military commission. The argument of inappropriate acquittal by juries should be afforded little weight given the enormity of crimes committed on September 11.

The other significant procedural changes—such as eliminating the requirement of unanimity for conviction and sentencing (at least in non-death penalty cases) and eliminating normal appellate review—seem designed only to facilitate quick guilty convictions. While there is a legitimate national interest in convicting guilty terrorists, that interest should be weighed against damage to the rule of law and concerns about convicting innocent persons. Obviously, it is difficult to answer the question of whether convicting terrorists is such a high priority that the United States should abandon due process protections, normally considered central to our justice system.

Questions as to the Appearance of Legitimacy

. . . .Problems concerning legitimacy may also impact on the trials themselves. For instance, Spain initially took the position that it would not extradite eight men charged with complicity in the September 11 attacks unless the United States agreed to try them in a civilian court. If countries are unwilling to extradite suspects, they may also be unwilling to assist in obtaining key witnesses and evidence. As a result, the United States' ability to conduct the actual trials could be hampered.

Thus, even if (a) military trials are conducted under well-planned, fairly neutral rules prescribed by the Secretary of Defense, (b) defendants are represented by able defense counsel, and (c) the proof is solid, it would be exceedingly difficult to counter allegations that the proceedings were illegitimate, especially if parts of the proceedings are closed to the public.

In *Hamdan*,[5] the Supreme Court held that the President Bush lacked congressional authorization to establish the commissions. The Court, in finding

---

5. Hamdan v. Rumsfeld, 548 U.S. 557 (2006).

several deficiencies, held the commissions' procedures violated basic fair trial standards established by the Geneva Conventions of 1949. According to the Court, the Geneva Conventions mandated humane treatment of all persons held by the U.S. in the "conflict with al Qaeda." The main thrust of the criticism was that "[t]he military commissions invalidated by the Court in *Hamdan* substantially deviated from regular court-martial practice and were thus found to have not been authorized by Congress. . . ."[6]

In response to *Hamdan*, Congress enacted the Military Commissions Act of 2006,[7] which purports to "facilitate bringing to justice terrorists and other unlawful enemy combatants through full and fair trials by military commissions, and for other purposes."[8]

The Act established a Combatant Status Review Tribunal to determine whether a detainee can be categorized as an "alien unlawful enemy combatant" under Section II of the Act. Criteria for this review are taken from the Detainee Treatment Act of 2005, and referenced in Section 10 of the Act. The Tribunal is made up of three neutral officers, one of whom is a judge advocate and another who, as senior ranking officer, is President of the tribunal. Detainees may testify, call witnesses, and introduce additional evidence. After the hearing, the Tribunal conducts a closed-door session to decide whether the detainee is properly held as an enemy combatant. The criteria for when other "competent tribunals" may review this status determination are specified in the Detainee Treatment Act of 2005, which essentially limits review to the United States Court of Appeals for the District of Columbia Circuit.[9]

1. The Geneva Convention and Rights Denied by the Act

A gap exists between the rights granted in criminal trials conducted by the military and rights accorded unlawful enemy combatants in military commissions. James G. Stewart makes the distinction clear:

> While an accused in a court-martial is protected from the admission of an involuntary statement, the unlawful enemy combatant before a military commission is only protected against statements obtained by cruel, inhuman or degrading interrogation, and then only if the interrogation occurred after the enactment of the Detainee Treatment Act of 2005. While the accused in a court-martial has the right to be warned before any interrogation of the nature of the accusation against him or her, as well as of his or her right to not make a statement concerning the offence and that any statement he or she does make may be used as evidence in a court-martial against him or her, the unlawful combatant has only the right to be free from irrelevant and degrading questions at a military commission. Under the UCMJ, a suspect or an accused can

---

6. Jack M. Beard, *The Geneva Boomerang: The Military Commissions Act of 2006 and U.S. Counterterrorism Operations*, 101 Am. J. Int'l L. 56 (2007), at 58.

7. Military Commissions Act of 2006, or Senate Bill 3930, signed September 22, 2006.

8. Military Commissions Bill, *available at* http://www.nytimes.com/2006/09/28/opinion/28thu1.html?ex=1317096000&en=3eb3ba3410944ff9&ei=5090&partner=rssuserland&emc=rss/.

9. Detainee Treatment Act of 2005, Section (e)(2)(A), *available at* http://jurist.law.pitt.edu/gazette/2005/12/detainee-treatment-act-of-2005-white.php.

terminate interrogation at any time by requesting counsel, while the only provision of the Military Commissions Act that provides defence [sic] counsel does so only after the swearing of charges. In an obvious effort to protect military intelligence and security based interrogations and ensure that they remain effective in obtaining information from unlawful enemy combatants, the Congress created a criminal system that is far less supportive of any right against self-incrimination or right to counsel.[10]

Under the Act, the detainee is protected from cruel, inhumane, or unusual treatment while in custody or while under the physical control of the United States, regardless of the detainee's nationality or physical location. Nevertheless, as initially established prosecutors may use evidence obtained under varying degrees of coercion, though this is expressly prohibited by the Geneva Conventions.[11]

Furthermore, the prosecution does not have to give the detainee prompt or detailed notice of the nature and cause of the charges against him.[12] In military commissions, pretrial hearings and investigations are severely limited compared to the courts-martial system.

Under the Act, detainees are explicitly denied the right to a speedy trial, meaning they may be held for indefinite periods without a finding of guilt.[13] Furthermore, case precedent is non-existent. The use of hearsay is specifically addresssed:

> A noteworthy departure from American jurisprudence in the potential rules for the military commissions is a new process for the admissibility of hearsay evidence. Unlike the MRE, which mirror the general prohibition against hearsay with numerous exceptions of the Federal rules, the military commissions adopt a curious burden-shifting approach for hearsay evidence that does not fit under one of the enumerated exceptions. The proponent of the hearsay must give advance notice to the opposing party of their intention to admit hearsay evidence that includes the particulars of the hearsay evidence, including how it was obtained, and provides that party with fair opportunity to "meet" the evidence. The opposing party then has the burden of showing that the evidence is unreliable or lacking in probative value in order to have the evidence excluded.[14]

Another frequently repeated critique is the Act's failure to define "competent tribunal." The U.S. Army Field Manual[15] requires a board of not less than three officers to determine if a person is a prisoner of war. Article 5 of the Third Geneva Convention grants all belligerents protection until their status is

---

10. James G. Stewart, *The Military Commissions Act of 2006 Inconsistency with the Geneva Conventions*, 5 J. Int'l Criminal Justice 19 (2007), at 56-57.

11. Beard, *supra* note 6, at 59.

12. Guénaël Mettraux, *Comparing the Comparable: 2006 Military Commissions v. The ICTY*, 5 J. Int'l Criminal Justice 59 (2007), at 62.

13. Richard V. Meyer, *When a Rose Is not a Rose: Military Commissions v. Courts-Martial*, 5 J. Int'l Criminal Justice 48 (2007), at 59.

14. *Id.* at 56.

15. Section 27-10.

determined by a competent tribunal.[16] However, the Act expressly revokes Article 5 and grants rights only to *lawful*, not unlawful, military combatants:

> (g) Geneva Conventions Not Establishing Source of Rights — No alien unlawful enemy combatant subject to trial by military commission under this chapter may invoke the Geneva Conventions as a source of rights.[17]

In other words, the Act restricts invocation of the Geneva Conventions when a detainee petitions for the writ of *habeas corpus*.[18] This provision applies to all cases pending at the time the Act was enacted, as well as to all future cases.

MICHAEL C. DORF, WHY THE MILITARY COMMISSION ACT
IS NO MODERATE COMPROMISE

FindLaw, Oct. 11, 2006[19]

Americans following the news coverage of the debate about how to treat captives in the ongoing military conflicts could be forgiven for believing that the bill recently passed by Congress, the Military Commissions Act ("MCA"), was a compromise between a White House seeking far-reaching powers, and Senators seeking to restrain the Executive. After all, prior to reaching an agreement with the President, four prominent Republican Senators — Susan Collins, Lindsey Graham, John McCain, and John Warner — had drawn a line in the sand, refusing to go along with a measure that would have redefined the Geneva Conventions' references to "outrages upon personal dignity" and "humiliating and degrading treatment." No doubt many Americans believe that because these four courageous Senators stood on moral principle, the bill that emerged, and which President Bush will certainly sign, reflects a careful balance between liberty and security. Yet if that is what Americans believe, they are sorely mistaken. On nearly every issue, the MCA gives the White House everything it sought.

Indeed, the Administration and many of its allies in Congress refuse even to say whether they think that the MCA prohibits *future* waterboarding. They argue that stating what specific practices are forbidden would give our enemies an advantage, because these enemies could then focus their training on methods of resisting only those harsh interrogation methods that are permitted; yet the Administration and its allies simultaneously argue that the MCA is needed to tell our own interrogators exactly what they can and cannot do. They do not explain how the same language of the law can somehow provide guidance to our troops and civilian interrogators, but not to the enemy.

The Constriction of the Writ of Habeas Corpus

There is, of course, an answer to that question, but it is not a pretty one: Perhaps the enemy will be kept guessing because the Administration does

---

16. Third Geneva Convention, Article 5 (Oct. 1950), *available at* http://www.unhchr.ch/html/menu3/b/91.htm (last visited July 24, 2007).

17. *Id.* at §984b(g).

18. *Id.* at §5(a).

19. *Available at* http://writ.news.findlaw.com/dorf/20061011.html (last visited July 24, 2007).

not actually intend to abide by the provisions of the MCA or DTA. After all, no alien can sue to enforce these provisions, and thus violations may never come to light. And that's before the President construes the MCA even more narrowly in a signing statement, as he is wont to do.

To be sure, if the government provides someone declared to be an enemy combatant with a combatant status review tribunal (CSRT), then the DTA authorizes judicial review of that determination. And the MCA does amend the DTA for the better in one important respect: Whereas the DTA only authorized civilian judicial review of CSRT determinations for detainees at Guantanamo, under the MCA, a person held by the United States pursuant to a CSRT anywhere in the world can appeal the CSRT's ruling to a civilian federal court. But, there is no statutory requirement that the government ever utilize a CSRT-and absent a CSRT ruling, there is no access to civilian court.

Thus, under the terms of the DTA as amended by the MCA, there would be no access to a civilian court whatsoever, even if the detainee were held within the United States, so long as the government determined that he or she were an unlawful enemy combatant by some means other than using a CSRT.

---

2. Military Commission Act 2009

In October 2009, Congress passed the Military Commission Act of 2009, which replaced the Bush-era Military Commission Act of 2006. The 2009 Act includes changes to the rules governing military commission proceedings, in particular evidentiary rules and rules regarding defense resources. Although the Obama administration has failed to resolve the conundrum of whether to shut down the Military Commissions permanently, the 2009 Act reforms the 2006 Act. The reforms — while granting defendants' additional rights — failed to satisfy the human rights community.

US: New Legislation on Military Commissions Doesn't Fix Fundamental Flaws

Humans Rights Watch, Oct. 8, 2009[20]

"Tinkering with the discredited military commissions system is not enough," said Joanne Mariner, Terrorism and Counterterrorism Program director at Human Rights Watch. "Although the pending military commissions legislation makes important improvements on the Bush administration's system, the commissions remain a substandard system of justice."

The Military Commissions Act of 2009 revises the procedures governing the use of military commissions to try alien "unprivileged enemy belligerents" (individuals labeled "unlawful enemy combatants" during the previous

---

20. *Available at* Human Rights Watch, *available at* http://www.hrw.org/en/news/2009/10/08/ us-new-legislation-military-commissions-doesn-t-fix-fundamental-flaws (last visited July 20, 2010).

administration). The draft legislation addresses some of the worst due-process failings of the Military Commissions Act of 2006.

Notably, the bill limits the admission of coerced and hearsay evidence and grants greater resources to defense counsel. The revised system would still, however, depart in fundamental ways from the trial procedures that apply in the US federal courts and courts-martial. Nor does it satisfy the constitutional and policy concerns set forth by the Obama administration in recent months. It does not, for example, include a sunset clause to set a time limit on military commission trials, a provision the administration had specifically requested.

Human Rights Watch warned that as the latest version of the military commissions created by the Bush administration, the revised tribunals would be viewed globally as unfair, harming international cooperation on counterterrorism. It noted that trying only non-US citizens before the commissions would raise further concerns about fairness and discrimination. And it pointed out that by allowing child suspects to be prosecuted in military proceedings, the US was bucking a global trend to end this practice.

The very purpose of the military commissions is to permit trials that lack the full due-process protections available to defendants in federal courts, Human Rights Watch said. Tinkering with the procedures of tribunals created from scratch forfeits the benefits of using long-established civilian criminal courts whose procedures and protections have been tried and tested via years of litigation.

The federal courts have shown themselves to be fully capable of trying terrorism cases while protecting intelligence sources and the due-process rights of the accused. In the more than seven years since the military commissions were announced, only three suspects have been prosecuted, while the federal courts have tried more than 145 terrorism cases during the same period.

Unlike the federal courts, which enjoy constitutional protection against executive pressure, the commissions lack independence. Indeed, the previous commissions were highly susceptible to improper political influence, leading several military prosecutors to resign in protest.

JEFFREY F. ADDICOTT, EFFICACY OF THE OBAMA POLICIES TO COMBAT AL-QA'EDA, THE TALIBAN, AND ASSOCIATED FORCES—THE FIRST YEAR

30 Pace L. Rev. 340, 350-52 (2010)

... On June 8, 2009, President Obama first indicated that he intended to reverse course from his January 2009 Executive Order halting military commissions and would restart the process for alleged al-Qa'eda enemy combatant war criminals. Of course, military commissions are only illegal unless the nation is, or has been, in a state of armed conflict under the law of war. On the other hand, President Obama was quick to repeat and actually advance the Bush Administration's confusion regarding the appropriate judicial forum to prosecute al-Qa'eda enemy combatants for their crimes. Obama first did this by directing the June 2009 transfer from Guantanamo Bay of one enemy combatant al-Qa'eda member to stand trial in New York federal district court to face murder charges for his role in the al-Qa'eda terrorist bombings in Africa in 1998. Then, in November 2009, the Obama Administration made the strange decision to prosecute Khalid Sheikh Mohammed and four other senior al-Qa'eda leaders in federal court in New York City. While President Bush could somewhat mask his confused decision about applying the proper rule of law to enemy combatants by asserting that the al-Qa'eda members that he had sent to federal district court—Zacarias Moussaoui and Richard Reid—had not been formally labeled as enemy combatants, President Obama could not. All five of the al-Qa'eda members slated for trial in New York had been detained for years as enemy combatants. In addition, to make matters even more confusing, the announcement by the Obama Administration, disclosing that five enemy combatant (now termed "unprivileged enemy belligerent" by the Administration) al-Qa'eda members—including Khalid Sheikh Mohammed—would be tried in federal district court, came in tandem with the announcement that another five enemy combatant al-Qa'eda members held at Guantanamo Bay would be tried by military commissions, caused a firestorm of debate and confusion. . . .

ISSUES TO CONSIDER

1. How should a proper judicial forum be identified?
2. What are the reasons the U.S. has failed to develop a consistent judicial paradigm policy?
3. What is the practical effect of MCA 2006 and MCA 2009?
4. What defendant rights are the most important to protect?
5. Does the lack of consistent decision making reflect an inability to determine terrorist status and rights?
6. From the initial military commissions premised on troubled case law, the administrations have denied detainees basic constitutional protections to detainees; what are the strategic consequences of this failure?

III. INTERNATIONAL COURTS

In addition to comparing the relative merits of civilian (Article III) courts and military commissions for terrorist-defendants, it is important to weigh the possibility of internationalizing the judicial process. Unlike war crime defendants who have been brought to trial before tribunals, terrorist-defendants have, to date, been brought to trial exclusively before domestic courts.

While not authorizing implementation of an international judicial regime to prosecute terrorists, the 15 member-nations of the United Nations Security Council adopted Resolution 1373 (Sept. 28, 2001), which mandated the following:

> On 28 September 2001, acting under Chapter VII of the United Nations Charter (concerning threats to international peace and security), the Security Council

adopted Resolution 1373 (2001), reaffirming its unequivocal condemnation of the terrorist attacks which took place in New York, Washington, D.C., and Pennsylvania on 11 September 2001, and expressing its determination to prevent all such acts. Resolution 1373 also established the Counter-Terrorism Committee (CTC), made up of all 15 members of the Security Council. The CTC monitors the implementation of resolution 1373 by all states and tries to increase the capability of states to fight terrorism. The CTC is an instrument to monitor the implementation of resolution 1373. The CTC is not a sanctions committee and does not have a list of terrorist organizations or individuals.

To establish an international tribunal primarily for the purpose of trying terrorist-defendants would deviate greatly from current domestic judicial regimes which manifest both sovereignty and national counterterrorism. In domestic judicial paradigms, the only considerations are the specific nation's goals, laws, and moral values. The question is whether international-ization of terror trials enhances counterterrorism while, admittedly, minimiz-ing sovereignty.

Would an international judicial regime better serve the interests of nations who purport to seek similar goals on a global scale? The relative advantages and disadvantages of bringing terrorists to trial before an international court are underscored in the following excerpt.

Peter Golding, The Transformation of Counter Terrorism

USAWC Strategy Research Project, April 9, 2002[21]

International Problem

Though domestic courts are not monolithic in their judicial regime, the defendant—regardless of which regime is adopted—is tried either by that country's national court system or in a military court established by that nation in its capacity as an occupying power. The authority for each of these judicial systems is therefore, a single nation's sovereign power. The only considerations are that nation's goals and means for achieving them in a judicial setting.

Although these terrorists targeted the United States on 11 September 2001, countering terrorism effectively is an international problem. The problem is international in scope because the terrorist network is itself international in scope; the continuing threat these terrorists pose is not con-fined to the Untied States. The victims of 11 September 2001 were not only United States citizens, but citizens of many countries. Indirectly, the terrorists' attacks affected all nations, thus the community of nations together ought to coalesce and deal with the terrorism problem. United Nations Security Coun-cil Resolution 1368 "calls on all states to work together to bring justice to the perpetrators." Indeed, Mary Robinson United Nations High Commissioner

---

21. *Available at* https://carlisle-www.army.mil/srp/ex_paper/Golding_P_A_02.pdf (last vis-ited Nov. 14, 2006).

for Human Rights said, "No one can argue that this isn't a crime against humanity."

Arguments Against Using an International Court

Practical Reasons

As the International Criminal Court does not yet exist, to pursue an ad-hoc International Court would necessitate developing court procedures, rules of evidence, standards of proof (beyond a reasonable doubt, clear and convincing, preponderance of the evidence or some other standard). As different countries have different procedures and traditions, for example the common law adversarial tradition versus the civil law inquisition tradition, establishing the ground rules could consume months if not years in simply creating the court. Furthermore, who would determine the rules and the selection of the judges? Would it be just the United States, or the combatants in the war in Afghanistan, or NATO or the United Nations?

For example, the crime of conspiracy could impose substantial difficulties from the point of view of the United States. It appears clear that the United States government is treating conspiracy to commit the terrorism on 11 September 2001 as a capital crime. However, most countries, including our European allies, would be unlikely to support the notion of conspiracy to commit murder as being a capital crime.

Proposals to develop and establish an international terror court have drawn attention to potential obstacles including the appropriate rules of evidence, particularly the right to confront the accuser; the right to self-representation; and determining whether the scope of the court's jurisdiction should include both domestic and international terrorism. Attempts to punish guilty individuals by sentencing them to death also stands out as a major source of conflict. The Presidential Order established the death penalty for those convicted by a military commission convened in Guantanamo Bay. European nations are unanimously opposed to the death penalty and have refused to extradite terror-suspects to the United States.

Yet perhaps the most difficult issue remains the definition of terrorism. As discussed previously, there are over 109 definitions and while a working definition has been offered for this book, the international community continues to be divided regarding what, exactly, constitutes terrorism. If nations cannot agree upon the very entity compelling the need for an international tribunal, it seems unlikely that other disagreements regarding the appropriate judicial process will be easily settled.

A. BARRIERS TO INTERNATIONAL TRIBUNALS

Professor Michael Newton's analysis emphasizes the definitional quandary inherent to the establishment of international tribunals and suggests that the failure to agree on terms may be the largest stumbling block.

Michael A. Newton, International Criminal Law Aspects of the War Against Terrorism

79 U.S. Naval War College International Law Studies 323 (2003)

Modern international law embodies a significant body of law and practice that empowers domestic states to adjudicate terrorist crimes. Recent arguments, however, have postulated that an internationalized enforcement mechanism is warranted simply by virtue of the international nature of the problems posed by transnational terrorism. International law often evolves in response to perceived weaknesses in the normative structure that are highlighted by current events. This is the pattern for the post-September 11 wave of thinking about the linkage between international terrorism and an internationalized trial process. Given the inability of domestic forums to eradicate transnational terrorism, it is understandable that the aftermath of September 11 saw a groundswell of support for the creation of an international judicial forum to prosecute such terrorists. Even as they acknowledge that national courts are the backbone for the systematic prosecution of international terrorists, some scholars have pointed out that an international forum would "symbolize global justice for global crimes."

However, this strain of thought is merely the current incarnation of an older set of discarded ideas. Despite nearly a century of discussion and debate, the nations of the world have not agreed on a comprehensive definition of terrorism, which is the obvious cornerstone of any international forum with jurisdiction over transnational terrorist acts. States instead shifted from a universal and general approach towards cooperative efforts to define and criminalize specific manifestations of terrorism through specific multilateral treaties which bind signatory states to proscribe and punish such acts using domestic systems.

As a logical corollary, states have repeatedly rejected proposals for an overarching international tribunal charged with prosecuting crimes of transnational terrorism. The repeated formal rejections of terrorism as an international problem that should be addressed in supranational judicial forums date back to the League of Nations era. In 1926, the International Congress of Penal Law recommended that the Permanent Court of International Justice "be competent to judge individual liabilities" incurred as a result of crimes considered as international offenses "which constitute a threat to world peace." This proposal died on the vine of international diplomacy.

The cries for an international tribunal imply that an international response is always appropriate for crimes grounded in international law that shock the conscience of mankind, which in turn implies an unseemly assertion that domestic prosecutions are always inappropriate and unfair. While terrorism is widespread, and may be impossible to eradicate, the compelling motivations that have required the formation of international forums in other contexts are notably absent.

In other words, despite the inherent difficulty of investigating and prosecuting international terrorists, there is no culture of impunity because one or several sovereign states will always have jurisdiction, political will, and a very strong motivation to prosecute that particular set of terrorists when there is available evidence sufficient to sustain conviction of persons who are within the substantive and personal jurisdiction of the sovereign state. Creation of an international forum specifically designed to respond to crimes of terrorism would be a wholly new development in the field of international criminal law because it would be the first time that an international forum was created solely due to the nature of the crimes committed. If the nations of the world are committed to combating the core problem of transnational terrorism, the best place is in the domestic forums of affected states. This approach will accomplish the most in the long term to ensure that the rule of law is strengthened and justice is done.

ISSUES TO CONSIDER

1. If one man's freedom fighter is another man's terrorist, can the international community articulate an agreed upon definition of terrorism?
2. How should the death penalty controversy be resolved?
3. What are the benefits for like-minded nations to establish an international terror court?
4. Is terrorism sufficiently international to justify the establishment of an international judicial regime?
5. If Chechen terrorists have different goals then terrorists responsible for the Madrid train bombings, would an international terror court be the appropriate forum for their respective trials?
6. What is the appropriate reach of an international terror court: the doers, the financiers, the providers of safe haven?

B. STATES, EVIDENCE, AND THE RIGHTS OF THE ACCUSED

The establishment of an international terrorism tribunal requires addressing evidentiary issues, in particular the admissibility of classified intelligence information. Gerald Gahima's testimony before the United States House Armed Services Committee explains how the various war crimes tribunals have struck a crucial balance between the rights of nations to use classified information and the rights of defendants to confront their accusers.

TESTIMONY OF GERALD GAHIMA'S BEFORE THE U.S. ARMED SERVICES COMMITTEE

July 26, 2006[22]

The rules of both the ICTR and the ICTY recognize the legitimacy of national security concerns of states assisting the two tribunals. It was understood and

---

22. *Available at* http://www.globalsecurity.org/security/library/congress/2006_h/060726-gahima.pdf (last visited July 20, 2010).

was provided for in the tribunals' rules of procedure and evidence that the sensitive nature of some of the assistance provided by states to the tribunals might preclude the conduct of public proceedings and or require restrictions on the submission of certain types of evidence. Rule 54(F) of the ICTY and ICTR's Rules of Evidence and Procedure ("RPE") were specifically constructed to address national security concerns of this nature. According to the rule, a state having concerns over the national security impact of a public hearing shall "file a notice of its objection not less than five days before the date of the hearing" and may request in camera or ex parte proceedings, or the use of documents submitted in redacted form accompanied by an affidavit signed by a senior official explaining the reasons for the document's restrictions.

Not every piece of information is subject to disclosure or exclusion based on national security. According to Rule 70(B) of both Tribunals on the production of evidence,

If the Prosecutor is in possession of information which has been provided to him on a confidential basis and which has been used solely for the purpose of generating new evidence, that initial information and its origin shall not be disclosed by the Prosecutor without the consent of the person or entity providing the initial information and shall in any event not be given in evidence without prior disclosure to the accused.

If rules of procedure of international criminal courts permit states which have assisted them to seek orders for the non-disclosure of information which might jeopardize their national interest, the availability of such remedies (the use of summaries and redactions of classified information, in camera proceedings and ex parte proceedings, etc.) in proceedings in U.S. courts trying suspected terror suspects would not by analogy violate international standards of fair trial.

ISSUES TO CONSIDER

1. What are the benefits of trying terrorists in an international tribunal?
2. Why should nation-states relinquish the right to try terrorists in a domestic criminal law court?
3. How should the lack of a unifying definition of terrorist be resolved?
4. Is international cooperation enhanced by international tribunals?

The development of an international tribunal would require the seven surveyed nations to make significant legal and policy decisions regarding counterterrorism. If the goal is to contribute to international cooperation in responding to global terror threats, then tribunals—whether existing tribunals such as the ICC or special terror tribunals—are an appropriate response. Conversely, if nation-states seek to punish terrorists who have attacked its citizens, then a domestic court paradigm—either civilian courts or military commissions—may be a more effective venue.

The policy ramifications of the globalization of counterterrorism are not insignificant. Establishing an international terror court requires nation-states to accept cooperation as not only a theme, but also a reality. The decision to establish such a tribunal is ultimately not a legal issue but rather a policy consideration requiring decision makers to implement a universal model in response to global terrorism.

LAURA A. DICKINSON, USING LEGAL PROCESS TO FIGHT TERRORISM: DETENTIONS, MILITARY COMMISSIONS, INTERNATIONAL TRIBUNALS, AND THE RULE OF LAW

75 S. Cal. L. Rev. 1407 (2002)

Terrorism is a transnational problem that spans virtually the entire world, and strong multilateral efforts are required if it is to be contained. The Al Qaeda network alone draws on the nationals of multiple countries who leave their homes to train in terrorist camps in host countries such as Afghanistan, Somalia, Sudan, and the Philippines, and who are then sent to target countries such as the United States, where they live in cells, waiting to be deployed.

Immediately following the September 11 attacks, the United States drew on the support of numerous countries around the globe in efforts to combat terrorism. On the day after the attacks, the UN Security Council issued a resolution strongly condemning the attacks and recognizing "the inherent right of individual or collective self-defence in accordance with the Charter." Shortly thereafter, the Security Council issued another resolution, explicitly invoking its authority under Chapter VII of the United Nations Charter, referring to the previous resolution's recognition of the right to self defense, reaffirming the need to combat by "all means" terrorist acts threatening international peace and security, requiring states to take steps to block terrorist finances and end any state support for terrorism, and calling on states to increase cooperative intelligence-gathering and law enforcement efforts.

An international legal process would help to build on these cooperative efforts. First, as discussed in more detail below, an international process would likely have greater legitimacy internationally than the proposed military commissions or even domestic trials within the United States. If other governments perceive the United States as acting fairly and with appropriate deference to international norms, they are more likely to continue as active members of a coalition to combat terrorism. Second, even beyond the question of perceived legitimacy, the international proceeding itself, by involving participants from many countries, would strengthen both formal and informal intergovernmental networks and institutions.

An international proceeding would involve participants from many nations in the prosecution and punishment of terrorism suspects, which would give those nations a stake in the process, lead to the development of a cadre of governmental, intergovernmental, and nongovernmental personnel with expertise in addressing the problem of terrorism, and foster channels of communication and collaboration among them.

In order to see how an international process helps to create a context for the development of intergovernmental networks, we can look at the problem of secret evidence. Critics have charged that an international process offers the greatest potential for damaging leaks, which will make countries reluctant to provide the intelligence information needed at trial. Due to the transnational nature of terrorism, however, information-sharing is absolutely essential, and countries will refuse to disclose information only at their peril, with or without an international legal process. Indeed, as UN Security Council Resolution 1373 recognizes, enhanced multilateral information-sharing is an intrinsic part of any serious effort to contain terrorism. In tracking down and locating Al Qaeda suspects, the United States has already relied considerably on intelligence provided by other countries.

To be sure, the United States might well be reluctant to disclose, even to a group of intelligence officials operating under conditions of secrecy, certain information that would be necessary to convict Al Qaeda operatives, if members of the panel included representatives from governments deemed less trustworthy. The circle of governments to which we might be willing to disclose such information could well be, and perhaps should be, quite narrow. Indeed, we may not even trust certain other countries enough to give credence to the information received from them, let alone enough to give them additional material. Nonetheless, there can be no doubt that information-sharing is already occurring and that it is necessary in the fight against terrorism. Moreover, even a multilateral panel with representatives from only a few countries would be an improvement over a purely unilateral approach.

ISSUES TO CONSIDER

1. What are the policy implications of establishing international tribunals?
2. How should "effective" be defined in the judicial paradigm with respect to terrorism?

IV. NATIONAL SECURITY COURTS

Some critics suggest that neither system currently in place in the United States—military commissions and Article III courts—can effectively try suspected terrorists and therefore a national security court, or domestic terror court, should be created.

AMOS GUIORA, CREATING A DOMESTIC TERROR COURT

48 Washburn L. J. 617 (2009)

. . . As an absolutely critical first step, President Obama *must* articulate criteria for determining—via a person-specific vetting process—which of the detainees presents a current or future threat to America's national security. Those deemed to present a threat must be brought to trial; those deemed not, must be released. Although the logistics of releasing thousands of detainees is a daunting task, it must not-under any circumstances- justify their continued detention. As the former President of the Israeli Supreme Court, Aharon Barak, once commented, "logistical requirements should never stand in the way of personal freedom."

There is one important caveat to this ironclad rule that requires careful consideration: What is the correct decision when the *only* information available against a particular detainee is classified information and therefore no judicial process is feasible? There are, I suggest, three options: (1) outright release of the individual in spite of the available information; (2) continued, indefinite detention thereby prolonging violation of constitutional rights; or (3) creation of an administrative detention paradigm, borrowing from the United Kingdom or Israeli models, subject to statutorily mandated periodic review by an independent judiciary.

. . . Detainees present a definitional challenge primarily because they are neither traditional criminal defendants nor prisoners of war as defined by international law. It is important, however, to define "detainee" not only to ensure their established rights, but also to articulate additional rights. I propose that "post-9/11 detainees" are "individuals suspected of involvement in terrorism." This term gives us a starting point toward creating a hybrid paradigm. This hybrid paradigm will contribute to resolving the difficult task of balancing legitimate national security concerns with the equally legitimate rights of the individual suspects. . . .

. . . The DTC [Domestic Terror Court] itself will be a restructured Foreign Intelligence Surveillance Act (FISA) court thereby enabling it to adjudicate guilt and innocence in addition to its primary statutorily mandated responsibility of considering governmental wire tap warrants. This added responsibility obviously will require the appointment of a significant number of additional judges to the FISA bench. The current FISA structure is clearly inadequate to support the increased needs inherent in the establishment of a DTC. These judges will be drawn from the pool of sitting United States District Court judges, as is the current practice, and the president will need to nominate, subject to Senate confirmation, new judges who will sit on the DTC. The DTC will have, in addition to considering wire tap requests, three primary responsibilities: (1) to rule on remand requests, from detention to indictment; (2) to determine whether to hold the defendant for trial based on the charging documents and evidence presented at a preliminary hearing; and (3) to adjudicate guilt or innocence.

One of the critical — and admittedly problematic — features of the DTC is the manner in which the government's interest in protecting legitimate national security concerns will be balanced against the obligation to simultaneously ensure the rights of individual suspects, particularly with respect to the right to confront an accuser. The DTC will not provide suspects with the same level of constitutional protection as traditional Article III courts. This measure will enable the government to keep intelligence information classified. Nevertheless, significant measures will be taken to ensure that the information received by the DTC is weighed by the bench in a manner intended to benefit the defendant, precisely because he is absent.

Although the evidence is presented by the prosecution and a member of the intelligence community, by applying a strict four-part test in weighing the submitted information, the judge will wear two hats: one as the court and the other as defense counsel. The information and the source must be held to be: (1) reliable; (2) viable; (3) valid; and (4) corroborated. If the intelligence meets the four-part test, then and only then is it admissible and available for use against the defendant at trial. However, a defendant's conviction may not be based solely on confidential intelligence information. This evidence may only be used to support an existing body of evidence known to the defendant and his counsel and introduced in open court proceedings. In every case, the sitting judge will make all decisions as to the admissibility of evidence while viewing the evidence in a light most favorable to the defendant.

Similarly, the sitting judge may determine through *in camera* review of intelligence evidence that introducing the information in open court proceedings does not pose a threat to national security. In these cases, the judge gives the prosecution the option of declassifying the information and presenting it in court or proceeding to trial without such evidence.

If a defendant is convicted in the DTC, sentencing will proceed just as in traditional courts with maximum and minimum sentencing terms. Furthermore, sentencing will not, under any circumstance, involve the death penalty. Appeals will be filed directly to the United States Court of Appeals.

A Critique of "National Security Courts"

The Constitution Project, June 23, 2008[23]

Advocates of national security courts that would try terrorism suspects claim that traditional Article III courts are unequipped to handle these cases. This claim has not been substantiated, and is made in the face of a significant — and growing — body of evidence to the contrary. A recent report released by Human Rights First persuasively demonstrates that our existing federal courts are competent to try these cases. The report examines more than 120 international terrorism cases brought in the federal courts over the past fifteen years. It finds that established federal courts were able to try these cases without sacrificing either national security or the defendants' rights to a fair trial. The report documents how federal courts have successfully dealt with classified evidence under the Classified Information Procedures Act (CIPA) without creating any security breaches. It further concludes that courts have been able to enforce the government's Brady obligations to share exculpatory evidence with the accused, deal with Miranda warning issues, and provide means for the government to establish a chain of custody for physical evidence, all without jeopardizing national security.

Of course, our traditional federal courts have not always done everything that the government would like them to do. They are, after all, constrained by well-established constitutional limits on prosecutorial power. For example, no federal court would permit the prosecution to present witnesses without protecting the defendant's constitutional right to confront those witnesses

---

23. *Available at* http://www.constitutionproject.org/pdf/Critique_of_the_National_Security_Courts.pdf (last visited Jan. 7, 2011).

against him or her. Nor would a federal court permit the prosecution to rely on a coerced confession in violation of a defendant's Fifth Amendment right against self-incrimination. But creating a new set of courts would not repeal existing constitutional rights. Conversely, to the extent that the existing rules are not constitutionally compelled, ordinary federal courts (or Congress, where applicable) can modify them when it is shown that the modification is necessary to accommodate the government's legitimate interests.

Most importantly, there is the intrinsic and inescapable problem of definition. Whereas the argument for specialized courts for tax and patent law is that expert judges are particularly necessary given the complex subject-matter, proposals for specialized courts for terrorism trials are based on the asserted need for relaxed procedural and evidentiary rules and are justified on the ground that terrorists do not deserve full constitutional protections. This creates two fundamental constitutional problems. First, justifying departures from constitutional protections on the basis that the trials are for terrorists undermines the presumption of innocence for these individuals. Second, if a conviction were obtained in a national security court using procedural and evidentiary rules that imposed a lesser burden on the government, then the defendant would be subjected to trial before a national security court based upon less of a showing than would be required in a traditional criminal proceeding. The result would be to apply less due process to the question of guilt or innocence, which, by definition, would increase the risk of error. And, if the government must make a preliminary showing that meets traditional rules of procedure and evidence in order to trigger the jurisdiction of a national security court, such a showing would also enable it to proceed via the traditional criminal process.

National security courts for criminal prosecutions are not just unnecessary; they are also dangerous. They run the risk of creating a separate and unequal criminal justice system for a particular class of suspects, who will be brought before such specialized courts based on the very allegations they are contesting. Such a system undermines the presumption of innocence for these defendants, and risks a broader erosion of defendants' rights that could spread to traditional Article III trials. It was Justice Frankfurter who wrote that "It is a fair summary of history to say that the safeguards of liberty have frequently been forged in controversies involving not very nice people." Committee members strongly believe that the shadow of terrorism must not be the basis for abandoning these fundamental tenets of justice and fairness.

In addition, these proposals are alarmingly short on details with respect to the selection of judges for these national security courts. Although there is a history of creating specialized federal courts to handle particular substantive areas of the law (e.g., taxation; patents), unlike tax and patent law, there is simply no highly specialized expertise that would form relevant selection criteria for the judges. Establishing a specialized court solely for prosecutions of alleged terrorists might also create a highly politicized process for nominating and confirming the judges, focusing solely on whether the nominee had sufficient "tough on terrorism" credentials — hardly a criterion that lends itself to the appearance of fairness and impartiality.

None of the above is to deny that there is a class of individuals who may be tried in appropriate military tribunals. Persons captured by the U.S. military as part of an armed conflict have traditionally been subject to military jurisdiction under the laws of war. This principle is well-established, but it has long coexisted with the complementary principle that only individuals who are properly subject to military jurisdiction under the laws of war may be so tried. Military tribunals may not try offenders or offenses unless they are encompassed by traditional laws of war.

Just as there is no need to establish national security courts to replace traditional Article III courts, so too there is no need to create such tribunals to handle cases that would normally be tried by military courts. Individuals should be tried either in our traditional criminal justice system or in properly constituted military courts.

V. CONCLUSION

The four options discussed — domestic criminal courts, military commissions, international tribunals, and national security courts — represent very diverse approaches to the bringing of terrorists to justice. Again, how nations balance diametrically opposing rights of the individual and the state represents the essential dilemma facing decision makers and jurists. By adopting a traditional criminal law approach, the state is guaranteeing the terrorist-defendant full rights and privileges, *potentially* at the cost of losing prosecutorial power. Conversely, by adopting a domestic military court, the state establishes a judicial framework that facilitates prosecution at the cost of denying the defendant universally accepted rights.

To balance these competing interests, each nation has adopted differing approaches to policy, operations, intelligence gathering, and the appropriate use of information gathered from detainees. These issues are directly related to the judicial paradigm adopted by each of the seven nations; any sustainable international paradigm would require some level of consensus regarding these different approaches.

How should the seven surveyed nations go forward? In the United States, amending FISA legislation so that suspected terrorists might be brought to trial before a special FISA court could resolve legal ambiguity. Such congressional initiative might enable suspects to be tried before a civilian court competent in issues specific to terrorist trials. As the *Moussaoui* trial clearly demonstrated, traditional Article III courts are ill-equipped for such trials. Individuals suspected of involvement in terrorism could be heard before a bench trial, without a jury, to allow the introduction of intelligence information that would not be made available to the defendant or counsel. While this would violate the Sixth Amendment right to confront the accuser, a court specifically trained in reading and analyzing the reliability of intelligence information would satisfy a balancing test whereby the state could introduce such information subject to strict judicial scrutiny by an independent court. Clearly, the U.S. is still struggling in deciding where and how to try terrorist suspects.

The judicial approaches adopted by Russia and India indicate that these nations prefer to apply a criminal law paradigm in which terrorists are brought before a civilian court. At the same time, these countries employ aggressive operational counterterrorism methods in contrast to traditional law enforcement. In other words, both Russia and India treat terrorists as a distinct entity in an operational sense, but as criminals once the suspected terrorists are caught. These countries have come under severe criticism for widespread allegations of human rights violations.

China's and Colombia's implementation of the criminal law paradigm extends to their policy regarding the proper judicial forum for suspected terrorists.

The Spanish government, on the other hand, treats terrorists as criminals in both the operational and judicial regimes. But Spain's traditional law enforcement is unique in that it allows for incommunicado detention, which has also been the subject of international criticism. Nevertheless, these three countries—Russia, India, and Spain—have largely resisted the adoption of a second judicial tier established by the United States and Israel.

Israel has the most fully developed two-track judicial approach to terrorism in that defendants may be brought either to court for a full criminal trial or detained administratively subject to independent judicial review. A terrorist defendant brought to trial in a military court is provided full criminal rights and protections akin to the judicial process before a civilian court; in administrative detention the detainee is not entitled to confront his accuser.

Implementation of methods extending beyond the criminal law paradigm suggests recognition that the traditional approach is inapplicable, but careful analysis of *how* each paradigm has been implemented hints at overreach and tweaking rather than a consistent legal policy. All of the seven surveyed nations articulate—subtly or clearly—a realization that terrorists are somehow *different* than common criminals. How different and how to articulate the difference is an issue with which nations continue to struggle. That struggle has resulted in policy inconsistency, ambiguity, and violations of human rights.

11

FUTURE CHALLENGES TO
COUNTERTERRORISM

This final chapter examines the threat that Mexican drug cartels pose to Mexico[1] and the United States, and the threat that pirates, primarily off the Somali coast, pose to international shipping.

Neither threat was addressed in the first edition and they are distinguishable from the terrorist model described in the preceding chapters. Unlike the terrorist threats largely faced by the seven surveyed nations, Mexican drug cartels and Somalia pirates are primarily motivated by economic gain rather than the ideological considerations generally associated with traditional terrorism. Yet, the direct and indirect threats posed by these actors to civil democratic society justify their incorporation in this book under the theme of future challenges.

The perpetual danger posed by terrorist actors described in the preceding chapters manifests the primary threat faced by nation-states. The continuing effort of al-Qaeda and its progeny to plan additional attacks against potential targets both in Europe and in the U.S. represents the most enduring viable threat. Whether that includes unconventional attacks (e.g., nuclear, chemical or biological), as has been suggested, cannot be determined at this time.

Assuming that tomorrow's attack will be similar to previous attacks reflects the adage "fighting yesterday's war." Precisely for that reason, decision makers must base operational counterterrorism on the rule of law, geopolitics, threat and risk assessment, resource allocation/prioritization, and cost-benefit analysis predicated on sophisticated intelligence gathering and analysis. Otherwise, operational counterterrorism will not only be ineffective but will also, inevitably, violate domestic and international law principles.

Essential to this process are the issues discussed throughout this book for they reflect the essence of counterterrorism. Those principles must be applied to a constant threat whose modes of operation can best be described as a moving target; reported attempts to conduct a Mumbai-style attack in Europe,

---

1. *Available at* http://www.washingtonpost.com/wp-dyn/content/article/2010/04/20/AR201004 2004961.html?wpisrc=nl_headline (last visited April 21, 2010).

loading cargo planes with explosive filled cartridges, and continued suicide bombings reflect threats that nations continue to face based on traditional terrorist motivation.

The last two examples below reflect attacks based on motivations *distinct* from the traditional model. Whether they represent an increasingly powerful motivation is unclear; that they represent powerful threats requiring operational responses is without doubt.

I. MEXICO

Mexican drug cartels pose a direct threat to the safety and security of individual Mexican citizens and to the stability of particular Mexican states and an indirect threat to the United States.[2] While the number of victims— approximately 22,000 killed in three years—is extraordinary, the future danger draws our attention. While the turf violence and illicit trade of drug cartels may reflect a traditional criminal law paradigm, the threats posed both externally and internally suggest an alternative paradigm is more appropriate.

From the perspective of U.S. decision makers, the threat posed by the drug cartels extends far beyond specific drug-related acts of crime in Mexico. Drug cartel-related kidnappings in American cities including Phoenix, Arizona are but one example of the cross-border range of the threat posed. While the targets are, reportedly, non-Americans the violence occurs on American soil with potential loss of life among Americans.

Therefore, the potential operational American responses to the threat raises significant international law questions: (1) whether Mexico is a failed (including partially) failed state and (2) the limits of Mexican sovereignty given the effect on America security predicated on the spillover of the violence from Mexico into America. Whatever the spillover's cause—primarily the *corruption* of Mexican law enforcement officials—it has a *direct* impact on the United States.

Precisely for that reason, possible American responses can be framed in accordance with self-defense as articulated by Article 51 of the United Nation's charter. While the drug cartels are distinct from the political insurrection in Colombia, the danger, nevertheless, to the U.S. and Mexico is not abstract. The danger is palpable and measurable; therefore an external reaction by the U.S. directly addressing the threat would be defined as legitimate according to international law.

Simply put: will the U.S. remain passive in the face of threats to American citizens originating in Mexico? If there are pockets in Mexico where neither local nor central government exercises authority—in conjunction with a disturbing lack of transparency in the Mexican judiciary—then a possible clear

---

2. *Available at* http://www.cnn.com/2010/WORLD/americas/05/02/mexico.drug.violence/index.html?hpt=Sbin (last visited May 3, 2010).

and present danger exists with respect to U.S. interests. In such a paradigm, an argument espousing the right to self-defense can be made.

Though President Calderon has taken a strong stand against the drug cartels and is actively seeking to combat corruption in law enforcement and the judiciary, drug-related violence continues to spread with repercussions potentially spilling out of control. By example: road blocks operated by drug cartels control traffic flow in specific areas. Unlike in Colombia where the government crackdown on narco-terrorism contributed to a decrease in the drug trade, the proactive measures in Mexico have had an opposite effect. This is largely the result of corruption and a significant increase in the number of arms dealers supplying weapons to the drug cartels.

In addition, the possibility that terrorists can utilize drug and human smuggling routes from Mexico to the U.S. suggests threats posed by drug cartels exceeds that of the traditional criminal law paradigm. Similar to the convergence of route usage among opium dealers and terrorists in Afghanistan, development of a similar model between Mexico and the U.S. demands the attention of decision makers on both sides of the border.

There remains, however, a strong possibility that drug cartels would resist terrorist organizations using similar routes because this would, potentially, negatively affect their financial interests. Nevertheless, the possibility of route convergence presents a significant national security threat to the U.S. justifying consideration of proactive measures.

Experts point to the increasing number of Hezbollah terrorists in Central America involved in the cocaine industry thereby reinforcing the convergence between drugs and terrorism. This further emphasizes that the Mexican model is not only domestic based narco-terrorism (similar to Colombia) but potentially has cross-border ramifications that present a threat to its neighboring country.[3]

According to international law, a nation-state is broadly defined as an entity with defined borders and territory with a functioning government and judiciary that provides services to those living within its territory. Failed states have been defined as "shattered social and political structure";[4] some experts suggest that "partial" failed state most accurately describes western Pakistan where Bin-Laden presumably is based. That is, while Pakistan's government is fully functioning in the majority of the country, it does not exercise control with respect to a specific region. That same analysis is appropriate to Lebanon as southern Lebanon is largely in the hands of Hezbollah with the central Lebanese government exercising neither control nor authority there. When asking experts whether this definition pertains to certain Mexican states, particularly those bordering the U.S., the response has been an all but uniform "no, but time will tell whether President Caldaron is able to

---

3. To that end, in the fall of 2010 the author was interviewed by a journalist writing an article addressing the possibility of U.S. drone attacks against specific targets based in Mexico.

4. *Available at* http://www.sourcewatch.org/index.php?title=Failed_state (last visited Apr. 19, 2010).

successfully minimize control the drug cartels impose on state institutions including the judiciary and law enforcement."

Terrorist organizations benefit from weakened state institutions; the ability to provide "cradle to grave" services—Hamas and Hezbollah are prime examples—enables them to step into the shoes of failed institutions. It is presently uncertain how the conflict between the drug cartels and the government will be resolved; what is certain is that the threat to government institutions and possible cross-border linkage between drug cartels and terrorist organizations represent profound threats to regional stability.

The possible confluence between drug cartels and terrorist organizations represents a threat different than that posed by religious-based terrorism. The latter appeals to a motivation predicated on a higher calling with eternal reward promised to the actor who acts in accordance with God's commands as articulated by a faith leader. The terrorism described above is based exclusively on earthly rewards, driven by pecuniary gain and its functional and well-documented rewards and costs. This model is clearly distinguishable from contemporary terrorism paradigms addressed in this book.

While not reflecting a trend, it is important to note that a similar model is observable in Somalia in general and piracy in specific. It is to that model we turn our attention.

II. SOMALIA

Piracy[5] has plagued the world for hundreds of years as seafarers have been the victims of attacks by sea pirates on the worlds' oceans. The primary motivation for pirates—historically and presently—has been pecuniary gain of goods, money, and weapons. Pirates are akin to private, roving gangs attacking the vulnerable with the difference that attacks are carried out on the sea, rather than city streets and alleys. While the location and technique are different, the motivation and result are fundamentally similar.

While reports indicate that the number of pirate attacks has decreased (2010 in comparison to 2009),[6] the range of the attackers has spread therefore increasing the number of ships and individuals potentially vulnerable to random attacks. The randomness is particularly important because any ship is "fair game" subject to attack literally "anywhere, anytime." In particular, piracy is acute off the coast of Somalia where pirates take full advantage of a weak, largely non-functioning nation-state to prey on ships in the Indian Ocean with their reach extending to the Oman waters.[7]

---

5. *Available at* http://www.cnn.com/2010/WORLD/africa/04/21/pirates.report/index.html?hpt=Sbin (last visited Apr. 22, 2010).

6. *Available at* http://www.cnn.com/2010/WORLD/africa/04/21/pirates.report/index.html?iref=allsearch (last visited May 3, 2010).

7. *Available at* http://allafrica.com/stories/201003301102.html(last visited May 3, 2010).

While piracy off the coast of Somalia is not a new phenomenon,[8] it has become Somalia's most important income-producing industry.[9] Precisely because of the fundamental weakness of the Somali government, pirates are able to operate devoid of any government control and restraint. However, recently Islamic groups — in lieu of government — have vowed to fight piracy which they consider "un-Islamic"[10] as part of their effort to impose Sharia law on Somalia.

While it has yet to be determined how these two distinct entities — pirates and extremist Islamic groups — resolve their potential conflict there are two other population groups at risk: hostages presently held by pirates and the international shipping industry. That is, akin to the ramifications of a significantly weakened Mexican government, the weak (at best) Somalia government similarly raises questions regarding terrorism and self-defense. Important to this discussion is the distinction between the terrorism discussed in previous chapters and the terrorism suggested in this chapter. While the other surveyed countries are largely confronted with terrorism not predicated on pecuniary gain (with the possible exception of Columbia), Mexico and Somalia are seeking to minimize — with limited resources and weak central government — a direct threat on their rule and authority motivated by financial interests.

Furthermore, in the case of Somalia (unlike Mexico) U.S. policy is increasingly aggressive as manifested by an extended and increased presence of the U.S. Navy in the Indian Ocean, Gulf of Aden, and off the Somali coast.[11]

The primary reasons for this extended, more aggressive military response are the financial impact on the shipping industry, the need to protect important international shipping lanes, and possible harm to innocent individuals. The threat to significant international resources, including the 2009 hijacking of a Saudi oil tanker,[12] raises the stakes both with respect to piracy and the threat it poses as evidenced by the rise in oil prices in the aftermath of the hijacking.[13] According to the U.S. State Department, piracy threatens maritime commerce and regional security,[14] which requires aggressive protection of shipping in the region.

At least one suspected pirate will be brought to trial in the United States.[15] The direct threat to commerce, resources, and innocent individuals suggests that piracy is an additional form of terrorism. While piracy has been a reality

---

8. *Availabe at* http://www.helium.com/items/1424309-history-of-piracy-in-somalia (last visited May 3, 2010).

9. *Available at* http://www.helium.com/items/1424309-history-of-piracy-in-somalia (last visited May 3, 2010).

10. *Available at* http://news.yahoo.com/s/ap/piracy (last visited May 3, 2010).

11. *Available at* http://www.csmonitor.com/USA/Military/2010/0402/Suspected-Somali-pirates-more-active-but-US-Navy-fighting-back (last visited May 4, 2010).

12. *Available at* http://news.bbc.co.uk/2/hi/africa/7733482.stm (last visited May 4, 2010).

13. *Available at* http://news.bbc.co.uk/2/hi/africa/7733482.stm (last visited May 4, 2010).

14. *Available at* http://www.state.gov/t/pm/ppa/piracy/index.htm (last visited May 4, 2010).

15. *Available at* http://www.nytimes.com/2009/04/22/nyregion/22pirate.html (last visited May 4, 2010).

for hundreds of years, its dramatic resurgence in Somalia in the past 20 years reflects a form of terrorism that justifies aggressive counterterrorism. Much like the Mexican government must develop effective measures to respond to the dramatic increase in drug cartel violence, the Somali government—or the international community—must develop effective operational measures to counter the pirates.

TABLE OF CASES

Principal cases denoted by italics.

INDEX